CWTS: Certified Wireless Technology Sp Study Guide

D0517655

CWTS Exam (PW0-070) Objectives

OBJECTIVE	CHAPTER

Wireless Technologies, Standards, and Certifications

1.1 Define the roles of the following organizations in providing direction and accountability within the wireless networking industry.
IEEE; Wi-Fi Alliance; Regulatory Domain Governing Bodies   1

1.2 Define basic characteristics of Wi-Fi technology.   4, 7
Range, coverage, and capacity; Frequencies/channels used; Channel reuse and co-location; Active and passive scanning; Power saving operation; Data rates and throughput; Dynamic rate selection; Authentication and association; The distribution system and roaming; Infrastructure and ad hoc modes; BSSID, SSID, BSS, ESS; Protection mechanisms

1.3 Summarize the basic attributes and advantages of the following WLAN standards, amendments, and product certifications.   1
Wi-Fi certification: 802.11a, 802.11b, 802.11g, 802.11n; Wi-Fi Multimedia (WMM) certification; WMM Power Save (WMM-PS) certification; Wi-Fi Protected Setup (WPS) certification: push-button, PIN-based; Wi-Fi Protected Access (WPA/WPA2) certification: enterprise, personal

Hardware and Software

2.1 Identify the purpose, features, and functions of the following wireless network components. Choose the appropriate installation or configuration steps in a given scenario.   2
Access points: lightweight, autonomous, mesh; Wireless LAN routers; Wireless bridges; Wireless repeaters; WLAN controller/switch: distributed AP connectivity, direct AP connectivity, Layer 2 and Layer 3 AP connectivity; Power over Ethernet devices: midspan, endpoint

2.2 Identify the purpose, features, and functions of the following client devices. Choose the appropriate installation or configuration steps in a given scenario.   3
PC Cards (ExpressCard, CardBus, and PCMCIA); USB2, CF, and SD devices; PCI, Mini-PCI, and Mini-PCIe cards; Workgroup bridges; Client utility software and drivers

2.3 Identify the purpose, features, and functions of and the appropriate installation or configuration steps for the following types of antennas.   6
Omnidirectional/dipole; Semidirectional; Highly directional

Sybex®
An Imprint of
WILEY

Security and Compliance

6.1 Identify and describe the following WLAN security techniques.   10
SSID hiding; Legacy security mechanisms: WEP and MAC filtering; User-based
security: 802.1X/EAP and RADIUS authentication; Passphrase-based security;
Push-button or PIN-based wireless security; Encryption – TKIP/CCMP; Role-based
access control (RBAC); Virtual private networking (VPN); Wireless intrusion
prevention systems (WIPS)

6.2 Regulatory compliance.   10
PCI compliance; HIPAA compliance; Enforcing compliance with WIPS

Sybex®
An Imprint of
WILEY

OBJECTIVE	CHAPTER

4.3 Define the need for and the use of a manual site survey tool and differentiate between the following manual site survey types.
Active surveys; Passive surveys — 9

4.4 Differentiate between manual and predictive site surveys.
Advantages and disadvantages of each site survey methodology — 9

4.5 Define the need for and use of a protocol analyzer in a manual site survey as it relates to the following.
Identifying, locating, and assessing nearby WLANs — 9

4.6 Differentiate between site surveys involving networks with and without a mesh access layer. — 9

4.7 Define the need for and use of a spectrum analyzer in a manual site survey.
Identification and location of interference sources; Differentiation of Wi-Fi and non-Wi-Fi interference sources — 9

4.8 Identify limitations on hardware placement .
Areas where APs or antennas cannot be placed; Areas beyond Ethernet/PoE distance limitations — 9

4.9 Understand industry-best practices for optimal use of directional and omnidirectional antennas in site surveys. — 9

Applications, Support, and Troubleshooting

5.1 Identify deployment scenarios for common WLAN network types.
Small office/home office (SOHO); Extension of existing networks into remote locations; Building-to-building connectivity; Public wireless hotspots; Mobile office, classroom, industrial, and health care; Municipal and law enforcement connectivity; Corporate data access and end-user mobility; Last-mile data delivery—wireless ISP; Transportation networks (trains, planes, automobiles) — 1

5.2 Recognize common problems associated with wireless networks and their symptoms, and identify steps to isolate and troubleshoot the problem. Given a problem situation, interpret the symptoms and the most likely cause. Problems may include:
Decreased throughput; Intermittent or no connectivity; Weak signal strength; Device upgrades — 11

5.3 Identify procedures to optimize wireless networks in specific situations.
Infrastructure hardware selection and placement; Identifying, locating, and removing sources of interference; Client load balancing; Analyzing infrastructure capacity and utilization; Multipath and hidden nodes — 11

Sybex®
An Imprint of
⊛WILEY

OBJECTIVE	CHAPTER

Radio Frequency (RF) Fundamentals

3.1 Define the basic units of RF measurements. 4
Milliwatt; Decibel (dB); dBm; dBi

3.2 Identify factors that affect the range and speed of RF transmissions. 4
Line-of-sight requirements; Interference (baby monitors, spread spectrum phones, microwave ovens); Environmental factors

3.3 Define and differentiate between the following Physical layer wireless technologies. 5
HR/DSSS; OFDM; MIMO

3.4 Define concepts that make up the functionality of RF and spread spectrum technology. 5
OFDM and HR/DSSS channels; Co-location of HR/DSSS and OFDM systems; Adjacent-channel and co-channel interference; WLAN/WPAN coexistence; CSMA/CA operation, half-duplex

3.5 Identify RF signal characteristics and the applications of basic RF antenna concepts. 6
Passive gain; Beamwidths; Simple diversity; Polarization

3.6 Describe the proper locations and methods for installing RF antennas. 6
Pole/mast mount; Ceiling mount; Wall mount

3.7 Identify the use of the following WLAN accessories and explain how to select and install them for optimal performance and regulatory domain compliance. 6
RF cables; RF connectors; Lightning arrestors and grounding rods

Site Surveying and Installation

4.1 Understand and describe the requirements to gather information prior to the site survey and do reporting after the site survey. 8
Gathering business requirements; Interviewing managers and users; Defining physical and data security requirements; Gathering site-specific documentation; Documenting existing network characteristics; Identifying infrastructure connectivity and power requirements; Understanding RF coverage requirements; Client connectivity requirements; Antenna use considerations

4.2 Define and differentiate between the following WLAN system architectures and understand site survey concepts related to each architecture. Identify and explain best practices for access point placement and density. 9
Multiple channel architecture (MCA); Single channel architecture (SCA)

Sybex®
An Imprint of
WILEY

CWTS™
Certified Wireless Technology Specialist
Official Study Guide

Robert J. Bartz

Wiley Publishing, Inc.

Acquisitions Editor: Jeff Kellum
Development Editor: Stef Jones
Technical Editors: Bryan Harkins and Marcus Burton
Production Editor: Rachel McConlogue
Copy Editor: Lunaea Hougland
Production Manager: Tim Tate
Vice President and Executive Group Publisher: Richard Swadley
Vice President and Publisher: Neil Edde
Media Project Manager 1: Laura Moss-Hollister
Media Associate Producer: Angie Denny
Media Quality Assurance: Josh Frank
Book Designers: Judy Fung and Bill Gibson
Compositor: Craig W. Johnson, Happenstance Type-O-Rama
Proofreader: Publication Services, Inc.
Indexer: Nancy Guenther
Project Coordinator, Cover: Lynsey Stanford
Cover Designer: Ryan Sneed

Library of Congress Cataloging-in-Publication Data

Bartz, Robert J., 1959-
 CWTS : certified wireless technology specialist official study guide (PW0-070) / Robert J. Bartz. — 1st ed.
    p. cm.
 ISBN-13: 978-0-470-43889-3 (pbk.)
 ISBN-10: 0-470-43889-4 (pbk.)
 1. Wireless LANs—Examinations—Study guides. 2. Telecommunications engineers—Certification—Study guides. I. Title. II. Title: Certified wireless technology specialist official study guide (PW0-070).
  TK5105.78.B37 2009
  621.384076—dc22
                    2009010840

Dear Reader,

Thank you for choosing *CWTS: Certified Wireless Technology Specialist Official Study Guide*. This book is part of a family of premium-quality Sybex books, all of which are written by outstanding authors who combine practical experience with a gift for teaching.

Sybex was founded in 1976. More than thirty years later, we're still committed to producing consistently exceptional books. With each of our titles we're working hard to set a new standard for the industry. From the paper we print on to the authors we work with, our goal is to bring you the best books available.

I hope you see all that reflected in these pages. I'd be very interested to hear your comments and get your feedback on how we're doing. Feel free to let me know what you think about this or any other Sybex book by sending me an email at nedde@wiley.com, or if you think you've found a technical error in this book, please visit http://sybex.custhelp.com. Customer feedback is critical to our efforts at Sybex.

Best regards,

Neil Edde
Vice President and Publisher
Sybex, an Imprint of Wiley

To my mother Kathryn, who taught me and my 11 brothers and sisters the meaning of hard work, honesty, and loyalty. At 86 years young she is still a great inspiration to me. I want to say thanks, Mom.

Acknowledgments

I would like to thank my wife, Jeannie, and two young adult children, Ashley and Jason, and to say how much I appreciate the support I received during the writing process of this book. This book was a huge task that took hundreds of hours and kept me locked away for days at a time. They made completing this project much easier for me because of their support, patience, and understanding.

I would also like to thank all the people at Sybex who helped with the creation of this book, including Acquisitions Editor Jeff Kellum, Production Editor Rachel McConlogue, Copy Editor Lunaea Hougland, Editorial Assistant Connor O'Brien and Editorial Manager Pete Gaughan. I owe all these individuals a ton of gratitude for their patience while working with me on this project, including having to deal with a few unexpected delays.

A very special thanks goes to the Development Editor Stef Jones for all her hard work in helping me with the editing, organization, and suggestions that allowed me to complete this book and still maintain my sanity. Her knowledge, expertise, and attention to detail were an enormous help to me.

The Technical Editor of this book is Bryan Harkins. I want to thank Bryan for his timely reviews, comments, and suggestions that helped make this book a valuable reference source for sales and technical support people. His years of experience as a technical trainer, engineer, and security specialist were a great contribution in creating a book I hope you will enjoy reading.

I would like to thank the thousands of students who have taken the time to attend the networking classes I was given the opportunity to teach. Educating, mentoring, and entertaining so many of these individuals gave me the inspiration and motivation to author this book.

Of course, this book would not exist if it were not for the people at CWNP. This group of individuals I have known for many years includes Kevin Sandlin, Scott Williams, Devin Akin, and Scott Turner as well as some of the newer members of the team, Cary Chandler, Marcus Burton, Trish Bruce, Abbey Cole, and all the others. They have realized the need for vendor-neutral wireless LAN training and certification and have done a great job of building a brand over the years that is now known worldwide.

Finally, a thank you to all the manufacturers, vendors, organizations, and individuals that provided the subject matter, allowing me the technology and tools needed to write this book.

Aerohive – www.aerohive.com
Stephen Philip and Adam Conway

AirMagnet – www.airmagnet.com
Joe Kuo and Dilip Advani

Aruba Networks – www.arubanetworks.com
Brad Day and Michael Tennefoss

Broadcom Corporation – www.broadcom.com

Cisco Systems – www.cisco.com

CompactFlash Association – www.compactflash.org

CWNP – www.cwnp.com
Devin Akin and Marcus Burton

HP ProCurve (Colubris Networks) – www.procurve.com

IEEE – www.ieee.org

Intel – www.intel.com

L-com Global Connectivity – www.l-com.com
Jim Corcoran

Linksys – www.linksys.com

MetaGeek – www.metageek.net
Mark Jensen and Ryan Woodings

Motorola – www.motorola.com
Tim Brophy and Bryan Harkins

Netgear – www.netgear.com

Network Stumbler – www.netstumbler.com

PCI-SIG – www.pcisig.com

PCMCIA Association – www.pcmcia.org
Mary Hain, Hain Communications

Proxim Wireless – www.orinocowireless.com

Psiber Data Systems – www.psiber.com
Bruce Nelson

SD Association – www.sdcard.org

TamoSoft – www.tamos.com
Michael Berg

TerraWave Solutions – www.terrawave.com
Jennifer Haltom

Trapeze Networks – www.trapezenetworks.com

USB Implementers Forum, Inc. – www.usb.org

Wi-Fi Alliance – www.wi-fi.org

WildPackets – www.wildpackets.com

Xirrus – www.xirrus.com
Douglas Haider

About the Author

Robert Bartz is a technical trainer and computer networking consultant. He is a graduate of California State University Long Beach, School of Engineering, with a Bachelor of Science degree in Industrial Technology. Prior to becoming a computer networking engineer and trainer, Robert was employed as an aerospace test engineer working with radar systems and satellite communications. He has attained many technical certifications over the years, including Master Certified Novell Engineer (MCNE), Certified Novell Instructor (CNI), Microsoft Certified Systems Engineer (MCSE), Microsoft Certified Trainer (MCT), CWNP Certified Wireless Network Administrator (CWNA), Certified Wireless Security Professional (CWSP), and Certified Wireless Network Trainer (CWNT), to name a few. He has been involved with the CWNP program since its inception and has taught this technology to thousands of people from various industries and markets across the United States and abroad.

Robert is the founder of Eight-O-Two Technology Solutions, LLC, a computer networking technical training and consulting services company providing education and services to various organizations both local and around the country. He spends his spare time learning new technology, working outside, and enjoying the beauty of his surroundings at his home in Monument, Colorado. Robert hopes one day to semi-retire and be the proprietor of a neighborhood eating and drinking establishment in a warm sunny beach community. He can be contacted by e-mail at robert@eightotwo.com.

Contents at a Glance

Foreword   *xxi*

Introduction   *xxiii*

Assessment Test   *xxxvi*

Chapter 1   Introduction to Wireless Local Area Networking   1

Chapter 2   Wireless LAN Infrastructure Devices   27

Chapter 3   Wireless LAN Client Devices   61

Chapter 4   Radio Frequency (RF) Fundamentals for
                Wireless LAN Technology   95

Chapter 5   Access Methods, Architectures, and
                Spread Spectrum Technology   131

Chapter 6   WLAN Antennas and Accessories   159

Chapter 7   WLAN Terminology and Technology   205

Chapter 8   Planning a WLAN Site Survey   249

Chapter 9   Performing a WLAN Site Survey   283

Chapter 10 WLAN Security   337

Chapter 11 Troubleshooting and Maintaining Wireless Networks   381

Appendix   About the Companion CD   421

Glossary   **427**

Index   *445*

Contents

Foreword   *xxi*

Introduction   *xxiii*

Assessment Test   *xxxvi*

Chapter 1   Introduction to Wireless Local Area Networking   1

Common WLAN Deployment Scenarios   3
    Small Office/Home Office (SOHO)   4
    Enterprise Deployments: Corporate Data Access
       and End-User Mobility   4
    Extending Existing Networks with Wireless LAN   5
    Mobile Office and Public Wireless Hotspots   5
    Educational Institutions: Classroom Deployments   6
    Healthcare   7
    Last-Mile Data Delivery: Wireless ISP   7
    Industrial, Municipal, Law Enforcement, and
       Transportation Networks   7
    Building-to-Building Connectivity   8
Radio Frequency Regulatory Domain Governing Bodies   9
    United States: Federal Communications Commission (FCC)   10
    Europe: European Telecommunications Standards
       Institute (ETSI)   11
IEEE and Wireless LAN Standards   11
    802.11   11
    802.11b   12
    802.11a   12
    802.11g   13
    802.11n   14
    Additional IEEE 802.11 Amendments   16
Interoperability Certifications   16
    Wi-Fi Alliance   17
    Wi-Fi Protected Access (WPA) Certification Overview   17
    Wi-Fi Protected Access 2 (WPA 2.0) Certification Overview   18
    Wi-Fi Multimedia (WMM) Certification Overview   18
    Wi-Fi Multimedia Power Save (WMM-PS) Certification
       Overview   19
    Wi-Fi Protected Setup (WPS) Certification Overview   19
Summary   20

		Key Terms	20
		Exam Essentials	21
		Review Questions	22
		Answers to Review Questions	26
Chapter	**2**	**Wireless LAN Infrastructure Devices**	**27**
		OSI Model Basics	28
		Access Points (AP)	29
		Autonomous Access Points	31
		Lightweight Access Points	38
		Mesh Access Points	38
		Wireless LAN Routers	40
		Wireless Bridges	42
		Wireless Repeaters	42
		Wireless LAN Controller/Switch	43
		Power over Ethernet (PoE)	47
		Summary	51
		Exam Essentials	52
		Key Terms	53
		Review Questions	54
		Answers to Review Questions	58
Chapter	**3**	**Wireless LAN Client Devices**	**61**
		PCMCIA	62
		Features of PCMCIA Cards	63
		Installation and Configuration of PCMCIA Cards	64
		ExpressCard	68
		Features of the ExpressCard	68
		Installation and Configuration of an ExpressCard	69
		USB 1.0, USB 1.1, and USB 2.0	69
		Features of USB	70
		Installation and Configuration of USB Devices	71
		CompactFlash (CF) Devices	73
		Features of CF Cards	73
		Installation and Configuration of a CF Card	74
		Secure Digital (SD)	74
		Features of SDIO Cards	75
		Installation and Configuration of SDIO Cards	75
		Peripheral Component Interconnect (PCI)	75
		Features of PCI	76
		Installation and Configuration of PCI Cards	77

Mini-PCI and Mini-PCIe (Mini-PCI Express)   79
    Features of Mini-PCI and Mini-PCIe Cards   79
    Installation and Configuration of Mini-PCI and
      Mini-PCIe Cards   80
Workgroup Bridges   81
    Features of Workgroup/Client Bridges   82
    Installation and Configuration of Workgroup/Client Bridges 83
Client Device Drivers   83
Client Utility Software   84
    Manufacturer-Specific Client Utilities   85
    Third-Party Client Utilities   86
Summary   86
Exam Essentials   87
Key Terms   88
Review Questions   89
Answers to Review Questions   93

**Chapter 4   Radio Frequency (RF) Fundamentals for
Wireless LAN Technology   95**

Understanding Radio Frequency (RF)   96
    Wavelength   98
    Frequency   99
    Amplitude   100
    Phase   100
    Frequencies Used for Wireless LANs   101
Coverage and Capacity   104
    Coverage   105
    Capacity   108
    Channel Reuse and Co-location   109
RF Range and Speed   110
    Line of Sight   111
    Interference   112
    Environment: RF Behavior   114
Basic Units of RF Measurement   118
    Absolute Measurements of Power   118
    Relative Measurements of Power   119
Summary   122
Exam Essentials   122
Key Terms   123
Review Questions   124
Answers to Review Questions   128

Chapter 5   **Access Methods, Architectures, and Spread Spectrum Technology**   **131**

Network Access Methods   132
  Detecting Network Traffic Collisions with CSMA/CD   133
  Avoiding Network Traffic Collisions with CSMA/CA   134
  Reserving Time for Data Transmission Using
    Distributed Coordination Function (DCF)   135
  Effects of Half Duplex on Wireless Throughput   135
  Narrowband vs. Spread Spectrum Communication   136
Spread Spectrum Technology   138
  Frequency-Hopping Spread Spectrum (FHSS)   138
  Direct-Sequence Spread Spectrum (DSSS)   140
  High Rate/Direct-Sequence Spread Spectrum (HR/DSSS)   140
  DSSS and HR/DSSS Channels   141
  Orthogonal Frequency Division Multiplexing (OFDM)   143
  OFDM Channels   144
  Multiple Input/Multiple Output (MIMO)   146
  MIMO Channels   147
  Co-location of HR/DSSS and ERP-OFDM Systems   147
  Adjacent-Channel and Co-channel Interference   148
  WLAN/WPAN Coexistence   148
Summary   150
Exam Essentials   151
Key Terms   152
Review Questions   153
Answers to Review Questions   157

Chapter 6   **WLAN Antennas and Accessories**   **159**

Basic RF Antenna Concepts   160
  RF Lobes   161
  Beamwidth   161
  Antenna Gain   163
  Passive Gain   164
  Active Gain   165
  Antenna Polarization   166
WLAN Antenna Types   167
  Omnidirectional Antennas   167
  Omnidirectional Antenna Specifications   168
  Semidirectional Antennas   170
  Highly Directional Antennas   181
  Highly Directional Antenna Specifications   182

RF Cables and Connectors 184
    Cable Types 184
    Cable Length 184
    Cable Cost 185
    Impedance and VSWR 186
    RF Connectors 186
Factors in Antenna Installation 187
    Addressing the Effects of Earth Curvature 187
    Antenna Placement 187
    Minimizing the Effects of Multipath Using
       Antenna Diversity 188
Combating Effects of Wind and Lightning on
   Wireless Connections 190
    Lightning Arrestors 190
    Grounding Rods 191
Installation Safety 191
Antenna Mounting 191
    Pole/Mast Mount 192
    Ceiling Mount 193
    Wall Mount 194
Maintaining Clear Communications 194
    Visual Line of Sight 194
    RF Line of Sight 194
    Fresnel Zone 194
Summary 195
Exam Essentials 196
Key Terms 197
Review Questions 198
Answers to Review Questions 202

Chapter   7   WLAN Terminology and Technology   205

Wireless LAN Modes of Operation 206
    Independent Basic Service Set (IBSS) 207
    Basic Service Set (BSS) 212
    Extended Service Set (ESS) 214
Connecting to a Wireless Network 216
    Frame Types 216
    Passive Scanning 217
    Active Scanning 218
    Authentication 219
    Association 223
    Deauthentication and Disassociation 224

Distribution System (DS)   225
Data Rates   226
Throughput   228
Dynamic Rate Switching (DRS)   231
WLAN Roaming   232
Power Saving Operation   234
    Active Mode (AM)   234
    Power Save (PS) Mode   234
    Automatic Power Save Delivery (APSD)   236
Protection Mechanisms   236
    Extended Rate Physical (ERP) Protection Mechanism   236
    High Throughput (HT) Protection Mechanism   237
Summary   239
Exam Essentials   241
Key Terms   242
Review Questions   243
Answers to Review Questions   247

Chapter   8   Planning a WLAN Site Survey   249

Wireless LAN Site Surveys   250
    Size of Physical Location   251
    Intended Use of the Network   251
    Number of Users   251
    Performance Expectations   252
Gathering Business Requirements   252
    General Office/Enterprise   253
    Manufacturing   254
    Warehousing   256
    Retail/Point of Sale (POS)   257
    Health Care/Medical   257
    Government/Military   259
    Education   260
    Public Access, Hotspots, Hospitality   261
Interviewing Managers and Users   262
    Manufacturer Guidelines and Deployment Guides   265
Defining Physical and Data Security Requirements   265
Gathering Site-Specific Documentation   266
    Floor Plans and Blueprints   266
    Furnishings   266
    Electrical Specifications   267
Documenting Existing Network Characteristics   267
Identifying Infrastructure Connectivity and Power Requirements   268

Understanding RF Coverage and Capacity Requirements   270
Client Connectivity Requirements   270
Antenna Use Consideration   271
Summary   274
Exam Essentials   275
Key Terms   275
Review Questions   276
Answers to Review Questions   280

Chapter   9   Performing a WLAN Site Survey   283

The Physical Site Survey Process   285
RF Spectrum Analysis   286
   Wi-Fi and Non-Wi-Fi Interference Sources 289
   Wi-Fi Interference   294
Performing a Manual Site Survey   299
   Obtaining a Floor Plan or Blueprint   300
   Identifying Existing Wireless Networks   300
   Testing Access Point Placement   301
   Analyzing the Results   303
   Advantages and Disadvantages of Manual Site Survey   303
   Software Assisted Manual Site Survey   303
   Manual Site Survey Toolkit   306
Performing a Predictive Site Survey   307
Protocol Analysis   312
Documenting Existing Network Characteristics   318
RF Coverage Requirements   319
Infrastructure Hardware Selection and Placement   320
Infrastructure Connectivity and Power Requirements   320
Received Signal Strength   321
Antenna Use Considerations   323
   Testing Multiple Antenna Types   323
   Choosing the Correct Antennas   324
Channel Architectures   325
   Multiple Channel Architecture (MCA)   326
   Single Channel Architecture (SCA)   326
Installation Limitations   327
Site Survey Report   328
Summary   328
Exam Essentials   329
Key Terms   330
Review Questions   331
Answers to Review Questions   335

Chapter	10	**WLAN Security**	**337**

Introduction to Wireless Security 339
Wireless LAN Threats and Intrusion 339
IEEE 802.11 Standards Security 341
  Open System Authentication 341
  Shared Key Authentication 342
Early WLAN Security Mechanisms 342
  Service Set Identifier (SSID) 343
  SSID Hiding 343
  Media Access Control (MAC) Address 344
Authentication and Encryption 346
  About Wired Equivalent Privacy (WEP) 346
  How to Use WEP 346
SOHO and Enterprise Security Solutions 348
PIN-Based or Push-Button Configuration (PBC)
  Wireless Security 348
  PIN-Based Security 348
  Push-Button Configuration (PBC) Security 348
Passphrase-Based Security 350
  Passphrase Features 351
User-Based Security 351
  802.1X 352
  EAP 353
  802.1X/EAP 353
  Remote Authentication Dial In User Service 354
Encryption: WEP/TKIP/CCMP 356
  WEP 356
  TKIP 357
  CCMP 359
Role-Based Access Control (RBAC) 360
Virtual Private Networking (VPN) 360
  PPTP 362
  L2TP 363
  Components of a VPN Solution 363
Wireless Intrusion Prevention Systems (WIPS) 367
Regulatory Compliance 369
  PCI Compliance 369
  HIPAA Compliance 370
  Other Regulatory Compliances 370
Summary 371
Exam Essentials 372
Key Terms 373
Review Questions 374
Answers to Review Questions 378

Chapter   11   Troubleshooting and Maintaining Wireless Networks   **381**

Identifying Wireless LAN Problems   382
   Transmitters and Receivers   384
   No Connectivity   384
   Intermittent Connectivity   390
   Throughput   394
   Software and Hardware Upgrades   398
Optimizing Wireless Networks   404
   Infrastructure Hardware Selection and Placement   405
   Identifying, Locating, and Removing Sources
     of Interference   405
   Client Load Balancing   406
   Analyzing Infrastructure Capacity and Utilization   407
   Multipath   408
   Hidden Node   408
Summary   412
Exam Essentials   413
Key Terms   413
Review Questions   414
Answers to Review Questions   418

Appendix   About the Companion CD   **421**

What You'll Find on the CD   422
   Demonstration Software Programs   422
   Demonstration Software Programs
     Available for Download   423
   Case Studies   423
   Case Studies Available for Download   424
   Generic Floor Plan   424
   Applications   424
   Sensor Placement Site Survey Form   424
   Sybex Test Engine   424
   Electronic Flashcards   425
System Requirements   425
Using the CD   425
Troubleshooting   426
   Customer Care   426

Glossary   **427**

Index   *445*

Table of Exercises

Exercise **3.1** PCMCIA Card Installation Steps 65

Exercise **3.2** Installing a USB 2.0 Wireless LAN Adapter 71

Exercise **3.3** PCI Card Installation Steps 77

Exercise **3.4** Mini-PCI and Mini-PCIe Installation Steps 81

Exercise **4.1** How to Demonstrate Fresnel Zone and Blockage 111

Exercise **6.1** Demonstrate Passive Gain 165

Exercise **6.2** Steps for Installing a Pole/Mast Mount 193

Exercise **7.1** How to Measure Throughput of a Wireless Network 229

Exercise **9.1** Spectrum Analysis Demonstration 290

Exercise **9.2** PC Card Spectrum Analyzer Demonstration 294

Exercise **9.3** Predictive Site Survey Demonstration 309

Exercise **9.4** Protocol Analyzer Demonstration 314

Exercise **10.1** VPN Setup 364

Exercise **11.1** Upgrading a Device Driver 399

Foreword

Manufacturers, value added resellers (VARs), and end-user organizations are now seeing the value of training and certifying not only "techies," but account managers, sales representatives, project managers, help desk professionals, and others with similar roles on Wi-Fi technology. For maximum ROI, it's important that this Wi-Fi training and certification be appropriate to these specific job roles. The Wi-Fi landscape is continually changing, and keeping abreast of trends, terminology, and technology has never been more important.

With all of this change, how can an organization be sure to train and certify its people on relevant and position-appropriate material? How can an organization provide an upwardly mobile learning path should its people change positions? How can an organization be sure that the training being provided to its people will continue to be relevant should they decide to partner with a different or additional vendor? These are valid concerns faced by large organizations every day, and CWNP has the answer. CWNP's new Certified Wireless Technology Specialist (CWTS™) certification has been targeted at these user groups with the modus operandi "*what it is, not how it works*." For example, in most organizations it's clear that a Wi-Fi account manager needs to understand what an RF site survey is and why it's important in given circumstances, but it's also clear why the account manager doesn't need to understand every nuance of performing an RF site survey in order to accomplish his or her own sales functions. The same applies to a plethora of topics, from understanding Wi-Fi equipment types to Wi-Fi security.

Wi-Fi terminology is a world of confusion in and of itself, but the confusion can be greatly reduced with even a minimal amount of targeted education. It doesn't help that marketing departments at various manufacturers create a new marketing term for every new technology offering, often changing their own terminology for the purpose of differentiation. Most technologies, devices, equipment features, architectures, and the like have industry-standard names. Such standardized naming conventions are facilitated by the IEEE, Wi-Fi Alliance, and by CWNP. For example, when implementing a single channel architecture (a term that also has various marketing terms in the industry) system, each channel is called a _____. This could be a *span*, *stack*, *layer*, *blanket*, *channel*, or perhaps something new in the near future. They all mean the same thing. How is the customer to compare apples-to-apples when Wi-Fi terminology is all over the map? This is where trained people make all the difference.

The book you now hold in your hand is an important step in studying for the CWTS certification. The *CWTS: Certified Wireless Technology Specialist Official Study Guide* covers the CWTS exam objectives step-by-step in a concise manner. It's a no-nonsense approach to obtaining a certification that will differentiate you from your peers and help you wins sales, better support your customers, and most of all, grow in your career.

Robert Bartz has been part of the CWNP program since day 1, when in our very first class in November 2001 he sat front-left paying close attention while I was explaining RF behavior. Thereafter, he very quickly passed the CWNA exam and moved on to become one of our first instructors. He has participated in CWNP in a variety of ways over the years and has added significant value to the program as a whole. He has taught CWNP classes at every level and to diverse audiences around the globe since 2001, and it's easy to give both Robert and his new book a big thumbs-up. I would also like to thank Sybex for producing such high-quality books for CWNP. They are a class act through and through, and we look forward to working with them more in the future. Now, what are you waiting for? Stop reading this foreword, and get on to Chapter 1. Your future in Wi-Fi awaits!

Devin Akin
Chief Technology Officer
The CWNP Program

Introduction

This book is intended to provide an introduction to the exciting and emerging world of wireless LAN technology. This technology continues to expand at a phenomenal pace with constant improvements in speed, reliability, and security. Reading this book will teach you the fundamentals of standards-based technology, giving you an overview of the design, communication, hardware components, and maintenance associated with wireless LAN technology, commonly referred to as Wi-Fi™.

In addition to providing an overview of the technology, this book will help you prepare for the Certified Wireless Technology Specialist (CWTS) certification exam available from the CWNP program. CWTS is an entry-level enterprise wireless LAN certification, and is recommended prior to the Certified Wireless Network Administrator (CWNA) certification. CWTS is designed as a replacement for the Wireless# Certification. This certification is geared specifically toward both wireless LAN (WLAN) sales and support staff for those in the enterprise WLAN industry.

Not only will this book help you prepare for the CWTS Certification exam, it will give you the fundamental knowledge, tools, and terminology to more effectively sell and support enterprise WLAN technologies. The main goal of this book is for you to learn "what it is," not "how it works." The "how" part comes later in other CWNP Study Guides and instructor-led courses. After reading this book and completing all the available practice exam tools included, you will have the knowledge needed to take the CWTS certification exam.

Finally, the CD included with this book contains evaluation software you can install in order to become familiar with RF spectrum analysis, perform some limited packet analysis, and explore site survey tools.

For more information about the CWTS and other vendor-neutral wireless LAN certifications from the CWNP program, visit www.cwnp.com.

About CWNP®

CWNP is the abbreviation for Certified Wireless Network Professional and is the industry standard for vendor-neutral, enterprise wireless LAN certifications. CWNP currently offers five levels of enterprise WLAN certifications, from novice to expert. The goal of CWNP is to provide educational resources and certifications that are recognized worldwide to information technology (IT) and sales professionals in the field of wireless networking technology. By acquiring this knowledge, these professionals will be able to enter any business and sell, design, install, manage, and support the wireless LAN infrastructure regardless of which manufacturer's solution is used.

In addition to CWTS, there are four other wireless certifications currently offered from CWNP:

CWNA®: Certified Wireless Network Administrator   The CWNA® (Certified Wireless Network Administrator) certification is the foundation-level enterprise wireless LAN certification for the CWNP program. The CWNA certification will validate one's skills to successfully administer enterprise-class wireless LANs. Passing the CWNA exam will earn one credit toward the more advanced CWNP certifications. The CWNA exam measures one's ability to understand the fundamentals of RF behavior and to describe the features and functions of various WLAN components. Passing the PW0-104, Wireless LAN Administration certification exam will satisfy the requirement to become CWNA certified.

CWSP®: Certified Wireless Security Professional   The CWSP® (Certified Wireless Security Professional) certification is an advanced-level WLAN certification offered by the CWNP program. Acquiring this certification will prove one's ability to successfully apply the most up-to-date wireless LAN security solutions to an organization's wireless LAN. This certification will ensure that the successful candidate understands the security weaknesses inherent in wireless LANs, the solutions available to address those weaknesses, and the steps necessary to implement a secure and manageable wireless LAN in an enterprise environment. Successfully passing two exams is required to become CWSP certified:

- Exam PW0-104 – Wireless LAN Administration
- Exam PW0-200 – Wireless LAN Security

CWNE®: Certified Wireless Network Expert   The CWNE® credential is the final certification step in the CWNP program. By successfully completing the CWNE requirements, one will have demonstrated that they have the most advanced skills available in today's wireless LAN market. CWNE assures that the skills mastered include the ability to administer, install, configure, troubleshoot, and design wireless network systems. Additional skills include protocol analysis, intrusion detection and prevention, performance and QoS analysis, spectrum analysis, and WLAN management.

In order to become CWNE certified, one must pass the PW0-104, PW0-200, and PW0-300 exams, and hold a valid CWSP certification at the time of application for CWNE. Successfully passing these exams is not all that is required. To maintain CWNE certification, the following criteria must be met:

- Pass all three exams, PW0-104, PW0-200, and PW0-300
- Professional experience
- Three letters of endorsement
- 60 points in the CWNE points schedule
- Continuing education requirement

 For additional information on the details required for CWNE certification, visit www.cwnp.com

CWNT®: Certified Wireless Network Trainer   Certified Wireless Network Trainers (CWNT®) are qualified instructors certified by the CWNP program to deliver CWNP training courses to IT professionals. CWNTs are technical and instructional experts in wireless technologies, products, and solutions. CWNP Training Partners are required to use CWNTs when delivering training using Official CWNP Courseware.

To become a CWNT, the requirements include:

- Attend an official class for the CWNP level to be taught
- Pass the appropriate level exam with a minimum score of at least 80%
- A minimum of 12 months of documented IT industry training experience

CWNP Learning Resources

There are a variety of resources available from CWNP to help one learn vendor-neutral wireless LAN technology. Listed are some of these resources:

- Self-study materials
- Official study guides from Sybex
- Online practice exams from www.cwnp.com
- Instructor-led training
- Online training
- Computer-based training (CBT)
- CWNP website
- CWNP forums
- CWNP blog
- CWNP learning center, 1,000+ white papers

How to Become a CWTS

To become a CWTS, you must complete the following two steps:

- Agree that you have read and will abide by the terms and conditions of the CWNP confidentiality agreement
- Pass the CWTS PW0-070 certification exam.

A copy of the CWNP confidentiality agreement can be found online at the CWNP website.

When you take the exam, you will be required to accept the confidentiality agreement before you can continue to complete the exam. After you have agreed, you will be able to continue with the exam. When you pass the exam with a score of 70 percent or higher, you will have met the requirements to become CWTS certified.

The information for the CWTS exam is as follows:

- Exam name: Certified Wireless Technology Specialist
- Exam number: PW0-070
- Cost: $125.00 (USD)
- Duration: 90 minutes
- Questions: 60
- Question types: Multiple choice/multiple answer
- Passing score: 70 percent (80 percent for instructors)
- Available languages: English
- Renewal: None—lifetime certification. Recommended prior to CWNA.
- Availability: Register at Pearson VUE (www.vue.com/cwnp)

When you schedule the exam, you will receive instructions regarding appointment and cancellation procedures, ID requirements, and information about the testing center location. In addition, you will receive a registration and payment confirmation e-mail. Exams can be scheduled weeks in advance or, in some cases, even as late as the same day.

After you have successfully passed the CWTS exam, the CWNP program will award you the lifetime certification. If the e-mail contact information you provided the testing center is correct, you will receive an e-mail from CWNP recognizing your accomplishment and providing you with a CWNP certification number. After you earn any CWNP certification, you can request a certification kit. The kit includes a congratulatory letter, a certificate, and a wallet-sized personalized ID card. You will need to log in to the CWNP tracking system, verify your contact information, and request your certification kit.

Who Should Buy this Book?

This book is intended to provide an overview of wireless LAN technology for sales and technical support professionals. This book is written with the CWTS exam objectives in mind and "what it is," not "how it works." The exam objectives were designed based on the skill set the intended audience should need in order to perform their job functions or roles in an organization. One thing to keep in mind is that this book will introduce and teach you a technology, a combination of local area networking and radio frequency.

If you follow the exam objectives, perform the hands-on exercises, and utilize all the available exam questions and practice exams included with the CD and on www.cwnp.com, this book should be enough to effectively prepare you to pass the CWTS certification exam. It will also serve as a stepping-stone to more advanced books that teach the technology in more depth as well as a reference guide for the technology.

How to Use this Book and the CD

This book includes a CD-ROM with exam questions and flashcards. These are designed to test your knowledge on the information you have learned from reading the book and performing the exercises. Although there is no guarantee you will pass the certification exam if you use this book and CD, you will have the tools necessary that effectively prepare you to do so.

Before you begin   At the beginning of the book (right after this introduction) is an assessment test you can use to check your readiness for the certification exam. Take this test before you start reading the book; it will help you determine the areas you may need to brush up on. The answers to the assessment test appear on a separate page after the last question of the test. Each answer includes an explanation and describes why the other options are incorrect.

Chapter review questions   To test your knowledge as you progress through this book, there are review questions at the end of each chapter. As you finish each chapter, answer the review questions and then check your answers—the correct answers appear on the page following the last review question. You can go back and revisit the section that deals with each question you answered wrong to ensure that you understand the material and answer correctly the next time you are tested on that topic.

Electronic flashcards   You will find flashcard questions on the CD for on-the-go review. These are short questions and answers, just like other flashcards you may be familiar with. You can answer them on your PC or download them onto a Palm device for quick and convenient reviewing.

Test engine   The CD also contains the Sybex Test Engine. With this custom test engine, you can identify weak areas up front and then develop a solid studying strategy that includes each of the robust testing features described previously. The readme file on the CD will walk you through the quick, easy installation process.

In addition to the assessment test and the chapter review questions, you will find two bonus exams. Use the test engine to take these practice exams just as if you were taking the actual exam (without any reference material). When you have finished the first exam, move on to the next one to solidify your test-taking skills. After you get a high percentage of the answers correct, it is an indication you are ready to take the actual certification exam.

Labs and exercises   Several chapters in this book have exercises that use evaluation software that is either provided on the CD-ROM included with this book or downloadable from the manufacturer's website. These exercises will provide you with a broader learning experience by providing hands-on experience and step-by-step problem solving.

White papers   Several wireless networking white papers are also provided on the CD-ROM included with this book or available for download. These white papers serve as additional reference material for preparing for the CWTS or other CWNP certification exams.

The CWTS Certification Exam (PWO-070) Is Based on the Exam Objectives

It is important to note that in order to pass the certification exam you should study from the currently posted exam objectives. Use this book as an learning aid to understand the exam objectives. For the most up-to-date certification exam objectives, visit the CWNP website at www.cwnp.com.

Exam Objectives

The Certified Wireless Technology Specialist (CWTS) certification, covering the current objectives, will certify that successful candidates know the fundamentals of RF behavior, can describe the features and functions of wireless components, and have the skills needed to install and configure wireless network hardware components. A typical candidate should have a basic understanding of data networking concepts.

The skills and knowledge measured by this examination are derived from a survey of wireless networking experts and professionals. The results of this survey were used in weighing the subject areas and ensuring that the weighting is representative of the relative importance of the content.

The following chart provides the breakdown of the exam, showing you the weight of each section:

Subject Area	% of Exam
Wi-Fi Technology, Standards, and Certifications	15%
Hardware and Software	25%
Radio Frequency (RF) Fundamentals	15%
Site Surveying and Installation	15%
Applications, Support, and Troubleshooting	15%
Security and Compliance	15%
Total	100%

Wireless Technologies, Standards, and Certifications—15%

1.1. Define the roles of the following organizations in providing direction and accountability within the wireless networking industry

- IEEE
- Wi-Fi Alliance
- Regulatory Domain Governing Bodies

1.2. Define basic characteristics of Wi-Fi technology

- Range, coverage, and capacity
- Frequencies/channels used
- Channel reuse and co-location
- Active and passive scanning
- Power saving operation
- Data rates and throughput
- Dynamic rate switching
- Authentication and association
- The distribution system and roaming
- Infrastructure and ad hoc modes
- BSSID, SSID, BSS, ESS
- Protection mechanisms

1.3. Summarize the basic attributes and advantages of the following WLAN standards, amendments, and product certifications

- Wi-Fi certification
  - 802.11a
  - 802.11b
  - 802.11g
  - 802.11n
- Wi-Fi Multimedia (WMM) certification
- WMM Power Save (WMM-PS) certification
- Wi-Fi Protected Setup (WPS) certification
  - Push-button
  - PIN-based
- Wi-Fi Protected Access (WPA/WPA2) certification
  - Enterprise
  - Personal

Hardware and Software—25%

2.1 Identify the purpose, features, and functions of the following wireless network components. Choose the appropriate installation or configuration steps in a given scenario.

- Access points
  - Lightweight
  - Autonomous
  - Mesh
- Wireless LAN routers
- Wireless bridges
- Wireless repeaters
- WLAN controller/switch
  - Distributed AP connectivity
  - Direct AP connectivity
  - Layer 2 and Layer 3 AP connectivity
- Power over Ethernet (PoE) devices
  - Midspan
  - Endpoint

2.2. Identify the purpose, features, and functions of the following client devices. Choose the appropriate installation or configuration steps in a given scenario.

- PC cards (ExpressCard, CardBus, and PCMCIA)
- USB2, CF, and SD devices
- PCI, Mini-PCI, and Mini-PCIe cards
- Workgroup bridges
- Client utility software and drivers

2.3. Identify the purpose, features, and functions of and the appropriate installation or configuration steps for the following types of antennas

- Omnidirectional/dipole
- Semidirectional
- Highly directional

Radio Frequency (RF) Fundamentals—15%

3.1 Define the basic units of RF measurements

- Milliwatt (mW)
- Decibel (dB)
- dBm
- dBi

3.2 Identify factors that affect the range and speed of RF transmissions

- Line-of-sight requirements
- Interference (baby monitors, spread spectrum phones, microwave ovens)
- Environmental factors

3.3 Define and differentiate between the following Physical layer wireless technologies

- HR/DSSS
- OFDM
- MIMO

3.4 Define concepts that make up the functionality of RF and spread spectrum technology

- OFDM and HR/DSSS channels
- Co-location of HR/DSSS and OFDM systems
- Adjacent-channel and co-channel interference
- WLAN/WPAN co-existence
- CSMA/CA operation – half duplex

3.5 Identify RF signal characteristics and the applications of basic RF antenna concepts

- Passive gain
- Beamwidths
- Simple diversity
- Polarization

3.6 Describe the proper locations and methods for installing RF antennas

- Pole/mast mount
- Ceiling mount
- Wall mount

3.7 Identify the use of the following WLAN accessories and explain how to select and install them for optimal performance and regulatory domain compliance

- RF cables
- RF connectors
- Lightning arrestors and grounding rods

Site Surveying and Installation—15%

4.1 Understand and describe the requirements to gather information prior to the site survey and do reporting after the site survey

- Gathering business requirements
- Interviewing managers and users
- Defining physical and data security requirements
- Gathering site-specific documentation
- Documenting existing network characteristics
- Identifying infrastructure connectivity and power requirements
- Understanding RF coverage requirements
- Client connectivity requirements
- Antenna use considerations

4.2 Define and differentiate between the following WLAN system architectures and understand site survey concepts related to each architecture. Identify and explain best practices for access point placement and density.

- Multiple channel architecture (MCA)
- Single channel architecture (SCA)

4.3 Define the need for and the use of a manual site survey tool and differentiate between the following manual site survey types

- Active surveys
- Passive surveys

4.4 Differentiate between manual and predictive site surveys

- Advantages and disadvantages of each site survey methodology

4.5 Define the need for and use of a protocol analyzer in a manual site survey as it relates to the following

- Identifying, locating, and assessing nearby WLANs

4.6 Differentiate between site surveys involving networks with and without a mesh access layer

4.7 Define the need for and use of a spectrum analyzer in a manual site survey

- Identification and location of interference sources
- Differentiation of Wi-Fi and non-Wi-Fi interference sources

4.8 Identify limitations on hardware placement

- Areas where APs or antennas cannot be placed
- Areas beyond Ethernet distance limitations

4.9 Understand industry best practices for optimal use of directional and omnidirectional antennas in site surveys

Applications, Support, and Troubleshooting—15%

5.1 Identify deployment scenarios for common WLAN network types

- Small office/home office (SOHO)
- Extension of existing networks into remote locations
- Building-to-building connectivity
- Public wireless hotspots
- Mobile office, classroom, industrial, and health care
- Municipal and law-enforcement connectivity
- Corporate data access and end-user mobility
- Last-mile data delivery, wireless ISP
- Transportation networks (trains, planes, automobiles)

5.2 Recognize common problems associated with wireless networks and their symptoms, and identify steps to isolate and troubleshoot the problem. Given a problem situation, interpret the symptoms and the most likely cause. Problems may include:

- Decreased throughput
- Intermittent or no connectivity
- Weak signal strength
- Device upgrades

5.3 Identify procedures to optimize wireless networks in specific situations

- Infrastructure hardware selection and placement
- Identifying, locating, and removing sources of interference
- Client load balancing
- Analyzing infrastructure capacity and utilization
- Multipath and hidden nodes

Security and Compliance—15%

6.1 Identify and describe the following WLAN security techniques

- SSID hiding
- Legacy security mechanisms: WEP and MAC filtering
- User-based security: 802.1X/EAP and RADIUS authentication
- Passphrase-based security
- Push-button or PIN-based wireless security
- Encryption: TKIP/CCMP
- Role-based access control (RBAC)
- Virtual private networking (VPN)
- Wireless intrusion prevention systems (WIPS)
- Captive Portal

6.2 Regulatory Compliance

- PCI compliance
- HIPAA compliance
- Enforcing compliance with WIPS

CWNP Exam Terminology

The CWNP program uses specific terminology when phrasing the questions on any of the CWNP exams. The terminology used most often mirrors the language that is used in the IEEE 802.11-2007 standard. While technically correct, the terminology used in the exam questions often is not the same as the marketing terminology that is used by the Wi-Fi Alliance or the manufacturers of WLAN equipment.

The most current IEEE version of the 802.11 standard is the IEEE 802.11-2007 document, which includes all the amendments that have been ratified prior to the document's publication. Standards bodies such as the IEEE often create several amendments to a standard before "rolling up" the ratified amendments (finalized or approved versions) into a new standard.

For example, you might already be familiar with the term *802.11g*, which is a ratified amendment that has now been integrated into the IEEE 802.11-2007 standard. The technology that was originally defined by the 802.11g amendment is called Extended Rate Physical (ERP). Although the name 802.11g effectively remains the more commonly used marketing terminology, exam questions may use the technical term ERP instead of 802.11g. A document with exam terms is available from the CWNP website. At the time of this writing, the URL to access this document is www.cwnp.com/exams/exam_terms.html.

Assessment Test

1. Which amendment to the standard operates in the 2.4 GHz ISM band and supports data rates up to 54 Mbps?

   A. 802.11a

   B. 802.11b

   C. 802.11g

   D. 802.11n

2. The access method that an IEEE 802.11a wireless network would use to get control of the wireless medium in order to transmit data is called what?

   A. CSMA/CD

   B. FHSS

   C. HR/DSSS

   D. CSMA/CA

   E. CSMA/DSSS

3. What will a protocol analyzer do during a manual site survey?

   A. Perform a RF analysis of the proposed area

   B. Help locate sources of RF interference

   C. Identify existing wireless networks

   D. Describe security requirements of the wireless LAN

4. IEEE 802.11g wireless networks can operate in which unlicensed RF band?

   A. 902 – 928 MHz ISM

   B. 2.400 – 2.500 GHz UNII

   C. 5.725 – 5.825 GHZ UNII

   D. 5.250 – 5.350 GHz UNII

   E. 2.400 – 2.500 GHz ISM

5. What could be the cause of intermittent connectivity for a wireless client device in an IEEE 802.11g wireless network?

   A. A weak received signal strength on the client

   B. A signal-to-noise ratio of 35 dB

   C. The access point power is set too high and overpowering the client device

   D. The radio in the client device is disabled

6. Which statement is accurate regarding mesh access points and mesh technology?

   A. Mesh is a legacy technology and the priority should be to select an appropriate upgrade path.

   B. In a full mesh network, all nodes connect together with at least two paths for every node.

   C. Mesh access points are unreliable communications and represent a single point of failure.

   D. Mesh access points require a separate radio for communications and therefore can be costly to implement.

7. PIN-based wireless LAN security is _____.

   A. Addressed in the Wi-Fi Protected Setup certification

   B. Required by the 802.11i amendment

   C. Best used in enterprise wireless networks

   D. A multifactor authentication mechanism for WLANs

8. Open system authentication is _____ in an IEEE 802.11 wireless network.

   A. Flawed

   B. Optional

   C. Secure

   D. Required

9. The amount of output power and useable frequency ranges for wireless devices is determined by which organization?

   A. Wireless Ethernet Compatibility Alliance

   B. Wi-Fi Alliance

   C. Institute of Electrical and Electronics Engineers

   D. Regulatory domain governing bodies

10. Which IEEE 802.11 standard or amendment can use three radio chains per band and multiple input/multiple output (MIMO) to transmit data?

    A. 802.11

    B. 802.11a

    C. 802.11g

    D. 802.11h

    E. 802.11n

11. What can contribute to voltage standing wave ratio (VSWR) in an IEEE 802.11g wireless LAN circuit?

    A. Output power of the access point

    B. Impedance mismatch

    C. Gain of an antenna

    D. Attenuation value of cable

12. Wireless repeaters are devices in wireless networking that are _____.

    A. Used to extend the radio frequency cell

    B. Used to repeat and strengthen the RF signal for better performance

    C. Used as a backup solution in the event of an access point failure

    D. Used to increase the bandwidth of the WLAN

13. What does the term *authenticator* identify in an IEEE 802.1X secure network?

    A. The RADIUS server

    B. The access point

    C. The client device

    D. The RAS server

14. An independent basic service set requires a minimum of how many access points?

    A. 0

    B. 1

    C. 2

    D. 3

15. An HR/DSSS channel used to transmit data an IEEE 802.11g wireless LAN is _____ wide.

    A. 2.412 GHz

    B. 5.160 GHz

    C. 11 MHz

    D. 22 MHz

16. What is the horizontal angle of measurement in degrees of an omnidirectional antenna with a gain of 2.2 dBi?

    A. 90

    B. 180

    C. 270

    D. 360

    E. 0

17. You are a wireless LAN engineer hired to perform a predictive analysis site survey for a 150,000-square-foot office building. This space includes walled offices as well as cubicles. What is an advantage of a predictive modeling site survey over a manual survey in this specific application?

    A. A predictive site survey is the most accurate available.

    B. The amount of time required for accurate results is much less than a complete manual walkthrough.

    C. Because of an extensive attenuation database, a predictive modeling site survey will be able to determine the interference values of any obstacles.

    D. A predictive modeling site survey will allow you to experiment with different access point criteria, including power settings, channels, and locations, without the need for a physical visit.

18. Which RF channels are considered non-overlapping for an IEEE 802.11g network?

    A. 1 and 4

    B. 6 and 9

    C. 1 and 6

    D. 3 and 7

    E. 11 and 13

19. The Service Set Identifier (SSID) in an IEEE 802.11 wireless LAN is also known as what?

    A. The name of the wireless network

    B. The media access control address of the radio

    C. The name of the access point

    D. The wireless medium identifier

20. What Layer 2 security mechanisms are weak and should not be used with IEEE 802.11 wireless LANs? (Choose three.)

    A. SSID hiding

    B. WPA

    C. VPN

    D. WEP

    E. WPA 2.0

    F. RBAC

    G. MAC filter

21. If an autonomous access point is set to what is commonly referred to as *root mode,* it will be able to perform which function?

   A. Connect to a distribution system and allow client devices to send information to other devices

   B. Connect to a distribution system as a root bridge and allow two or more LANs to connect wirelessly

   C. Connect to a distribution system but is seldom used as this mode requires extensive configuration

   D. Connect to a distribution system as a repeater which allows the RF cell to be extended

22. What could cause low throughput in an 802.11g wireless network?

   A. Access point output power is too high

   B. Too many associated client devices

   C. Load-balancing features are moving clients

   D. The clients are too close to the access points and are overpowered

23. Some common wireless personal network (WPAN) devices such as Bluetooth use a communication technology that has the potential to interfere with IEEE 802.11g wireless LANs. What is the name for this technology?

   A. FHSS

   B. DSSS

   C. HR/DSSS

   D. HR/FHSS

   E. ERP-OFDM

24. A virtual private network (VPN) operates at what layer of the OSI model?

   A. Physical, Layer 1

   B. Data Link, Layer 2

   C. Network, Layer 3

   D. Transport, Layer 4

   E. Application, Layer 7

25. An antenna will propagate RF energy in specific radiation patterns, both horizontal and vertical. How do antenna manufacturers identify the horizontal radiation patterns?

   A. Elevation

   B. Azimuth

   C. Dipole

   D. Longitude

26. Wi-Fi Protected Access 2 (WPA 2.0) requires _____ for the cipher suite and _____ for the encryption mechanism.

   A. TKIP, RC4

   B. TKIP, RC5

   C. WEP, RC4

   D. CCMP, RC4

   E. CCMP, AES

27. Antenna diversity will _____.

   A. Provide an RF signal additional range

   B. Reduce the effects of multipath

   C. Increase the effects of VSWR

   D. Provide active gain

28. The manual site survey process allows the site surveyor to perform the survey in one of two modes. What are these two modes? (Choose two.)

   A. Passive

   B. Visual

   C. Predictive

   D. Active

   E. Placement

29. A beacon is an example of what type of frame used in an IEEE 802.11 wireless LAN?

   A. Control

   B. Management

   C. Data

   D. Null function

30. What can have a negative effect on the capacity of an IEEE 802.11g wireless LAN access point?

   A. Reflections caused by furnishings

   B. Frequency range in use

   C. Number of associated users

   D. Output power of access point

Answers to Assessment Test

1. **C.** The IEEE 802.11g amendment to the standard and the 802.11a amendment both support up to 54 Mbps maximum data rates. However, of the two only 802.11g operates in the 2.4 GHz ISM band. 802.11b also operates in the 2.4 GHz ISM band but only supports a maximum data rate of 11 Mbps. The IEEE 802.11n amendment currently in draft supports up to 300 Mbps but eventually 600 Mbps. For more information, see Chapter 1.

2. **D.** CSMA/CA stands for Carrier Sense Multiple Access/Collision Avoidance and is used as an access method for wireless LANs to share the communication medium, which is the air. CSMA/CD is Carrier Sense Multiple Access Collision/Detection Avoidance and is used with Ethernet networks. FHSS and HR/DSSS are spread spectrum technologies used with some standards or amendments. CSMA/DSSS does not exist. For more information, see Chapter 5.

3. **C.** A protocol analyzer will help identify existing wireless networks in an area and provide other information about these networks that can be used in the site survey/design process. An RF analysis is performed by a spectrum analyzer, which will also help locate sources of RF interference. A protocol analyzer can help identify security-related issues from existing wireless networks but will not describe security requirements of a new wireless LAN. For more information, see Chapter 9.

4. **E.** IEEE 802.11g networks operate in the 2.4 GHz ISM band. 802.11a networks operate in the 5 GHz UNII band. IEEE standards-based wireless networks do not use the 900 MHz ISM band or the 2.4 GHz UNII band. For more information, see Chapter 4.

5. **A.** The received signal strength represents how much of a transmitted signal is being received. If this signal is weak, the difference between the signal and noise may not be high enough to recover the data. If the power on an access point is high, it would provide more received signal. A signal-to-noise ratio of 35 dB is more than adequate. If the radio on the client was disabled, it would not be able to connect at all. For more information, see Chapter 11.

6. **B.** In a full mesh network, all nodes connect together with at least two paths for every node. This technology is on the increase in outdoor installations and starting to appear in indoor installations as well. It is common in metropolitan area networks and campus area networks. Many access points and wireless LAN switches/controllers have the capability built in. For more information, see Chapter 2.

7. **A.** PIN-based security is designed for home networks or small office installations to help ease the burden of setting up wireless LAN security. The IEEE 802.11i amendment to the standard requires CCMP/AES and is used in enterprise installations. Enterprise installations use more sophisticated solutions such as user-based and 802.1X/EAP. Multifactor authentication requires at least two parts to be authenticated, such as something you have and something you know. A bank automated teller machine (ATM) card is an example of multifactor authentication. For more information, see Chapter 10.

8. D. Open system authentication is addressed in the original IEEE 802.11 standard and requires a wireless client device to authenticate to an access point in order to associate. Shared key authentication is legacy and flawed and either cannot or should not be used. Open system authentication is a "null" authentication, is automatic and not secure. For more information, see Chapter 7.

9. D. Regulatory domain governing bodies manage the RF spectrum used in both unlicensed and licensed applications. The IEEE creates standards and the Wi-Fi Alliance certifies devices for interoperability. Wireless Ethernet Compatibility Alliance is the former name of the Wi-Fi Alliance. For more information, see Chapter 1.

10. E. 802.11n and MIMO will use up to three radios in either the 2.4 GHz ISM or the 5 GHz UNII band. 802.11a/g uses one radio per band but can use two antennas for diversity. 802.11h is for spectrum management. For more information, see Chapter 5.

11. B. An impedance mismatch between connections in a WLAN system will cause VSWR. The gain of an antenna is a relative value that has to do with the size or shape of the RF pattern emitted. Attenuation of cable adds to the overall loss of the system. For more information, see Chapter 6.

12. A. A wireless repeater—which in most cases is a function of an access point—will extend the RF cell to allow users at a greater distance to connect. This will have an impact on throughput for users connected to the repeater and this solution is recommended only when necessary. For more information, see Chapter 2.

13. B. 802.1X is for port-based access control and the terminology for the access point is *authenticator*. The RADIUS server is the authentication server and the client device is a supplicant. The RAS server is the predecessor to RADIUS. For more information, see Chapter 10.

14. A. An independent basic service set (IBSS) is an ad hoc network that is used for peer-to-peer communications. No access points are used in an IBSS implementation. For more information, see Chapter 7.

15. D. Both DSSS and HR/DSSS channels are 22 MHz wide. 2.412 GHz and 5.160 GHz is the center frequency of some channels used. For more information, see Chapter 5.

16. D. An omnidirectional antenna has a horizontal radiation pattern of 360 degrees. For more information, see Chapter 6.

17. B. A predictive analysis site survey will minimize the time required on-site for testing and analysis. This site survey will be accurate if the information about the location input is accurate. A manual site survey requires a walkthrough on the area and can be time consuming. For more information, see Chapter 9.

18. C. To be considered non-overlapping, channels in the 2.4 GHz ISM band need to be separated by 5 or 25 MHz. For more information, see Chapter 4.

19. A. The SSID is the name that identifies a wireless network. The MAC address of the access point radio is the BSSID. For more information, see Chapter 7.

20. A,D,G. SSID hiding, WEP, and MAC filtering are legacy security mechanisms for IEEE 802.11 wireless networks and should not be used. WPA and WPA 2.0 are Wi-Fi certifications and are more advanced. Virtual private network (VPN) is a Layer 3 security solution typically used for remote access. RBAC is role-based access control. For more information, see Chapter 10.

21. A. Most enterprise-level autonomous access points have the capability to operate in root, repeater, or bridge modes. Root mode is the most common. Root mode allows devices to authenticate, associate, and access network resources and services. For more information, see Chapter 2.

22. B. Low throughput may occur when too many client devices are associated to an access point and cause overloading. Load balancing would help to solve this problem. Because of DRS, the closer the client device is to an access point, the better the throughput. For more information, see Chapter 11.

23. A. Some wireless personal networks (WPANs), such as Bluetooth, use FHSS for communications. This will potentially interfere with IEEE 802.11 wireless networks. DSSS, HR/DSSS, ERP-OFDM are all used in wireless LANs. HR/FHSS does not exist. For more information, see Chapter 5.

24. C. A virtual private network (VPN) is a Layer 3 (Network) security solution and is commonly used for remote access connectivity from unsecured networks such as hotspots. For more information, see Chapter 10.

25. B. The technical term for the horizontal radiation pattern is *azimuth*. The elevation is the vertical radiation pattern. For more information, see Chapter 6.

26. E. Wi-Fi Protected Access 2 (WPA 2.0) requires CCMP/AES. TKIP/RC4 is optional. WEP/RC4 is legacy and should not be used. It cannot be used with a robust secure network. RC5 is a stream cipher and not used with IEEE 802.11 wireless LANs. CCMP uses AES, not RC4. For more information, see Chapter 1.

27. B. Antenna diversity will reduce the effects of multipath caused by reflections. An antenna will provide additional coverage and range based on the gain. VSWR is caused by an impedance mismatch, and active gain is provided by amplifiers and other powered devices. For more information, see Chapter 6.

28. A,D. Passive and active are the two modes in which a manual site survey can be performed. Passive mode monitors all RF, and active mode requires a client association. For more information, see Chapter 9.

29. B. A beacon frame is a management frame and is used to advertise information about the wireless LAN. For more information, see Chapter 7.

30. C. The number of associated users will affect the capacity of an access point. The frequency range will affect the propagation as well as the output power. Reflections will cause multipath. For more information, see Chapter 4.

Chapter

1

Introduction to Wireless Local Area Networking

THE FOLLOWING CWTS EXAM OBJECTIVES ARE COVERED IN THIS CHAPTER:

✓ **Identify deployment scenarios for common WLAN network types**

- Small office/home office (SOHO)
- Extension of existing networks into remote locations
- Building-to-building connectivity
- Public wireless hotspots
- Mobile office, classroom, industrial, and healthcare
- Municipal and law-enforcement connectivity
- Corporate data access and end-user mobility
- Last-mile data delivery: wireless ISP
- Transportation networks (trains, planes, automobiles)

✓ **Define the roles of the following organizations in providing direction and accountability within the wireless networking industry**

- IEEE
- Wi-Fi Alliance
- Regulatory Domain Governing Bodies

✓ **Summarize the basic attributes and advantages of the WLAN standards, amendments, and product certifications**

- Wi-Fi certification

- 802.11a

- 802.11b

- 802.11g

- 802.11n

- Wi-Fi Multimedia (WMM) certification

- WMM Power Save (WMM-PS) certification

- Wi-Fi Protected Setup (WPS) certification

- Push-button

- PIN-based

- Wi-Fi Protected Access (WPA/WPA2) certification

- Enterprise

- Personal

Wireless computer networks have taken computer communication to a new level. This communication technology is the combination of computer local area networking (LAN) and radio frequency (RF) technology. By combining these two technologies, computer users have the opportunity to access and share information in ways that would seem unattainable a few years ago.

This chapter will look at various ways in which wireless local networks are used and deployed. We will also cover organizations responsible for managing and creating wireless LAN standards. Details of the 802.11 standard and amendments will be discussed illustrating the communications and functional aspects. Finally, we will discuss interoperability certifications available for communications, quality of service, and security of IEEE 802.11 wireless networks.

Common WLAN Deployment Scenarios

The availability of wireless LAN technology has increased while the cost continues to decrease, making wireless LANs a viable solution for many business models, including small offices, home offices, and personal use. This chapter will look at scenarios in which wireless networking is used, and provide an overview of standards-based solutions and interoperability certifications. The following are some common applications utilizing wireless local area networks (WLANs):

- Small office/home office (SOHO)
- Enterprise: corporate data access and end-user mobility
- Extension to remote locations
- Mobile office
- Public wireless hotspots
- Classroom
- Healthcare
- Last-mile data delivery: wireless Internet service provider (ISP)
- Industrial
- Municipal and law-enforcement connectivity
- Transportation networks
- Building-to-building connectivity

Small Office/Home Office (SOHO)

Many small office/home office (SOHO) businesses have the same needs as those of larger businesses with regard to technology, computer networking, and communication. Computer networking technology is common regardless of the size of the business. Whether there are 1 or 100 employees or even more, many are categorized as small businesses. Wireless LANs can play a major role in small businesses. Many of these locations will have a high speed Internet connection such as DSL (digital subscriber line) or cable modem for access outside the local network.

With the number of work-at-home professionals continuing to grow at a very high rate, the need for wireless networking in this environment is also continuing to grow. The same goes for the small office environment. Deployments such as these typically involve a small number of users. Therefore, the equipment used may be consumer brands sold in consumer electronics and department stores.

Figure 1.1 shows a SOHO configuration with a wireless LAN router connected to an Internet service provider allowing access to the necessary network/Internet resources.

FIGURE 1.1   Example of a SOHO wireless LAN configuration

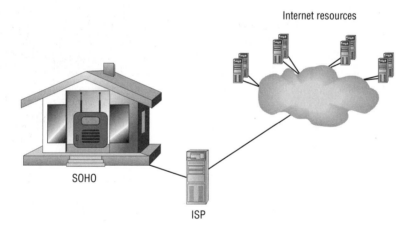

Enterprise Deployments: Corporate Data Access and End-User Mobility

Enterprise organizations have used wired local area networks for many years. With the increased need for mobility, wireless LANs within enterprise organizations have also increased in popularity. In earlier years, due to lack of interoperability and security features, many enterprise organizations limited wireless LAN deployments to extensions of networks where wired connectivity was either not feasible or too costly. Because of advancements in wireless LAN technology over the recent years, deployments in enterprise organizations are now growing at a rapid pace.

Wireless LANs in the enterprise are used with—but not limited to—client workstation connectivity (desktop and notebook), printers, barcode scanners, voice handsets, and location services. The cost of this technology has decreased while capabilities, performance, and security have increased, making wireless a very attractive solution for many enterprise organizations. The cost savings over hard-wired solutions are enormous, adding to the attractiveness. Finally, wireless connectivity is the only option in some cases, such as mobile Voice over Wi-Fi handsets for voice communications.

Extending Existing Networks with Wireless LAN

Early wireless networking technology was typically deployed to allow an extension of an existing wired network infrastructure. For example, some users who required access to the computer network exceeded the distance the IEEE 802.3 Ethernet standard allowed for a copper-wired connection, therefore other solutions were needed to provide connectivity. Other wired technology, such as fiber optics and leased lines, were sometimes cost prohibitive or not logistically feasible. Wireless local area networks were an excellent alternative.

Mobile Office and Public Wireless Hotspots

Mobility is one of the major benefits of wireless networking. Mobility allows users to access information from a variety of locations, either public or private. One example is wireless hotspots. These days, it is rare to visit any public location, be it a restaurant, hotel, coffee shop, or airport, and not be able to find a public wireless hotspot.

A *wireless hotspot* is defined as a location that offers 802.11 wireless connectivity for devices (computers, PDAs, phones, etc.) to connect to and access the Internet. Many users work from remote locations and require Internet access as part of their job.

A typical wireless hotspot will be configured with at least one wireless LAN router connected to an Internet service provider (ISP). In some cases, this setup could be as simple as a location offering free Wi-Fi Internet access for its customers. More sophisticated hotspots will have several wireless routers or a complete wireless infrastructure and will be connected to a remote billing server that is responsible for collecting revenue from the potential user. In many cases, when a user connects to the hotspot router, they will be prompted with a web page for authentication. At this point they might be asked to enter information such as an account number, username and password, or a credit card number to allow usage for a limited period of time. In the case of a free hotspot, typically this web page lists terms and conditions the user agrees to prior to accessing the Internet. This type of web page configuration is known as a *captive portal*.

Wireless hotspots can raise security concerns for the user. Without a secure connection, all information is passed in clear text through the air via radio frequency, allowing an intruder to capture usernames and passwords, credit card numbers, or other information that could lead to identity theft. Most hotspots do not have the capability to provide a secure connection for the user from their computer or wireless device to the wireless router or network. The secure connection then becomes the responsibility of the user. Many corporations allow employees to work remotely from wireless hotspot connections. In this case, usually a *virtual private network* (VPN) is used to ensure security. A VPN creates a secure tunnel between the user and the corporate network, allowing for a secure encrypted connection for the user from the wireless hotspot to their corporate network over the Internet or public network.

For users who connect to wireless hotspots, it is very important for their wireless devices to be secured with the appropriate antivirus software, firewall software, and up-to-date operating system patches or service packs. Following these guidelines will help protect the user from attacks when they are connected to and using a wireless hotspot.

Figure 1.2 shows a simple wireless hotspot implementation.

FIGURE 1.2   Wireless hotspot allows users to connect to the Internet from remote locations.

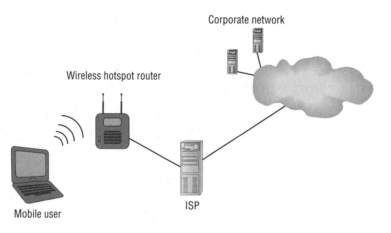

Educational Institutions: Classroom Deployments

Educational institutions can benefit from wireless networking in many ways. Wireless LAN deployments are common in elementary and high schools. Universities have deployed campus-wide wireless LANs amounting to thousands of access points servicing tens of thousands of users on a single campus.

Wireless LAN technology allows for increased mobility in the educational environment, providing huge cost savings on technology refresh. Mobile carts with notebook computers are one example. A high school can deploy infrastructure devices such as access points in classrooms and purchase several mobile carts with notebook or tablet computers to be used when and where needed. This is beneficial since it will save on supplying many classrooms with computers where continual utilization may be low. Some school buildings may be older or historic buildings and installing cabling is not possible or cost prohibitive. Wireless provides the solution.

Healthcare

The growth of wireless LAN deployments in the healthcare industry is quite impressive. Healthcare installations have many challenges when it comes to design, deployment, and support of wireless networking.

Hospitals in many cases run $7 \times 24 \times 365$ days a year. Wireless LANs have numerous applications in hospitals, including:

- Patient registration
- Patient charting
- Prescription automation
- Treatment verification
- Inventory tracking

One of the obstacles to take into consideration is interference. Hospitals use many devices that operate in the unlicensed industrial, scientific, and medical (ISM) RF band. This can create challenges for design and reliability of the wireless network.

Legislative compliance such as the Health Insurance Portability and Accountability Act of 1996 (HIPAA) also needs to be taken into consideration when designing wireless installations for healthcare.

Last-Mile Data Delivery: Wireless ISP

Last-mile data delivery is a common term used in telecommunications to describe the connection from a provider to an endpoint such as home or business. (Last-mile is not necessarily a mile in distance.) This can be a costly solution in many applications since each endpoint needs a separate physical connection. Wireless provides a more cost-effective solution for last-mile data delivery.

Some communication technology, such as DSL, has physical limitations that prohibit connections in some cases. It may not be cost effective for telecommunication service providers to supply connections in rural or semi-rural areas due to return on investment. Wireless LANs can service areas that may not be part of a last-mile run. Providing Internet access from a wireless ISP is one application. Things to consider for feasibility are line of site, obstacles, and interference.

Industrial, Municipal, Law Enforcement, and Transportation Networks

Wireless LANs are valuable technology in the industrial, municipal, and law enforcement fields, and in transportation networks.

Some industrial deployments have been using wireless LAN technology for many years, even prior to the development of standards-based solutions. Examples include barcode and scanning solutions for manufacturing, inventory and retail.

Federal and local law enforcement agencies frequently maintain state-of-the-art technology utilizing computer forensics and wireless LAN technology. Technologies that use 19.2 Kbps connectivity are becoming obsolete due to slower data transfer rates. Municipal deployments that include police, fire, utilities, and city or town services are often all connected to a common wireless LAN.

Transportation networks are no exception. Wireless LAN installations are becoming more common in places like commuter buses, trains, and airplanes. Users can connect for free or by paying a nominal fee. This type of connectivity now allows a user to better employ idle time. This is especially helpful to the mobile user or "road warrior" who needs to make the best use of available time.

Building-to-Building Connectivity

Connecting two or more wired LANs together over some distance is often necessary in computer networking. Depending on the topology, this can be an expensive and time-consuming task. Wireless LAN technology is often used as an alternative to copper cable, fiber optics, or leased line connectivity between buildings. Whether connecting two or multiple locations together, point-to-point or point-to-multipoint links can be a quick and cost-effective solution for building-to-building connectivity.

Antenna selection plays an important role in this type of connectivity and will be discussed further in Chapter 6, "WLAN Antennas and Accessories." Other factors to consider in either point-to-point or point-to-multipoint connections are radio frequency and distance, both of which will determine if a link is feasible.

Point-to-Point Link

Connecting at least two wired LANs together is known as a *point-to-point link* (see Figure 1.3). Some WLAN equipment manufacturers claim the distance of point-to-point links can be up to 25 miles—sometimes further depending on terrain and other local conditions. These links can serve both wired and wireless users on the connected local area networks. Point-to-point links typically call for semidirectional or highly directional antennas. When an omnidirectional antenna is used in this configuration, it is considered a special case, called a *point-to-multipoint link*. This will be discussed in Chapter 6.

FIGURE 1.3   A point-to-point link using directional antennas

LAN1   LAN2

Point-to-Multipoint Link

A network connecting more then two LANs together is known as a *point-to-multipoint link* (see Figure 1.4). This configuration usually consists of one omnidirectional antenna and multiple semi- or highly directional antennas. Point-to-multipoint links are often used in campus-style deployments where connections to multiple buildings or locations may be required.

FIGURE 1.4   A typical point-to-multipoint link using an omnidirectional antenna

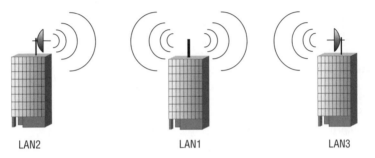

LAN2   LAN1   LAN3

Radio Frequency Regulatory Domain Governing Bodies

Wireless networks use radio frequency (RF) to communicate. The RF spectrum needs to be regulated in order to ensure correct use of the allocated frequency bands. The International Telecommunication Union–Radiocommunication Sector (ITU-R) is responsible for global management of RF spectrum, in addition to satellite orbits. This organization currently comprises 191 member states and over 700 sector members. It manages five regions, one of which is Region A, North and South America, Inter-American Telecommunication Commission (CITEL).

Figure 1.5 shows all five regions and the geographic area they encompass.

FIGURE 1.5   ITU-R region map

For additional information, visit www.itu.int/ITU-R.

Table 1.1 shows the five regions, the geographic areas they cover, and the website uniform resource locator (URL) address for each region.

TABLE 1.1   ITU-R Regions, Geographic Locations and Website URLs

Region	Location	URL
Region A	America	www.citel.oas.org
Region B	Western Europe	www.cept.org
Region C	Eastern Europe and Northern Asia	www.rcc.org
Region D	Africa	www.atu-uat.org
Region E	Asia and Australia	www.aptsec.org

United States: Federal Communications Commission (FCC)

The regulatory body that manages RF spectrum for the United States is the *Federal Communications Commission (FCC)*. The FCC, founded in 1934, is responsible for regulating licensed and unlicensed radio frequency spectrum. IEEE 802.11 wireless networks may use licensed or unlicensed RF spectrum for communication. A benefit of using unlicensed radio spectrum is no cost to the end user. The IEEE uses two of three unlicensed RF bands allowed by the FCC:

- 2.4 GHz industrial, scientific, and medical (ISM) band
- 5 GHz Unlicensed National Information Infrastructure (UNII) band

This will be illustrated further in looking at details of standards-based wireless communications.

For additional information, visit www.fcc.gov.

Europe: European Telecommunications Standards Institute (ETSI)

The European Telecommunications Standards Institute (ETSI) is a European standards organization responsible for producing standards for information and communications technologies, including fixed, mobile, radio, converged, broadcast, and Internet technologies. ETSI was created by the European Conference of Postal and Telecommunications Administrations (CEPT) in 1988.

In Europe, radio frequency use is managed by CEPT. CEPT develops guidelines and provides national administrations with tools for coordinated European radio frequency spectrum management.

IEEE and Wireless LAN Standards

The *IEEE* (originally known as the *Institute of Electrical and Electronics Engineers*) is a nonprofit organization responsible for generating a variety of technology standards, including those related to information technology. Since 1997 the IEEE has released a series of standards related to WLAN networking.

The IEEE wireless networking standards are described in the order in which they were released. They define communication: range, power, and speed. Some of these standards will be explained more thoroughly later in this book.

For additional information, visit www.ieee.org.

802.11

The 802.11 standard, released in 1997, is what defined the wireless LAN communication standards. The data rates used in this standard (1 and 2 Mbps) are considered slow by today's standards and technology.

The IEEE Standard 802.11-2007 (previously known as 802.11ma) is the most current standard. This standard rolled up the 802.11 standard and various amendments such as 802.11a/b/e/g/h/I, and others into one document. However, many in the industry still refer to the original names: 802.11b, 802.11a, 802.11g, and so on.

User and application requirements for 802.11 are discussed in Chapter 4, "Radio Frequency (RF) Fundamentals for Wireless LAN Technology."

The following list provides details such as frequency range, spread spectrum technology, and data rates for the 802.11 standard.

- 2.4 GHz ISM band
- Frequency-hopping spread spectrum (FHSS)
- Direct-sequence spread spectrum (DSSS)
- Infrared (IR)
- 1 and 2 Mbps

Frequency-hopping spread spectrum is considered legacy technology. However, some companies still manufacture a limited line of equipment to support legacy implementations.

802.11b

The 802.11b amendment to the 802.11 standard works in the 2.4–2.5 GHz ISM band. This amendment, released in 1999, specifies high rate DSSS (HR/DSSS)

The 802.11b amendment was released before the 802.11a amendment.

The following list provides details such as frequency range, spread spectrum technology, and data rates for the 802.11b amendment.

- 2.4 GHz ISM band
- Direct-sequence spread spectrum (DSSS)
- High rate–direct-sequence spread spectrum (HR/DSSS)
- 5.5 and 11 Mbps
- Backward compatible to 802.11 DSSS for 1 and 2 Mbps

With the release of the 802.11b amendment, wireless LAN technology became more affordable and mainstream. This amendment introduced two higher rate data speeds of 5.5 and 11 Mbps, making the technology more desirable.

802.11a

This amendment to the 802.11 standard operates in the 5 GHz UNII band. Released in 1999, this standard operates over four frequency ranges in three bands—UNII-1, UNII-2, and UNII-3. UNII-1 is for indoor use only, UNII-2 is for indoor or outdoor use, and UNII-3 may be used indoors or outdoors but is typically used outdoors. The data rates for 802.11a are up to 54 Mbps using orthogonal frequency division multiplexing (OFDM).

The following list provides details such as frequency range, spread spectrum technology, and data rates for the 802.11a amendment.

- 5GHz UNII band
    - 5.150–5.250 GHz UNII-1
    - 5.250–5.350 GHz UNII-2
    - 5.725–5.825 GHz UNII-3
- Orthogonal frequency division multiplexing (OFDM)
- 6, 12, 24 Mbps OFDM required data rates
- 9, 18, 36, 48, and 54 Mbps OFDM data rates are supported but not required.

A benefit to using the 5 GHz UNII band is less interference. Currently, many fewer devices use 5 GHz UNII license-free band than those using the 2.4 GHz ISM band. Less interference means increased performance and reliability.

 In late 2003, the FCC made changes regarding the 5 GHz unlicensed band. Additional frequencies above those described in the IEEE 802.11a amendment can now be used for IEEE 802.11 wireless networking. These changes will be discussed further in Chapter 6.

802.11g

This amendment to the 802.11 standard was released in 2003. It operates in the 2.4 GHz ISM band as do 802.11 and 802.11b. This amendment addresses extended data rates with OFDM and is backward compatible to 802.11 and 802.11b.

The following list provides details such as frequency range, spread spectrum technology, and data rates for the 802.11g amendment:

- 2.4 GHz ISM band
- Direct-sequence spread spectrum (DSSS)
- High rate–direct-sequence spread spectrum (HR/DSSS)
- Extended rate physical–orthogonal frequency division multiplexing (ERP-OFDM)
- Packet binary convolutional code (PBCC; optional)
- 1 and 2 Mbps (compatible with DSSS)
- 5.5 and 11 Mbps complementary code keying (CCK; compatible with HR/DSSS)
- 6, 12, 24 Mbps OFDM required data rates
- 9, 18, 36, 48, and 54 Mbps OFDM data rates are supported but not required.

802.11g is backward compatible to 802.11 and 802.11b because it operates in the same 2.4 GHz ISM band and supports the same access methods. One benefit of 802.11g compatibility is many established infrastructures and devices have used 802.11 and 802.11b for years. This allows them to continue to operate as normal with upgrades or replacement as appropriate.

In order to allow the slower DSSS data rates of 1, 2, 5.5, and 11 Mbps to operate in an 802.11g network, the amendment addresses the use of protection mechanisms. These protection mechanisms will degrade the performance of 802.11g clients to some degree when 802.11b radios are present.

Table 1.2 provides a summary and comparison of details regarding the currently released 802.11 communication standards.

TABLE 1.2   Summary of 802.11 Communications Standards and Amendments

Details	802.11	802.11a	802.11b	802.11g
2.4 GHz ISM band	x		x	x
5 GHz UNII bands		x		
FHSS	x			
DSSS	x		x	x
HR/DSSS			x	x
ERP-OFDM				x
OFDM		x		
1 and 2 Mbps	x		x	x
5.5 and 11 Mbps			x	x
6, 9, 12, 18, 24, 36, 48, 54 Mbps		x		x

802.11n

The 802.11n amendment is currently in draft and has not yet been ratified. As of this writing, the 802.11n amendment is expected to be ratified in Q4 2009. However, the 802.11n draft 2.0 is available, and products for both SOHO and enterprise are Wi-Fi certified and available to the market under draft 2.0.

⊕ **Real World Scenario**

How to Maximize the Throughput in an 802.11g Network

In certain cases the only way to maximize the throughput of an 802.11g network is to set the data rates of the access points to support 802.11g data rates only. The tradeoff is that 802.11b devices will not be able to connect to the network because the access point will not recognize the 802.11b data rates. This would work well where backward compatibility to 802.11b is not required and all equipment in use supports 802.11g. An analogy would be a group of individuals all speaking one language. They all understand the same language so they have no need to accommodate a second language.

Due to protection mechanisms defined in the 802.11g amendment, throughput will degrade in an 802.11b/g mixed mode environment when 802.11b devices are present. This is because the 802.11b devices have a maximum data rate of 11 Mbps (HR/DSSS) and they share the medium with the 802.11g devices that have a maximum data rate of 54 Mbps (OFDM). Think of the language analogy. If a group of individuals are speaking two different languages, a translator may be required. A discussion among the group would take longer because the translator would need to translate the languages. Likewise, protection mechanisms will have an impact on the throughput for the 802.11g devices since the 2.4 GHz medium is shared. If there are no 802.11b devices in the radio range of an access point in an 802.11b/g mixed mode environment, then protection mechanisms should not affect throughput, since the access point will not have to share the medium with the two different technologies

If you do not have any 802.11b devices on your network, you can set your access point to 802.11g only mode by disabling the 802.11b data rates. In this configuration, your 802.11g devices will perform better since protection mechanisms will not be enabled. However, if there are any 802.11b devices not belonging to your network in the "listening" range of the access point, data collisions will increase at the access point. This is because 802.11b and 802.11g operate in the same RF range, and the 802.11g (OFDM) access point does not understand the 802.11b (HR/DSSS) transmissions. (It sees them as RF noise.) In this configuration, overall throughput will still exceed that of an access point set to 802.11b/g mixed mode in the presence of 802.11b devices. The access point will hear the 802.11b transmissions, but they will not be serviced because they are only seen as RF noise. Thus they will have less impact on throughput.

The following list provides details such as frequency range, spread spectrum technology, and data rates for the 802.11n amendment.

- 2.4 GHz ISM band
- 5 GHz UNII bands
- MIMO (multiple input multiple output)
- Up to 600 Mbps
- HT-OFDM

Additional IEEE 802.11 Amendments

In addition to communications, the IEEE creates amendments regarding specific functionality including security and quality of service. The following amendments discuss some of these functions.

802.11e

The original 802.11 standard lacked quality of service (QoS) functionality features. In the original 802.11 standard, Point Coordination Function (PCF) mode provided some level of QoS. PCF mode is a function of the access point and allows for polling of connected client devices. This creates a contention-free period for data transmissions and provides QoS-like functionality. However, few if any vendors implemented this mode of operation.

The 802.11e amendment defines enhancements for QoS in wireless LANs. 802.11e introduced a new coordination function, hybrid coordination function (HCF). HCF defines traffic classes and assigns a priority to the information to be transmitted. For example, voice traffic is given a higher priority than data traffic, such as information being sent to a printer.

802.11i

The 802.11i amendment addresses advanced security solutions for wireless LAN, since the original 802.11 standard was known for several security weaknesses.

Manufacturers of WLAN equipment addressed the following security features:

- Service Set Identifier (SSID) Hiding
- Media Access Control (MAC) address filtering
- Wired Equivalent Privacy (WEP)

Each of these had known vulnerabilities, allowing for security weaknesses in 802.11 wireless LANs. The 802.11i amendment addressed these weaknesses by several enhancements, discussed in Chapter 10, "WLAN Security."

Interoperability Certifications

By creating standards, the IEEE is encouraging technology progression. Vendors often implement wireless devices and networks in a proprietary manner, within or outside the standard. This model often leads to a lack of interoperability among devices. In the wireless community, such practices are not widely accepted. Users want all of their devices to function well together. The combination of proprietary implementations and user dissatisfaction fostered the creation of interoperability testing and certification.

This section will discuss vendor interoperability certifications related to IEEE 802.11 standard equipment. These certifications address communications, quality of service, and security.

Wi-Fi Alliance

As mentioned in the previous section, the IEEE is responsible for generating the standards for wireless networking. However, equipment manufacturers are not required to provide proof that their equipment is compliant to the standards. Starting with the release of the 802.11b amendment, several early WLAN equipment manufacturers—including Symbol Systems, Aironet, and Lucent—formed an organization known as Wireless Ethernet Compatibility Alliance (WECA) to promote the technology and to provide interoperability testing of wireless LAN equipment manufactured by these and other companies. In 2000, WECA was renamed the *Wi-Fi Alliance*. The term *Wi-Fi* represents a certification and is often misused by people in the industry. Wi-Fi is a registered trademark, originally registered in 1999 by WECA and now registered to the Wi-Fi Alliance.

 For additional information, visit www.wi-fi.org.

Figure 1.6 shows an example of a Wi-Fi certified logo.

FIGURE 1.6   Wi-Fi Certified logo for devices that are Wi-Fi certified

Wi-Fi Protected Access (WPA) Certification Overview

The *Wi-Fi Protected Access (WPA)* certification was derived from the fact that security in the original 802.11 standard was weak and had many security vulnerabilities. This certification was designed as an interim solution until an amendment to the 802.11 standard addressing security improvements was released. The 802.11i amendment addressed security for the 802.11 family of standards. The bottom line is that WPA is a pre-802.11i certification introducing more advanced security solutions such as Temporal Key Integrity Protocol (TKIP), passphrase, and 802.1X/EAP.

   This pre-802.11i certification addressed two options for wireless LAN security. The two options are personal mode and enterprise mode. Personal mode is intended for the small office/home office (SOHO) and home users. Enterprise mode is intended for larger deployments.

Wi-Fi Protected Access 2 (WPA 2.0) Certification Overview

The WPA certification by the Wi-Fi Alliance worked out so well that it was decided to certify wireless LAN hardware after the 802.11i amendment was released. This new certification, known as *Wi-Fi Protected Access 2 (WPA 2.0),* is a post-802.11i certification. Like WPA, WPA 2.0 addresses two options for wireless LAN security: personal mode and enterprise mode. This certification addresses more advanced security solutions and is backward compatible with WPA. We will take a look at both WPA and WPA 2.0 in more detail in Chapter 10.

- The personal mode security mechanism uses a passphrase for authentication, which is intended for SOHO and personal use. The use of a passphrase to generate a 256-bit preshared key provides strong security.

- The enterprise mode mechanism uses 802.1X/EAP for authentication, which is port-based authentication designed for enterprise implementations. 802.1X/EAP provides strong security using external authentication and Extensible Authentication Protocol (EAP). This works well as a replacement for legacy 802.11 security solutions.

Table 1.3 provides a high-level description of the WPA and WPA 2.0 certifications.

TABLE 1.3 DETAILS OF THE WPA AND WPA 2.0 CERTIFICATIONS

Wi-Fi Alliance Security Mechanism	Authentication Mechanism	Cipher Suite/ Encryption Mechanism
WPA – Personal	Passphrase	TKIP/RC4
WPA – Enterprise	802.1X/EAP	TKIP/RC4
WPA 2.0 – Personal	Passphrase	CCMP/AES or TKIP/RC4
WPA 2.0 – Enterprise	802.1X/EAP	CCMP/AES or TKIP/RC4

Wi-Fi Multimedia (WMM) Certification Overview

The *Wi-Fi Multimedia (WMM)* certification was designed as a proactive certification for the 802.11e amendment to the 802.11 standard. As mentioned earlier in this chapter, the 802.11e amendment addresses quality of service in wireless LANs. The WMM certification verifies the validity of features of the 802.11e amendment and allows for a vendor-neutral approach to quality of service.

Quality of service is needed to ensure delivery of information for time-sensitive, time-bounded applications such as voice and streaming video. If a wireless network user were to send a file to a printer or save a file to a server, it is unlikely they would notice any minor latency. However, in an application that is tuned to the human senses such as hearing or eyesight, latency would more likely be noticeable.

Wi-Fi Multimedia Power Save (WMM-PS) Certification Overview

Wi-Fi Multimedia Power Save (WMM-PS) is designed for mobile devices and specific applications that require advanced power-save mechanisms for extended battery life. Listed are some of these devices and applications that benefit from it:

- Voice over IP (VoIP) phones
- Notebook computers
- PDAs
- Headsets
- Mice
- Keyboards

Power-save mechanisms allow devices to conserve battery power by "dozing" for short periods of time. Depending on the application, performance could suffer to some degree with power-save features enabled. WMM Power Save consumes less power by allowing devices to spend more time in a "dozing" state—an improvement over legacy power save mode that at the same time improves performance by minimizing transmission latency.

Wi-Fi Protected Setup (WPS) Certification Overview

Wi-Fi Protected Setup (WPS) was derived from the fact that small office and home office users wanted a simple way to provide the best security possible for their installations without the need for extensive technical knowledge of wireless networking. Wi-Fi Protected Setup provides strong out-of-the-box setup adequate for many SOHO implementations.

The Wi-Fi Protected Setup certification requires support for two types of authentication that enable users to automatically configure network names and strong WPA2 data encryption and authentication:

- Push-button configuration (PBC)
- PIN-based configuration, based on a personal identification number

Support for both PIN and PBC configurations are required for access points; client devices at a minimum must support PIN. A third, optional method, Near Field Communication (NFC) tokens, is also supported.

Summary

This chapter discussed many applications in which wireless LANs are currently used, from small office/home office to corporate deployments and last-mile connectivity. Standards-based wireless deployments continue to grow at a fast pace, replacing proprietary and legacy-based implementations.

The IEEE is an organization that creates standards and amendments used for 802.11 wireless LANs. This chapter described the released communication standards that address range, power, and speed including:

- 802.11a
- 802.11b
- 802.11g

Also some details regarding 802.11n were discussed which at the time of this writing is in draft 2.0.

Standards that addressed quality of service and security were also discussed. The IEEE creates standards based on radio frequency regulations. We also looked at radio frequency regulatory domain governing bodies and their role in regulation of the RF spectrum used for IEEE 802.11 wireless networking.

As discussed in this chapter, the Wi-Fi Alliance is an organization addressing interoperability testing for equipment manufactured to the IEEE standards. This testing results in a variety of certifications for

- Communication
- Quality of service
- Security

Key Terms

Before you take the exam, be certain you are familiar with the following terms:

captive portal

Federal Communications Commission (FCC)

IEEE (Institute of Electrical and Electronics Engineers)

last-mile data delivery

point-to-multipoint link

point-to-point link

virtual private network

Wi-Fi Alliance

Wi-Fi Multimedia (WMM)

Wi-Fi Multimedia Power Save (WMM-PS)

Wi-Fi Protected Access (WPA)

Wi-Fi Protected Access 2 (WPA 2.0)

Wi-Fi Protected Setup (WPS)

wireless hotspot

Exam Essentials

Understand details of common WLAN applications.   These common WLAN applications can include small office/home office (SOHO), corporate data access, end-user mobility, and building-to-building connectivity.

Understand the function and roles of organizations that are responsible for the regulation and development of WLAN technology.   The IEEE, FCC, ETSI, ITU-R, and Wi-Fi Alliance play important roles with wireless technology. Know the function and role of each organization.

Remember frequency ranges, data rates, and spread spectrum technologies for IEEE 802.11 communication standards.   Understand the details of the 802.11, 802.11b, 802.11a, 802.11g, and 802.11n standard and amendments. It is important to know the supported data rates and operating radio frequency of each.

Know the purpose of IEEE specific function amendments.   Be familiar with the details of 802.11e and 802.11i specific function amendments. Know that 802.11e is for quality of service and 802.11i addresses security.

Understand the differences among interoperability certifications by the Wi-Fi Alliance.   Know the purpose of the WPA, WPA 2.0, WMM, WMM-PS, and WPS Wi-Fi Alliance certifications. Understand which address security, quality of service, and power-save features.

Review Questions

1. Point-to-point links typically use which antenna types? (Choose 2.)
   A. Semidirectional
   B. Omnidirectional
   C. Highly directional
   D. Long range omnidirectional

2. Typically a point-to-multipoint link consists of _____ connections.
   A. Two
   B. Three
   C. Four
   D. Five

3. True or false? A point-to-point link always uses an omnidirectional antenna.
   A. True
   B. False

4. What organization is responsible for unlicensed frequency band regulation in the United States?
   A. ETSI
   B. Wi-Fi Alliance
   C. IEEE
   D. FCC
   E. WPA

5. 802.11g LANs operate in what frequency range?
   A. 900 MHz
   B. 5.15–5.25 GHz
   C. 5.25–5.35 GHz
   D. 2.4–2.5 GHz

6. Which of the following organizations is responsible for standards compliance?
   A. FCC
   B. ETSI
   C. IEEE
   D. WPA2
   E. Wi-Fi Alliance

7. 802.11a uses which spread spectrum technology?

  A. ERP-OFDM

  B. HR/DSSS

  C. OFDM

  D. FHSS

8. 802.11b is capable of which of the following data rates? (Choose 3.)

  A. 1 Mbps

  B. 6 Mbps

  C. 5.5 Mbps

  D. 11 Mbps

  E. 12 Mbps

9. 802.11g is backward compatible to which of the following IEEE wireless LAN standards? (Choose 2.)

  A. 802.11 DSSS

  B. 802.11a OFDM

  C. 802.11a ERP-OFDM

  D. 802.11b HR/DSSS

  E. 802.3af

10. In the 802.11a amendment, the UNII-3 band can be used for which of the following WLAN applications?

  A. Indoor and outdoor

  B. Outdoor only

  C. Indoor only

  D. The UNII-3 band cannot be used for WLANs.

11. The 802.11i amendment to the standard addresses which of the following technologies?

  A. Quality of service

  B. DSSS

  C. Security

  D. MIMO

12. Which of the following best describes the Wi-Fi Alliance?

  A. U.S.-based standards organization

  B. Interoperability testing organization

  C. Works with the FCC to verify compliance

  D. Local regulatory body for Europe

13. Which of the following is addressed by the Wi-Fi Multimedia (WMM) certification? (Choose 2.)

   A. Security

   B. WPA and WPA2

   C. QoS

   D. Quality of service

14. Wi-Fi Protected Setup was designed for which of the following wireless applications?

   A. Small office/home office (SOHO) organizations

   B. Enterprise organizations

   C. FCC interoperability

   D. Security organizations

15. The 802.11g standard uses which two spread spectrum technologies?

   A. FHSS

   B. OFDM

   C. ERP-OFDM

   D. DSSS

   E. MIMO

16. WPA was developed as an interim solution for which amendment to the 802.11 standard?

   A. 802.11a

   B. 802.11n

   C. 802.11e

   D. 802.11i

   E. 802.11g

17. Which of the following is correct regarding 802.11e?

   A. Only operates in the 5 GHz frequency range

   B. Only operates at 1, 2, 5.5, and 11Mbps

   C. Addresses wireless security

   D. Addresses wireless quality of service

18. According to the 802.11a amendment, which of the following data rates are mandatory?

   A. 1, 2, 5.5, and 11 Mbps

   B. 6, 24, and 54 Mbps

   C. 6, 9, 12, 18, 24, 36, 48, and 54 Mbps

   D. 6, 12, and 24 Mbps

   E. 1, 6, 12, and 24 Mbps

19. You support a wireless network for an office of five employees. The installation consists of one access point, three notebook computers, and two desktop computers. The access point and computers in the office have wireless adapters that are Wi-Fi WPA 2.0 Certified. You want to use the highest level security possible without additional cost or administration. Which of the following solutions would be best for this deployment? (Choose 2.)

    A. WEP

    B. WPA 2.0 personal

    C. WPS

    D. WMM

    E. WPA 2.0 enterprise

20. Which two of the following options are for Wi-Fi Protected Access 2 (WPA 2.0)?

    A. Personal mode

    B. Protection mode

    C. Professional mode

    D. Enterprise mode

    E. WPA 2 mode

Answers to Review Questions

1. A, C. Semidirectional and highly directional antennas are used for point-to-point links. Omnidirectional antennas are for point-to-multipoint links. Long range omnidirectional antennas do not exist.

2. B. Point-to-multipoint links typically have three or more connections.

3. B. Point-to-multipoint links use omnidirectional antennas, but point-to-point links do not.

4. D. The FCC is the local regulatory body responsible for frequency regulation in the U.S.

5. D. 802.11g LANs operate in the 2.4–2.5 GHz ISM band. 900 MHz is not used with 802.11 wireless LANs, and 5 GHz is 802.11a.

6. E. The Wi-Fi Alliance performs interoperability testing and verifies standards compliance.

7. C. 802.11a uses OFDM; ERP-OFDM is used in 802.11g.

8. A, C, D. 802.11b can use 1, 2, 5.5 and 11 Mbps. 6 and 12 Mbps are used in 802.11a and 802.11g.

9. A, D. 802.11g is backward compatible to DSSS and HR/DSSS

10. A. The UNII-3 band can be used indoors or outdoors, but typically is used outdoors only.

11. C. 802.11i addresses security. 802.11e addresses quality of service.

12. B. Wi-Fi Alliance performs interoperability testing for IEEE 802.11 wireless LAN standards.

13. C, D. Both C and D are both correct since QoS is an acronym for quality of service. WMM is a proactive Wi-Fi Alliance certification for quality of service. WPA and WPA are certifications that address security.

14. A. Wi-Fi Protected Setup was designed with SOHO users in mind.

15. C, D. 802.11g can use ERP-OFDM and DSSS.

16. D. WPA was designed as a pre-802.11i solution for wireless security.

17. D. 802.11e is a specific function amendment addressing quality of service.

18. D. The IEEE requires 6, 12, and 24 Mbps for 802.11a OFDM.

19. B, C. WPA 2.0 Personal and WPS are both designed with the small business in mind.

20. A, D. WPA 2.0 consists of personal mode using passphrase and enterprise mode using 802.1X/EAP.

Wireless LAN Infrastructure Devices

THE FOLLOWING CWTS EXAM OBJECTIVES ARE COVERED IN THIS CHAPTER:

✓ Identify the purpose, features, and functions of the following wireless network components. Choose the appropriate installation or configuration steps in a given scenario.

- Access Points

  Lightweight

  Autonomous

  Mesh

- Wireless LAN Routers

- Wireless Bridges

- Wireless Repeaters

- WLAN Controller/Switch

  Distributed AP Connectivity

  Direct AP Connectivity

  Layer 2 and Layer 3 AP Connectivity

- Power over Ethernet Devices

  Midspan

  Endpoint

 Wireless LAN infrastructure devices are an important and critical part of a successful wireless LAN deployment. In this chapter, we will look at a variety of infrastructure devices, including access points, bridges, repeaters, and wireless LAN controllers/switches. This chapter will describe some of the features, benefits, and advantages of these and other infrastructure devices. In order to fully understand how these devices operate, an introduction to some basic networking concepts such as the Open Systems Interconnection (OSI) model will also be discussed. Power over Ethernet (PoE) is commonly used in enterprise wireless LAN deployments. The concepts of PoE will be discussed in this chapter.

OSI Model Basics

Some background on computer networking theory is necessary prior to continuing on with wireless infrastructure devices. The basics of computer networking discussion start with the OSI model. The *Open Systems Interconnection (OSI) model* has been around for several decades. It describes the basic concept of computer communications in the computer network environment.

There are seven layers to the OSI model. Each layer is made up of many protocols and serves a specific function. Only layers that pertain to wireless networking will be discussed in this book. Figure 2.1 illustrates the seven layers of the OSI model.

At this point it would be best to understand that wireless networking functions at the two lowest layers of the OSI model, Layer 1 (Physical) and Layer 2 (Data Link). However, to some degree Layer 3 (Network) plays a role as well, generally for TCP/IP capabilities.

- Layer 1 (PHY, the *Physical layer*) consists of bit-level data streams and computer network hardware connecting the devices together. This hardware consists of network interface cards, cables, switches, and bridges. In the case of wireless networking, radio frequency (RF) uses air as the medium for wireless communications.

- Layer 2 (*Data Link layer*) is responsible for organizing bit-level data for communication between devices on a network and detecting and correcting Physical layer errors. This communication is accomplished through Media Access Control (MAC) addressing. A *MAC address* is a unique identifier of each device on the computer network.

- Layer 3 (*Network layer*) is where the IP protocol resides and is responsible for addressing and routing functions of data. An IP address is defined as a numerical identifier or logical address assigned to a network device.

FIGURE 2.1 OSI model illustration

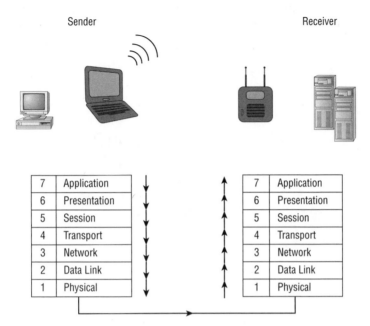

In order for computers and other network devices to communicate with one another, a communication infrastructure of some type is necessary. In a wired network, such an infrastructure consists of cables, repeaters, bridges, and Layer 2 switches. In a wireless network, these devices are access points, bridges, and repeaters. All will be discussed in more detail in this chapter.

Access Points (AP)

The *access point* (AP) is a major player in the wireless LAN network infrastructure. Access points are available in three types, autonomous, lightweight, and mesh. Autonomous access points are self-contained units and can function as independent network infrastructure devices. Lightweight access points function as part of the wireless LAN controller/switch. Mesh access points connect together to form a self-forming, self-healing intelligent network. Both lightweight and mesh access points will be discussed later in this chapter. The AP provides computers and other wireless devices access to the local area network using RF as the connection medium.

When a wireless device is connected to an access point, it is said to be in *infrastructure mode*. In this operation mode, all wireless data traffic is passed through the access point.

An access point can operate as a standalone network device. It can also operate as part of a larger wireless network by sharing some of the same configurations, such as Service Set Identifier (SSID). The SSID is the name or identifier all devices connected to the access point will share. Figure 2.2 shows an access point connected to an Ethernet network.

FIGURE 2.2 Access point connected to an Ethernet network

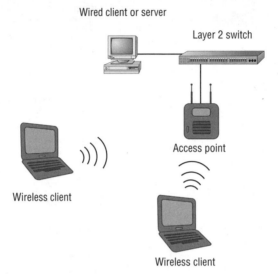

Access points are *half-duplex* devices. Half duplex in computer terminology is defined as two-way communication that occurs in only one direction at a time. (By contrast, full duplex allows for two-way communication to occur between devices simultaneously.) Communication only one way at a time means less data throughput for the connected device(s). An access point is a network infrastructure device that connects to a distribution system (DS)—typically an Ethernet segment or Ethernet cable—and allows users from a wireless communication perspective to access network resources. According to the IEEE 802.11 standards, access points are considered stations (abbreviated STA). Full duplex is another communication method used in computer networking. In a completely Ethernet-switched network, devices will communicate directly with the Ethernet switch. Figure 2.3 illustrates half-duplex communication in a wireless network.

 The CWNP program uses the terms Autonomous AP and Lightweight AP to identify the following devices. In the industry they may also be known as Intelligent AP and Thin AP, or various other terms based on how the manufacturer chooses to identify them.

FIGURE 2.3   Half duplex—Communication one direction at a time

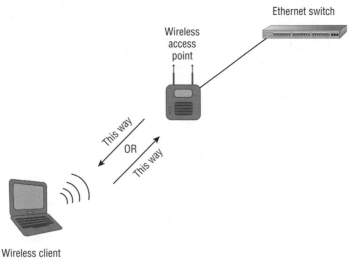

Half duplex—Two-way communication in only one direction at a time.

Autonomous Access Points

Autonomous access points are self-contained units with all the intelligence necessary to provide devices wireless access to the wired network infrastructure and to the resources they have permission to use. There are two grades of autonomous access points—enterprise and SOHO. Each grade has a different feature set.

SOHO Access Points

Although very powerful devices, SOHO-grade access points have a less extensive feature set than enterprise-grade access points. However, most consumer (SOHO) grade and enterprise-grade access points now support the highest security features available, including Wi-Fi Protected Access 2.0 (WPA 2.0). Consumer-grade access points are best used in the SOHO or home environment and usually will have a limited number of connections for computers and devices. Listed are some of the features in SOHO-grade access points:

- IEEE 802.11 standards support
- Wi-Fi certifications
- Removable antennas
- Static output power
- Security

- Bridge functionality
- Repeater functionality
- DHCP server
- Configuration and settings options

Figure 2.4 shows a typical SOHO access point.

FIGURE 2.4   DLink DWL-2100AP SOHO access point

IEEE 802.11 Standards Support

Most later-model SOHO access points support current 802.11 standards, while others require firmware updates for compliance. Some older devices have no firmware update available, causing implementation challenges where interoperability with newer and legacy devices is required. The standards supported will vary based on several factors, including the cost and complexity of the unit. The most common SOHO access points will support the 802.11g and 802.11b communication standards. Dual-band access points (which support both 802.11a and 802.11b/g) are not as common in the SOHO market. Some equipment manufacturers do make dual-band models, but the cost is normally higher.

Wi-Fi Certifications

Wi-Fi certifications are a common feature of SOHO access points. These certifications include WPA/WPA 2.0 and WPS for Security, WMM and WMM-PS for QoS. Selecting a SOHO access point that is Wi-Fi certified ensures compliance to IEEE standards and interoperability with other devices.

Removable Antennas

Some SOHO access points are equipped with *removable antennas*. This allows the end user to change to a larger (higher gain) antenna thereby creating a larger radio frequency coverage area. Conversely, connecting a smaller (lower gain) antenna will decrease the coverage area. Antennas will be discussed in Chapter 6, "WLAN Antennas and Accessories."

RF coverage of an access point can be increased by adding a higher gain antenna to an access point. For more information, see Chapter 6.

Static Output Power

Occasionally an end user will have the ability to adjust the transmit output power in a SOHO access point. The transmit output power will determine in part the area of radio frequency coverage, also known as the *cell*. The typical transmit output power of a SOHO model access point is about 15 dBm or 32 mW. An access point model with static output power cannot be adjusted, which will limit the ability to decrease or increase the size of the radio frequency cell. In this case, changing the cell size can only be accomplished by changing the gain of the antenna in models that have the removable antenna feature.

Security

Newer SOHO access points should support the highest security features. These security features include WPA 2.0 personal and enterprise modes, which give users with limited technical knowledge the ability to provide the most up-to-date security for their wireless network. For those users who have greater technical know-how, more advanced security features such as 802.1X/EAP or virtual private network (VPN) pass-through are also options.

Bridge Functionality

SOHO access points occasionally can be configured in bridge mode. Either point-to-point or point-to-multipoint settings are available, giving the ability to connect two or more wired LANs together wirelessly.

Repeater Functionality

A SOHO access point may have the ability to be configured to function as a repeater. Configuring an access point as a repeater enables administrators to extend the size of the radio frequency cell. This allows users not in hearing range of an access point to connect to the wireless network. However, this comes at the cost of reduced throughput for the users accessing the network through a repeater.

DHCP Server

Another common feature for SOHO access points is the ability to act as a *Dynamic Host Configuration Protocol (DHCP)* server. A DHCP server will automatically issue an Internet Protocol (IP) address to allow upper layer communications between devices on the network. As mentioned in "OSI Model Basics," earlier in this chapter, IP addresses are a function of Layer 3 of the OSI model.

Configuration and Settings Options

SOHO access points are configured via a web browser either through *HTTP (Hypertext Transfer Protocol)* or *HTTPS (Hypertext Transfer Protocol Secure Sockets Layer)*. This type of browser-based configuration is an easy way for the novice user to make all the necessary settings based on the application in which the access point will be used. Figure 2.5 shows a sample of a configuration page from a SOHO access point.

FIGURE 2.5   SOHO access point configuration page in a web browser

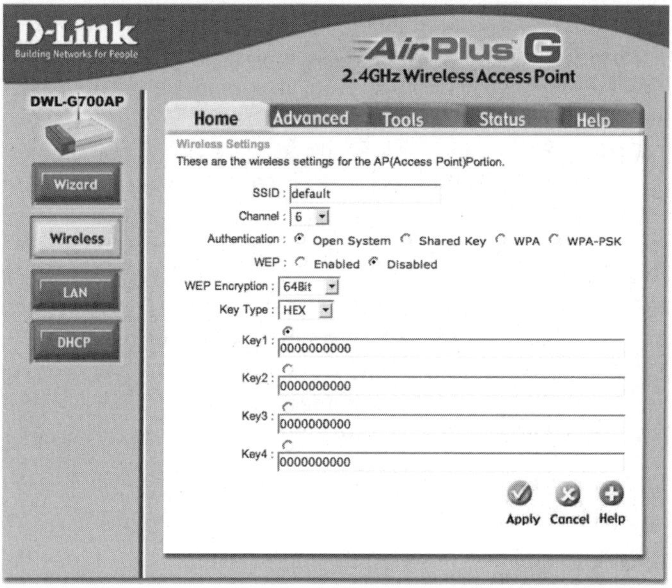

For security purposes, best practices include configuration of the access point from the wired side of the network whenever possible. Configuration should only be done wirelessly if absolutely necessary. If configuring the access point from the wireless side is the only option, a secure connection should be in place to prevent unauthorized access.

> Some manufacturers of SOHO wireless equipment have online emulators that allow customers to view a sample of the configuration process for a device. This gives a user the ability to go through the configuration of the device prior to making a purchase.

Enterprise Access Points

Enterprise access points typically have a much more extensive feature set than the previously mentioned SOHO access points. This section will look at some of the more advanced features available in enterprise-grade access points.

Figure 2.6 shows an enterprise-grade access point.

FIGURE 2.6   Motorola AP7131 IEEE 802.11n access point

Enterprise-grade access points can include the following features:

- IEEE 802.11 standards support
- Wi-Fi certifications
- Removable or expandable antennas
- Adjustable transmit output power
- Advanced security
- Multiple operation modes, including root, bridge, and repeater capabilities
- Command-line interface (CLI) configuration

IEEE 802.11 Standards Support

Just as SOHO access points support IEEE standards, enterprise access points support standards as well. Enterprise access points have a more extensive feature set and, depending on the manufacturer and model, they will support all communication standards by utilizing 802.11a and 802.11b/g dual-band radios.

Wi-Fi Certifications

Wi-Fi certifications are an important feature of enterprise grade access points. These certifications include WPA/WPA 2.0 for Security, WMM and WMM-PS for QoS. Selecting an enterprise-grade access point that is Wi-Fi certified ensures compliance with IEEE standards and interoperability with other devices.

Removable or Expandable Antennas

Many enterprise access points have removable or expandable antennas. These antenna configurations provide a lot of flexibility—an installer can choose the appropriate antenna based on the deployment scenario. Enterprise-quality access points that use internal antennas may offer options for connecting external antennas should they be required. Antennas will be discussed in more detail in Chapter 6.

Adjustable Transmit Output Power

Unlike some SOHO-grade access points, enterprise-grade access points have the capability to adjust transmit output power. This feature allows an installer to select the correct amount of transmit power based upon the installation needs of the access point. One benefit of having adjustable output power is that an installer can adapt to the environment in which the access point was installed. If the radio frequency dynamics of an area change, the ability to change the access point settings, such as output power, without physical intervention is very beneficial.

Advanced Security

Compared to access points used in the SOHO environment, enterprise access points will have more advanced security features, such as a built-in user database for local *Remote Authentication Dial-In User Service (RADIUS)* authentication. This local RADIUS authentication feature allows small to medium businesses to provide their own advanced authentication features without the need of external RADIUS authentication services. This reduces costs and lowers administration overhead. RADIUS is just one example of the more advanced security features available in enterprise-level access points.

Some other configuration options available for one model of enterprise access point are shown in Figure 2.7.

Multiple Operation Modes

In addition to the above-mentioned features, enterprise access points typically have several operation modes. These modes are:

- Root access point mode—the most common configuration
- Bridge mode—for connecting LANs together
- Repeater mode—to extend the RF cell

Root Access Point Mode   *Root access point mode* is typically the default operation mode in which an enterprise access point is set. Root access point mode involves connecting the access point to a distribution system (DS) such as an Ethernet segment or backbone. This allows computers and other devices to connect to the access point and use network resources based on the assigned permissions of the user, computer, or device.

FIGURE 2.7   Enterprise-grade access point configuration page in a web browser

Bridge Mode   This configuration allows for an access point to be set in bridge mode for point-to-point or point-to-multipoint configurations connecting two or more LANs together. Benefits of using wireless access points to bridge LANs together include cost savings and high data transfer rates.

Repeater Mode   An access point configured in repeater mode can act to extend the radio frequency cell. This allows computers and devices outside the radio hearing range to connect to the network and access network resources.

Command-Line Interface (CLI) Configuration

Most enterprise access points have command-line interface (CLI) capabilities to allow configuration of the device. Browser-based administration is also available. In some cases, the CLI command set allows an administrator to perform additional configuration because of a higher level command set. This allows consistency in configuring other network infrastructure devices because many manufacturers share commands among devices. CLI capabilities vary depending on the manufacturer, but most enterprise models have a very extensive set of commands.

Lightweight Access Points

Lightweight access points differ from autonomous access points in that they are used with wireless LAN controllers/switches and not as standalone devices. (As discussed in the section "Autonomous Access Points," earlier in this chapter, an autonomous access point is a self-contained unit with all the intelligence needed to provide computer and device access to a wireless network.) Lightweight access points have shifted much of the intelligence to the wireless LAN controller/switch. Since a lightweight access point contains less intelligence than an autonomous access point, the cost of a lightweight access point can be significantly lower.

Depending on the manufacturer, lightweight access points may have a more extensive feature set than autonomous access points, and include many of the features of those devices. Lightweight access points are centrally managed from the wireless LAN controller/switch. One of these features is Layer 3 virtual private network (VPN) connectivity for computers and other devices. Figure 2.8 shows a typical lightweight access point.

FIGURE 2.8 Aruba Dual-radio 802.11a/n + 802.11b/g/n using 3 antennas

Mesh Access Points

Wireless mesh networking is growing at a steady pace. The term *mesh networking* has been in existence for many years. In a full mesh network, all nodes connect together with at least two paths for every node. This allows for reliable communications in the event of a device or path failure.

Wireless mesh networking is very popular in the outdoor market. Some examples where wireless mesh networks are currently utilized are:

- Metropolitan
- University campuses

- Public safety
- Transportation
- Government
- Amphitheaters

Most outdoor mesh access points provide the highest levels of wireless security and are usually inside a rugged weatherproof enclosure for protection from the elements.

Currently many wireless LAN manufacturers use proprietary mechanisms and protocols for mesh networking. The IEEE 802.11 standard will be amended to include wireless mesh networking. This amendment to the standard will be 802.11s. Many enterprise grade access points have the ability to operate in mesh mode, while others have a dedicated mesh function.

Wireless mesh networking for indoor deployments is still in the early stages, mostly due to lack of standards, which leads to interoperability problems. Some manufacturers recommend using both unlicensed bands for mesh operation. One common solution is to use the 2.4 GHz ISM band for device access and the 5 GHz UNII band for mesh device connectivity. The use of a third radio is also an option in some cases. Figure 2.9 shows an illustration of mesh access points connected to a wired infrastructure.

FIGURE 2.9   Illustration of mesh access points/routers connected to a common infrastructure and may also be connected to the Internet.

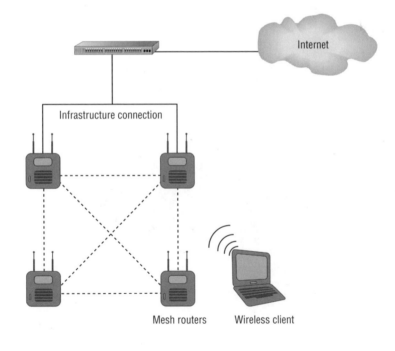

Wireless LAN Routers

Wireless LAN routers can be defined differently depending upon the application. In the SOHO or home market, a wireless LAN router may also be known as a wireless broadband router. The CWNP program and associated material refer to these devices as wireless residential gateways. In the enterprise environment, a wireless LAN router may have similar functionality plus extended features, and may be known as a wireless VPN router.

Wireless Residential Gateway

SOHO or home broadband routers (also known as wireless residential gateways) are usually equipped with an Internet port, several ports for an Ethernet switch, and a wireless access point. These routers are configured through a web browser using either the HTTP or the HTTPS protocol. Configuration of the devices is fairly simple for the novice user using a web browser via a built-in web server. In most cases, a broadband wireless router connects to either a cable modem or a digital subscriber line (DSL) connection available from an Internet service provider (ISP). In this configuration, a router is able to accept wired and wireless connections for computers and other devices allowing access to the LAN or the Internet. Some of the features of a broadband router include:

- Network Address Translation (NAT)
- DHCP server
- IP routing
- Domain Name System (DNS) services
- Firewall

A wireless broadband router has many of the same features as a SOHO access point. An example of a wireless broadband router is shown in Figure 2.10.

FIGURE 2.10   Netgear WNDR3300 RangeMax Dual Band Wireless-N router

Wireless VPN Router

A *wireless VPN router* typically has three ports available:

- Ethernet port to connect to a LAN

- Internet port to connect to the wide area network (WAN)

- Wireless port to allow IEEE 802.11 computers and devices to connect to a network

Wireless VPN routers have a more extensive feature set than wireless broadband routers, including Layer 3 VPN tunnels between devices and the router on each side acting as a VPN endpoint. Other features include:

- Point-to-point Tunneling Protocol (PPTP)

- Layer 2 Tunneling Protocol/Internet Protocol Security (L2TP/IPSec)

- SSH2

- Advanced IP networking services

- Edge router capability

Figure 2.11 shows a typical wireless VPN router.

FIGURE 2.11   Colubris wireless VPN router

Wireless Bridges

Wireless bridges connect two or more wired LANs together. As discussed in Chapter 1, "Introduction to Wireless Local Area Networking," typically there are two configurations for wireless bridges: point-to-point or point-to-multipoint. A wireless bridge is a dedicated device that functions in much the same way as an access point in bridge mode. Wireless bridges have many of the same features as enterprise access points, including removable antennas and selectable power levels.

Connecting locations together using wireless bridges has many benefits, including fast installation, cost savings, and high data transfer rates. Depending on the circumstances, a wireless bridge can be installed in as little as one day. Cost savings can be enormous compared to installing and maintaining a physical wired connection between locations, such as copper, fiber optics, or a leased line from a service provider.

Wireless bridges work in either the 2.4 GHz ISM or 5 GHz UNII band. The distance can span long distances. Since wireless bridges can potentially span long distances, it is important to take security into consideration.

Figure 2.12 illustrates wireless bridges connecting two LANs.

FIGURE 2.12   Wireless bridges connecting two LANs

LAN 1

LAN 2

 When connecting LANs together using wireless bridges, the bridges must be set to the same RF channel and have the same SSID.

Wireless Repeaters

Wireless repeaters are used to extend the radio frequency cell. In a wired Ethernet network, repeaters function at Layer 1 of the OSI model to extend the Ethernet segment. An Ethernet repeater lacks intelligence—that is, it cannot determine data traffic types and simply passes all data traffic across the device.

Just as an Ethernet segment has a maximum distance for successful data transmission, wireless LANs do as well. A wireless repeater provides the ability for computers and other devices to connect to a wireless LAN even though they are not within the normal hearing range of the access point connected to the network.

Figure 2.13 illustrates how a wireless repeater can extend the range of a wireless network.

FIGURE 2.13   Wireless repeater extends the range of a wireless network

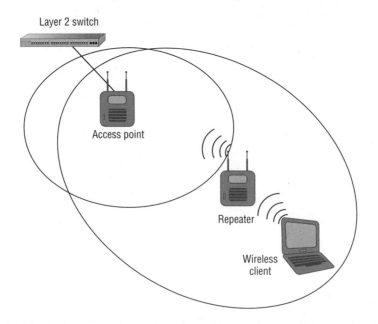

Layer 2 switch

Access point

Repeater

Wireless
client

Using Wireless Repeaters Reduces Throughput

Before using a wireless repeater, one needs to consider if this would be the best solution. Since wireless LANs are half duplex (two-way communication but only one way at a time), data throughput will suffer when using repeaters. Every time the data traverses a wireless link, the data throughput is reduced by about 50 percent. The Ethernet port on a wireless repeater should be disabled since it is not connected to an infrastructure and for security purposes.

Wireless LAN Controller/Switch

Wireless controllers/switches are growing in popularity in wireless LAN deployments. Wireless LAN controllers/switches range from branch office models with a few lightweight access points to large scale enterprise devices with hundreds or thousands of lightweight access points. The branch office models are typically used in remote office installations or small/medium business (SMB) applications with a limited number of access points. Listed are some of the many benefits, features, and advantages that may be available on wireless LAN controllers/switches.

- Centralized administration
- Lightweight access points

- Virtual LAN (VLAN)
- Power over Ethernet (PoE) capability
- Improved roaming
- Security profiles
- Captive portal
- Built-in RADIUS services
- Site survey tools
- Radio frequency spectrum management
- Firewall
- Quality of service
- Redundancy
- Intrusion prevention system (IPS)
- Direct or distributed AP connectivity
- Layer 2 and Layer 3 AP connectivity

Centralized Administration

A wireless LAN controller/switch with *centralized administration* gives an administrator the ability to completely control the wireless network from a single location. Unlike autonomous access points that require intervention at each device for configuration, a wireless LAN controller/switch can be a "one stop shop" for configuration and management. A Wireless Network Management System (WNMS) may be used as a centralized tool to manage autonomous access points. This may be used to help scale the autonomous access point architecture but is not required.

Lightweight Access Points

The benefits of lightweight access points are similar to those of autonomous access points, including radio frequency management, security, and quality of service. But lightweight access points cost less than autonomous access points, and very little or no information is contained within the devices. Lightweight access points are PoE capable for ease of deployment in either mid-size or large organizations.

Virtual LAN (VLAN)

According to the IEEE standards, *virtual local area networks (VLANs)* define broadcast domains in a Layer 2 network. Layer 2 Ethernet switches can create broadcast domains based upon how the switch is configured by using VLAN technology. This allows an administrator to separate physical ports into logical networks to organize traffic according to the use of the VLAN for security profiles, QoS, or other applications. The concept of a Layer 2 wired VLAN is extended to wireless LANs. Wireless LAN controllers/switches have the ability to configure broadcast domains and segregate broadcast and multicast traffic between VLANs.

Power over Ethernet (PoE) capability

Wireless LAN controllers/switches support Power over Ethernet (PoE), allowing power and data to be sent over the same cable. Details regarding Power over Ethernet (PoE) will be discussed later in this chapter in the section "Power over Ethernet."

Improved Roaming

Fast seamless Layer 2 and Layer 3 *roaming* between access points is another common feature of wireless LAN controllers/switches. This feature is beneficial in order for computers and other devices connected to the wireless LAN to maintain a connection while physically moving throughout the service set.

Security Profiles

A wireless LAN controller/switch can provide network administrators the ability to create a variety of security profiles. Security profiles can work in conjunction with VLANs to allow or deny access based on requirements for the computer, device, or user access.

 Using security profiles, you can allow legacy devices that may be limited to Wired Equivalent Privacy (WEP) to be located on a separate VLAN without compromising the security of the entire network.

Captive Portal

Captive portal capability is a common feature in wireless LAN controllers/switches. A Captive portal will intercept a user's attempt to access the network by redirecting them to an authorization web page. This web page will request account credentials or payment information from a user before granting access to the network.

Built-in RADIUS Services

Another common feature of wireless LAN controllers/switches is RADIUS services for 802.1X/EAP authentication supported by WPA and WPA 2.0. Built-in RADIUS allows a network administrator to utilize the most advanced security features available today to secure the wireless network. Built-in RADIUS server databases typically have a limited number of users that can be created, therefore built-in RADIUS is a good solution for small/medium business (SMB) or remote office locations, but not for very large organizations.

Site Survey Tools

Predictive site survey tools assist in placement of access points and other infrastructure devices. These tools are sometimes a feature of a wireless LAN controller/switch. Performing a predictive site survey will assist in planning to determine coverage and capacity for data and voice for both indoor and outdoor deployments.

Radio Frequency Spectrum Management

Keeping an eye on the radio frequency environment is another responsibility of the wireless network administrator. RF spectrum management consists of adjusting radio frequency parameters such as channel (frequency) and RF power after deployment. This allows the network to adapt to changes in the environment and assist in the event of hardware failures.

Firewall

Integrated stateful *firewall* features help protect your network from unauthorized Internet traffic yet allow authorized traffic. Firewalls can be hardware-based, software-based or a combination of both. Stateful firewalls, which keep records of all connections passing through the firewall, help protect against broadcast storms, rogue DHCP server attacks, Address Resolution Protocol (ARP) poisoning, and other potential attacks against the wireless LAN.

Quality of Service (QoS)

Quality of service features help time-bounded applications such as voice and video communications to minimize latency and allow for traffic prioritization.

Redundancy

Redundancy allows for fault tolerant deployments and uninterrupted access in the event of access point or wireless LAN controller/switch failure. Complete redundancy will prevent a major outage due to hardware failure for mission critical or other deployments. Coverage is maintained by alternating access points between the redundant devices, minimizing interruption for user access in the event of a hardware failure.

Intrusion Prevention System (IPS)

An intrusion prevention system (IPS) monitors all activity across the wireless network for potential intrusion and malicious activities, and can take appropriate action based on the type of intrusion.

Direct and Distributed AP Connectivity

Connecting access points that are not directly plugged into a port on the wireless LAN controller/switch is known as distributed AP connectivity. This is beneficial in large scale deployments. Many manufacturers support distributed AP connectivity. Direct AP connectivity is defined as a direct connection to ports on the switch. A typical model with distributed connectivity is shown in Figure 2.14.

FIGURE 2.14   Meru MC5000 Large Scale Enterprise wireless LAN controller

Layer 2 and Layer 3 AP Connectivity

Early wireless network implementations were built with dedicated Layer 2 connectivity, which meant limited wireless mobility. Layer 2 roaming occurs when a computer or other wireless device moves out of the radio cell of the currently connected AP and connects to a different AP maintaining Layer 2 connectivity.

As wireless networking technology evolved, so did the need for Layer 3 connectivity and roaming. Internet Protocol (IP) addresses are Layer 3 addresses that identify devices on a network. All IP devices on the same network or subnet are considered to be in the same IP boundary. Layer 3 roaming occurs when a client moves to an AP that covers a different IP subnet. After roaming, the client will no longer have a valid IP address from the original subnet and the device will be issued an IP address from the new subnet while maintaining Layer 3 connectivity. Figure 2.15 illustrates Layer 2 and Layer 3 connectivity.

Power over Ethernet (PoE)

Power over Ethernet (PoE) sends direct current (DC) voltage and computer data over the same Ethernet cable, enabling a device to receive DC power and computer data simultaneously. PoE is an IEEE standard, described in *802.3-2005 Clause 33*, also known as IEEE 802.3af, and allows devices used in wired or wireless networking to receive DC power from the Ethernet connection without the need for an external DC power source.

An Ethernet cable has four copper wire pairs or eight copper wires. Depending on the technology in use, either two or all four wired pairs may be used to carry data traffic. Figure 2.16 shows an example of a standard Ethernet cable pin assignment.

The PoE standard allows electrical power to be supplied in one of two ways, either over the same wired pairs that carry computer data or over the pairs that do not carry data. 10BASE-T and 100BASE-T (Fast Ethernet) implementations use only two wired pairs (four wires) to carry data. 1000BASE-T (Gigabit Ethernet) uses all four pairs (eight wires) to carry computer data.

FIGURE 2.15 Wireless client device roaming across Layer 2 and Layer 3 boundaries

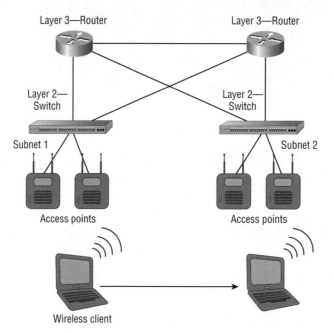

FIGURE 2.16 Standard Ethernet pin assignment

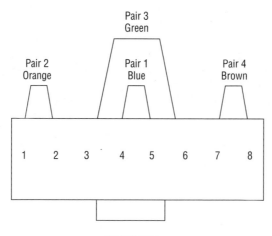

The nominal voltage for PoE is *48 VDC*, but the standard allows for a range of 36 to 57 VDC. The PoE standard addresses two types of devices: power sourcing equipment (PSE) and powered device (PD).

> Prior to standardized PoE some manufacturers used proprietary implementations. These solutions used various voltages, polarities, and pin assignments and may still be in the market today. It is recommended to verify PoE standard compliance prior to utilizing this technology to prevent potential hardware failures.

The current IEEE 802.3-2005 Clause 33 standard was released in 2003 and allows for 15.4W per port maximum. The soon to be released IEEE 802.3at standard, also known as PoE Plus, will allow for approximately 30W per port maximum.

Power Sourcing Equipment (PSE)

Power sourcing equipment is the device that supplies the DC voltage to the end devices. The DC voltage (power) can be delivered to the device in one of two ways:

- An endpoint device (usually a wireless LAN controller/switch or an Ethernet switch) delivers DC power directly.
- A *midspan* device (usually a single port or multiple port injector) injects DC power into the Ethernet cable over the unused wire pairs.

Powered Device (PD)

The *powered device* is defined as the device receiving DC power, such as an access point, wireless bridge, IP camera, IP phone, and so on. Equipment manufacturers have the option of defining a classification signature. This classification signature determines the maximum amount of power a device requires, thereby allowing the PSE to better manage the amount of power delivered to a specific port. The PoE standard makes five classes of powered device available (class 0 through class 4). Table 2.1 shows the available classes, and the amount power in watts for each class.

Figure 2.17 shows an example of a power sourcing equipment (PSE) and powered device (PD).

TABLE 2.1   Classes of Powered Device Described in the PoE amendment to the Ethernet standard, 802.3-2005 clause 33.

Class	Use	PSE Power Output in Watts	PD Max Levels in Watts
0	Default	15.4W	0.44 W to 12.95 W
1	Optional	4.0W	0.44 W to 3.84 W

TABLE 2.1   Classes of Powered Device Described in the PoE amendment to the Ethernet standard, 802.3-2005 clause 33. *(continued)*

Class	Use	PSE Power Output in Watts	PD Max Levels in Watts
2	Optional	7.0W	3.84 W to 6.49 W
3	Optional	15.4W	6.49 W to 12.95 W
4	Reserved for future use	n/a	n/a

FIGURE 2.17   Motorola PSE single-port injector and PD Motorola access port

Single port injector

Powered device—
thin access point

Benefits of PoE

There are many benefits to using devices that support PoE, including cost savings and convenience. The IEEE 802.3 standard (Ethernet) specifies a maximum distance of 100 meters or 328 feet for *unshielded twisted pair (UTP)* category 5 (CAT5) Ethernet cable. Power over Ethernet provides the ability for a PoE device to receive DC power and computer data at this distance without the need for electrical power at the point where the device is installed or located. This can amount to a large cost savings if a voltage source is not available where the device is located, because there is no need to install electrical power at that point.

Midspan Devices

Midspan devices inject the required DC voltage (48V nominal) into the Ethernet cable allowing the AP, bridge, etc., to receive electrical power and computer data. There are two types of midspan device—single port injectors and multiport injectors. A single port injector will supply power to a single device. This is useful in an implementation that may have only a few PoE devices. A single port injector is an in-line device that adds DC power to the Ethernet cable. A multiport injector will supply DC power to many devices. A multiport injector is an in-line device that functions like a patch panel. Two ports on this device are required to supply both DC power and computer data to a single powered device access point, such as a bridge or IP camera.

Endpoint Devices

Endpoint devices will supply DC power and computer data directly at the Ethernet port rather than relying on an intermediate device to supply the power. Wireless LAN controllers/switches and Ethernet switches are examples of endpoint devices. A benefit of endpoint PoE is that no intermediate adapter to inject power is necessary. Figure 2.18 shows an example of an endpoint device.

FIGURE 2.18   Aruba 2400 Mobility Controller with Power over Ethernet endpoint capability

Summary

This chapter discussed wireless LAN infrastructure devices that are commonly used to provide wireless connectivity to a network for computers and other wireless devices. These devices include the access point—the heart of the wireless LAN—available either as a self-contained intelligent (autonomous) device or as a lightweight device for use with a wireless LAN controllers/switches providing user access to network resources. Other infrastructure devices include wireless LAN routers for SOHO or home use, wireless bridges for connecting LANs together, and wireless repeaters for extending the RF cell. This chapter explained some of the features, benefits, and applications of these infrastructure devices. Finally, the chapter covered the Power over Ethernet PoE standard (IEEE 802.3-2005 Clause 33), its components, the DC voltage and amount of power supplied (in watts), and how the power is delivered to an end device.

Exam Essentials

Remember the function and features of three different access point technologies. Compare and contrast the differences and features between autonomous, lightweight, and mesh access points. Know that autonomous access points are self-contained units, and lightweight access points work with wireless LAN controllers/switches.

Understand differences in various infrastructure devices. Identify the features and applications of access points, bridges, repeaters, and wireless LAN controller/switches.

Explain the function of other infrastructure devices. Understand the different modes in which wireless infrastructure devices operate as well as the uses for specific devices such as wireless bridges and repeaters.

Explain the differences regarding Power over Ethernet devices. Know the differences between power sourcing equipment (PSE) and powered device (PD), and know their use in wireless networking.

Know details of the IEEE 802.3-2005 Clause 33 Power over Ethernet standard. Know that the IEEE 802.3-2005 Clause 33 PoE standard uses 48 volts nominal. Identify different classifications. Understand the difference between midspan and endpoint solutions.

Key Terms

48 VDC

802.3-2005 Clause 33

access point

autonomous access points

cell

centralized administration

Data Link layer

Dynamic Host Configuration Protocol (DHCP)

endpoint devices

firewall

half duplex

HTTP (Hypertext Transfer Protocol)

HTTPS (Hypertext Transfer Protocol Secure Sockets Layer)

infrastructure mode

lightweight access points

MAC address

midspan devices

Network layer

Open Systems Interconnection (OSI) model

Physical layer

powered device

Power over Ethernet (PoE)

power sourcing equipment

redundancy

Remote Authentication Dial-In User Service (RADIUS)

removable antennas

Roaming

root access point mode

unshielded twisted pair (UTP)

virtual local area networks (VLANs)

wireless bridges

wireless controllers/switches

wireless LAN routers

wireless mesh networking

wireless repeaters

wireless VPN router

Review Questions

1. Wireless LANs function at which of the following layers of the OSI model? (Choose 2.)
   - **A.** Layer 5
   - **B.** Layer 4
   - **C.** Layer 3
   - **D.** Layer 2
   - **E.** Layer 1

2. In computer network terminology, the definition of half duplex is closest to which of the following?
   - **A.** One-way communication one way only
   - **B.** One-way communication one way at a time
   - **C.** Two-way communication both directions simultaneously
   - **D.** Two-way communication one way at a time

3. A self-contained intelligent access point is:
   - **A.** Lightweight
   - **B.** Heavyweight
   - **C.** Autonomous
   - **D.** Thin

4. SOHO access points have which of the following features? (Choose 3.)
   - **A.** WPA 2.0 support
   - **B.** CLI configuration
   - **C.** Static output power
   - **D.** Wi-Fi certifications

5. Wireless bridges must be configured with _____ and _____. (Choose 2.)
   - **A.** Null SSID
   - **B.** Same SSID
   - **C.** Same RF channel
   - **D.** Channel scanning
   - **E.** Wired Equivalent Privacy

6. Which of the following is a benefit of a wireless repeater? (Choose 2.)

A. Higher data transfer rate

B. Larger cell size allows for more devices to access the medium

C. Smaller cell size allows for less devices to access the medium

D. Less data throughput

E. Extends cell size

7. True or false: A benefit of a wireless LAN controller/switch is distributed administration.

A. True

B. False

8. Static output transmit power of a SOHO access points is typically:

A. 32dBm

B. 15dBm

C. 23mW

D. 15mW

9. The 802.3-2005 Clause 33 standard specifies _____ VDC as the nominal voltage.

A. 32

B. 57

C. 48

D. 12

10. Which of the following devices is an in-line device that will inject DC voltage into the Ethernet cable?

A. Midspan

B. Midpoint

C. Endspan

D. Endpoint

11. Which layer of the OSI model is responsible for delivering data to a unique hardware address?

A. Layer 1

B. Layer 2

C. Layer 3

D. Layer 4

E. Layer 5

F. Layer 6

G. Layer 7

12. SOHO access points are typically configured by using _____. (Choose 2.)

   A. HTTP

   B. FTP

   C. HTTPS

   D. CLI

   E. SMTP

13. True or false: An administrator should always configure an access point from the wireless network.

   A. True

   B. False

14. Access points (APs) work at which layers of the OSI model? (Choose 2.)

   A. Layer 1

   B. Layer 2

   C. Layer 3

   D. Layer 4

   E. Layer 5

   F. Layer 6

   G. Layer 7

15. Enterprise access points may contain which of the following features? (Choose 3.)

   A. WPA 2.0 support

   B. RADIUS server

   C. Static output power

   D. Repeater mode

   E. Power sourcing equipment

16. Which of the following statements is true regarding a wireless LAN controller/switch?

   A. Virtual local area networks (VLANs) involve physical separation of ports.

   B. Virtual local area networks (VLANs) involve a logical separation of ports.

   C. Virtual local area network (VLAN) is another name for a repeater.

   D. Virtual local area networks (VLANs) require Power over Ethernet (PoE).

17. A lightweight access point connected to a port on the wireless LAN controller/switch and not to an intermediate device is considered to have which of the following?

   A. Direct connectivity

   B. Distributed connectivity

   C. Decentralized connectivity

   D. Centralized connectivity

18. Power sourcing equipment delivers which of the following?

    A. RF power to the access point

    B. DC power to the end device

    C. RF power to an antenna

    D. DC power to an antenna

19. Which access point mode involves connecting the access point to a distribution system for user access to the LAN?

    A. Bridge only mode

    B. Repeater only mode

    C. Root access point mode

    D. Access mode

20. Which of the following are midspan PoE devices? (Choose 2.)

    A. Single port injectors

    B. Multiport injectors

    C. Endpoint injectors

    D. Endspan injectors

Answers to Review Questions

1. D, E. Wireless LAN technology functions at Layer 1 and Layer 2 of the OSI model.

2. D. In computer terminology, half duplex is two-way communication but only one way at a time. Full duplex is two-way communication in both directions simultaneously.

3. C. An autonomous access point is an intelligent, self-contained network infrastructure device. Lightweight access points (also called thin access points) work with a wireless LAN controller/switch.

4. A, C, D. A, C, and D are correct. SOHO access points typically are managed from a web browser and do not have a command-line interface feature.

5. B, C. Bridges must be on the same RF channel and have the same SSID in order to communicate.

6. B, E. Wireless repeaters do extend the cell size and will potentially allow more users to connect. However, using a wireless repeater will decrease throughput.

7. B. A wireless LAN controller/switch uses centralized administration, not distributed administration.

8. B. Many SOHO access points use 15dBm or 32mW for transmit output power.

9. C. The PoE standard specifies 48 VDC as nominal. The range is 32–57 VDC.

10. A. A midspan device will inject power into an Ethernet cable. Endpoint power is delivered directly from a switch or controller.

11. B. Layer 2 is the Data Link layer. A MAC address is a unique identifier of the network card.

12. A, C. SOHO use HTTP or HTTPS for configuration. Enterprise can also use CLI. SMTP is Simple Mail Transfer Protocol.

13. B. An administrator should avoid configuring an access point from the wireless side of the network unless absolutely necessary.

14. A, B. Depending on the specific function, APs operate at Layers 1 and 2. Repeaters function only at Layer 1.

15. A, B, D. Enterprise access points have adjustable output power. Power sourcing equipment is used in PoE to deliver power and data.

16. B. VLANs involve logical separation of ports.

17. A. A lightweight access point connected to a port on the switch is considered to have direct connectivity.

18. B. PSE delivers DC power, not RF power. The DC power is delivered to an end device such as an access point.

19. C. Root access point is the default mode in most cases. An access point in root access point mode allows users to connect to the network.

20. A, B. Single port and multiport injectors combine power and data in the same cable. Endpoint power is out of the switch port. There is no such thing as an endspan injector.

Chapter

3

Wireless LAN Client Devices

THE FOLLOWING CWTS EXAM OBJECTIVES ARE COVERED IN THIS CHAPTER:

✓ **Identify the purpose, features, and functions of the following client devices. Choose the appropriate installation or configuration steps in a given scenario.**

- PC Cards (ExpressCard, CardBus, and PCMCIA)

- USB2, CF, and SD devices

- PCI, Mini-PCI, and Mini-PCIe cards

- Workgroup bridges

- Client utility software and drivers

Client devices are often thought of as computers—either desktop or notebook—connected to a network.

However, there are many other devices, both wired and wireless, that can connect to a computer network. Wireless LAN client devices include various types of computers, scanners, print servers, cameras, and other devices that are used to send data to a computer network. This chapter will look at the features of various wireless LAN client adapter types and the software for configuration and management of these devices.

Devices that connect to wireless networks use various types of adapters. Which adapter is used depends on the device it connects to. You can connect to such devices as a notebook PC, pocket PC, desktop computer, or barcode scanner. Wireless LAN adapters are available in various types, both external and internal. External adapters connect either to an available port or into a slot in the device. Examples of external adapter types are:

- PCMCIA
- ExpressCard
- USB 2.0
- CompactFlash (CF)

Some devices use internal adapters that may require some level of disassembly or removal of a panel prior to the installation. Examples of internal adapter types are:

- PCI
- Mini-PCI
- Mini-PCIe

Wireless LAN client adapters differ from other networking adapters (such as Ethernet adapters) because they contain radio hardware. The radio hardware uses radio frequency (RF) to send the computer data over the air. Chapter 4, "Radio Frequency (RF) Fundamentals for Wireless LAN Technology," will discuss RF fundamentals in more detail.

PCMCIA

PCMCIA technology was developed in the early 1990s because the portable computer industry demanded smaller, lighter, and more mobile technology. The international standards organization developed to promote the growth of such technology is the Personal Computer Memory Card International Association (PCMCIA).

Features of PCMCIA Cards

The PCMCIA standard addresses three types of cards—Type I, Type II, and Type III. These cards are named after the PCMCIA organization that promotes this card technology and is responsible for the standards. You might also see the term *PC Card* used to describe these cards. PC Card describes the physical card or peripheral. All three types are the same width and length and have a 68-pin connector.

Figure 3.1 shows an example of a PCMCIA card that allows a computer to connect to a wireless network.

FIGURE 3.1   Netgear WN511T Wireless PCMCIA adapter

The only difference among the three types of cards is their thickness. Table 3.1 lists the different thickness and common uses of the card types.

TABLE 3.1   Features of the Three Types of PCMCIA Card

Card Type	Thickness	Common Use
Type I	3.3 millimeters	RAM, flash, OTP, and SRAM memory cards
Type II	5.0 millimeters	LANs, data/fax modems, and mass storage I/O devices
Type III	10.5 millimeters	Rotating mass storage devices

There are five versions of the PCMCIA standard. The release numbers are 1.0, 2.0, 2.1, 5.0, and 8.0. Releases 1.0 through 2.1 support 16-bit applications. Releases 5.0 and up address a 32-bit interface.

 For additional details on the PCMCIA releases, visit the PCMCIA website at www.pcmcia.org.

Installation and Configuration of PCMCIA Cards

Installation of a PCMCIA card is a fairly simple process. The first consideration is to verify the physical characteristics of the card, such as the type (Type I, II, or III) and device in which it will be used—a notebook computer, for example. The devices need to be physically compatible with each other to ensure correct operation. Another consideration is the device driver. A *device driver* is software required for a component such as a PCMCIA card to communicate with the computer operating system. The installer should have the latest version of the device driver accessible. The card comes with an installation CD (compact disc) that contains the device driver. It is best to follow the manufacturer's installation recommendations for the installation process, which may involve updating the driver from the manufacturer's website.

 It is important to verify compatibility and minimum system requirements prior to installing a wireless network adapter in a device. Refer to the owner's manual or manufacturer's website for this information.

Configuration Using Installer Software

In many cases, a user will be required to first install a software program from the card manufacturer. This software will usually load the device driver within the computer operating system and install the configuration utility for the card.

Configuration Using a Wizard

In some cases, when the PCMCIA card is inserted into the correct slot, the computer operating system will automatically install the required device driver. If the operating system cannot find the correct driver, the user will be prompted to search the Internet or insert a CD or other source from the manufacturer with the software device driver. Figure 3.2 shows a wizard that the Microsoft Windows XP operating system will display to help load the device driver.

The manual device driver installation process described in Exercise 3.1 for PCMCIA is also applicable for other types of adapters explained in this chapter.

Exercise 3.1 illustrates how a common PCMCIA wireless LAN card will be installed. Do not insert the adapter until instructed to do so by the installation program.

FIGURE 3.2   Microsoft Windows XP Found New Hardware Wizard

EXERCISE 3.1

PCMCIA Card Installation Steps

The following steps are typical for installation of a PCMCIA wireless LAN card. Installation steps are specific to the manufacturer, and it is recommended to follow the manufacturer's installation instructions. Always read the manufacturer's manual regarding setup and safety before attempting installation.

1. Insert the Setup CD-ROM into the CD-ROM drive. The program should start automatically, and a welcome screen may appear.

    The graphic shows the welcome screen for the Linksys Wireless-G Notebook Adapter Setup Wizard.

EXERCISE 3.1 *(continued)*

2. After reading and accepting the license agreement, click to continue the installation and the program will begin copying the files onto your computer.

3. The setup program will now prompt the installer to install the adapter into the PC. This image illustrates inserting the adapter into a notebook computer.

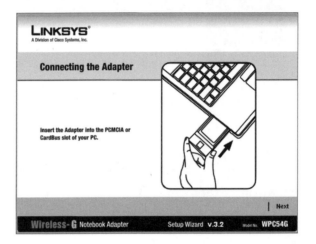

4. After the card has been identified, the program will copy the driver files to the computer.

5. The setup program will display the available wireless networks in the area or mode for connecting. Create a profile by selecting or typing in the desired wireless network. The following image shows the Linksys Setup Wizard's Wireless Mode connection screen.

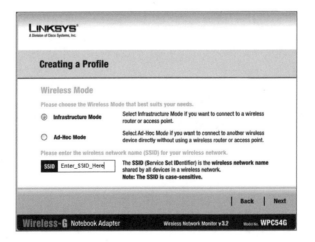

6. On the Wireless Security screen of the wizard, select the appropriate security settings—in this case, WPA2-personal. Enter the preshared key of the wireless network. The key must be 8 to 63 characters and must match the network key.

7. Connect to the wireless network using the created profile. The wizard summary screen shows the results of the installation.

8. Setup is complete. Remove the Setup CD-ROM from the CD-ROM drive.

In some cases, the installation and setup may require the computer to be restarted in order for the adapter to operate correctly. Follow the manufacturer's recommendations.

ExpressCard

ExpressCard is the next generation of PC Card technology. Hewlett Packard, Dell, Intel, and Microsoft are some of the PCMCIA member companies responsible for creating the ExpressCard standard. This technology is used in a large percentage of notebook computers to add new hardware capabilities.

Lower cost, smaller size, and higher performance were the driving forces behind ExpressCard technology. Applications include wired and wireless networking and communications, multimedia, and additional memory storage.

Features of the ExpressCard

The ExpressCard standard is built on the 16-bit and 32-bit PC Card standards. ExpressCard modules are available in four types: 34mm, 34mm extended, 54mm, and 54mm extended. The extended modules can be used for external connectors, television tuners, and wireless broadband, whereas standard modules will have specific functionality such as a wireless network adapter. Figure 3.3 shows the four types of ExpressCards.

FIGURE 3.3   The four types of ExpressCard module

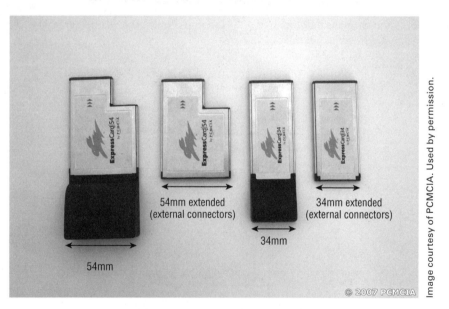

Users can install or remove an ExpressCard without having to power down the computer or device. This technology is known as *hot-plug*. Hot-plug technology is also commonly supported by USB and other adapters.

For additional details and information, visit the ExpressCard website at www.expresscard.org.

Installation and Configuration of an ExpressCard

The installation and configuration steps for an ExpressCard are similar to those for installing a PCMCIA card. (See the earlier section, "Installation and Configuration of PC Cards.") Figure 3.4 shows an ExpressCard plugged into a notebook computer.

FIGURE 3.4   ExpressCard installed in a notebook computer

USB 1.0, USB 1.1, and USB 2.0

Introduced in 1995, the *Universal Serial Bus* (USB 1.0) standard was designed as a replacement for legacy serial and parallel connections.

Serial communication is the process of transmitting one data bit at a time. *Parallel communication* has the capability of transmitting several data bits at a time. Imagine a single lane road versus a four-lane highway. On a single lane road, only one car at a time can travel, whereas on a four-lane highway, many cars can traverse the same path at the same time.

USB allows connectivity for various devices that once used serial and parallel data connection ports. These devices include but are not limited to:

- Keyboard
- Mouse
- Digital camera
- Printer
- PDA

USB 1.0 specified data rates from 1.5 Mbps to 12 Mbps. USB 1.0 was replaced by USB 1.1 in 1998. Devices using this version of the standard were more common in the market.

USB standards are implemented by the USB Implementers Forum (USB-IF). This organization consists of companies from the computer and electronics industries, including Intel, Microsoft, NEC, and Hewlett Packard.

The *USB 2.0* specification was released in April 2000. The first revision appeared in December 2000 and the standard has been revised several times since. USB 2.0 incorporates several changes, including connector types. Data rates now allow for a maximum speed of up to 480 Mbps (USB 1.0 supported a maximum of 12 Mbps).

Figure 3.5 shows an example of a USB 2.0 port.

FIGURE 3.5   USB 2.0 port on notebook computer panel

USB 2.0 port

Features of USB

USB uses a standard connector that replaces 9-pin serial, 25-pin parallel, and various other connector types. External configuration allows the installer to plug in the USB device and power it with one cable. The operating system will guide the installer through the device driver installation process. External installation minimizes the need to open up a computer case and make adjustments within the computer such as switch or jumper settings. USB also supports hot-swapping of devices, allowing connection and disconnection without the need to power down the device or the computer. In some cases, USB allows for power to be delivered to the peripheral device, eliminating the need for an external power supply.

For additional information and specifications regarding the USB standards, visit the USB Implementers Forum (USB-IF) at www.usb.org.

Installation and Configuration of USB Devices

Exercise 3.2 walks you through the steps for installation of the D-Link Wireless N USB 2.0 Adapter. Many USB wireless LAN adapters use installation procedures similar to this one. Installation steps are specific to the manufacturer, and it is recommended to follow the manufacturer's installation instructions. Always read the manufacturer's manual regarding installation and safety before attempting installation.

EXERCISE 3.2

Installing a USB 2.0 Wireless LAN Adapter

To install the D-Link Wireless N USB 2.0 Adapter on a computer running Microsoft Windows, follow these steps:

1. Insert the Setup CD-ROM into the CD-ROM drive. The program should start automatically and an autorun screen will appear. Click to start the installation, and the Installation Wizard window will appear.

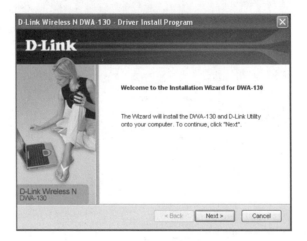

2. Accept the default location to install the files or browse for an alternate file location.

3. When prompted, insert the USB adapter into an available USB port on your computer.

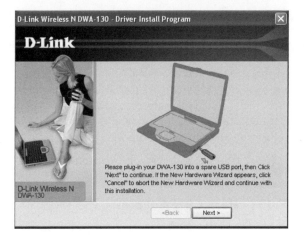

4. When prompted, enter the network name (SSID) manually. If you don't know the SSID, click Scan to see the site survey page.

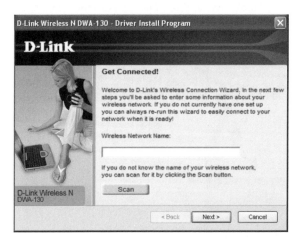

The site survey page will also appear if the SSID is entered incorrectly. Click on the network name (SSID) and click Next.

5. Click Finish to continue. If prompted to restart the computer, select Yes, Restart The Computer Now.

CompactFlash (CF) Devices

CompactFlash (CF) was originally designed as a mass storage device format used in portable electronic devices. SanDisk introduced this format in 1994. The CF format is now used for a variety of devices and technologies including Ethernet networks, Bluetooth, digital cameras, RFID, and wireless LANs.

Features of CF Cards

CF cards are available in two types, Type I and Type II. Both types have the same length and width, 36mm × 43mm. The only difference is the thickness.

Table 3.2 lists physical characteristics and typical uses of CompactFlash cards.

TABLE 3.2   Characteristics and Uses of CF Cards

Card Type	Thickness	Common Use
Type I	3.3 millimeters	RAM, flash memory cards
Type II	5.0 millimeters	Wireless LANs, microdrives

Figure 3.6 shows the front and back of a CompactFlash wireless LAN card supporting IEEE 802.11a/b/g wireless connectivity.

FIGURE 3.6   Motorola LA-5137 IEEE 802.11a/b/g CompactFlash card

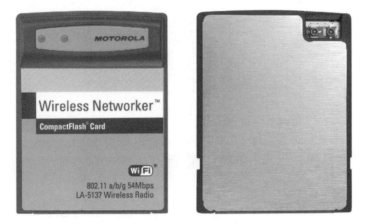

For additional information regarding this technology, visit the Compact-Flash organization at www.compactflash.org.

Installation and Configuration of a CF Card

Installing a CF IEEE 802.11 wireless LAN card differs from some of the previous installation examples. These differences may include connecting a handheld personal computer running a Microsoft operating system (*Pocket PC*) or personal digital assistant (*PDA*) to another computer in order to complete the installation process. It is recommended to follow the manufacturer's setup instructions for installing the specific card.

Secure Digital (SD)

Like CompactFlash cards, Secure Digital (SD) was designed as a flash memory storage device with storage capacities from 8 MB to 4 GB. The SD memory card was a joint venture among SanDisk, Toshiba, and Panasonic in 1999.

Even though the SD card was designed as a flash memory card, the slot will allow for connection of other devices such as cameras, global positioning system (GPS) units, FM radios, TV tuners, Ethernet networks, and of course wireless LANs. In this format the SD card is known as *Secure Digital Input Output (SDIO)*. This card is designed to provide high-speed data I/O with low power consumption for mobile electronic devices. Figure 3.7 is an example of an SDIO wireless LAN adapter.

FIGURE 3.7   SanDisk SDIO Wi-Fi card

Features of SDIO Cards

SDIO cards are available in two sizes:

- The full-size SDIO card is 24mm × 32mm × 2.1mm in size—approximately the size of a postage stamp. This SDIO card is targeted for portable and stationary applications.

- The mini-SDIO is 27mm × 20mm × 1.4mm in size and used with wireless LAN and Bluetooth adapters.

> For additional information regarding SD and SDIO technology, visit the SD Association at www.sdcard.org.

Installation and Configuration of SDIO Cards

Installing an SDIO 802.11 wireless LAN card is similar to installing a CompactFlash card, and differs from the installation of PCMCIA and ExpressCard. These differences may include connecting a Pocket PC or PDA to another host PC running ActiveSync in order to complete the installation process. It is recommended to follow the manufacturer's setup instructions for installing a specific card. Following are the typical steps for installing an SDIO wireless LAN card:

1. Connect the Pocket PC or PDA to the host PC running ActiveSync.

2. Install the software using the host PC.

3. Insert the SDIO Wireless LAN card.

4. Start the program on the Pocket PC or PDA.

5. Find a wireless LAN to connect and create a profile.

6. Connect to the wireless LAN.

> Always read the manufacturer's manual regarding installation and safety before attempting installation.

Peripheral Component Interconnect (PCI)

PCI is the abbreviation for *Peripheral Component Interconnect*, a standard for computer interface cards that was developed by Intel. A PCI card is inserted into a slot in a desktop computer, allowing for the attachment of peripheral devices. Installing a *PCI* card may require tools and the installer might need to remove the cover from the desktop computer case. Figure 3.8 shows an example of an IEEE 802.11 wireless PCI card.

FIGURE 3.8   Netgear WG311T IEEE 802.11g wireless PCI adapter

Features of PCI

PCI connects to what is known as a *data bus*. In basic terms, a data bus allows connection of devices to the computer's processor or "brain." In the early days of personal computers, many devices used a data bus. These devices included video, hard disks, serial ports, Ethernet adapters, and parallel ports for printers. These interfaces connected to what is known as an *Industry Standard Architecture* (ISA) bus.

Modern computers have integrated many of these interfaces directly into the motherboard, system board, or main board. As PC technology evolved, so did the data bus architecture, going to 32-bit and now 64-bit bus. Wireless networks are no stranger to PCI. Even though wireless is often thought of as portable or mobile, in many cases stationary desktop computers can utilize wireless LAN connectivity through the use of wireless PCI interface cards.

 PCI-SIG (Peripheral Component Interconnect–Special Interest Group) is the industry organization for development and management of the PCI standards. For additional information, visit www.pcisig.com.

Installation and Configuration of PCI Cards

In 1995, Microsoft introduced a feature in the Windows 95 operating system called Plug and Play (PnP). This new feature accelerated the interest in PCI. PnP made installing a PCI card a snap. All that was required was for the installer to plug the card into the motherboard and it would be recognized and automatically work with the operating system. However, this still required user intervention to open the case in order to physically install the card. Exercise 3.3 describes the steps for installing a PCI card in a desktop computer.

EXERCISE 3.3

PCI Card Installation Steps

The following steps are typical for installation of a PCI wireless LAN card. Installation steps are specific to the manufacturer, and it is recommended to follow the manufacturer's setup instructions. Always read the manufacturer's manual regarding setup and safety before attempting installation.

1. Insert the Setup CD-ROM into the CD-ROM drive. The program should start automatically, and a welcome or autorun screen may appear. When this screen appears, click Next to continue and follow the instructions to install and configure the wireless PCI adapter. The installation wizard will appear on the screen.

2. The setup program will copy the required files to the desktop computer.

EXERCISE 3.3 *(continued)*

Turn off the computer to install the card. Once the computer is turned off, unplug the power cord from the wall jack.

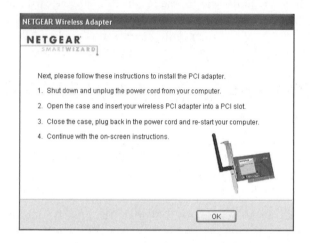

3. Open the case and identify an available PCI slot. Using the appropriate tool, remove the cover over the slot. Insert the wireless PCI adapter into the available PCI slot and securely fasten in place. The image shows an available PCI slot in a desktop computer.

4. Once the card is securely mounted, close the case and insert the power cable into the wall jack. Turn on the computer.

5. The setup program will appear on the screen. Follow the on-screen instructions to complete the installation.

In some cases, the installation and setup may require the computer to be restarted in order for the adapter to operate correctly. Follow the manufacturer's recommendations.

Mini-PCI and Mini-PCIe (Mini-PCI Express)

Mini-PCI is a variation of the PCI standard. However, Mini-PCI was designed for laptops and other small-footprint computer systems. One common example of a Mini-PCI card is the IEEE 802.11 Mini-PCI adapter shown in Figure 3.9.

FIGURE 3.9   IEEE 802.11 Mini-PCI adapter

Mini-PCI cards are common in many applications such as Fast Ethernet networks, Bluetooth, modems, hard drive controllers, and wireless LANs. In the wireless world, Mini-PCI cards are used in access points and client devices such as laptops or notebooks.

Mini-PCI Express (Mini-PCIe) cards are a replacement for the Mini-PCI card and are based on PCI Express.

Many notebook and portable computers with built-in wireless LAN will use either Mini-PCI or Mini-PCIe cards for wireless IEEE 802.11 wireless LAN connectivity.

Features of Mini-PCI and Mini-PCIe Cards

Mini-PCI cards are available in three types; Type I, Type II, and Type III. Two of the three types (Type I and Type II) use a 100-pin stacking connector. Type III cards use a 124-pin edge connector. Type II cards have RJ11 and RJ45 connectors for telephone and Ethernet network connections. These cards are commonly located at the edge of the computer or docking station so that the connectors can be mounted for external access such as modem or computer network access.

Mini-PCIe cards are 30mm × 56mm in length and width and have a 52-pin edge connector, consisting of two staggered rows on a 0.8mm pitch. These cards are 1.0mm thick excluding components. Table 3.3 summarizes the features of Mini-PCI and Mini-PCIe cards.

TABLE 3.3 Features of Mini-PCI and Mini-PCIe Cards

Card Type	Connectors	Size
Mini-PCI Type IA	100-pin stacking	7.5mm × 70mm × 45mm
Mini-PCI Type IB	100-pin stacking	5.5mm × 70mm × 45mm
Mini-PCI Type IIA	100-pin stacking, RJ11, RJ45	17.44mm × 70mm × 45mm
Mini-PCI Type IIB	100-pin stacking, RJ11, RJ45	5.5mm × 78mm × 45mm
Mini-PCI Type IIIA	124-pin edge	5mm × 59.75mm × 50.95mm
Mini-PCI Type IIIB	124-pin edge	5mm × 59.75mm × 44.6mm
Mini-PCIe	52-pin edge, two staggered rows on 0.8mm pitch	30mm × 56mm × 1mm (excluding components)

Figure 3.10 shows a Mini-PCIe adapter.

FIGURE 3.10   Intel 3945 IEEE 802.11a/b/g Mini-PCIe adapter

Installation and Configuration of Mini-PCI and Mini-PCIe Cards

As with the PCI card installation process, Mini-PCI and Mini-PCIe installation may require the user to physically install hardware in the computer. Location of the Mini-PCI or Mini-PCIe interface varies depending on the computer manufacturer. On some computers you just have to remove a panel on the bottom of the notebook. On others you need to disassemble the case. Exercise 3.4 describes the typical installation steps.

EXERCISE 3.4

Mini-PCI and Mini-PCIe Installation Steps

The following steps are typical for installation of a Mini-PCI and Mini-PCIe wireless LAN card on a notebook computer. Installation steps are specific to the manufacturer, and it is recommended to follow the manufacturer's setup instructions.

1. Shut down the computer. Verify the computer is not in Hibernation mode. If so, turn on the computer and perform a complete shutdown.

2. Disconnect the AC power cord from the wall jack.

3. Disconnect all connected peripherals and remove the battery pack.

4. Remove the panel covering the Mini-PCI–Mini-PCIe compartment (details of this step will depend on the computer model).

5. Insert the Mini PCI or Mini-PCIe card into the correct slot. Note the correct pin orientation.

6. Connect the wireless antenna cables to the Mini PCI or Mini-PCIe card.

7. Replace the panel for the Mini-PCI–Mini-PCIe compartment.

8. Replace all peripheral devices and battery pack. Plug in the AC power cord to the wall jack.

9. Power on the computer and insert the Setup CD-ROM into the CD-ROM drive. The program should start automatically, and a welcome or autorun screen may appear. When this screen appears, click Install Drivers and follow the on-screen instructions to install and configure the wireless Mini PCI or Mini-PCIe card.

Always read the manufacturer's manual regarding installation and safety before attempting installation.

Workgroup Bridges

A wireless workgroup or client bridge is a wireless client device that will allow several Ethernet devices on an Ethernet segment (devices connected to a common physical layer boundary) to connect to a wireless infrastructure. This is accomplished without the need to upgrade each device on the Ethernet segment to wireless. Figure 3.11 illustrates an application of a wireless workgroup or client bridge.

FIGURE 3.11 Typical application for a wireless workgroup/client bridge

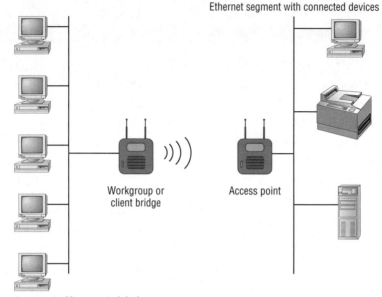

Features of Workgroup/Client Bridges

The *wireless workgroup bridge* (WWB), also known as a *wireless client bridge*, can be used in a variety of business applications, including enterprise, medical, retail, education, and warehouse. Supported devices include computers, printers, scales, medical equipment, barcode readers, and point-of-sale machines such as cash registers. Workgroup bridge devices will have a limited number of clients that can connect. The access point sees a wireless workgroup bridge as a single station even if several stations are connected, because the wireless workgroup bridge multiplexes the signal to a single connection. Figure 3.12 is a picture of a wireless client bridge.

Wireless workgroup/client bridges may include these features:

- Fixed or detachable antennas
- Security features such as WEP, WPA, or WPA 2.0
- Web browser and/or command-line interface management utilities
- MAC filtering options
- Multiple connectivity modes
- Power over Ethernet
- Support for connection of a limited number of client devices

FIGURE 3.12   Motorola CB3000 client bridge

Installation and Configuration of Workgroup/Client Bridges

The following are the steps usually necessary for installing and configuring a workgroup or client bridge:

1. Connect the workgroup or client bridge to the Ethernet segment that needs to have a wireless connection.

2. If Power over Ethernet (PoE) is not a feature of the device, connect the bridge power adapter to the wall jack.

3. Using a web browser, connect to the assigned IP address. In some cases it may be necessary to assign an IP address to the workgroup or client bridge from a CLI prior to configuring the bridge.

4. From the web management interface, assign the correct Service Set Identifier (SSID) and radio frequency channel in order to associate to the correct access point.

5. Verify association of the workgroup/client bridge to the desired access point.

    Always read the manufacturer's manual regarding installation and safety before attempting installation.

Client Device Drivers

All devices connected to a computer require a device driver. Components requiring drivers include keyboard, mouse, video card, USB port, printer, network interface card (NIC), IEEE 802.11 wireless LAN card, and many others. The device driver is software that allows the installed device to communicate with or take instructions from the operating system installed on the computer in order to provide correct functionality.

It is important to verify the latest revision of the device driver from the client device manufacturer. Having the latest revision installed will ensure correct operation and sometimes add additional features. Figure 3.13 shows a device listing in the Windows XP operating system.

FIGURE 3.13 Microsoft Windows XP Device Manager

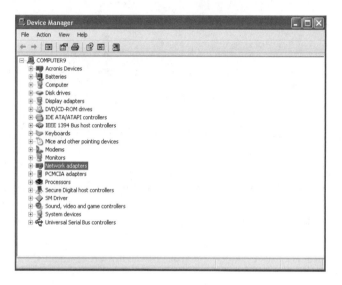

Client Utility Software

All IEEE 802.11 wireless LAN cards require configuration in order to connect to a wireless network. The configuration capabilities of device drivers are usually very limited. Therefore a user needs additional configuration software. The user can choose from either manufacturer-specific utilities or third-party client utilities built into some operating systems. When IEEE 802.1X port-based authentication is used, the client device is known as the supplicant. The supplicant will provide authentication credentials to the authenticator, which in wireless networking is the access point. 802.1X authentication will be discussed in more detail in Chapter 10, "WLAN Security." Regardless of the client utility installed, a user has the capability to create a profile that will retain the connection/session parameters. A profile will contain information regarding a specific connection, including network name or SSID and security settings.

Manufacturer-Specific Client Utilities

Most manufacturers of wireless LAN adapters provide a software client utility for the wireless adapter. The features of the utility depend on whether the client is SOHO grade or enterprise grade. SOHO-grade client utilities have basic connection and security parameters. The installation usually is part of the adapter install process and is typically performed through a setup wizard. Figure 3.14 shows a screenshot from a SOHO client utility.

FIGURE 3.14 Linksys Dual-Band Wireless-N USB client utility

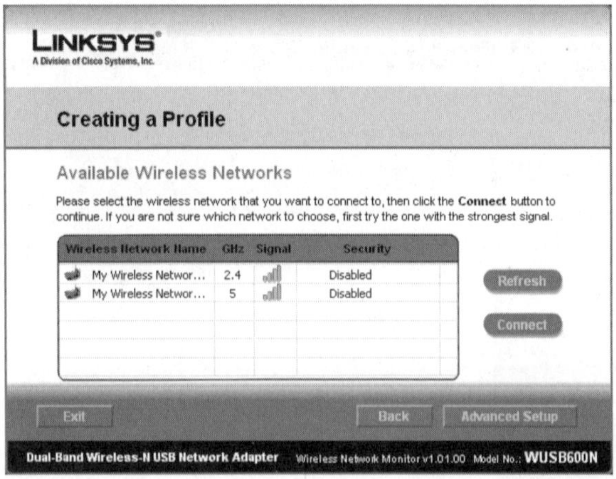

Enterprise-grade client utilities may have a more advanced feature set, including connection statistics and site survey. Typically, a user can install the device driver and client utility simultaneously or may be able to choose separate installation procedures. In most enterprise-grade client utilities, profile setup is a manual process requiring a user to have a basic understanding of the adapter's capabilities as well as the network configuration. Figure 3.15 shows an enterprise-grade client utility.

FIGURE 3.15 Proxim client utility for 8480-WD 802.11a/b/g

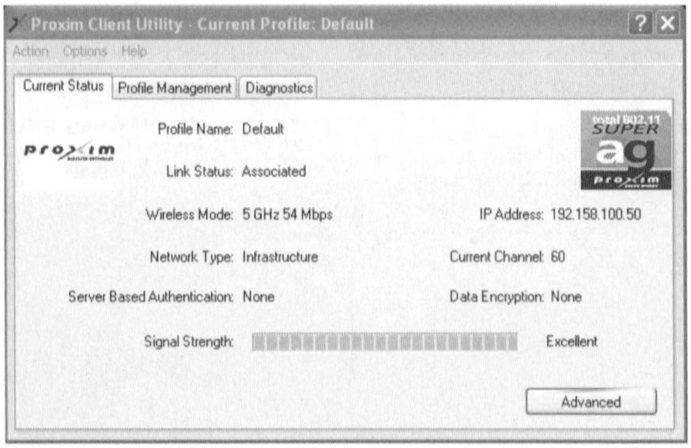

Third-Party Client Utilities

Another option for a wireless LAN adapter client utility is a third-party utility built into a computer operating system. Recent versions of the Microsoft Windows operating system—Windows XP and Vista, for example—have a client utility built in and running as a service. This client utility is called the *Wireless Zero Configuration (WZC) utility*. After the wireless adapter is installed, a user may select a wireless network to connect to and supply security parameters if required. Figure 3.16 shows the Windows XP WZC client utility.

FIGURE 3.16   Microsoft Windows XP WZC client utility

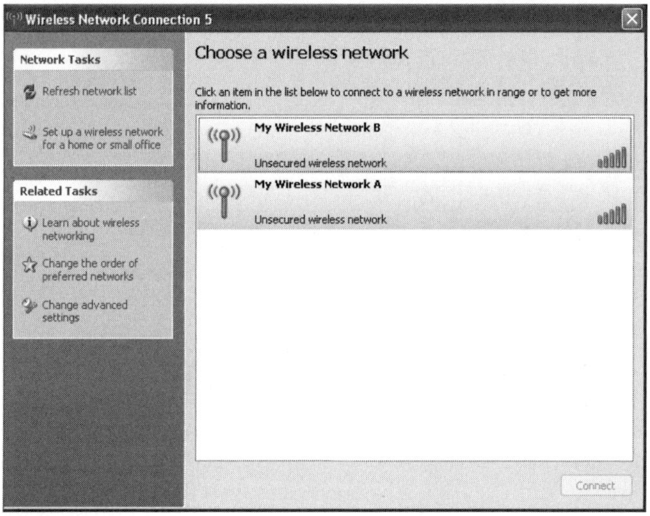

Summary

There are many different types of wireless LAN client devices used in various applications. These device types include desktop and notebook computers, printers, and barcode scanners, to name a few. This chapter looked at some of the various IEEE 802.11 wireless LAN adapter types, explaining the features, common hardware, software, and configuration procedures. External adapters with wireless LAN functionality include:

- PCMCIA
- ExpressCard
- USB 2.0
- CompactFlash (CF)

Wireless LAN adapters are also available as internal adapters. These adapters may require some disassembly or removal of a panel for installation. Internal adapters include:

- PCI
- Mini-PCI
- Mini-PCIe

Wireless LAN adapters require a device driver in order to communicate with the operating system, and in most cases software utilities will need to be installed and configured in order to connect the wireless network. This chapter described several installation scenarios for various types of wireless LAN adapters, including PCMCIA and USB. We also looked at how a wireless workgroup bridge can be used to connect computers and other devices on an Ethernet segment to a network by connecting to an access point.

Finally, this chapter showed how wireless LAN client utilities simplify the process of connecting to a wireless network. Client utilities are sometimes supplied by the manufacturer of the adapter or may part of the operating system. Windows Wireless Zero Configuration (WZC) is a commonly used operating system client utility.

Exam Essentials

Know the various types and features of external client adapters used in wireless LAN clients.   Understand the features and function of external client adapters, including PCMCIA, ExpressCard, USB 2.0 and CompactFlash (CF).

Know the various types and features of internal client adapters used in wireless LAN clients. Be familiar with internal adapter cards used with 802.11 wireless LAN technology, including PCI, Mini-PCI, and Mini-PCIe cards. Understand the installation factors involved with internal network adapters.

Understand the installation process of client adapters and client software.   PCMCIA, ExpressCard, USB2, CompactFlash (CF), SDIO, PCI, Mini-PCI, and Mini-PCIe cards require software components such as a device deriver and client utility software to be installed in order to function correctly.

Explain the function and features of specialty client devices.   Specialty client devices such as a wireless workgroup or client bridge can be used to connect devices on a common physical layer cable to a wireless network.

Know the differences among software components of wireless client adapters.   Device drivers, client utility software, third-party client software all play important roles in the successful installation of a wireless client adapter. Understand the details of software components used in wireless networking.

Key Terms

CompactFlash (CF)

data bus

device driver

ExpressCard

hot-plug

Industry Standard Architecture

Mini-PCI

Mini-PCI Express (Mini-PCIe)

Parallel communication

PCI

PCMCIA

PDA

Peripheral Component Interconnect

Pocket PC

Secure Digital Input Output (SDIO)

serial communication

Universal Serial Bus

USB 2.0

wireless client bridge

wireless workgroup bridge

Wireless Zero Configuration (WZC) utility

Review Questions

1. You have a notebook computer and wish to connect to an IEEE 802.11g wireless network. The computer does not have a built-in wireless LAN card. You do not want any peripherals connected to the notebook that use wires and do not want to disassemble the computer. Which wireless adapter would be the best solution?

    A. Wireless PCI

    B. Wireless PCMCIA

    C. Wireless Mini-PCI

    D. Wireless WSB 2.0

2. You need to select a wireless LAN card for a notebook computer to connect to an IEEE 802.11n network. The notebook has a slot on the side that will accept one of three physical types of adapter. Which card would work best in this case?

    A. PCI

    B. Mini-PCIe

    C. PCMCIA

    D. CompactFlash

3. In addition to wireless networking, which card was designed for flash memory storage and can be used in a digital camera?

    A. PCI

    B. PCMCIA

    C. ISA

    D. SD

4. A _____ computer requires the user to disassemble the computer case to install a wireless PCI network adapter. Which computer would be the best candidate in this situation?

    A. Notebook

    B. Desktop

    C. Pocket PC

    D. PDA

5. Which step is required for installation of a wireless 802.11n PCMCIA adapter card?

    A. Install device driver

    B. Install client utility

    C. Install profile software

    D. Install Windows WZC

6. You want to connect a desktop computer to an IEEE 802.11g wireless network. Which wireless LAN adapter would be the best solution if you do not want to disassemble the computer?

    A. Mini-PCI

    B. USB 2.0

    C. Mini-PCIe

    D. PCMCIA

7. Which client device will allow a user to connect several Ethernet devices on a common segment to an access point?

    A. PCMCIA

    B. PCI bridge

    C. Wireless client bridge

    D. Ethernet bridge

8. USB was designed as a replacement for which two legacy communication connections?

    A. Serial and PCI

    B. Serial and parallel

    C. Parallel and ISA

    D. Parallel and EISA

9. How many data bits does serial communications transmit at a time?

    A. 1

    B. 3

    C. 4

    D. 8

10. Which wireless adapter may require some disassembly of a notebook computer to install?

    A. PCI

    B. PCMCIA

    C. PC Card

    D. Mini-PCI

11. Most manufacturers recommend installing a PCMCIA adapter at what point?

    A. When the computer not powered on

    B. When instructed by the setup utility

    C. After calling technical support

    D. Before starting the setup process

12. Enterprise-grade IEEE 802.11g client utilities typically contain which advanced feature?

   A. PCI configuration

   B. Spectrum analyzer

   C. Setup wizard

   D. Site survey

13. Which item is required for an IEEE 802.11g PCI card to communicate with a computer connected to an unsecured wireless LAN?

   A. Mini-PCI card

   B. Device driver

   C. Third -party utility

   D. Enterprise utility

14. A wireless workgroup/client bridge will allow which of the following?

   A. Connect two LANs together

   B. Connect a wired LAN to an AP

   C. Connect a PCI card to a LAN

   D. Connect two client bridges

15. CompactFlash (CF) cards are available in two types. What is the main difference between the two types?

   A. Length

   B. Width

   C. Thickness

   D. Height

16. Which two wireless LAN adapters can be installed in a computer without the need to disassemble the computer in any way? (Choose 2.)

   A. PCI

   B. PCMCIA

   C. USB 1.1

   D. PCIe

   E. Mini-PCI

17. Secure Digital Input Output (SDIO) cards are typically installed in which device?

   A. Desktop computer

   B. Access point

   C. Notebook computer

   D. Pocket PC

18. A device driver can be used in wireless networking. Which is an example of a device driver?

    A. Software to control a wireless NIC

    B. Software to control the OS

    C. Hardware to install a PCI card

    D. Hardware to install a client bridge

19. Six wired clients can connect to a wireless LAN by using which device?

    A. Workgroup/client bridge

    B. PCI bridge

    C. Mini-PCI adapter

    D. PCI adapter

20. Which is required in order to successfully install an IEEE 802.11g wireless LAN adapter?

    A. Security profile

    B. Device driver

    C. Third-party client utility

    D. SOHO utility

Answers to Review Questions

1. B. Wireless PCMCIA adapters connect through a slot in the notebook computer.

2. C. PCMCIA cards are available in three types. The only difference in the three types is the thickness.

3. D. SDIO cards were originally designed for flash memory storage used in digital cameras and evolved to be used in IEEE 802.11 wireless devices.

4. B. A PCI adapter is a 32-bit card that requires a PCI slot inside a desktop computer. Notebook computers, Pocket PCs, and PDAs will use external cards such as Mini-PCI.

5. A. A device driver is required for the PCMCIA card to function with the operating system.

6. B. A USB 2.0 adapter can be connected to a port on the outside of the computer. Mini-PCI and Mini-PCIe are typically used in notebook computers and other portable devices and require some level of disassembly. PCMCIA cards can be used in desktop computers only if an internal PCI adapter is used, which will require disassembly of the computer case.

7. C. A wireless client bridge will connect an Ethernet segment to a wireless network, allowing all devices connected to a common physical layer boundary to communicate wirelessly.

8. B. The original USB standard was intended to replace serial and parallel ports.

9. A. Serial communications transmits one bit at a time. Parallel transmits several bits at a time.

10. D. A Mini-PCI card may be mounted in a panel or within the computer case.

11. B. Most manufacturers recommend installing a PCMCIA card at a specific point. This is usually after the device driver has been copied to the computer during the setup process.

12. D. Enterprise client utilities have more advanced features such as a site survey utility. PCI configuration includes physical settings prior to installation. A spectrum analyzer is a separate product used to analyze radio frequency. A setup wizard can be a part of a SOHO-grade adapter as well as an enterprise-grade adapter.

13. B. Device drivers are required in order for the network adapter to communicate with the operating system.

14. B. A wireless workgroup/client bridge will connect an Ethernet segment to an access point.

15. C. CF cards are identical in length and width. Type I is 3.3 mm thick and Type II is 5.0 mm thick.

16. B, C. PCMCIA and USB devices connect to a slot on the outside of the computer.

17. D. Pocket PCs have SD slots and can use SDIO cards.

18. A. Wireless network cards require device drivers in order for the card to work with the computer operating system.

19. A. Wireless workgroup/client bridges can connect wired devices to a wireless LAN.

20. B. Device drivers are required. A third-party client utility is optional because manufacturers usually include a utility with the device.

Chapter 4

Radio Frequency (RF) Fundamentals for Wireless LAN Technology

---

THE FOLLOWING CWTS EXAM OBJECTIVES ARE COVERED IN THIS CHAPTER:

✓ **Define basic characteristics of Wi-Fi technology**

- Range, coverage, and capacity
- Frequencies/channels used
- Channel reuse and co-location

✓ **Identify factors that affect the range and speed of RF transmissions**

- Line-of-sight requirements
- Interference (baby monitors, spread spectrum phones, microwave ovens)
- Environmental factors

✓ **Define the basic units of RF measurements**

- Milliwatt (mW)
- Decibel (dB)
- dBm
- dBi

Radio frequency (RF) plays an essential role in wireless LAN technology. Radio waves are passed through the air (which is the medium) and are used to get information from one wireless device to another. Technically speaking, with respect to wireless LANs, RF consists of high frequency alternating current (AC) signals passing over a copper cable connected to an antenna. The antenna then transforms the signal into radio waves that propagate through the air from a transmitter to a receiver.

Unlike wired devices, which use physical cable to communicate, wireless LANs use the radio waves and the air to communicate. This chapter will discuss the characteristics of RF, explain how far a radio signal will travel, the area covered by the radio frequency propagation, and some of the factors determining how many clients or devices can use the RF signals for data communications. Understanding RF units of measure such as watts (W), milliwatts (mW), and decibels (dB) is important to RF work, just as understanding denominations of money such as U.S. dollars and British pounds is an important part of daily life. This chapter will also explain the range and speed of RF transmissions. Range (how far radio waves will travel) and speed (how fast radio waves will travel) can be affected by several environmental conditions, such as reflection and refraction. Finally, this chapter will examine some of the conditions that will affect the transmission of information across the airwaves, including interference.

Understanding Radio Frequency (RF)

Radio frequency (RF) waves are used in a wide range of communications, including radio, television, cordless phones, wireless LANs, and satellite communication. RF is around everyone and everything, and comes in many forms. RF energy is emitted from the numerous devices that use it for various types of communications. For the most part, it is invisible to humans. There is so much of it around, if you could actually see RF, it would probably scare you. Don't let it scare you, however, because the amount of regulated RF power transmitted from the devices used in daily lives is harmless. Figure 4.1 shows some of the many ways RF is used. Studies have shown that the amount of power emitted from many of these devices, such as cordless telephones or wireless network adapters, will not cause any physical harm if the devices are manufactured based on the maximum regulated power allowed for the device.

Remember, RF consists of high frequency alternating current (AC) signals passing over a copper cable connected to an antenna. This antenna will then transform the received signal into radio waves that propagate through the air. The most basic AC signal is a sine wave. This wave is the result of an electrical current varying in voltage over a period of time. Figure 4.2 shows a basic sine wave.

FIGURE 4.1   RF is used in many different devices and applications to provide communications

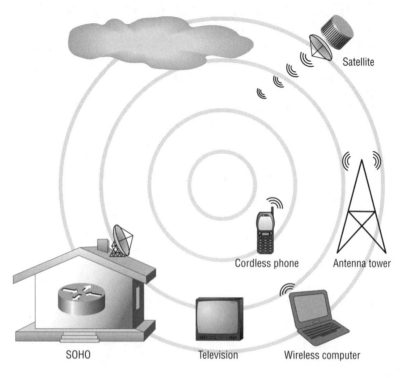

FIGURE 4.2   A basic sine wave, one complete cycle varying voltage at a point in time

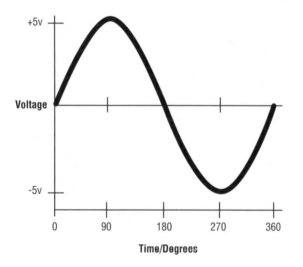

Successful radio transmissions consist of a minimum of two components, a transmitter and receiver. (See Figure 4.3.) These two components work together: for every radio transmitter there must be one or more radio receivers. It is important to understand the basic characteristics of radio frequency transmissions. These characteristics work together to form alternating current signals and include the wavelength, frequency, amplitude, and phase. The antenna will transform these signals into radio waves that travel through the air carrying information from the transmitter to the receiver. This is accomplished in different ways depending on the wireless technology in use. This theory will be discussed more in Chapter 6, "WLAN Antennas and Accessories."

FIGURE 4.3   RF transmitter and receiver. In a wireless LAN the transmitter and receiver could be an access point and client device

Wavelength

The wavelength is the distance of one complete cycle or one oscillation of an AC signal. Wavelength is typically identified by the Greek symbol lambda (λ), which is used in formulas for calculations. This distance is usually measured in centimeters or inches. Figure 4.4 shows an example of wavelength.

FIGURE 4.4   The wavelength is the distance of one complete cycle, measured in centimeters or inches.

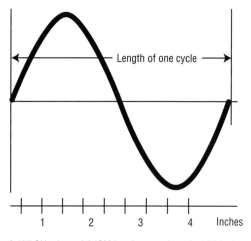

2.437 GHz channel 6 ISM band, approximately 4.85 inches

IEEE 802.11 wireless LANs use both the 2.4 GHz and 5 GHz unlicensed frequency ranges for transmission. Table 4.1 lists some examples of wavelengths for IEEE 802.11 wireless LANs using unlicensed frequencies.

TABLE 4.1   Typical Radio Transmission Wavelengths for WLANs

RF Channel	Frequency (GHz)	Length (in)	Length (cm)
6	2.437 GHz	4.85 in	12.31 cm
40	5.200 GHz	2.27 in	5.77 cm
153	5.765 GHz	2.05 in	5.20 cm

Frequency

Frequency is defined as how many complete cycles occur in one second. Low frequencies correspond to long waves, high frequencies to short waves, so the higher the frequency, the shorter the wavelength (range). In formulas, frequency is typically identified by the lower-case letter f.

Figure 4.5 illustrates an example of frequency.

FIGURE 4.5   Frequency is the number of complete cycles in 1 second.

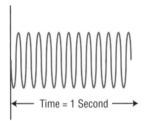

Time = 1 Second

How Far Can a Signal Travel?

A few years back, 900 MHz cordless phones were very popular. With a 900 MHz phone you could hypothetically go up to 500 feet away from the cordless phone's base station before losing the signal and no longer being able to make a phone call. In the past few years, higher frequency phones have increased in popularity. After upgrading to a 2.4 GHz phone you may have noticed you can only get about 250 feet away (half the distance compared to a 900 MHz phone) in the same environment before losing the signal and no longer being able make a phone call. This is because the 2.4 GHz wavelength is about half the distance of a 900 MHz wavelength, assuming both phones are operating at the same output power.

IEEE 802.11 wireless LANs work in several unlicensed frequency ranges. The unlicensed ranges used for WLANs are 2.4 GHz to 2.5 GHz and 5.15 GHz to 5.825 GHz. There are some areas in the 5.15 GHz to 5.825 GHz range that are not used for wireless networking.

Amplitude

Amplitude is the height or the voltage of the sine wave. As mentioned earlier, a basic sine wave is a change in voltage over a period of time. Using a formula, the voltage at the peak of the signal can be used to calculate the amount of RF power. So an increase in amplitude is equal to an increase in RF power. An increase in power is also known as the *gain*. Conversely, any decrease in amplitude will be a decrease in power. A decrease in power is also known as loss. If a transmitter outputs a certain amount of RF power—for example, 100 mW—it has a specific amplitude of some value. As this signal travels through an RF cable, it will have a specific level of loss based on the cable in use. Therefore the result will be less amplitude at the end of the cable due to the loss value of the cable.

Figure 4.6 shows two signals operating at the same frequency with different amplitudes. The signal with the higher amplitude (Signal A) is more powerful than the signal with the lower amplitude (Signal B).

FIGURE 4.6   Two signals at the same frequency with different amplitudes

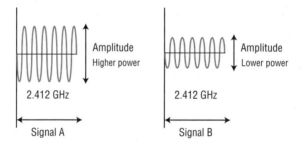

Phase

Phase is the difference in degrees designating the start and end of two different overlapping sine waves. For example, if a second sine wave starts a quarter of a wavelength after the first sine wave, it is considered to be 90° out of phase with the first sine wave. Figure 4.7 shows an example of the phase relationship between two AC signals. Two radio waves that have the same frequency but start at different times are known to have a phase difference and are considered out of phase with one another. The amount of the phase difference is typically measured in degrees ranging from 0° to 360°. If two waves are 180° out of phase, this will usually cause a cancellation effect or null the signals.

FIGURE 4.7   Phase is the difference in degrees between two signals.

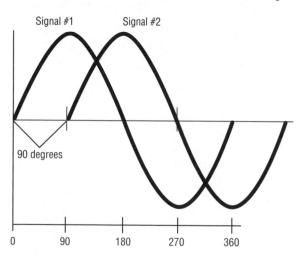

Frequencies Used for Wireless LANs

As discussed in Chapter 1, "Introduction to Wireless Local Area Networking," RF spectrum is governed by local regulatory bodies. The country where the RF is used determines the regulations, such as frequency use and maximum power. Table 4.2 illustrates examples of some local RF regulatory bodies.

TABLE 4.2   Local RF Regulatory Bodies

Location	Regulation
Canada	ISC RSS-210
China	RRL/MIC Notice 2003-13
Europe (ETSI)	ETS 300.328 ETS 301.893
Israel	MOC
Japan (MKK)	TELEC 33B TELEC ARIB STD-T71
Singapore	IDA/TS SSS Issue 1
Taiwan	PDT
USA	FCC (47 CFR) Part 15C, Section 15.247 FCC (47 CFR) Part 15C, Section 15.407

U.S. (FCC) Unlicensed Frequency Bands

In the United States, the Federal Communications Commission (FCC) is the local regulatory body responsible for regulating licensed and unlicensed radio spectrum. Listed are the unlicensed RF bands available in the U.S. for use with wireless communications:

- ISM: Industrial, Scientific, and Medical
  - 902–928 MHz
  - 2.400–2.4835 GHz
  - 5.725–5.875 GHz
- UNII: Unlicensed National Information Infrastructure
  - 5.15–5.25 GHz: UNII-1, lower
  - 5.25–5.35 GHz: UNII-2, middle
  - 5.470–5.725 GHz: UNII-2e, middle
  - 5.725–5.825 GHz: UNII-3, upper

The IEEE 802.11 standard addresses the 2.4 GHz ISM band and the 5 GHz UNII bands. In the United States, the 2.4 GHz ISM band allows for 11 of 14 channels to be used for wireless LAN communications. The 5 GHz UNII band consists of three bands utilizing four frequency ranges. The three bands are UNII-1, the lower band; UNII-2 and UNII-2e, the middle bands; and UNII-3, the upper band. Table 4.3 shows unlicensed frequency bands and channels used by IEEE 802.11 wireless LAN technology.

TABLE 4.3   IEEE 802.11 Frequency and Channel Allocations

Band	Frequency	Number of Channels
ISM	2.400–2.4835 GHz	11
UNII-1	5.150–5.250 GHz	4
UNII-2	5.250–5.350 GHz	4
UNII-2e	5.470–5.725 GHz	11
UNII-3	5.725–5.825 GHz	4
ISM	5.725–5.850	1

A chart of the United States Frequency Allocation is available from the National Telecommunications and Information Administration. To view this chart, visit www.ntia.doc.gov/osmhome/allochrt.pdf

Channels

As we have seen, radio frequency is divided into bands. These bands can be further separated into channels. One familiar application in which this is accomplished is television. Until over the air television became available in digital format, television was allocated certain frequency ranges. Common television channels operated in the very high frequency (VHF) band—for example, channels 2 through 13 operated from 54 through 216 MHz. This frequency range was divided into 12 channels, allowing optimal use of the frequency range for the application, in this case television signals. A viewer can change channels on a television to watch different programs running simultaneously. However, only one program can be viewed at any one time depending on which channel is currently selected. (Picture-in-picture televisions can show two channels at once on the screen, but each picture is still being received on a different channel.)

Wireless LANs use channels in the same way. Certain unlicensed frequency ranges are allocated for wireless networking and those frequency ranges are subdivided into channels. In order for a transmitter and receiver to communicate with one another they must be on the same channel. The 2.4 GHz ISM band has a total of 14 channels available for wireless networking. The locale where they are used will determine which of the 14 channels can be legally used for wireless networking. In the United States, IEEE 802.11b/g/n wireless networks use 11 of the 14 channels available in the 2.4 GHz ISM band. Each of these 11 channels for DSSS are 22 MHz wide and channels for OFDM are 20 MHz wide. Simple mathematics show there will be overlap in order to accommodate all of the 20 MHz or 22 MHz wide channels in this frequency range. Figure 4.8 shows the 14 channels in the 2.4 GHz range.

FIGURE 4.8   Channels in the 2.4 GHz ISM band

2.4 GHz ISM Band

Channel number	Frequency in GHz	USA	Europe	Israel*	China	Japan
1	2.412	X	X	X	X	X
2	2.417	X	X	X	X	X
3	2.422	X	X	X	X	X
4	2.427	X	X	X	X	X
5	2.432	X	X	X	X	X
6	2.437	X	X	X	X	X
7	2.442	X	X	X	X	X
8	2.447	X	X	X	X	X
9	2.452	X	X	X	X	X
10	2.457	X	X	X	X	X
11	2.462	X	X	X	X	X
12	2.467		X	X		X
13	2.472		X	X		X
14	2.484					X

* Israel only allows 5–13 outdoors, but 1–13 indoors.

The 5 GHz UNII band is also divided into channels. This band consists of three bands—lower, middle, and upper. These three bands consist of four different frequency ranges. Since there are fewer channels in the same amount of space, channels in the UNII bands do not overlap. In the 5 GHz UNII bands, channels are 20 MHz wide. Figure 4.9 shows the 5 GHz UNII bands for the FCC and ETSI locales.

FIGURE 4.9   Channels in the 5 GHz bands

Locale	Frequency	Number of Channels
Americas/EMEA	UNII-1 band (5.15–5.25)	4
Americas/EMEA	UNII-2 band (5.25–5.35)	4
Americas/EMEA	UNII-2e band (5.470–5.725)	11
Americas/EMEA (with restrictions)	UNII-3 band (5.725–5.825)	4
Americas	ISM (5.725–5.850)	1

Range

Range for wireless LANs is based on the wavelength or distance of a single cycle. The higher the frequency, the shorter the range of the signal. The lower the frequency, the longer the range of the signal. At the same output power level, a 2.4 GHz signal will travel almost twice as far as a 5 GHz signal. If a network design is planning to use dual-band access points, range will need to be considered to ensure proper coverage for both the 2.4 GHz ISM and 5 GHz UNII bands. A wireless site survey will help determine the useable range an access point will produce. A survey can involve physically walking around the proposed space and/or predictive modeling using one of many software programs. This process is discussed further in Chapter 9, "Performing a WLAN Site Survey."

Coverage and Capacity

Coverage and capacity are two key factors to take into consideration when designing and implementing an IEEE 802.11 wireless LAN. During the design phase of an IEEE 802.3 wired network, the design engineer will take capacity into consideration, verifying and validating that there are enough capacity switches, ports, etc., for the user base of the network.

The same is true for a wireless network. The number of users connected to an access point is something that needs to be carefully considered. The fact that wireless networks use a shared medium is an issue because the more users who are connected to an access point, the lower the performance may be, depending on what the users are doing. This capacity consideration will ensure satisfied end users and good network performance—proof of a successful network design and deployment.

In wireless networks, coverage also needs to be considered. Coverage is determined by the RF cell size. In IEEE 802.11 wireless networks, a cell is the area of RF coverage of the transmitter, in most cases an access point. Depending on implementation, wide coverage or large cell size may not be the best solution. A large space covered by a single access point could result in less than adequate performance based on factors such as the users' distance from the access point. The farther away from an access point, the less throughput a device or user will experience. If users will be scattered throughout a large space, it may be best to have several access points covering the space to allow for optimal performance.

 The term *cell* has several different meanings depending on the context. In the world of IEEE 802.11 wireless networks, a cell is the radio coverage area for a transmitter such as an access point.

Coverage

The term *coverage* has different meanings depending on the context in which it used. For example, if you buy a gallon of paint, the label will specify the approximate coverage area in square feet. If one gallon of paint covers 300 sq ft and the room you wish to paint is 900 sq ft, simple math shows at least three gallons of paint would be needed to effectively cover the room.

The concept is similar in IEEE 802.11 wireless networks. However, unlike with paint, there is no simple rule that determines how much space an access point will cover with the RF energy it is transmitting. This coverage will depend on many factors, some of which include:

- Size of area
- Number of users
- Bandwidth-intensive applications in use or hardware applications
- Obstacles and propagation (the way radio waves spread through an area)
- Radio frequency range
- WLAN hardware in use (this affects coverage because higher frequencies, e.g., 5 GHz, do not travel as far as lower ones, e.g., 2.4 GHz)
- Power output of transmitter

You might initially assume that you want the RF signal to propagate over the largest area possible. But this may not be the best solution. A very large cell may allow too many devices to connect to a single access point. For those clients connected at a greater distance, the performance will be lower than for stations closer to the access point. Figure 4.10 shows a large coverage area, approximately 11,250 sq ft (1,058 sq m) covered with a single access point. This is an example of too large an area for a single access point.

FIGURE 4.10   Wide coverage with only a single access point is not recommended.

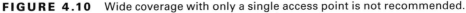

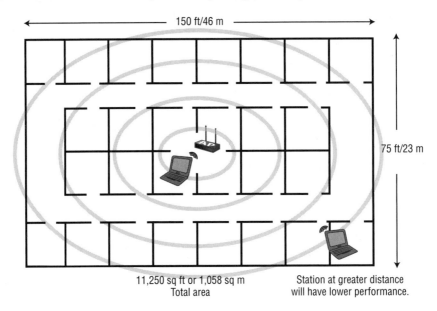

150 ft/46 m

75 ft/23 m

11,250 sq ft or 1,058 sq m
Total area

Station at greater distance
will have lower performance.

Size of Area

Rarely, if at all, will a manufacturer of IEEE 802.11 wireless LAN hardware commit to the amount of area an access point will cover. There are too many variables to take into consideration. However, some manufacturers may estimate the range of the device or access point. A site survey of the area will help determine the coverage area of an access point. A manual survey will allow for testing to verify the distance a signal will travel. A predictive site survey will model the environment and determine the signal propagation. This concept will be discussed further in Chapter 9.

Number of Users

The number of users in an area will also affect the RF coverage. A single access point covering a large area will potentially allow for a large number of users connecting to the AP. For example, an office of 8,000 sq ft may consist of 100 people, each with their own wireless computer. This is an example of wide coverage. The applications in use on the wireless network will have an impact on the overall performance. If all 100 people are using a CAD/CAM application, which is bandwidth intensive, the overall performance will be poor because this type of application requires a lot of resources. Therefore more access points, each covering less space, would parlay into better overall performance for the users. Wide coverage in a densely populated area may allow too many users to connect to a single access point, resulting in poor performance overall as explained with the CAD/CAM application example. As mentioned earlier, wireless LANs use what is known as a shared medium. In other words, all users connected to an access point will share the available bandwidth. Too many users using powerful applications will overload the access point, adding to the poor performance issues. This scenario can also be considered a capacity issue. In this situation more access points with each AP covering a smaller area would be a better solution.

Applications in Use

The application types in use—either software or hardware—can affect the bandwidth of an access point. If the users connected to an access point use bandwidth-intensive applications such as the CAD/CAM application mentioned earlier, this could result in poor throughput for all users connected to that access point. This is another example where more access points, with each covering a smaller area, could be a better solution than a single access point covering a large area. Multiple access points could allow the high-bandwidth users to be separated from other parts of the network, increasing overall performance of the network.

Obstacles, Propagation, and Radio Frequency Range

Obstacles in an area, such as walls, doors, windows, and furnishings, as well as the physical properties of these obstacles—thickness of the walls and doors, density of the windows, and type of furnishings—can also affect coverage. The radio frequency used—either 2.4 GHz or 5 GHz—will determine how well a signal will propagate and handle an obstacle. Partitions, walls, and other obstacles will also determine the coverage pattern of an access point because of the way RF behaves as it travels through the air. Behaviors of RF will be discussed later in this chapter in the section "Environment: RF Behavior."

WLAN Hardware and Output Power

The wireless LAN hardware in use can also have an impact on the coverage area. Examples include the antenna type, antenna orientation, and gain of the antenna. The higher the gain of an antenna, the greater the coverage area; conversely, the lower the gain of an antenna, the smaller the coverage area. The polarization of an antenna (horizontal vs. vertical) will also have an effect on the coverage area because of the different shapes of the radiation patterns. The output power of the transmitter or access point will also have an effect on coverage. The higher the output power, the greater distance a signal will propagate. A higher power signal will provide more coverage. Most enterprise-grade access points provide the capability to control or adjust the output power.

Capacity

One definition of capacity is the maximum amount that can be received or contained. An example of this would be an elevator in a building. Typically an elevator will have a maximum number of people or amount of weight it can hold; this is usually stated on a panel within the elevator. To ensure safety, the elevator may have a safety mechanism to prevent overloading. Likewise, a restaurant has a certain number of chairs to hold customers; therefore, they would have a maximum capacity of customers who can be served at any one time. Does this mean that when a restaurant fills its seats to capacity, the doors close and no other customers can enter the building? Not necessarily. In some cases, a restaurant could have customers standing and waiting to be seated.

Just as an elevator or a restaurant has a limited number of people they can accommodate comfortably, wireless access points also have a capacity. The capacity of an access point is how many users the AP can service effectively, offering the best performance. This capacity depends on several factors, including:

- Software applications in use
- Desired throughput or performance
- Number of users

The following sections discuss how these factors affect the capacity of an access point.

What Happens When an Access Point Is Overloaded

If the capacity of a single access point has exceeded the maximum number of users or devices based on the performance metrics, additional access points may need to be added. If a wireless network is installed correctly, an access point will not be overloaded with an excessive number of users. An overloaded access point will result in poor performance and therefore unhappy users.

To understand why, look back at the restaurant example. If a restaurant seats 20 customers and all 20 seats are taken, the restaurant has reached its capacity. Let's say the restaurant is short-staffed because two servers did not show up for work. The servers who did show up will have to work extra hard to handle the customers. This may cause delays in service because the servers need to handle more than their normal number of tables. The delays may result in unhappy customers.

The same is true for wireless access points. If a wireless access point has reached its capacity, it could get overloaded. This would result in its taking longer to handle any individual request for access. The delays may result in unhappy users. Therefore this situation could justify another access point in the area to handle the additional users. Just as a restaurant will not close its doors when all seats are taken, an access point will continue to accept users to connect unless restrictions such as load balancing are implemented.

Software Applications in Use

The software applications in use may affect the capacity of an access point. Some applications are more bandwidth-intensive than others. For example, word processing applications may not require much bandwidth whereas database or CAD/CAM applications may require much more bandwidth than other applications. If high-bandwidth applications are in use, the contention among the connected users will increase because they are using a shared medium (air and RF). Therefore performance will potentially be reduced for all users connected to the access point. The access point is providing the same amount of bandwidth, but the overall performance has been decreased for the connected users because the software applications are all using a lot of bandwidth.

Desired Throughput or Performance

The desired throughput or performance can also affect capacity. A large number of users connected to an access point using a bandwidth-intensive application will cause poor performance. Therefore, it may be necessary to limit the capacity to a certain number of users to give the connected users the best performance possible. Any software application that is bandwidth-intensive, such as CAD/CAM, streaming video, or file transfer protocol (FTP) downloads, can have an effect on overall performance. One way to help resolve this would be to use load balancing to limit the number of users that can connect to an access point. Another way would be to add more access points.

Channel Reuse and Co-location

Earlier in this chapter, it was noted that the 2.4 GHz ISM band has a total of three non-overlapping channels. In the U.S. FCC implementation of this band, the three non-overlapping channels are 1, 6, and 11. This means there must be a separation of five channels in order for them to be considered non-overlapping. In the 2.4 GHz ISM band, channels are separated by 5 MHz. Taking this into consideration, channels must be separated by 25 MHz in order to be considered non-overlapping. This is calculated from five channels of separation multiplied by 5 MHz ($5 \times 5 = 25$). With deployments larger than a few access points, a channel plan may be necessary. A channel plan will minimize the chance of interference due to two transmitters set to the same or adjacent overlapping channels.

Figure 4.11 illustrates a 2.4 GHz deployment with no channel planning. Users in the areas where the circles overlap will experience interference. This interference will result in lower overall throughput for the connected users because of the spread spectrum technologies that wireless LANs use. This interference basically has the same effect as collisions in an Ethernet network, resulting in retransmissions of data. A correct channel plan will implement channel reuse and ensure overlapping cells will not use overlapping channels. Channel reuse is using non-overlapping channels—for example 1, 6, and 11 in the 2.4 GHz range—in such a way that the overlapping cells are on different RF channels. Figure 4.12 shows a 2.4 GHz deployment utilizing proper channel reuse. This channel reuse may be accomplished by mapping out the access points on a floor plan and verifying that the RF cells propagated by the access points do not overlap on the same RF channels. This type of channel plan can de done manually or with site survey software applications. Site survey applications will be discussed in more detail in Chapter 9.

FIGURE 4.11   Users of these access points will experience overlapping channel interference because they are all set to the same channel.

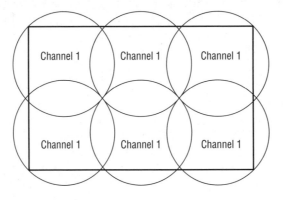

FIGURE 4.12   Co-location of access points with proper channel reuse. Overlapping areas use different channels to prevent interference.

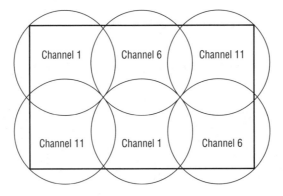

RF Range and Speed

How far and fast an RF signal can travel depends on a variety of factors, including line of sight, interference, and the types of materials in the environment. This section discusses these factors.

Line of Sight

RF communication between devices in 802.11 wireless networking requires a line of sight. There are two types of line of sight to take into consideration: visual and RF.

Visual line of sight is the ability of the transmitter and receiver to see each other. In order for wireless networking direct link communication to be successful there should be a clear, unobstructed view between the transmitter and receiver. An unobstructed line of sight means few or no obstacles blocking the RF signal between these devices.

Direct, RF line of sight is an unobstructed line between a radio transmitter and receiver. This line will be surrounded by an area of radio frequency transmissions known as the Fresnel zone.

The *RF line of sight,* or the radio transmissions between a transmitter and receiver, could be affected if the total area of the Fresnel zone is blocked by more than 40 percent. This blockage could be from a variety of sources such as trees, buildings, terrain, or other obstacles, including the curvature of the earth. Figure 4.13 illustrates a Fresnel zone.

FIGURE 4.13 Oval area represents the Fresnel zone RF coverage area between a transmitter and receiver.

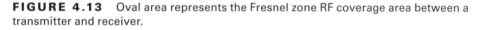
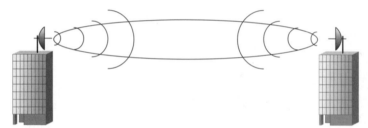

One way to think about this line of sight is by way of an analogy of two people looking at each other. If two people about the same height standing some distance apart are making direct eye contact, they have a good visual line of sight. In addition to being able to see directly in front of them, people also have peripheral vision. This peripheral vision gives people the ability to see movement and objects outside of their direct line of sight or direct eye contact. This peripheral vision or side vision is similar to the Fresnel zone theory.

EXERCISE 4.1

How to Demonstrate Fresnel Zone and Blockage

Here is one way to demonstrate Fresnel zone. Focus your eyes at a location on a wall. Make sure there are obstacles or movement off to both left and right sides of your view. Hold your hands down to your sides. Continue to focus your eyes for a minute or so then take your right, left, or both hands and slowly raise them from your sides toward the side of your head while blocking your peripheral vision. You'll notice as your hands get closer to the side of your head the view of the objects or movement to the sides will be blocked by your hands. This is an example of a blocked Fresnel zone.

Sixty percent of the total area of the Fresnel zone must be clear of obstacles in order to have RF line of sight.

Interference

Interference from a radio frequency point of view occurs when a receiver hears two different signals on the same or similar frequencies. Interference causes distortion. In wireless LANs, this interference can have a severe impact on the quality of signal received by the wireless device. This corrupted signal will decrease the amount of data the device can effectively receive, thereby causing less data throughput. A wireless LAN receiver has similar characteristics to the human ear. Both can hear a range of frequencies. If one person is speaking and a number of people are listening to this speaker, this is similar to a single transmitter and multiple receivers. If a second person started to speak at the same time, people listening may not be able to understand both speakers. In a sense they are experiencing interference.

As discussed earlier in this chapter, an IEEE 802.11 wireless network may use the unlicensed 2.4 GHz industrial, scientific, and medical (ISM) band. This band is also used for many other devices, including:

- Cordless phones
- Microwave ovens
- Medical devices
- Industrial devices
- Baby monitors
- Other WLANs

Because these devices also use radio frequency to operate, and the frequency is in the same unlicensed band as IEEE 802.11 wireless networks, they have potential to interfere with one another. Although they may coexist in the same RF space, the interference factor needs to be taken into consideration. This can be done as part of the site survey process.

Co-channel and Adjacent Channel Interference

Co-channel or adjacent channel interference occurs when two devices in the same physical area are tuned to a close or same radio frequency channel. For example, an access point on channel 1 and another access point on channel 2 in close or hearing range of each other will experience adjacent channel interference. Some of the symptoms of this type of interference are reduced throughput compared to what is normal, and the equivalent of collisions causing data retransmissions.

Co-channel interference is defined as two different radio transmitters using the same frequency. The IEEE 802.11-2007 standard, however, defines interference between channels 1 and 2 as co-channel interference caused by overlapping channels. According to the standard, adjacent channel interference for HR/DSSS and ERP in the 2.4 GHz ISM band is caused by frequencies greater than or equal to 25 MHz separation, such as channels 1 and 6. The terms *co-channel* and *adjacent* are used loosely in the wireless LAN industry. Please consult specific manufacturer's documentation for their definition. The CWNP program complies with the IEEE standards definition.

Overlapping interference is defined as two devices (such as access points) on the same frequency overlapping one another. For example, two access points in close proximity to each other, one on channel 1 and the other on channel 3, might interfere with each other.

Both adjacent channel interference and co-channel channel interference will cause poor throughput on a wireless network. In a wireless network, co-channel or adjacent channel interference can have the same impact. Figure 4.14 shows that 2.4 GHz ISM band channel 4 and channel 6 overlap.

FIGURE 4.14   Channel overlap in the 2.4 GHz ISM band

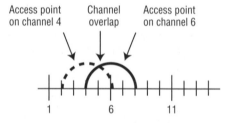

Representation of 2.4 GHz ISM band, consisting
of 14 channels. Channels 1, 6, and 11 are labeled.

A properly designed wireless LAN will have overlapping RF cells. Overlapping cells provide continuous coverage for the entire area where the access points are placed. Overlapping cells allow devices to move from one access point to another and maintain a connection. A well-designed wireless LAN will also minimize or eliminate overlapping channel interference. This design includes assigning non-overlapping RF channels to cells that do overlap with each other. The frequency in use is determined by how many non-overlapping channels are available in the band. For example, in the United States, the 2.4 GHz band used for 802.11b/g/n has three non-overlapping channels—1, 6, and 11. Figure 4.15 shows 2.4 GHz ISM band with three non-overlapping channels, channels 1, 6, and 11.

FIGURE 4.15   Five channels of separation and 25 MHz of separation between non-overlapping channels

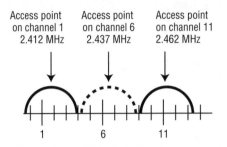

Representation of 2.4 GHz ISM band, consisting of
14 channels. Channels 1, 6, and 11 are non-overlapping.

WLAN/WPAN Interference

The performance of IEEE 802.11 wireless networks can be affected when they are co-located with IEEE 802.15 wireless personal area networks or WPANs. Bluetooth is an example of a personal area network. Like 802.11, Bluetooth devices operate in the 2.4 GHz frequency range and use frequency hopping spread spectrum (FHSS). This functionality could interfere with IEEE 802.11 wireless networks. Newer versions of Bluetooth that use adaptive frequency hopping (AFH) have less of a chance of interfering with other wireless networks. Adaptive frequency hopping allows devices such as Bluetooth to adapt to the RF environment by seeking areas of interference and not operating in those specific frequency ranges.

Bright Sunlight Interference

The IEEE 802.11 standard does address infrared (IR) communications. IR uses near visible light at a very high band on the radio spectrum to communicate. Since the CWTS exam only explores RF used in the ISM and UNII bands, IR will not be discussed in this book. Bright sunlight will not affect wireless LAN communications that use the 2.4 GHz ISM and 5 GHz UNII bands; however, it could have an impact on infrared communications.

Environment: RF Behavior

In addition to various types of RF interference, the interaction between RF and the surrounding environment can also affect the performance of IEEE 802.11 wireless networks. RF behavior is the result of environmental conditions including:

- Reflection
- Refraction
- Diffraction

- Scattering
- Absorption
- Diffusion

Reflection

Reflection occurs when an RF signal bounces off a smooth, nonabsorptive surface such as a table top and changes direction. Reflections can affect indoor wireless LAN installations fairly significantly in certain cases. Depending on the interior of the building—such as the type of walls, floors, or furnishings—there could be a large number of reflected signals. If not properly handled, reflections could cause a decrease in throughput and poor network performance. Figure 4.16 illustrates reflection.

FIGURE 4.16   RF reflection

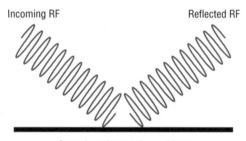

Incoming RF   Reflected RF

Smooth surface such as table top

 Think of a ping-pong game when it comes to reflection. When a ping-pong ball is served or hit, it comes in contact with the table—a smooth, hard surface—and bounces off in a different direction. This is similar to how reflection works with radio frequency.

Refraction

When an RF signal passes between mediums of different densities, it may change speeds and also bend. This behavior of RF is called *refraction*. Glass is an example of material that may cause refraction. When an RF signal comes in contact with an obstacle such as glass, the signal is refracted (bent) as it passes through and some of the signal is lost. The amount of loss depends on the type of glass, thickness, and other properties. Figure 4.17 shows refraction.

FIGURE 4.17   RF refraction

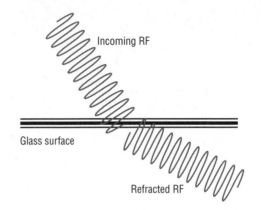

Diffraction

When an RF signal passes an obstacle, the wave changes direction by bending around the obstacle. This RF behavior is called *diffraction*. A building or other tall structure could cause diffraction, as could a column in a large open area or conference hall. Figure 4.18 illustrates diffraction. When the signal bends around a column, building, or other obstacle, the signal weakens, resulting in some level of loss.

FIGURE 4.18   RF diffraction

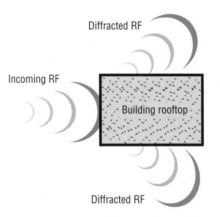

Demonstrating Diffraction: Rock in a Pond

You can demonstrate diffraction by using a pond of still water. Place a large object such as a two-by-four piece of lumber in a pond of still water. After the water settles, try to drop a pebble or small rock off to the side of the piece of lumber. Watch closely and you will see the ripple of the water diffract around the lumber.

Scattering

When an RF signal strikes an uneven surface, wavefronts of the signal will reflect off the uneven surface in several directions. This is known as *scattering*. Figure 4.19 illustrates scattering. Scattering is another form of loss that may severely degrade the RF signal.

Absorption

When material absorbs an RF signal, no signal penetrates through the material. An example of *absorption* is the human body. The human body has a high water content and will absorb RF signals. This type of absorption can be a problem for wireless network deployments in certain environments. Densely populated areas such as airports and conference halls need to consider absorption when designing a wireless LAN deployment. Figure 4.20 shows absorption.

FIGURE 4.19   RF scattering

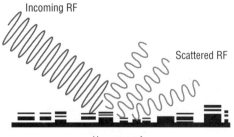

FIGURE 4.20   RF absorption

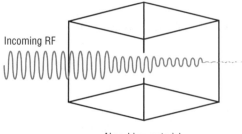

Diffusion

Diffusion occurs when the RF signal naturally widens as it leaves an antenna element. This is known as free space path loss (FSPL). FSPL is the greatest form of loss factor in an RF link. FSPL is calculated using frequency and distance as variables. The receiving antenna is only able to receive a small amount of the transmitted signal because of this widening effect of the diffused signal as it propagates through the air. Any signal that is not received is considered loss.

Basic Units of RF Measurement

If a person were given a dollar bill, they would be one dollar richer. If this person were given 100 cents, they would still be one dollar richer. From this example, we see 1 dollar = 100 cents and 1 cent = 1/100th of a dollar. One dollar and 100 cents are the same net amount, but a cent and a dollar are different units of currency.

The same is true for radio frequency measures of power. The basic unit of measure for radio frequency is the watt. A wireless access point may be set to an output of 30 mW (milliwatts) of power. A milliwatt is 1/1000 of a watt. Just as in currency cents and dollars are both denominations of money, watts and milliwatts are measurements of RF power. Other units of measurement for RF are dB, dBi, dBd, and dBm.

Absolute Measurements of Power

The amount of power leaving a wireless access point is one example of an *absolute measure of power*. This is an actual power measurement and not a ratio or a relative value. A typical amount of output power from an access point is 100 mW.

The measure of AC power can be calculated using a very basic formula. The formula is:

P = E * I

Power (P) equals voltage (E) multiplied by current (I).

A simple example would be to calculate the power from 1 volt and 1 amp. Using the given variables, the formula is:

P = 1 volt * 1 amp

The answer would be power = 1 watt.

The formula P = E * I is for reference only to demonstrate calculation of power. You will not need to know this formula for the CWTS exam.

Watt (W)

The watt is a basic unit of power measurement. This is an absolute value or measurable value. Most wireless networks function in the milliwatt range. Power level in watts is a common measurement in long distance point-to-point and point-to-multipoint applications.

Milliwatt (mW)

One milliwatt is 1/1000 of a watt. This is a common value used in RF work and IEEE 802.11 wireless LANs. The output power of an access point typically ranges from 1 mW to

100 mW. Most enterprise-grade access points allow you to change the output power. Most SOHO-grade access points have a fixed output power, typically 30 mW. The milliwatt is also an absolute unit of power measurement.

Decibel Relative to a Milliwatt (dBm)

dBm is the power level compared to 1 milliwatt. This is based on a logarithmic function. A good rule to remember is 0 dBm = 1 mW. This value is considered as absolute zero. Using a formula or basic RF calculation rules, one can easily convert any milliwatt value to decibels. For example 100 mW = 20 dBm. The dBm is also an absolute unit of power measurement. A dB is an example of a change in power or relative measurement of power where dBm is measured power referenced to 1 milliwatt or an absolute measure of power. The next section discusses relative measurements of power.

Remember, absolute values are measurable values of power such as watt, milliwatt, and decibel milliwatt.

Relative Measurements of Power

Changes in RF power are known as relative. dB and dBi are relative measurements of power. An example would be an RF amplifier. If the input power to an amplifier is 10 mW and the output power is 100 mW, the gain of the amplifier is 10 dB—a change in power.

If the input power to an antenna is 100 mW and the output power is 200 mW, the gain of the antenna is 3 dBi—a change in power. Both of these are examples of changes in power and are known as relative.

Decibel (dB)

The decibel (dB) is a ratio of two different power levels caused by a change in power. Figure 4.21 shows how an amplifier will provide an increase or change in power.

FIGURE 4.21   Output doubled in power from 100 mW to 200 mW from amplifier with a gain or change in power of +3 dB

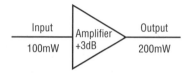

Basic RF Math: The 3s and 10s Rule

This section is beyond the scope of the CWTS exam objectives and is for informational purposes only.

There is a simple way to perform any RF math calculation without having to use logarithms and mathematical formulas. This method is known as the 3s and 10s Rule (or sometimes the 10s and 3s Rule). If you remember five basic steps you can perform any RF math calculation. The five basic steps are as follows:

- 0 dBm = 1 mW (starting point)

- Increase by 3 dBm and power in mW doubles or × 2

- Decrease by 3 dBm and power in mW is cut in half or ÷ 2

- Increase by 10 dBm and power in mW is multiplied by 10 or × 10

- Decrease by 10 dBm and power in mW is divided by 10 or ÷ 10

Decibel Isotropic (dBi)

Decibel isotropic (dBi) is the unit that represents the gain or increase in signal strength of an antenna. The term *isotropic* in the RF world means energy broadcast equally in all directions in a spherical fashion. An imaginary, perfect antenna is known as an *isotropic radiator*. This is a theoretical concept and is used in reference and calculations. dBi will be discussed and used in more detail in Chapter 6. Table 4.4 shows a summary of absolute and relative power measurements.

TABLE 4.4   Absolute and Relative Measures of Power

Absolute Power	Relative Power
Watt	dB
Milliwatt	dBi
dBm	dBd

Remember, relative values are changes in power from one value to another value. dB, dBi, and dBd measure relative power.

Decibel Dipole (dBd)

The gain of some antennas may be measured in decibel dipole (dBd). This unit of measurement refers to the antenna gain with respect to a reference dipole antenna. The gain of most antennas used in wireless LANs is measured in decibel isotropic (dBi); however some manufacturers may reference gain in dBd. The following simple formula derives the dBi value from the dBd value:

dBi = dBd + 2.14

This formula converts from dBi to dBd:

dBd = dBi − 2.14

🌐 Real World Scenario

dBd vs. dBi

You are a procurement agent working for a manufacturing company. An engineer orders some antennas to be used in a wireless LAN deployment. The part number you received from the engineer on the bill of materials is for antennas that are currently out of stock at your normal supplier. The order has to be placed as soon as possible, but technical support for the vendor is gone for the day and you are not able to get any assistance.

You found what appears to be a reasonable alternate for the requested antennas. However, the gain of the antennas does not exactly match what the engineer documented on the bill of materials. The engineer requested omnidirectional antennas with a gain of 6 dBi. You found what appears to be a comparable alternate with a gain of 6 dBd. It will be necessary for you to determine if these antennas will work. Not quite understanding the difference, you do some research to determine the difference between dBd and dBi. After searching various websites you find a formula to convert the two different units:

dBi = dBd + 2.14

Using your calculator, you enter the value from the specification sheet for the alternate antennas:

6 dBd + 2.14 = 8.14 dBi

Unfortunately, the antennas found will not be a good alternate in this example. Back to the drawing board!

Summary

This chapter looked at radio frequency basics and the essential role RF plays in the world of IEEE 802.11 wireless LANs. You learned the definition and understanding of RF as it pertains to wireless networking and the basic characteristics or properties of RF such as wavelength, frequency, amplitude, and phase. This chapter described devices such as transmitters and receivers and how they communicate. In wireless LAN technology, an example of a transmitter and receiver is an access point and client device. This chapter also discussed the unlicensed RF bands and channels used in the 2.4 GHz ISM and 5 GHz UNII ranges for wireless LAN communications. Coverage and capacity are two important areas that should be closely looked at in order to ensure a wireless deployment will offer reliable connectivity and perform well for the user base. This chapter also looked at correct channel reuse to minimize interference from co-location of access points. This chapter explored cause and effect of co-channel interference from sources other than wireless networks operating in the ISM and UNII bands. We also looked at RF behaviors such as reflection, refraction, and absorption, and the impact of propagation on radio waves. Finally, we discussed RF units of measure, including watt, milliwatt, dB, and dBi.

Exam Essentials

Know the basic characteristics or properties of radio frequency.   Understand the characteristics of radio frequency such as wavelength, phase, frequency, and amplitude.

Be familiar with the frequencies used for wireless networks.   Know the unlicensed ISM and UNII bands available for use with wireless networks.

Understand wireless network coverage and capacity.   Know the difference between coverage and capacity and the factors that will have an impact on both.

Know what RF factors will affect the range and speed of wireless networks.   Understand the effects of interference and the devices that cause interference. Be familiar with the environmental conditions that cause reflection, refraction, diffraction, scattering, and absorption. Understand their impact on the propagation of RF signals.

Identify basic RF units of measurement.   Understand the difference between absolute and relative measures of RF power. Define W, mW, dB, dBm, and dBi.

Key Terms

absolute measure of power

absorption

diffraction

gain

isotropic radiator

reflection

refraction

RF line of sight

scattering

visual line of sight

Review Questions

1. What is the term defining the amount of times a cycle of an RF signal will oscillate in one second?

   A. Phase

   B. Frequency

   C. Amplitude

   D. Wavelength

2. How many non-overlapping channels are available in the unlicensed 2.4 GHz ISM band?

   A. 1

   B. 3

   C. 6

   D. 11

3. The capacity of an access point is dependent upon which factors? (Choose two.)

   A. Number of users

   B. Channel reuse

   C. Co-location

   D. Software applications

   E. Frequency

4. When an RF signal passes between mediums of different densities and may change speeds and bend, the behavior is:

   A. Refraction

   B. Reflection

   C. Scattering

   D. Diffraction

5. What two devices use RF to communicate? (Choose two.)

   A. Transmitter

   B. Transistor

   C. Reactor

   D. Reflector

   E. Receiver

6. Which are relative measures of RF power? (Choose two.)

    A. mW

    B. dB

    C. dBm

    D. dBi

    E. Watt

7. In the 2.4 GHz range, what distance between the center frequencies (in megahertz) is required for two channels to be considered non-overlapping for HR/DSSS?

    A. 5 MHz

    B. 22 MHz

    C. 25 MHz

    D. 30 MHz

8. Two characteristics of RF signals are:

    A. Amplitude

    B. Reflection

    C. Phase

    D. Refraction

    E. Diffraction

9. How many channels are available for wireless LANs to use in the unlicensed UNII-1 band?

    A. 2

    B. 4

    C. 6

    D. 11

10. Which are absolute measures of RF power? (Choose two.)

    A. Watt

    B. dB

    C. mW

    D. dBi

    E. dBd

11. Which two channels are considered non-overlapping in the 2.4 GHz band?

    A. 1 and 6

    B. 2 and 6

    C. 6 and 10

    D. 11 and 13

12. How many channels are available for wireless LAN use in the unlicensed 2.4 GHz ISM band?

   A. 8

   B. 10

   C. 11

   D. 14

13. The range of a 2.4 GHz signal is mostly dependent on which RF characteristic?

   A. Frequency

   B. Wavelength

   C. Amplitude

   D. Phase

14. Which item has an effect on RF line of sight?

   A. Phase

   B. Obstacles

   C. Interference

   D. Amplitude

15. How many channels are available for wireless LAN use in the unlicensed middle UNII-2e band?

   A. 4

   B. 6

   C. 11

   D. 14

16. The amplitude of an RF signal is:

   A. Height

   B. Length

   C. Shift

   D. Width

17. An 802.11b channel is how wide in MHz?

   A. 5 MHz

   B. 22 MHz

   C. 25 MHz

   D. 30 MHz

18. When an RF signal bounces off a smooth non-absorptive surface, the behavior is:

    A. Refraction

    B. Reflection

    C. Scattering

    D. Diffraction

19. What is the gain of an antenna measured in?

    A. dB

    B. dBc

    C. dBi

    D. dBm

20. When RF passes or bends around an obstacle such as a building or column, the behavior is:

    A. Reflection

    B. Refraction

    C. Scattering

    D. Diffraction

Answers to Review Questions

1. B. Frequency is the number of times in one second a signal will oscillate. Phase is a shift, amplitude is height, and wavelength is a distance of one cycle.

2. B. There are three non-overlapping channels in the 2.4 GHz ISM band. Fourteen channels are available in this band. The locale will determine which channels can be used.

3. A, D. The capacity of an access point is dependent upon the number of users and software applications in use. Too many users or too many bandwidth-intensive applications will affect the performance of an access point.

4. A. Refraction is when a signal will change speeds and bend when passing between mediums of different densities. Reflection bounces off a smooth surface, diffraction will pass around, and scattering bounces off an uneven surface.

5. A, E. RF communications require a transmitter and receiver. A transistor is an electronic component; a reactor does not exist in RF.

6. B, D. dB and dBi are relative measures of RF power. mW, dBm, and watt are absolute measures of RF power.

7. C. 25 MHz is required for channels to be considered non-overlapping. 22 MHz is the width of a DSSS channel in the 2.4 GHz band.

8. A, C. Amplitude and phase are two characteristics of RF signals. Reflection, refraction, and diffraction are behaviors of RF.

9. B. UNII -1 band has four channels available for wireless LAN use. Eleven channels are available in UNII-2e.

10. A, C. Watt and mW are absolute measures of RF power. dB, dBi, and dBd are relative measures.

11. A. Channels 1 and 6 are non-overlapping. There must be a separation of five channels (with the exception of channel 14) to be considered non-overlapping in the 2.4 GHz band.

12. D. There are 14 channels available in the unlicensed 2.4 GHz ISM band. The channels used are determined by the locale.

13. B. The wavelength is the distance of an RF signal. Frequency is how many times it oscillates per second, amplitude is the height, and phase is a shift.

14. B. Obstacles affect the RF line of sight. Phase and amplitude are characteristics of radio frequency, and interference affects the throughput.

15. C. There are 11 channels available for wireless LAN use in the unlicensed UNII-2e band. The other three 5 GHz bands have only 4 channels each.

16. A. The amplitude is the height of an RF signal. The length of one cycle is the wavelength, the shift is phase, and width is not a valid factor.

17. B. A 2.4 GHz 802.11b signal is 22 MHz wide. 25 MHz is the distance required to be considered non-overlapping.

18. B. An RF signal that bounces off a smooth surface is reflection. Refraction passes through, diffraction bends around, and scattering bounces off a non-smooth surface.

19. C. The gain of an antenna is measured in dBi. This is a relative measure of power.

20. D. Diffraction passes or bends around an obstacle. Reflection bounces off a smooth surface, refraction passes through, and scattering bounces off an uneven surface.

Chapter 5

Access Methods, Architectures, and Spread Spectrum Technology

---

THE FOLLOWING CWTS EXAM OBJECTIVES ARE COVERED IN THIS CHAPTER:

✓ **Define concepts which make up the functionality of RF and spread spectrum technology**

- OFDM & HR/DSSS channels

- Co-location of HR/DSSS and OFDM systems

- Adjacent-channel and co-channel interference

- WLAN / WPAN co-existence

- CSMA/CA operation – half duplex

✓ **Define and differentiate between the following physical layer wireless technologies**

- HR/DSSS

- OFDM

- MIMO

It is important to understand how digital data is sent from one device to another. Whether on a wired network or a wireless network, an access method is used to transfer this type of information. Two common access methods are CSMA/CD and CSMA/CA. The type of medium in use—wired or wireless—will determine which of these two access methods is best suited for the application. We saw in previous chapters that wireless LANs use radio frequency with the communication medium. This chapter will discuss the various techniques and methods used to get digital computer data from one device to another using spread spectrum and modulation technologies. It is important to understand that different spread spectrum technologies such as FHSS, DSSS, and others will allow for various data rates. The spread spectrum technology in use will determine the maximum amount of data transfer as well as the resilience to noise and other interfering sources. We will look at the number of channels available, channel spacing, and the frequencies of unlicensed radio frequency band used. We will also discuss the implications of overlapping channels and interference. Finally, this chapter will discuss co-location of different technologies used in various amendments to the standard as well as interference from wireless LANs and other sources, including WPANs.

Network Access Methods

Network access methods allow devices connected to a common infrastructure the opportunity to communicate and transmit data across a network medium from one device to another. Several different types of network access methods are used in computer networks. The two types we will discuss in this chapter are:

- *Carrier Sense Multiple Access/Collision Detection (CSMA/CD)*
- *Carrier Sense Multiple Access/Collision Avoidance (CSMA/CA)*

Because Ethernet networks have the capability to detect collisions, 802.3 Ethernet networks use CSMA/CD as the access method. Devices on a wireless LAN do not have the capability to detect collisions; therefore 802.11 wireless LANs use CSMA/CA for the access method. Since multiple wireless devices can use an access point at the same time, wireless devices that connect to an AP are competing to share the medium; therefore, it is important to control the medium in order to minimize collisions. The CSMA/CA process provides this control.

Detecting Network Traffic Collisions with CSMA/CD

802.3 Ethernet networks use CSMA/CD to share the medium. The name of this access method describes how it functions.

The abbreviation CSMA/CD is broken down as follows:

- Carrier Sense—Devices sense the medium (in this case, Ethernet cable) to see if it is clear (no data being transmitted).

- Multiple Access—Many accessing the medium at the same time.

- Collision Detection—Detecting collisions that occur on the medium during the transmission of data.

CSMA/CD is a contention-based media access control method that Ethernet devices use to share the medium. This method allows only one device to transmit at any one time.

In computing terminology, *contention* is defined as multiple devices competing for a chance to send data on the network. CSMA/CD functions like this:

1. A device with data to transmit checks whether any data is being transmitted on the Ethernet cable (sensing).

2. If the device senses that the medium is clear and no data is being transmitted, it transmits its own data.

3. If more than one device transmits simultaneously, a collision occurs and the data is lost. The devices detect the collision and each backs off for a random amount of time.

4. After a random amount of time, the device checks the cable and attempts to send the data again.

This contention of the Ethernet segment is one reason for decreased data throughput of the transmitting devices. Figure 5.1 demonstrates CSMA/CD with desktop computers connected to an Ethernet segment.

FIGURE 5.1   Computers connected to Ethernet cable using CSMA/CD

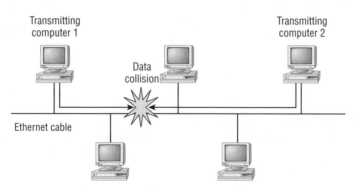

Conversation as a Form of CSMA/CD

An analogy for CSMA/CD is conversation among a group of people in which all the individuals in the group would like a chance to speak. Everyone is listening to each other (sensing the carrier). Only one person at a time gets a chance to say something. This is an example of a multiple access shared medium (MA). If there is a pause in the conversation, two or more people listening may notice the opportunity and may say something at the exact same time, in which case neither may be heard by the rest of the group. This is an example of a collision. At this point, the collision is detected (CD) and those involved in the failed communication wait a few seconds and attempt to speak again later (CSMA/CD).

Avoiding Network Traffic Collisions with CSMA/CA

Wireless LANs use CSMA/CA to share the medium. The main difference from CSMA/CD is the CA—collision avoidance. Just as in CSMA/CD, the abbreviation CSMA/CA gives an idea of how it functions:

- Carrier Sense—Sensing the medium, in this case the air.
- Multiple Access—Many accessing the medium at the same time.
- Collision Avoidance—Avoiding collisions that may occur on the medium during transmission.

Because wireless LAN devices have no way to detect collisions, the CSMA/CD access method is not an adequate solution for wireless LAN communications. If wireless LANs were to use CSMA/CD, collisions would occur at the wireless access point and all data would be lost. At this point, a transmitting device would not know that it should retransmit the information because the receiving device would be unaware that a collision occurred.

Instead of detecting transmission collisions, CSMA/CA uses mechanisms that attempt to avoid collisions. Although these mechanisms impose some overhead, the overall benefit is better data throughput because data collisions are minimized. This overhead occurs because devices have a countdown timer that requires them to wait a period of time before they are able to transmit again. This helps avoid collisions.

Lecture Q&A as a Form of CSMA/CA

An analogy for CSMA/CA is the question-and-answer period following a lecture. The lecture hall is filled with many people (multiple access). A presenter has finished giving a speech and it is now question-and-answer time. The presenter shouts out, "Does anyone have a question?" An attendee by the name of Marvin listens (sensing the carrier). He does not hear anyone speaking, so he yells out a question. Although many people are in the room (again, multiple access), they can hear that Marvin has the floor and this time is dedicated to him. So they defer and do not ask their question until Marvin's question has been answered by the speaker (collision avoidance).

Reserving Time for Data Transmission Using Distributed Coordination Function (DCF)

One of the access methods wireless LAN devices use to communicate is known as *distributed coordinated function (DCF)*. This method of access employs a contention period for devices competing to send data on the network. This collision avoidance mechanism is part of a detailed process requiring certain criteria to be met in order for a frame (a Layer 2 digital transmission unit) to be transmitted across the medium, in this case the air, using radio frequency.

To avoid collisions, the devices are required to

- Announce how much time is required for the frame exchange

- Detect RF energy

- Wait for a predetermined period of time between frames

- Back off and retry if the medium is busy

In short, these devices are reserving the medium so that transmissions can take place and avoid collisions. Figure 5.2 illustrates wireless LAN devices using CSMA/CA for an access method.

FIGURE 5.2   Wireless LAN devices using CSMA/CA and DCF

Access point

"I am transmitting."

"I am waiting until you are finished."

Wireless client 1

Wireless client 2

Effects of Half Duplex on Wireless Throughput

As discussed in Chapter 2, "Wireless LAN Infrastructure Devices," wireless LANs use half duplex to communicate. To review, *half duplex* in computer terminology is defined as two-way communication that occurs in only one direction at a time. Communication only one way at a time means less data throughput for the connected device(s). Half-duplex communication is part of the reason why in wireless LANs the amount of data being transferred is sometimes less than half of the advertised data rate; collisions and additional overhead are other factors to consider. An 802.11b device may only get 5.5 Mbps or less data transfer even though this technology is rated at 11 Mbps. On a good day, 802.11a or 802.11g devices will also average less than half of the advertised data rates. Figure 5.3 shows the half-duplex communication method and some of the effect it has on throughput. The data rate in this example is 54 Mbps, but the throughput is less than half of that, about 22 Mbps.

FIGURE 5.3 Half-duplex operation has some effect on throughput

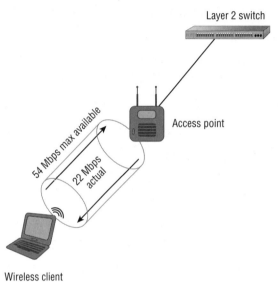

Layer 2 switch

Access point

54 Mbps max available

22 Mbps actual

Wireless client

Narrowband vs. Spread Spectrum Communication

Narrowband and spread spectrum are two examples of how devices can communicate using radio frequency.

One example of *narrowband communication* is an FM radio station. FM radio stations use licensed frequency ranges that are tuned to a certain radio frequency in the FM band. A station can transmit a signal at high power at tens of thousands of watts in a very narrow frequency. The receiver can hear the station for tens or even possibly hundreds of miles.

Figure 5.4 shows the high amount of output power over a narrowband frequency of a potential FM radio station.

In contrast, spread spectrum technology uses less power over a wider range of frequency. Figure 5.5 illustrates how spread spectrum uses low power over a wide frequency range.

FIGURE 5.4   Narrowband frequency—high power, narrow frequency

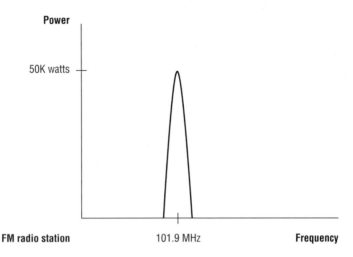

FIGURE 5.5   Spread spectrum technology

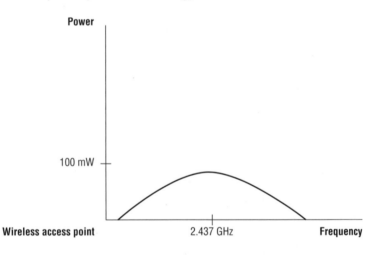

Lecturer vs. Breakout Discussions

Narrowband communication is similar to a lecture presented in a large room filled with several hundred attendees. The presenter may have a microphone connected to an amplifier or PA system to address the large audience. All attendees at this event will pay attention to the presenter, who will get the message across to the entire audience in this very large venue.

> Spread spectrum communication is similar to what happens when the same audience breaks out into small groups in which each member is communicating only with other members of that group. These groups of individuals will be speaking at a much lower volume without the help of a high-power microphone and the conversation volume will not exceed the area in which this group is contained.

Spread Spectrum Technology

Two types of *spread spectrum* technology are used in the original IEEE 802.11 wireless LAN standard:

- Frequency-hopping spread spectrum (FHSS)
- Direct-sequence spread spectrum (DSSS)

These spread spectrum technologies communicate in the 2.4 GHz ISM frequency range. There are advantages and disadvantages to each of these spread spectrum types.

Spread spectrum technologies take the digital information generated by a computer and, through the use of modulation technologies, send it across the air between devices using radio frequency.

In order for devices to effectively communicate and understand one another they must be using the same spread spectrum technology. This would be analogous to two people trying to talk with each other. If the two people don't know the same language, they will not be able to understand each other and a conversation could not take place.

Frequency-Hopping Spread Spectrum (FHSS)

Frequency-hopping spread spectrum (FHSS) is used in a variety of devices in computers and communications. FHSS was used by many early adopters of wireless networking, including computers, scanners, and other handheld and portable devices. Although defined in the original IEEE 802.11 standard, this technology is considered "legacy" (out of date) in wireless networking. However, FHSS is still common today in many devices such as cordless telephones and 802.15 wireless personal area networks (WPANs), including Bluetooth mice, cameras, phones, and older wireless LAN technology devices.

FHSS operates by sending small amounts of information such as digital data across the entire 2.4 GHz ISM band. As the name implies, this technology changes frequencies ("hops") constantly. A transmitter and receiver will be synchronized with the same hopping sequence, therefore allowing the devices to communicate.

The data rate for FHSS is only 1 and 2 Mbps, which is considered slow in most modern computer applications. However, the data rate is more than adequate for many applications—for example, some devices in retail and manufacturing still use FHSS in handheld scanners and other portable technology. The cost of upgrading these devices to support higher data rates is cost prohibitive and unnecessary in many cases and therefore is still used in such environments.

Figure 5.6 illustrates what FHSS would look like if you could see the RF hopping through the band.

FIGURE 5.6   FHSS hops the entire 2.4 GHz ISM band

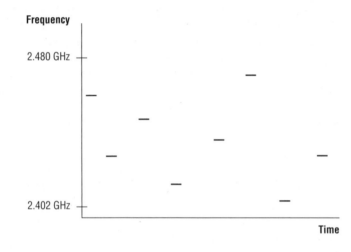

Sales

FHSS use in IEEE 802.11 wireless networking is considered legacy and is rarely supported. Therefore, if a customer wishes to purchase any FHSS wireless LAN equipment, they should be directed to the proper upgrade path for a more current and supported solution.

Technical Support

There is still a number of legacy IEEE 802.11 wireless networking FHSS devices in operation in various industries today. For whatever reason that these are still in use, it is important to understand replacement devices will be difficult to find if they can be found at all. It is best to consider the appropriate upgrade path for a more current and supported solution.

Direct-Sequence Spread Spectrum (DSSS)

Direct-sequence spread spectrum (DSSS) is a spread spectrum technology used with wireless LANs and defined by the original IEEE 802.11 standard. Like FHSS, DSSS supports data rates of 1 and 2 Mbps and is considered slow by today's computer networking requirements.

DSSS uses special techniques to transmit digital data across the air using radio frequency. This is accomplished by modulating or modifying the radio frequency characteristics such as phase, amplitude, and frequency (see Chapter 4, "Radio Frequency Fundamentals for Wireless LAN Technology").

In addition to modulation, DSSS uses technology known as a *spreading code* to provide redundancy of the digital data as it traverses through the air. The spreading code transmits information on multiple subcarriers, and the redundancy helps the receiver detect transmission errors due to interference. This spreading of information across the 22 MHz–wide channel is what helps makes DSSS resilient to interference. The spreading code technology allows the receiver to determine if a bit of digital data received is a binary 0 or binary 1. Depending on the data rate, the transmitter and receiver understand the spreading code in use and therefore are able to communicate.

An example of a coding technique is Barker code. Barker code is used as the spreading code for DSSS at the data rates of 1 and 2 Mbps.

DSSS operates within a range of RF frequency also known as a *channel*. Unlike narrowband communication, which operates on a single frequency, a DSSS channel is 22 MHz wide and is one of 14 channels in the 2.4 GHz to 2.5 GHz ISM band. The country and location of the device will determine which of the 14 channels are available for use.

Figure 5.7 shows that channel 6 is 22 MHz wide in the ISM unlicensed RF band.

 FHSS and DSSS both operate in the same frequency range. If devices that use both technologies are occupying the same physical area, the devices may encounter some interference.

High Rate/Direct-Sequence Spread Spectrum (HR/DSSS)

High rate/direct-sequence spread spectrum (HR/DSSS) is defined in the IEEE 802.11b amendment to the 802.11 standard. HR/DSSS introduced higher data rates of 5.5 and 11 Mbps. At the time this amendment was released, because of the higher data rates, this technology helped fuel the acceleration of IEEE standards based on wireless LAN technology.

Like DSSS, HR/DSSS uses one of 14 channels 22 MHz wide to transmit and receive data. The main difference between these two technologies is that HR/DSSS supports higher data rates.

HR/DSSS (802.11b) uses a different spreading code or an encoding technique than DSSS. HR/DSSS uses complementary code keying (CCK) for transmitting data at 5.5 and 11 Mbps. The detailed operation of CCK is beyond the scope of this book.

FIGURE 5.7   DSSS is limited to a 22 MHz–wide channel in the 2.4 GHz ISM band.

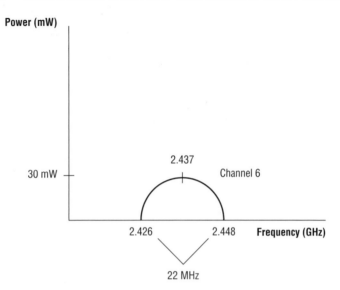

DSSS and HR/DSSS Channels

DSSS and HR/DSSS operate in the 2.4 GHz industrial, scientific, and medical (ISM) license free band. This band has 14 available channels. Depending on the country and location, all 14 channels may not be available. Table 5.1 shows the 14 available channels in the 2.4 GHz ISM band.

TABLE 5.1   2.4 GHz ISM Band Consists of 14 Available Channels

Channel	Frequency (GHZ)	Americas	EMEA	Israel*	China	Japan
1	2.412	✓	✓	✓	✓	✓
2	2.417	✓	✓	✓	✓	✓
3	2.422	✓	✓	✓	✓	✓
4	2.427	✓	✓	✓	✓	✓
5	2.432	✓	✓	✓	✓	✓
6	2.437	✓	✓	✓	✓	✓

TABLE 5.1   2.4 GHz ISM Band Consists of 14 Available Channels *(continued)*

Channel	Frequency (GHZ)	Americas	EMEA	Israel*	China	Japan
7	2.442	✓	✓	✓	✓	✓
8	2.447	✓	✓	✓	✓	✓
9	2.452	✓	✓	✓	✓	✓
10	2.457	✓	✓	✓	✓	✓
11	2.462	✓	✓	✓	✓	✓
12	2.467		✓	✓		✓
13	2.472		✓	✓		✓
14	2.484					✓

* Israel allows channels 1–13 indoors, but outdoors only 5–13.

Figure 5.8 shows the 14 available channels and the amount of overlap in the 2.4 GHz ISM band.

FIGURE 5.8   2.4 GHz ISM band allows 14 channels.

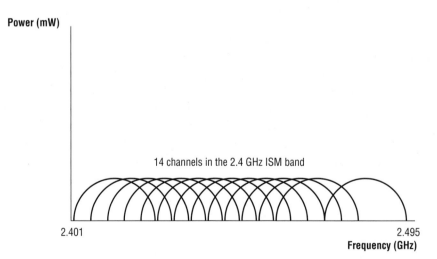

Of these 14 channels, mathematically there are only 3 adjacent non-overlapping channels, with the exception of channel 14. Per the IEEE 802.11-2007 standard, "Channel 14 shall be designated specifically for operation in Japan." There are 3 MHz of separation where the radio frequency of one channel ends and the next adjacent non-overlapping channel begins. For example, channel 1 and channel 6 are adjacent non-overlapping channels. Channel 1 ends at 2.423 GHz and channel 6 begins at 2.426 GHz. Mathematically this is a separation of 3 MHz. This means that three access points can be co-located in the same physical space without overlapping channel interference. However, there is still theoretically a small amount of overlapping RF or harmonics between these two channels. This small level of overlap is not large enough to cause any real interference issues. Figure 5.9 illustrates 3 of the first 14 channels that do not overlap in the 2.4 GHz ISM band.

FIGURE 5.9   3 Non-overlapping channels possible in the 2.4 GHz ISM band

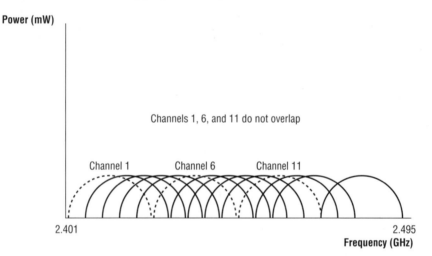

Each DSSS channel is 22 MHz wide. Using spread spectrum technology, a 22 MHz–wide channel helps add resiliency to interference for data transmissions and gives the capability to move large amounts of data with a small amount of power.

Orthogonal Frequency Division Multiplexing (OFDM)

Orthogonal frequency division multiplexing (OFDM) is used by the IEEE 802.11a (OFDM) and IEEE 802.11g Extended Rate Physical Orthogonal Frequency Division Multiplexing (ERP-OFDM) and IEEE 802.11n Draft amendments to the IEEE 802.11 standard. OFDM allows for much higher data rate transfers than DSSS and HR/DSSS, up to 54 Mbps higher for 802.11n. *Orthogonal frequency division multiplexing (OFDM)* is a technology designed to transmit many signals simultaneously over one transmission path in a shared medium and is used in wireless and other transmission systems. Every signal travels within its own unique frequency *subcarrier* (a separate signal carried on a main RF transmission). OFDM distributes computer data over 52 subcarriers equally spaced apart, and 4 of the 52 subcarriers do not carry data and are used as pilot channels. The many subcarriers allows for high data rates in wireless LAN IEEE 802.11a and IEEE 802.11g devices. 802.11n Draft devices (HT-OFDM) may use *spatial multiplexing (SM)*, which uses several antennas to transmit different pieces of the same information simultaneously, greatly increasing throughput. In addition to high data rates, OFDM also helps provide resiliency to interference from other wireless devices.

OFDM Channels

OFDM functions in either the 2.4 GHz ISM or the 5 GHz UNII bands. The channel width is smaller than DSSS or HR/DSSS. The width of an OFDM channel is only 20 MHz compared to 22 MHz for DSSS. Figure 5.10 shows a representation of a 20 MHz–wide OFDM channel.

FIGURE 5.10   OFDM 20 MHz–wide channel

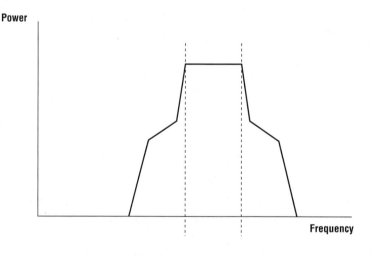

20 MHz wide channel (not to scale)

Like DSSS, the 2.4 GHz ISM band allows for only three non-overlapping channels if OFDM is used. In the 5 GHz Unlicensed National Information Infrastructure (UNII) bands, the channel spacing is such that there is no overlap. The frequency range used will determine how many non-overlapping channels are available for use. In the lower and upper UNII bands, there are 4 non-overlapping channels available. The middle UNII band has 15 non-overlapping channels available. All UNII band channels are 20 MHz wide and separated by 20 MHz from the center frequencies of each channel. Table 5.2 shows the 23 available channels in the 5 GHz UNII bands.

TABLE 5.2   5 GHz UNII Band Channels

Regulatory Domain	Frequency Band (GHz)	Frequency Center (GHz)	Channel Number
Americas/EMEA (4 channels)	5.150–5.250	5.180	36
		5.200	40
		5.220	44
		5.240	48
Americas/EMEA (4 channels)	5.250–5.350	5.260	52
		5.280	56
		5.300	60
		5.320	64
Americas/EMEA (11 channels)	5.470–5.725	5.500	100
		5.520	104
		5.540	108
		5.560	112
		5.580	116
		5.600	120
		5.620	124
		5.640	128
		5.660	132
		5.680	136
		5.700	140
Americas/EMEA (4 channels)	5.725–5.825	5.745	149
		5.765	153
		5.785	157
		5.805	161

Some regulatory domains allow the use of a 5.8GHz ISM band (5.725–5.850 GHz). This band does overlap the upper UNII band. The use of this ISM band is regulated separately with some similarities to the 2.4 GHz ISM band and allows for the use of more devices such as cordless telephones.

Multiple Input/Multiple Output (MIMO)

Multiple input/multiple output (MIMO) is a technology used by IEEE 802.11n Draft 2.0 certified devices. MIMO technology promises data rates up to 600 Mbps. Currently, wi-fi certified technology based on Draft 2.0 is capable of data rates of up to 300 Mbps. MIMO provides users better overall experience for data, voice, and video communications with throughput up to five times more than current 802.11 a/g, *single input/single output (SISO)* networks. SISO is the most basic wireless antenna technology used in a wireless LAN system. One antenna is used at the transmitter to transmit data, and one antenna is used at the receiver to receive the data. Coverage is more predictable and consistent with MIMO networks because devices using this technology are able to utilize reflected signals, which are a problem for wireless networks using other WLAN technologies.

MIMO also allows 802.11n networks better throughput at the same distance than DSSS or OFDM-based networks. IEEE 802.11n MIMO-based networks offer backward compatibility with 802.11a/b/g networks and devices in both the 2.4 GHz ISM and the 5 GHz UNII bands, allowing for deployments to continue using their existing hardware.

Some of the benefits of 802.11n MIMO networks include throughput, reliability, and predictability:

- Five times more throughput

  Enhanced file transfer and download speeds for large files

- 2x more reliable

  Lower latency for mobile communications

- 2x more predictable

  More consistent coverage and throughput for mobile applications

Unlike IEEE 802.11b (HR/DSSS) and IEEE 802.11a/g (OFDM) access points, MIMO access points use multiple radios with multiple antennas. The multiple radio chains and some additional intelligence are what give 802.11n MIMO access points the capability to process reflected signals. Since MIMO works with both 802.11g and 802.11a, a dual-band IEEE 802.11n MIMO access point will have up to six radio chains—three for 2.4 GHz and three for 5 GHz—and six antennas (one for each radio). Figure 5.11 shows that MIMO uses multiple radio chains and multiple antennas to transmit and receive data.

802.11n systems use MIMO technology; they have more receivers and are much more sensitive than the average 802.11a or 802.11g radio. The following techniques are what allow for much higher data rates (currently up to 300 Mbps and eventually up to 600 Mbps):

- Maximal ratio combining (MRC)
- Transmit beam forming (sometimes abbreviated TxBF)
- Spatial multiplexing (sometimes abbreviated SM)

FIGURE 5.11   MIMO hardware uses separate radio chains for each band and one antenna for each radio.

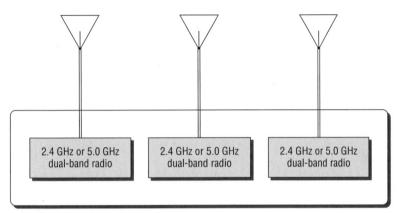

2.4 GHz or 5.0 GHz dual-band radio

2.4 GHz or 5.0 GHz dual-band radio

2.4 GHz or 5.0 GHz dual-band radio

802.11a/b/g networks are known as single input/single output (SISO), which allows for performance to degrade as a result of multipath, poor reception because of obstacles and RF interference sources. 802.11n MIMO networks can take advantage of multipath to help increase throughput at range providing much higher throughput at the same range.

MIMO Channels

IEEE 802.11n MIMO networks can operate in both the 2.4 GHz ISM and 5 GHz UNII bands and are capable of either 20 or 40 MHz–wide channels. Even while operating in 40 MHz channel width mode, many frames are still transmitted with a 20 MHz channel width. The 20 and 40 MHz channel widths are defined by the IEEE for transmission of OFDM modulated data. As one would expect, wider channels mean more data can be transmitted over the RF medium simultaneously. Therefore, wider channels allow higher data throughput. Think of this like cars traveling on a two-lane or a four-lane highway. A 20 MHz–wide channel can be looked at as the two-lane highway and a 40 MHz wide channel the four-lane highway. More cars can pass through four lanes in the same amount of time than can pass through two lanes. The 20 MHz or 40 MHz channels can be used in either the 2.4 GHz or 5 GHz frequency ranges. Because of the limited amount of frequency space in the 2.4 GHz ISM band, there is only one 40 MHz–wide channel without any adjacent-channel overlap.

Co-location of HR/DSSS and ERP-OFDM Systems

All IEEE-based wireless LANs can be *co-located*—that is, they can function in the same RF space. The technologies the devices use determine how well they work together. HR/DSSS (802.11b) as well as ERP-OFDM (802.11g) networks operate in the 2.4 GHz frequency range ISM band. 802.11g-compliant devices are backward compatible with 802.11b-compliant devices. However, this backward compatibility comes at a price: reduced data throughput. Because of protection mechanisms, ERP-OFDM devices used in 802.11g will suffer in performance when an HR/DSSS device is in the same radio or hearing range of the ERP-OFDM device.

HR/DSSS and ERP-OFDM systems have many common features:

- Both operate in the 2.4 GHz ISM band.
- Both have three non-overlapping channels.
- Both are subject to interference from other devices operating in the same frequency range.

HR/DSSS and ERP-OFDM (802.11b-compliant and 802.11g-compliant) devices are backward compatible. ERP-OFDM is rated at 6, 9, 12, 18, 24, 36, 48, and 54 Mbps. Actual throughput in an environment relatively free of interference will be about 18 to 22 Mbps. If a DSSS or HR/DSSS device is introduced in the radio range of the ERP-OFDM device, the throughput will decrease significantly because of protection mechanisms. How much of an impact this makes depends on many factors in the environment. Typically, the decrease in throughput is about 25 percent to 30 percent.

Adjacent-Channel and Co-channel Interference

Adjacent-channel and co-channel interference (two or more RF signals interacting with each other and causing a degradation of performance) is a concern in the design, development, and deployment of IEEE-based 802.11 wireless networks. This type of interference will have an impact on the amount of actual throughput between devices over a wireless network. As mentioned earlier in this chapter, the 2.4 GHz ISM band has only three non-overlapping channels. Careful channel planning is required when designing or implementing a wireless network. This type of planning will minimize issues such as poor throughput as a result of adjacent and co-channel interference. *Channel planning* involves designing wireless networks so that overlapping RF cells are on different (non-overlapping) channels—for example, channels 1, 6, and 11 in the 2.4 GHz ISM band. This will help optimize performance and minimize degradation of throughput because of adjacent and co-channel interference. RF energy propagates in several directions simultaneously. A well-designed wireless network will account for a three-dimensional propagation. In other words, in a three-story building, the RF from an access point on the second floor building may pass through to the first and third floors; therefore interference could be an issue if the network is not planned properly.

WLAN/WPAN Coexistence

Wireless personal networks (WPANs) typically consist of portable devices such as personal digital assistants (PDAs), cell phones, headsets, computer keyboards, and mice. As mentioned in Chapter 4, the performance of IEEE 802.11 wireless LANs can be affected when co-located with WPAN devices. The IEEE 802.15 standard addresses WPANs and includes Bluetooth and Zigbee networks. Bluetooth is one of the most popular WPAN network technologies and operates in the 2.4 GHz ISM band using frequency-hopping spread spectrum (FHSS).

Early Bluetooth devices can cause significant interference while operating in close proximity of IEEE 802.11 wireless LANs. Bluetooth was designed to hop at a rate of 1,600 times per second across the entire 2.4 GHz band, potentially causing significant interference with 802.11 wireless networks. As mentioned in Chapter 4, newer versions of Bluetooth use adaptive frequency hopping (AFH) and thus are less likely to interfere with IEEE 802.11 wireless networks, even though they still operate in the 2.4 GHz ISM band. Devices that use adaptive frequency hopping will try to avoid using the same frequencies, decreasing the chance of interference. Since these devices operate at low power, most WPANs communicate in small, close-range, peer-to-peer networks.

🌐 Real World Scenario

Taking Adjacent-Channel and Co-channel Interference into Consideration when Planning a New Wireless Network

As a wireless network engineer, you are tasked with deploying a new wireless network in a multi-tenant building. The area to be covered is approximately 50,000 square feet.

Your first task, prior to the procurement and deployment of the wireless network, should be to perform a spectrum analysis and site survey. This will help determine the best frequency and channels to be used in the new deployment.

A survey reveals that tenants on the floors above and below where the new deployment is to be installed are also using IEEE 802.11b/g networks with many access points on channels across the entire 2.4 GHz ISM band. A situation such as this may make the deployment difficult. There is an increased possibility of adjacent-channel and co-channel interference.

Upon further evaluation, it is determined that the lower band of the 5 GHz UNII band is not being utilized to any large extent. Since this is a new deployment, you have the opportunity to purchase equipment that will utilize the 5 GHz UNII band as well as the 2.4 GHz ISM band. Some of the items that need to be evaluated include:

- Are any devices limited to 802.11b/g capability only?

- Does the network require backward compatibility to 802.11b/g?

- Does the network need to support guest access?

- What impact would a network using only 5 GHz 802.11a have on the business?

- Is it possible to utilize both frequency bands in this deployment to maximize throughput while limiting interference?

These are just some questions that need to be considered prior to making any final decisions on the network to be installed and the equipment to be purchased.

Summary

In this chapter, we looked at access methods used to get data from one device to another. These access methods consist of collision avoidance and collision detection with multiple users sharing the medium. These two access methods are:

- CSMA/CD
- CSMA/CA

WLANs have no way of detecting collisions; therefore they must use collision avoidance or CSMA/CA. Wireless LANs use half-duplex communication, which decreases the performance of the communication data transfer.

This chapter also looked at the various spread spectrum technologies used with WLANs and the differences among them. The IEEE standard and various amendments use different spread spectrum technologies and unlicensed radio spectrum allowing for data rates up to 300 Mbps. The spread spectrum technologies include:

- FHSS—For data rates of 1 and 2 Mbps
- DSSS—For data rates of 1 and 2 Mbps
- HR/DSSS—For data rates of 5.5 and 11 Mbps
- OFDM—For data rates up to 54 Mbps
- HT-OFDM—Currently, for data rates of up to 300 Mbps

Even though FHSS is considered legacy technology when it comes to WLANs, it is still important to understand some of the basics of this technology since it is still in use today in many industries in different types of wireless technologies.

Some of the spread spectrum technologies discussed in this chapter are more susceptible to interference than others. This can make installations in some industries challenging. We also looked at co-location of HR/DSSS and ERP-OFDM systems and some of the challenges it can pose. Finally, this chapter also discussed the coexistence of WPANs and WLANs and the various devices and technology that can cause interference when working in the same RF space.

Exam Essentials

Know the frequencies and channels HR/DSSS and OFDM use.   Understand that HR/DSSS operates in the 2.4 GHz ISM band and can use 14 channels depending on the country/location used. Be familiar with the fact that ERP-OFDM is used for the 2.4 GHz band and OFDM is used for the 5 GHz band. Know the three UNII bands OFDM uses for the 802.11a amendment. Understand that MIMO systems may use HT-OFDM and can operate in either the 2.4 GHz ISM band or the 5 GHz UNII band.

Understand the difference between CSMA/CD and CSMA/CA.   Know the differences between access methods and that they can either detect or attempt to avoid collisions. Also understand that IEEE 802.11 wireless networks use distributed coordination function (DCF) mode as a contention method to send data.

Know the differences among various physical layer wireless technologies, such as FHSS, DSSS, HR/DSSS, OFDM, ERP-OFDM, and MIMO.   The uses of physical layer technologies vary depending on radio frequency, applications, and desired data rates. Understand the standard or amendment each physical layer technology uses as well as advantages and disadvantages of each, including co-location and interference.

Understand that co-location of WPAN and WLAN devices may cause interference and affect performance.   WPAN and WLAN devices might be co-located in the same RF space. Know the potential impact of co-location on performance and other factors. Some WPAN and WLAN devices use the same frequency and spread spectrum technology. Understand that this can cause interference.

Key Terms

Carrier Sense Multiple Access/Collision Avoidance (CSMA/CA)

Carrier Sense Multiple Access/Collision Detection (CSMA/CD)

channel

channel planning

co-location

contention

direct-sequence spread spectrum (DSSS)

distributed coordinated function (DCF)

Extended Rate Physical Orthogonal Frequency Division Multiplexing (ERP-OFDM)

frequency-hopping spread spectrum (FHSS)

high rate/direct-sequence spread spectrum (HR/DSSS)

interference

multiple input/multiple output (MIMO)

narrowband communication

network access methods

orthogonal frequency division multiplexing (OFDM)

single input/single output (SISO)

spatial multiplexing (SM)

spread spectrum

spreading code

subcarrier

Review Questions

1. IEEE 802.11a/b/g devices use what type of communication?

   A. Half diplex

   B. Full diplex

   C. Half duplex

   D. Full duplex

2. DSSS devices operate in which frequency range?

   A. 2.40 GHz

   B. 5.25 GHz

   C. 5.35 GHz

   D. 5.75 GHz

3. How many access points can be co-located without channel reuse in the same radio frequency area to maximize total system throughput while minimizing RF interference in an IEEE 802.11b network?

   A. Two

   B. Three

   C. Four

   D. Six

4. Devices compliant with which amendment to the IEEE standard use multiple radio chains and multiple antennas?

   A. 802.11a

   B. 802.11b

   C. 802.11g

   D. 802.11n

5. What technology is used to send WLAN data over a wireless medium using many subcarrier frequencies?

   A. Wireless broadband

   B. Narrowband

   C. Spread spectrum

   D. Spectral masking

   E. Wideband

6. Which two channels could be used so that the access points do not interfere with each other in an 802.11b wireless network? (Choose three.)

   A. Channel 1 and channel 5

   B. Channel 3 and channel 9

   C. Channel 6 and channel 11

   D. Channel 2 and channel 8

   E. Channel 4 and channel 7

7. Which network access method attempts to avoid collisions?

   A. CSMA/CA

   B. CSMA/CD

   C. CSMA/CR

   D. CSMA/DSSS

8. DSSS uses which spreading code at 1 Mbps?

   A. Barker

   B. CCK

   C. DBPSK

   D. DQPSK

9. FM radio stations use what type of RF communication?

   A. High power, narrow bandwidth

   B. High power, wide bandwidth

   C. Low power, narrow bandwidth

   D. Low power, wide bandwidth

10. An HR/DSSS channel is how wide?

    A. 1 MHz

    B. 20 MHz

    C. 22 MHz

    D. 40 MHz

11. Bluetooth devices use _____, which can potentially cause interference with WLANs.

    A. Bluetooth spread spectrum (BTSS)

    B. Orthogonal frequency division multiplexing (OFDM)

    C. Direct-sequence spread spectrum (DSSS)

    D. Frequency-hopping spread spectrum (FHSS)

12. OFDM is used in 802.11a and 802.11g and supports a maximum data rate of _____ Mbps.

   A. 11

   B. 22

   C. 33

   D. 54

13. Which wireless LAN technology can be used to obtain the highest data transfer rate possible?

   A. DSSS

   B. Ethernet

   C. HT-OFDM

   D. OFDM

14. Which frequency ranges are used in an IEEE 802.11a-compliant wireless LAN? (Choose two.)

   A. 900 MHz ISM range

   B. 2.40 GHz ISM range

   C. 5.25 GHz UNII range

   D. 5.35 GHz UNII range

15. Which two IEEE 802.11 amendments are interoperable?

   A. 802.11 and 802.11a

   B. 802.11a and 802.11b

   C. 802.11a and 802.11g

   D. 802.11b and 802.11g

16. Without any regulatory domain taken into consideration, the 2.4 GHz frequency range allows for how many channels using 802.11b?

   A. 3

   B. 6

   C. 11

   D. 14

17. FHSS uses which communication method to exchange data?

   A. 1 MHz–wide subcarriers

   B. 20 MHz–wide subcarriers

   C. 22 MHz–wide subcarriers

   D. 40 MHz–wide subcarriers

18. What is the maximum data rate of HR/DSSS 802.11b devices?

   A. 5.5 Mbps

   B. 11 Mbps

   C. 24 Mbps

   D. 54 Mbps

19. What IEEE 802.11 spread spectrum technology specifies that frequencies change regularly while transmitting and receiving data?

   A. DSSS

   B. OFDM

   C. FHSS

   D. ERP-OFDM

20. Which technology used in wireless LANs uses the effects of multipath to provide data rates of 300 Mbps?

   A. OFDM

   B. HR/DSSS

   C. HT/DSSS

   D. MIMO

Answers to Review Questions

1. C. IEEE wireless LAN devices use half-duplex communication. Half duplex is defined as two-way communication only one way at a time. Wired LANs can use full-duplex communication, which is two-way communication transmitting in both directions simultaneously. An example of diplex is to combine signals from two different frequencies into a single transmitter/receiver.

2. A. DSSS devices operate in the 2.4 to 2.5 GHz ISM band. OFDM devices operate in the 5GHz UNII bands.

3. B. 802.11b operates in the 2.4 GHz ISM band. A total of three access points can be co-located before interference becomes an issue.

4. D. The IEEE 802.11n draft 2.0 amendment devices use MIMO, multiple radio chains, and antennas to operate. 802.11a/b/g devices use one radio and may use multiple antennas for diversity.

5. C. Spread spectrum technology sends data over many subcarrier frequencies. Narrowband technology is not used in IEEE-based WLANs but is used in other technology such as radio and TV. Wireless broadband provides high-speed wireless data communications and wireless internet over a wide area network. Wideband uses a wide range of frequencies, and spectral mask refers to the signal levels of the radio frequency.

6. B, C, D. 802.11b channels need to be separated by at least five channels or 25 MHz to be considered non-overlapping. Channels 3 and 9 are separated by six channels, channels 6 and 11 are separated by five channels, and channels 2 and 8 are separated by six channels. All of these scenarios are non-overlapping channels.

7. A. CSMA/CA uses collision avoidance. CSMA/CD uses collision detection. CSMA/CR and CSMA/DSSS do not exist.

8. A. DSSS uses Barker code at 1 Mbps. CCK is for 5.5 Mbps. DBPSK and DQPSK are modulation technologies, not spreading codes.

9. A. FM radio stations use narrowband communication, which is high power and narrow frequency. WLANs use spread spectrum technology, which is low power and wide frequency.

10. C. HR/DSSS channels are 22 MHz wide. FHSS uses 1 MHz subcarrier frequencies. OFDM, ERP-OFDM, and HT-OFDM use 20 MHz–wide channels, and HT-OFDM can also use 40 MHz–wide channels.

11. D. Bluetooth operates in the 2.4 GHz band and can cause interference with WLAN devices that operate in the 2.4 GHz band, including FHSS, DSSS, and OFDM.

12. D. OFDM can be used in 802.11a or 802.11g and supports a maximum data rate of 54 Mbps. 802.11b supports a maximum data rate of 11 Mbps. OFDM is also used with 802.11n Draft devices, but the maximum data rate is 300 Mbps.

13. C. HT-OFDM can support data rates as high as 300 Mbps, OFDM supports a maximum of 54 Mbps, and DSSS supports a maximum of 11 Mbps. Ethernet is not a wireless LAN technology.

14. C, D. IEEE 802.11a wireless LANs operate in the 5 GHz UNII bands. 802.11b/g wireless LANs operate in the 2.4 GHz ISM band.

15. D. IEEE 802.11b and 802.11g amendments are interoperable. 802.11a networks operate in the 5 GHz UNII bands and therefore are incompatible with 802.11b/g.

16. D. 802.11b operates in the 2.4 GHz ISM band and will allow for 14 channels. The channels that can be used will depend on where the wireless LAN is located.

17. A. FHSS uses 1 MHz subcarrier frequencies to transfer data. 20 MHz–wide, 22 MHz–wide, and 40 MHz–wide channels are used with other technologies.

18. B. The IEEE 802.11b amendment specifies data rate of 5.5 and 11 Mbps. OFDM allows for data rates up to 54 Mbps and is used in IEEE 802.11a and IEEE 802.11g amendments.

19. C. FHSS constantly changes frequencies while transmitting data in a WLAN. DSSS, OFDM, and MIMO use set channels and frequencies to transmit data.

20. D. Current MIMO technology allows for up to 300 Mbps. One way this is accomplished is by using multipath as a benefit rather than a hindrance.

WLAN Antennas and Accessories

THE FOLLOWING CWTS EXAM OBJECTIVES ARE COVERED IN THIS CHAPTER:

✓ **Identify RF signal characteristics and the applications of basic RF antenna concepts**

- Passive gain

- Beamwidths

- Simple diversity

- Polarization

✓ **Identify the purpose, features, and functions of and the appropriate installation or configuration steps for the following types of antennas**

- Omnidirectional/dipole

- Semidirectional

- Highly directional

✓ **Identify the use of the following WLAN accessories and explain how to select and install them for optimal performance and regulatory domain compliance**

- RF cables

- RF connectors

- Lightning arrestors and grounding rods

✓ **Describe the proper locations and methods for installing RF antennas**

- Pole/mast mount

- Ceiling mount

- Wall mount

Antennas are an essential part of a successful wireless LAN deployment. From the transmitter perspective, an antenna will take the energy from the transmission system, transform it into radio waves, and propagate it through the free air. From the receiver perspective, an antenna performs the opposite task—it receives the radio waves, transforms them back to AC signals, and finally sends the information to a computer or other device.

Many factors are involved in determining the proper antenna to be used in an application or deployment of a wireless LAN. These factors include:

- Indoor or outdoor installation
- Distance between transmitter and receiver
- Frequency to be used
- Horizontal or vertical polarization
- Aesthetics
- Cost
- Manufacturer
- Intended use
- Mounting brackets
- Electrical characteristics
- Height
- Location
- Local ordinances

Basic RF Antenna Concepts

It is important to understand some of the basic theory, characteristics, and terminology associated with antennas prior to learning how they operate. Becoming familiar with this will help in making decisions when it comes to sales and support of antennas and wireless LAN systems. Some of the terminology for characteristics of antennas is listed here:

- RF lobes—Shape of the RF patterns
- Beamwidth—Horizontal and vertical measurement angles

- Antenna charts—Azimuth and elevation
- Gain—Changing the RF coverage pattern
- Polarization—Horizontal or vertical

RF Lobes

The term *lobe* has many meanings depending on the context in which it is used. Typically it is used to define the projecting part of an object. In anatomical terms, an example would be part of the human ear known as the ear lobe. In botanical terms, a lobe is the divided part of a leaf. As a radio frequency technology term, lobe refers to the shape of the RF energy emitted from an antenna element. RF lobes are determined by the physical design of the antenna. Antenna design also determines how the lobes project from an antenna element.

The effect of antenna design and the shape of the RF lobes are two reasons why choosing the correct antenna is a critical part of a wireless LAN design. Antennas may project many lobes of RF signal, some of which are not intended to be usable areas of coverage. The type of antenna utilized—omnidirectional, semidirectional, or highly directional parabolic dish—will determine the usable lobes. These antennas as well as the RF radiation patterns they project will be discussed in more detail later in this chapter. Figure 6.1 shows an example of RF lobes emitted from an antenna element.

FIGURE 6.1   RF lobes' shape and coverage area are affected by type of antenna.

Highly directional parabolic dish antenna

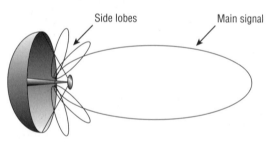

Beamwidth

The design of an antenna will determine how RF propagates and the specific patterns in which it propagates from an antenna element. As mentioned earlier, the patterns of energy emitted from an antenna are known as lobes. For antennas, the beamwidth is the angle of measurement of the main RF lobe measured at the half-power point or –3 dB point. Beamwidth is measured both horizontally and vertically, in degrees.

Azimuth and elevation charts available from the antenna manufacturer will show the beamwidth angles.

The *azimuth* refers to the horizontal RF coverage pattern, and the *elevation* is the vertical RF coverage pattern. The azimuth is the view from above or the "bird's-eye view" of the RF pattern; in some cases it will be 360°. Think of the elevation as a side view. If you were to look at a mountain from the side view, it would have a certain height or elevation measured in feet or meters. For example, Pikes Peak, a mountain in the front range of the Rocky Mountains, has an elevation of 14,115 feet (4,302 meters). Figure 6.2 shows a representation of horizontal and vertical beamwidths.

FIGURE 6.2   Horizontal (azimuth) and vertical (elevation) beamwidths measured at the half power point

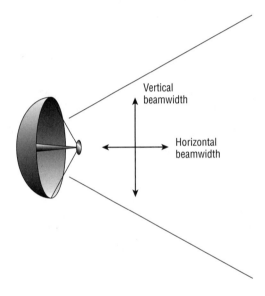

Real World Scenario

Reading Azimuth and Elevation Charts

Understanding how to read an azimuth and elevation chart is good to know from a technical sales, design, or integration perspective. Knowing these patterns will help when making hardware recommendations for customers based upon needed coverage and device use. These charts show the angles of RF propagation from both the azimuth (horizontal or looking down) and the elevation (vertical or side view). These charts give a general idea of the shape of the RF propagation lobe based on antenna design.

Antenna manufacturers test antenna designs in a laboratory. Using the correct instruments, an engineer is able to create the azimuth and elevation charts. These charts show only approximate coverage area based on the readings taken during laboratory testing and do not take into consideration any environmental conditions such as obstacles or interference. The following image shows an example of an azimuth and elevation chart.

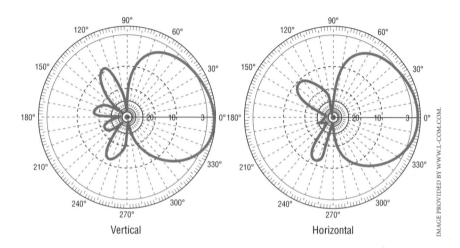

Vertical   Horizontal

Understanding how to read one of these charts is not very complicated. Notice the chart is a circular pattern with readings from 0° to 360°, and there are many rings within these charts. The outermost ring shows the strongest signal from the testing process of this antenna. The inner rings show measurements and dB ratings less than the strongest measured signal from the outside ring. A good-quality chart will show the most accurate readings from the testing process. A sales or technical support professional can use these charts to get an idea of how the radiation pattern would look based on a specific antenna type and model.

Antenna Gain

The *gain* of an antenna provides a change in coverage that is a result of the antenna focusing the area of RF propagation. This gain is produced from the physical design of the antenna element. In Chapter 4, "Radio Frequency (RF) Fundamentals for Wireless LAN Technology," we looked at various characteristics of radio frequency. One of these characteristics is amplitude, which was defined as the height (voltage level) of a sine wave. The amplitude is created by varying voltage over a period of time and is measured at the peaks of the signal from top to bottom. Amplification of an RF signal will result in gain. An antenna is a device that can change the coverage area, therefore propagating an RF signal further. Antenna gain is measured in decibels isotropic (dBi), which is a change in power as a result of increasing the isotropic energy. Isotropic energy is defined as energy emitted equally in all directions. The sun is a good example of isotropic energy, emitting energy in a spherical fashion equally in all directions. Figure 6.3 shows an example of energy being emitted from an isotropic radiator.

FIGURE 6.3   A perfect isotropic radiator emits energy equally in all directions.

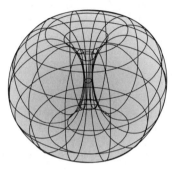

Passive Gain

It's actually quite intriguing how an antenna can provide *passive gain*, a change in coverage without the use of an external power source. Because of how antennas are designed, they focus isotropic energy into a specific radiation pattern. Focusing this energy increases coverage in a particular direction. A common example used to describe passive gain is a magnifying glass. If a person is standing outside on a beautiful sunny day, the sun's energy is not very intense because it is being diffused across the entire earth's hemisphere. Therefore, there is not enough concentrated energy to cause any harm or damage in a short period of time. However, if this person was to take a magnifying glass and point one side of the magnifying glass toward the sun and the other side toward a piece of paper, more than likely the paper would start to heat very quickly. This is because the convex shape of the magnifying glass focuses or concentrates the sun's energy into one specific area, therefore increasing the heat to that area.

Antennas are designed to function in the same way by focusing the energy they receive from a signal source into a specific RF radiation pattern. Depending on the design of the antenna element, as the gain of an antenna increases, both the horizontal and vertical radiation patterns will also increase. Figure 6.4 shows a drawing of a wireless LAN system with 100 mW of power at the antenna. Because of passive gain, the antenna emits 200 mW of power.

FIGURE 6.4   Access point supplying 100 mW of power and an antenna with a gain of 3 dBi for an output at the antenna of 200 mW

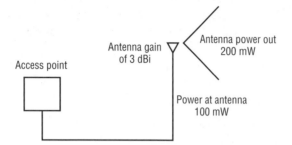

Exercise 6.1 is a simple way to demonstrate passive gain.

EXERCISE 6.1

Demonstrate Passive Gain

You can demonstrate passive gain by using a standard 8.5″ × 11.0″ piece of notebook paper or cardstock.

1.   Roll a piece of paper into a cone or funnel shape.

2.   Speak at your normal volume and notice the sound of your voice as it propagates through the air.

3.   Hold the cone-shaped paper in front of your mouth.

4.   Speak at the same volume.

5.   Notice that the sound of your voice is louder. This occurs because the sound is now focused into a specific area or radiation pattern, hence passive gain occurs.

Active Gain

Active gain will also provide an increase in signal strength. *Active gain* is accomplished by providing an external power source to a device in the wireless LAN system. An example of such a device is an amplifier. An amplifier is placed in series in the wireless LAN system and will increase the signal strength based on the gain of the amplifier.

If an amplifier is used in a wireless LAN system, certain regulatory domains require that the amplifier must be certified as part of the system. It is best to carefully consider whether an amplifier is necessary before using such a device in an IEEE 802.11 wireless LAN system. Using an amplifier may nullify the system's certification and potentially exceed the allowed RF limit.

Antenna Polarization

Antenna *polarization* describes how a wave is emitted from an antenna and the orientation of the electrical component or electric field of the waveform. To maximize signal, the transmitting and receiving antennas should be polarized in the same direction or as closely as possible. Antennas polarized the same way ensure the best possible signal.

If the polarization of the transmitter and receiver are different, the power of the signal will decrease depending how different the polarization is. Figure 6.5 shows an example of horizontal and vertical polarized antennas.

FIGURE 6.5   Horizontally and vertically polarized antennas

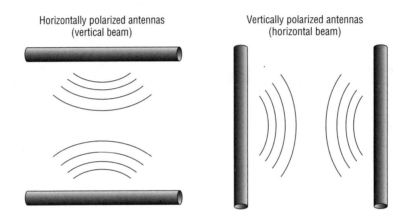

With the large number of wireless LAN devices available, it is a challenging task to accomplish the same polarization for all devices on the network. Performing a wireless LAN site survey will show signal strength based upon several factors, including polarization of access point antennas. This survey will help determine the received signal strength of the wireless LAN devices. Site surveys and antenna polarization will be discussed in more detail in Chapter 9, "Performing a WLAN Site Survey."

🌐 Real World Scenario

Antenna Polarization Example/Experiment

It is fairly simple to demonstrate antenna polarization with a notebook computer or other wireless LAN device and either a wireless network adapter client utility or other third-party software that shows signal strength and/or signal to noise ratio. One such utility is InSSIDer, a free open source Wi-Fi network scanner for Windows Vista and Windows XP. The InSSIDer program is included on the CD that comes with this book. InSSIDer displays the received signal strength from the access points in the receiver area.

You can visualize polarization by performing the following steps. This experiment should be performed using a notebook computer within close proximity to an access point.

1. Verify that you have a supported wireless network adapter.

2. Install and launch the InSSIDer program or other utility that shows signal strength.

3. Monitor the received signal strength (RSSI) value.

4. While monitoring the RSSI value, change the orientation of the notebook computer.

5. Notice the change in the RSSI value (either an increase or decrease) when the orientation of the computer changes with respect to the access point.

This demonstrates how polarity can affect the received signal of a device.

WLAN Antenna Types

The type of antenna that is best for a particular installation or application will depend on the desired RF coverage pattern. Making the correct choice is part of a good wireless LAN design. Using the wrong type of antenna can cause undesirable results, such as interference to neighboring systems, poor signal strength, or incorrect coverage pattern for your design.

Three common types of antennas for use with wireless LANs are:

- Omnidirectional/dipole antennas
- Semidirectional antennas
- Highly directional antennas

This section describes each type of antenna in more detail and provides specifications and installation or configuration information about these antennas.

Omnidirectional Antennas

Omnidirectional antennas are very common on most access points of either SOHO or enterprise grade. An *omnidirectional antenna* has a horizontal beamwidth (azimuth) of 360°. This means that when the antenna is vertically polarized (perpendicular to the earth's surface) the horizontal radiation pattern is 360° and will propagate RF energy in every direction horizontally. The vertical beamwidth (elevation) will vary depending on the antenna's gain. As the gain of the antenna increases, the horizontal radiation pattern will increase, providing more horizontal coverage. However, the vertical radiation pattern will decrease, therefore providing less vertical coverage.

The shape of the radiation pattern from an omnidirectional antenna looks like a donut. Figure 6.6 shows an example of the radiation pattern of an omnidirectional antenna.

FIGURE 6.6   The omnidirectional radiation pattern has a donut shape.

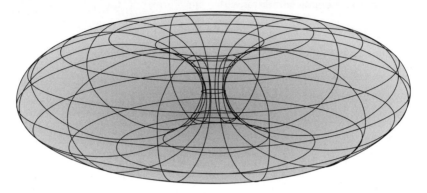

Omnidirectional antennas are one of the most common type of antennas for indoor wireless LAN deployments. Most access points use omnidirectional antennas. Access points come with either fixed or removable antennas. If the antenna is removable, the installer can replace it with one of different gain. Enterprise-grade access points typically have removable antennas that are sold separately.

Some regulatory domains require the use of proprietary connectors with respect to antennas. These connectors limit access points to the specific antennas tested with the system. Therefore it is best to consult with the manufacturer of the access point or other wireless LAN transmitting device to determine which antennas may be used with the system.

The most common type of omnidirectional antenna used indoors is known as the "rubber duck antenna." This type of antenna typically has a low gain of 2 dBi to 3 dBi and connects directly to an access point. Rubber duck antennas usually have a pivot point so the polarization can be adjusted vertically or horizontally regardless of how the access point is mounted.

Some antennas function in both the 2.4 GHz ISM band and the 5 GHz UNII band and can thus work with a multiband device.

Figure 6.7 Shows a rubber duck omnidirectional antenna.

Omnidirectional Antenna Specifications

In addition to the beamwidth and gain, omnidirectional antennas have various other specifications to be considered, including:

- Frequency range
- Voltage standing wave ratio (VSWR)
- Polarization
- Cable length
- Dimensions
- Mounting

Table 6.1 is an example of a specification sheet for a rubber duck omnidirectional antenna.

FIGURE 6.7   2.4 GHz Rubber Duck Omnidirectional Antenna

IMAGE PROVIDED BY WWW.L-COM.COM.

TABLE 6.1   Omnidirectional Antenna Specifications

Electrical Specifications	
Frequency ranges	2400–2500 MHz
Gain	2.2 dBi
Horizontal beamwidth	360°
Impedance	50 ohm
Maximum power	50W
VSWR	<2:0

TABLE 6.1   Omnidirectional Antenna Specifications *(continued)*

Mechanical Specifications

Weight	0.52 oz. (15g)
Length	4.7″ (105 mm)
Maximum diameter	0.4″ (10 mm)
Finish	Matte black
Connector	Reverse polarity SMA plug
Operating temperature	−40° C to 60° C (−40° F to 140° F)
Polarization	Vertical
Flame rating	UL 94HB
RoHS-compliant	Yes

A physical representation of the antenna is also helpful for sales and integration professionals. Figure 6.8 shows the physical specifications diagram for a rubber duck omnidirectional antenna.

Azimuth and elevation charts are usually available to allow visualization of the RF radiation pattern emitted from the antenna. This is useful for a wireless LAN professional to determine the approximate RF propagation pattern. The purpose of these charts as well as how to read them was explained in "Reading Azimuth and Elevation Charts" earlier in this chapter. Figure 6.9 shows the charts for a rubber duck omnidirectional antenna.

Semidirectional Antennas

Semidirectional antennas take power from the transmitting system and focus it into a more specific pattern than an omnidirectional antenna offers. *Semidirectional* antennas are available in various types, including patch, panel, sector, and Yagi. These antennas are manufactured for either indoor or outdoor use and are designed to provide more specific coverage by focusing the horizontal radiation pattern to a value of less than 360°. A semidirectional antenna will allow the wireless LAN designer to provide RF coverage to a specific area within a deployment. This coverage area may consist of rooms or areas in which an omnidirectional antenna may not be the perfect solution. For indoor installations, such areas include rectangular rooms or offices, hallways, and long corridors. For outdoor deployments, they include point-to-point and point-to-multipoint bridging installations.

FIGURE 6.8   Rubber duck omnidirectional antenna physical specifications

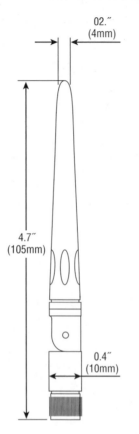

02.″
(4mm)

4.7″
(105mm)

0.4″
(10mm)

FIGURE 6.9   Vertical (elevation) and horizontal (azimuth) charts for omnidirectional antenna

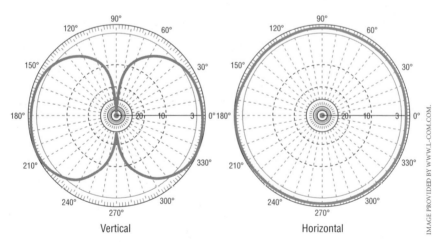

Vertical   Horizontal

IMAGE PROVIDED BY WWW.L-COM.COM.

The measurement unit for radio waves is named after Heinrich Rudolf Hertz (February 22, 1857, to January 1, 1894). He was a German physicist and the first to satisfactorily show the existence of electromagnetic waves.

Patch/Panel Antennas

In the wireless LAN world, the terms *patch* and *panel* are commonly used to describe the same type of antenna. The intended use will affect the choice of patch/panel antenna to be used in a specific application. Choosing the correct patch/panel antenna will require knowing the dimensions of the physical area to be covered as well as the amount of gain required. A *patch/panel antenna* can have a horizontal beamwidth of as high as 180°, but usually the horizontal beamwith is between 35° and 60°. The vertical beamwidth usually ranges between 30° and 80°. Figure 6.10 shows a 2.4 GHz flat patch antenna.

FIGURE 6.10   2.4 GHz 8 dBi flat patch antenna

IMAGE PROVIDED BY WWW.L-COM.COM.

🌐 Real World Scenario

Appropriate Use of a Semidirectional Antenna

A small business consultant is tasked with providing wireless LAN access to several offices in a multi-tenant building. The client wants to provide adequate coverage for the offices they lease but would like to minimize the number of access points. The client wishes to use access points and antennas that are aesthetically pleasing since these offices allow public access. The areas to be covered are rectangular, as shown below.

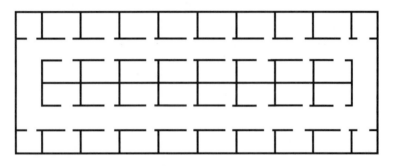

One solution would be to provide several access points using low-gain omnidirectional antennas. The following image illustrates how several access points could be used to provide coverage to this area.

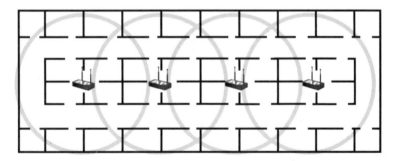

However, the consultant believes that if low-gain rubber duck omnidirectional antennas are used, an access point with significant output power would be required to cover the length of the rooms. In addition, the client wants to minimize the number of access points and make the installation aesthetically pleasing.

An alternate solution is to use a patch antenna on both sides of the office, thereby providing adequate coverage and minimizing the use of access points. The following image shows patch antennas mounted at both ends of the office area as well as the projected coverage area of both antennas.

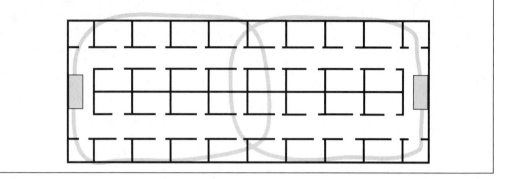

Patch/Panel Antenna Specifications

The specifications for semidirectional antennas such as patch or panel vary based on the design of the antenna. Semidirectional antennas are available in single or dual band capability. Semidirectional antennas may be used indoors or outdoors depending on the application. Table 6.2 is an example of a specification sheet for a 2.4 GHz 8 dBi flat patch antenna.

TABLE 6.2   Flat Patch Antenna Specifications

Electrical Specifications	
Frequency ranges	2400–2500 MHz
Gain	8 dBi
Horizontal beamwidth	75°
Vertical beamwidth	65°
Impedance	50 ohm
Maximum power	25 W
VSWR	<1.5:1 avg
Mechanical Specifications	
Weight	0.4 lb. (.18 Kg)
Dimensions	4.5 x 4.5 x 0.9″ (114 x 114 x 23 mm)

TABLE 6.2   Flat Patch Antenna Specifications *(continued)*

Radome material	UV-inhibited polymer
Connector	12″ N-female
Operating temperature	−40° C to 85° C (−40° F to 185° F)
Mounting	Four ¼″. (6.3 mm) holes
Polarization	Horizontal or vertical
Flame rating	UL 94HB
RoHS-compliant	Yes
Wind survival	>150 mph (241 kph)

WIND LOADING DATA

Wind Speed (mph)	Loading
100	5 lb.
125	7 lb.

Azimuth and elevation charts are also available for patch/panel antennas. Figure 6.11 shows the charts for the 2.4 GHz 8 dBi flat patch antenna.

FIGURE 6.11   Vertical (elevation) and horizontal (azimuth) charts for 2.4 GHz 8 dBi patch antenna

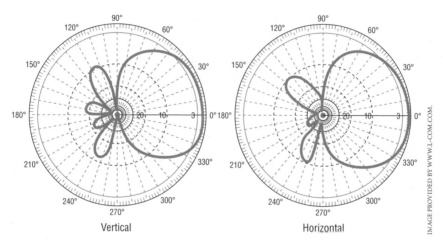

Vertical   Horizontal

IMAGE PROVIDED BY WWW.L-COM.COM.

Sector Antennas

Sector antennas can be used to create omnidirectional radiation patterns using semidirectional antennas. These antennas are often used for base station connectivity for point-to-multipoint connectivity. *Sector antennas* have an azimuth that varies from 90° to 180°. These are typically configured to offer a total azimuth of 360°. For example, using sector antennas with an azimuth of 120° each would require three antennas in order to get omnidirectional or 360° coverage. This is a common configuration used with cellular phone technology. Figure 6.12 shows a sector panel antenna.

FIGURE 6.12 2.4 GHz 14 dBi 90° sector panel antenna

IMAGE PROVIDED BY WWW.L-COM.COM.

Sector Antenna Specifications

As mentioned earlier, sector antennas are commonly configured in an array to allow semidirectional antennas to provide omnidirectional coverage. This is useful in a campus environment or community arrangement to provide wireless LAN access such as Internet access. Table 6.3 is an example of a specification sheet for a 2.4 GHz 14 dBi 90° sector panel WLAN antenna.

TABLE 6.3   90° Sector Panel WLAN Antenna Specifications

Electrical Specifications	
Frequency ranges	2400–2500 MHz
Gain	14 dBi
Horizontal beamwidth	90°
Vertical beamwidth	15°
Impedance	50 ohm
Maximum input power	300 W
VSWR	<1.5:1 avg
Front to back ratio	>23 dB
Lightning protection	DC ground

Mechanical Specifications	
Weight	4.4 lbs. (2 kg)
Dimensions	20 x 7 x 3.5″ (500 x 180 x 90 mm)
Radome material	UV-inhibited plastic
Connector	Integral N-female
Operating temperature	−40° C to 85° C (−40° F to 185° F)
Mounting	2^2 (50 mm) diameter mast maximum
Polarization	Vertical
Flame rating	UL 94HB
RoHS-compliant	Yes
Wind survival	>130 mph (210 Km/h)

TABLE 6.3   90° Sector Panel WLAN Antenna Specifications *(continued)*

WIND LOADING DATA

Wind Speed (mph)	Loading
100	32 lb.
125	49 lb.

Figure 6.13 shows the charts for the 2.4 GHz 14 dBi 90° sector antenna.

FIGURE 6.13   Vertical (elevation) and horizontal (azimuth) charts for 2.4 GHz 14 dBi 90° sector panel antenna

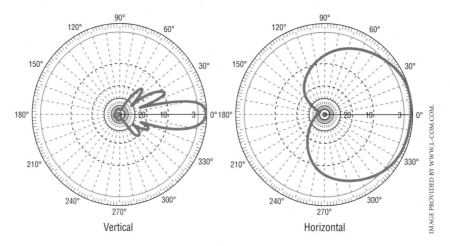

Vertical   Horizontal

IMAGE PROVIDED BY WWW.L-COM.COM.

Yagi Antennas

Yagi antennas are designed to be used indoors in long hallways and corridors, or outdoors for short-range bridging (typically less than two miles). *Yagi antennas* have vertical and horizontal beamwidths ranging from 25° to 65°. The radiation pattern may look like a funnel or a cone. As the signal propagates away from the antenna, the RF coverage naturally widens (diffusion). The aperture of the receiving antenna is much narrower than the signal at that point. This is a result of diffusion, which is the biggest form of loss in an RF link. Figure 6.14 shows a Yagi antenna.

FIGURE 6.14   2.4 GHz 15 dBi Yagi antenna

IMAGE PROVIDED BY WWW.L-COM.COM.

Yagi Antenna Specifications

Table 6.4 is an example of a specification sheet for a 2.4 GHz 15 dBi Yagi WLAN antenna.

TABLE 6.4   15 dBi Yagi Antenna Specifications

Electrical Specifications	
Frequency ranges	2400–2500 MHz
Gain	14.5 dBi
–3 dB beamwidth	30°
Impedance	50 ohm
Maximum power	50 W
VSWR	<1.5:1 avg
Lightning protection	DC short
Mechanical Specifications	
Weight	1.8 lbs. (.81 kg)
Dimensions – Length x diameter	18.2 x 3″ (462 x 76 mm)

TABLE 6.4   15 dBi Yagi Antenna Specifications *(continued)*

Mechanical Specifications *(continued)*

Radome material	UV-inhibited polymer
Connector	12² N-female
Operating temperature	–40° C to 85° C (–40° F to 185° F)
Mounting	1-1/4" (32 mm) to 2" (51 mm) diameter masts
Polarization	Vertical and horizontal
Flame rating	UL 94HB
RoHS-compliant	Yes
Wind survival	>150 mph (241 kph)

WIND LOADING DATA

Wind Speed (mph)	Loading
100	12 lb.
125	19 lb.

Figure 6.15 shows the charts for the 2.4 GHz 14 dBi Yagi antenna.

FIGURE 6.15   Vertical (elevation) and horizontal (azimuth) charts for 2.4 GHz 14 dBi Yagi antenna

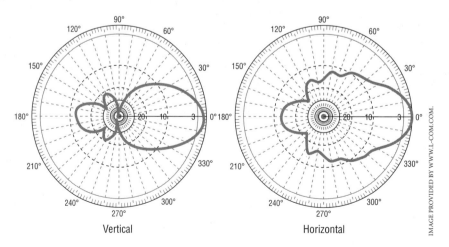

Vertical   Horizontal

IMAGE PROVIDED BY WWW.L-COM.COM.

Outdoor Installation of Yagi Antennas

A Yagi antenna may be in a weatherproof enclosure. This is not required, but may be useful in outdoor installations. The weatherproof enclosure will prevent collection of certain elements such as snow and ice. Radome covers are available for parabolic dish antennas for the same purpose.

Highly Directional Antennas

Highly directional antennas are typically *parabolic dish antennas* used for long-range point-to-point bridging links. These antennas are available with a solid reflector or a grid. Some manufacturers of parabolic dish antennas advertise ranges of 25 miles or more depending on the gain and the environmental conditions. Parabolic dish antennas have very narrow horizontal and vertical beamwidths. This beamwidth can range from 3° to 15° and has a radiation pattern similar to that of a Yagi with the appearance of a funnel. The beamwidth starts very narrow at the antenna element and naturally widens because of diffusion. Because these antennas are designed for outdoor use, they will need to be manufactured to withstand certain environmental conditions including wind rating and appropriate mounting. Figure 6.16 shows a parabolic dish antenna.

FIGURE 6.16   5 GHz 28.5 dBi parabolic dish antenna

Highly Directional Antenna Specifications

Table 6.5 is an example of a specification sheet for a 2.4 GHz 30 dBi grid parabolic dish antenna.

TABLE 6.5 2.4 GHz 30 dBi Grid Parabolic Dish Antenna Specifications

Electrical Specifications	
Frequency ranges	2400–2500 MHz
Gain	30 dBi
Horizontal beamwidth	5.3°
Vertical beamwidth	5.3°
Impedance	50 ohm
Maximum power	100 W
VSWR	<1.5:1 avg
Mechanical Specifications	
Weight	35 lbs. (16 kg)
Dimensions	59″ diameter (1.5 m)
Grid material	Galvanized steel
Operating temperature	−40° C to 85° C (−40° F to 185° F)
Mounting	1-1/4″ (32 mm) to 2″ (51 mm) diameter masts
Polarization	Vertical
Flame rating	UL 94HB
Wind survival	>134 mph

TABLE 6.5   2.4 GHz 30 dBi Grid Parabolic Dish Antenna Specifications *(continued)*

Shipping Specifications

Shipping carton size	(L x W x H) 62" x 17" x 32" (1.6m x 0.43m x 0.81m)
Shipping weight	50 lbs. (22.7 kg)

WIND LOADING DATA

Wind Speed (mph)	Loading
100	61.8 lb.
125	97 lb.

Figure 6.17 shows the charts for the 15 2.4 GHz 30 dBi grid parabolic dish antenna.

FIGURE 6.17   Vertical (elevation) and horizontal (azimuth) charts for 2.4 GHz 30 dBi grid antenna

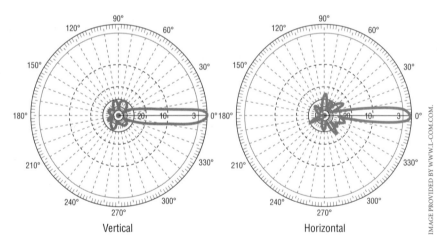

IMAGE PROVIDED BY WWW.L-COM.COM.

Shipping a Parabolic Dish Antenna

One thing to consider regarding the sale and procurement of a highly directional parabolic dish antenna is the size and shipping weight. Since these antennas are much larger and heavier than other antennas used in wireless LANs, shipping may be a factor. Some specification sheets will detail shipping information for this reason.

RF Cables and Connectors

RF cables play a role in various wireless LAN deployment situations. For example, cables may be used to connect access points and client devices to antennas or to connect other devices that may used in wireless networking. Several factors need to be taken into consideration when using cables in a wireless LAN system, including:

- Type
- Length
- Cost
- Impedance

Choosing the correct cable for use in wireless LAN systems is an important part of a wireless LAN deployment. The right cable for the right job will help ensure that *signal loss*—a decrease in signal strength—is minimized and performance is maximized.

Cable Types

The type of cable used will depend on the application. Many systems use cables to extend from the wireless device such as an access point to an antenna located outside of a building. It is important to choose the correct type of cable in order to optimize the performance of the wireless LAN system. Cables vary in diameter, and the application will determine the type of cable to use. For example, connecting a wireless LAN adapter on a notebook computer to an external antenna requires a specific type of cable that should be short and flexible. Thick rigid cables are best used for longer runs. The radio frequency range in which the cable will be used also is important to consider. Where the cable is used will determine the radio frequency rating of the cable. For example, wireless LANs use 50 ohm cable, whereas television (such as satellite and cable) will use 75 ohm cable. Using cable with the correct rating will minimize voltage standing wave ratio (VSWR). Figure 6.18 shows a spool of high-quality 50 ohm cable.

Cable Length

The length of a cable used in a wireless LAN system is another factor to consider. A cable of even a very short length will have some level of loss. As a reminder, loss is a decrease in signal strength. This decrease in signal strength means less overall performance and throughput for users of the wireless LAN. Professionally manufactured cables typically are available in many standard common lengths. Best practices recommend using the correct length and minimizing connections. For example, if a run from an access point to an external antenna is 27 feet in length, it would be best to use a single cable as close to that link as possible. Connecting two or more pieces of cable together will increase the loss to the system. One might be tempted to use a longer piece such as 50 feet, but this is not recommended since the extra length will add loss to the system. Figure 6.19 shows a short length of cable known as a pigtail used to connect a standard cable to a proprietary cable.

FIGURE 6.18   L-com spool of low loss 400-series coaxial bulk cable

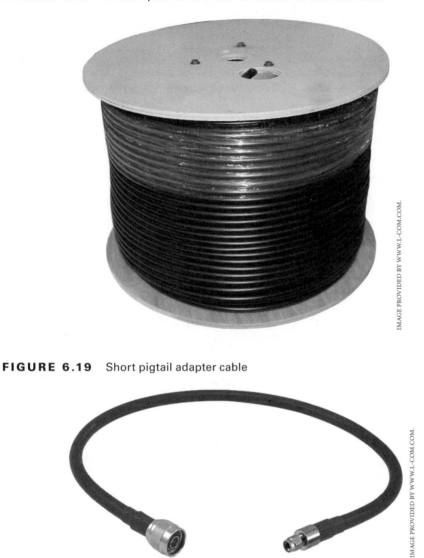

FIGURE 6.19   Short pigtail adapter cable

Cable Cost

Cable cost may also play a role in the type of cable to be used. The old saying "you get what you pay for" is true with cables as well. It is recommended to use high-quality name-brand RF cables to optimize the performance of the system. Premium cables may come at a higher price, but the benefit of better quality signal is the main advantage.

Impedance and VSWR

Impedance is the measurement of alternating current (AC) resistance. It is normal to have some level of impedance mismatch in a wireless LAN system, but the impedances of all components should be matched in order to optimize performance of the system. Impedance mismatches can result in what is called *voltage standing wave ratio (VSWR)*. A large impedance mismatch can cause high level of VSWR and will have an impact on the wireless LAN system and transmitted or received signal.

Electrical resistance is measured in ohms. IEEE 802.11 wireless LAN devices have an impedance of 50 ohms.

RF Connectors

In a wireless LAN system, RF connectors are used to join devices together. These devices may connect access point to antenna, antenna to cable, cable to cable, or various other components to each other. RF connectors also increase the level of VSWR. To minimize the effects of VSWR, best practices suggest keeping the use of connectors to a minimum. Using connectors can also result in *insertion loss*. Insertion loss is usually minor by itself, but it can contribute to overall loss in a system thereby resulting in less signal and less throughput.

Using Proprietary Connectors for Regulatory Domain Compliance

Some regulatory domains require the use of *proprietary connectors* on antennas and antenna connections in wireless LAN systems. These proprietary connectors prevent an installer or integrator from unintentionally using an antenna that might exceed the maximum amount of power allowed for the transmission system. Although these connectors are considered proprietary, many manufacturers will share proprietary connectors.

- MC connectors are used by Dell, Buffalo, IBM, Toshiba, and Proxim-Orinoco.

- MMCX connectors are used by 3Com, Cisco, Proxim, Samsung, Symbol, and Motorola.

- MCX connectors are used by Apple and SMC devices.

- RP-MMCX connectors are used by SMC devices.

Standard RF connectors may be used in wireless LAN systems to connect devices that are not part of the point connecting to the antenna. For example, an access point connecting to a length of cable then connected to an amplifier could use a standard RF connector. The cable connecting the amplifier to the antenna would require a proprietary connector. Figure 6.20 shows examples of common RF connectors.

FIGURE 6.20   Several common RF connectors used with wireless LANs

Factors in Antenna Installation

Several factors are important to consider when you are planning to install a wireless network. These include earth curvature, multipath, and RF line of sight. This section includes information about how to take these factors into account when planning a wireless installation.

Addressing the Effects of Earth Curvature

After seven miles, the curvature of the earth will have an impact on point-to-point wireless LAN links. Therefore, it is important to add height to the antenna in order to compensate for the *earth curvature*, sometimes referred to as earth bulge. There is a formula used to calculate the additional height of antennas when a link exceeds seven miles. However, this is beyond the scope of the CWTS exam objectives and is not shown in this book.

Antenna Placement

The installation location and placement of antennas depend on the type of antenna and application in which it will be used.

Omnidirectional Placement

Placement of an omnidirectional antenna will depend on the intended use. Some omnidirectional antennas can be connected directly to an access point. In this configuration, the installation is fairly straightforward; it is simply attaching the antenna to the access point. High-gain omnidirectional antennas are typically used in outdoor installations for point-to-multipoint configurations. This configuration is more involved because more than likely it requires mast or tower mounting. The exact placement depends on the intended coverage area as well as the gain of the antenna.

Semidirectional Placement

Semidirectional antennas may be used for either outdoor or indoor installations. When mounted indoors, a patch/panel antenna typically will be mounted flat on a wall with the connector upward for connections to a cable or directly to an access point. A template with the hole placement may be included for ease of installation. These antennas usually will use four mounting holes (one in each corner) to securely fasten the antenna to the wall. Yagi antennas can also be mounted either indoors or outdoors. The most common installation is outdoors for short range point-to-point or point-to-multipoint bridging solutions. This will require a mounting bracket such as a tilt and swivel for wall mounting or U-bolts and plate for mast or pole mounting.

Highly Directional Placement

Highly directional antennas such as a parabolic dish are almost always used exclusively in outdoor installations. This type of antenna is used mostly for long-range point-to-point bridging links and will require installation on building rooftops or antenna towers. Alignment for long-range links is critical for reliable communications. Software and hardware tools are available for the installer to use for accurate alignment. As with other outdoor installations, secure mounting is essential in order to maintain safety and link reliability.

Minimizing the Effects of Multipath Using Antenna Diversity

In Chapter 4, we discussed some of the behaviors of radio frequency, including reflection, refraction, scattering, and diffraction. To review, reflection is caused by an RF signal bouncing off a smooth, nonabsorptive surface and changing direction. Indoor environments are areas that are very prone to reflections. Reflections are caused by the RF signal bouncing off walls, ceilings, floors, and furniture; therefore some installations will suffer from reflections more than others. The effect of reflection will be a decrease in signal strength due to a phenomenon called *multipath*. Multipath is the result of several wavefronts of the same transmission signal received out of phase at slightly different times. This can cause the receiver to be confused about the received signals. The result is corrupted signal and less overall throughput. Figure 6.21 illustrates multipath.

FIGURE 6.21   Effects of multipath

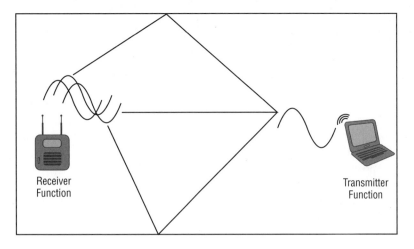

  Think of multipath as an echo. If you were to stand near a canyon and speak to somebody at a high volume some distance away, the other person would notice an echo. This echo is due to the fact that the sound of your voice is reflecting off the canyon walls. Therefore the other person is hearing variations of your voice at slightly different times.

Antenna diversity is one way to reduce the effects of multipath. *Antenna diversity* is a technology used in wireless LANs where a station (access point or client device) will utilize two antennas combined with one radio to decrease the effects of multipath. Using multiple antennas and some additional intelligence, the receiver will be able to determine which antenna will receive the best signal. In diversity systems, two antennas are spaced at least one wavelength apart. This allows the receiver to use the antenna with the best signal to transmit and receive. The antennas are required to be of the same design, frequency, gain, and so on.

Diversity Antenna Orientation

When using a diversity system such as an access point, it is important to have both antennas oriented the same way. They cannot be used to cover different areas. Using diversity antennas in an attempt to provide coverage for different areas will defeat the purpose of the diversity design.

Combating Effects of Wind and Lightning on Wireless Connections

Weather conditions such as rain, snow, and sleet typically do not affect wireless LAN communications unless the conditions are extreme or snow and sleet collect on antenna elements. However, some weather conditions that can affect wireless communications are wind and lightning.

Most outdoor antennas that can be affected by wind will have wind-loading data in the specification sheet. *Wind loading* is the result of wind blowing at high speeds and causing the antenna to move.

Lightning can destroy components connected to a network if the antenna takes either a direct or an indirect lightning strike. A properly grounded lightning arrestor will help protect wireless LAN and other networking equipment from indirect lightning strikes.

Lightning Arrestors

Transient or induced electrical currents are the result of an indirect lightning strike in the area of a wireless LAN antenna system. *Lightning arrestors* are an in-series device installed after the antenna and prior to the transmitter/receiver. Although this device will not provide protection from a direct lightning strike, it will help protect against an indirect lightning strike. When the induced electrical currents from a lightning strike travel to the antenna, a lightning arrestor will shunt this excess current to ground, protecting the system from damage. Figure 6.22 shows a lightning arrestor.

FIGURE 6.22   L-com AL6 series 0-6 GHz coaxial lightning and surge protector

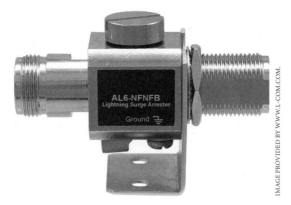

IMAGE PROVIDED BY WWW.L-COM.COM.

Grounding Rods

A *grounding rod* is a metal shaft used for grounding a device such as an antenna used in wireless networking. The rod should be driven into the ground at least eight feet deep. Grounding rods are available in various types of steel, including stainless, galvanized, and copper clad. They are also available in a variety of diameters and lengths. Depending on the local electrical code, the grounding system should measure resistance between 5 and 25 ohms. Local code should also be consulted regarding material, diameter, and length of grounding rods. It is recommended not to share grounding rods with other equipment as interference or damage may occur.

WARNING It is imperative to install a grounding rod properly to ensure correct operation. If installing a grounding rod and other lightning protection equipment is beyond the knowledge level of the wireless engineer or installer, it is best to have a professional contractor perform the job.

Installation Safety

Professional contractors should be considered in the event you are not comfortable with performing the installation of a wireless LAN antenna yourself. Installing antennas may require bonded or certified technicians. Be sure to check local building codes prior to performing any installation of a wireless LAN antenna. Never underestimate safety when installing or mounting antennas. All safety precautions must be adhered to while performing an installation. The following are some general guidelines and precautions to be considered for a wireless LAN antenna installation:

- Read the installation manual from the manufacturer.
- Always avoid power lines. Contact with power lines can result in death.
- Always use the correct safety equipment when working at heights.
- Correctly install and use grounding rods when appropriate.

Antenna Mounting

In addition to choosing the correct antenna to be used with a wireless LAN system, the antenna mounting also needs to be taken into consideration. The required antenna mounting fixture will depend on the antenna type, whether it will be used indoors or outdoors, and whether it will be used for device/client access or bridging solutions such as point-to-point or point-to-multipoint. It is best to consult with the antenna or device manufacturer to determine which mounting fixture is appropriate for use based on the intended deployment scenario. The following are several mounting types that may be used for a wireless LAN antenna solution:

- Pole/mast mount

- Ceiling mount

- Wall mount

Pole/Mast Mount

Pole/mast mounts typically consist of a mounting bracket and U-bolt mounting hardware. The mounting bracket is L-shaped. One side of the bracket has a hole to mount an omnidirectional or similar antenna. The other side of the bracket has predrilled holes for fastening the bracket to a pole using U-bolts. Figure 6.23 shows an example of a heavy-duty mast mount.

FIGURE 6.23 Heavy-duty mast mount with U-bolts

IMAGE PROVIDED BY WWW.L-COM.COM.

Exercise 6.2 describes the basic steps for installing a patch antenna using a mast mount adapter.

EXERCISE 6.2

Steps for Installing a Pole/Mast Mount

1. Attach mounting bracket to mast using hardware supplied.

2. Remove the antenna mounting bolt and washer from the base of the antenna.

3. Insert the antenna into the hole in the top of the mounting bracket. Without overtightening, securely fasten the antenna to the mounting bracket using the washer and antenna mounting bolt.

4. For outdoor installations, remember to use the proper sealant for weatherproofing when connecting the cable to the antenna.

Ceiling Mount

It may be necessary to mount certain antennas or access points with attached antennas from a ceiling. Many antennas have the capability to be mounted directly to a hard ceiling made from concrete, drywall, etc. Another possibility is a drop ceiling with acoustic tiles. Regardless of the type of ceiling in question, follow the manufacturer's instructions on the appropriate fixture to be used for mounting and detailed instructions for ceiling mounts. Figure 6.24 shows an example of a ceiling mount antenna.

FIGURE 6.24 L-com 2.3 GHz to 6 GHz 3 dBi omni ceiling antenna

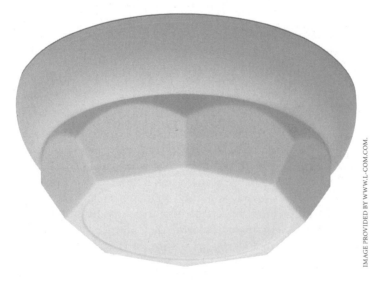

IMAGE PROVIDED BY WWW.L-COM.COM.

Wall Mount

Antennas or access points with attached antennas may need to be mounted to a wall based on the application or site survey results. Just as with a ceiling mount, it is recommended to follow the manufacturer's instructions on the appropriate fixture for wall mounting. When mounting an antenna to the wall it is important to consider the polarization of the antenna. Keep in mind some antennas are designed to be mounted on the ceiling; these types should not be mounted on a wall. Choosing the correct antenna and mounting position is typically part of a wireless LAN site survey. Site surveys will be discussed in more detail in Chapter 9.

Maintaining Clear Communications

Several factors affect whether two wireless devices can communicate with each other. These factors include line of sight (both visual and RF) and Fresnel zone.

Visual Line of Sight

Visual *line of sight* (LoS) is defined as the capability of two points to have an unobstructed view of one another. A visual line of sight is usually not necessary for communications using IEEE 802.11 wireless LAN systems; it is implied with RF line of sight. If a wireless LAN engineer was planning on connecting two buildings together using a wireless LAN link, one of the first things he would do is to verify there is a clear unobstructed view between the planned locations in order to provide an RF line of sight.

RF Line of Sight

For two devices to successfully communicate via radio frequency, a clear path for the RF energy to travel between the two points is necessary. This clear path is called RF line of sight. This RF line of sight is the premise of the Fresnel zone.

Fresnel Zone

The *Fresnel zone* for an RF signal is the area of radio frequency coverage surrounding the visual line of sight. The width or area of the Fresnel zone will depend on the specific radio frequency used as well as the length or distance of the signal path. There is a formula used to calculate the width of the Fresnel zone at the widest point. However, this is beyond the scope of the CWTS exam objectives and is not shown in this book.

It is important for the Fresnel zone to be clear of obstructions for successful communications to take place between a transmitter and receiver. Best practices recommend maintaining an obstruction-free clearance of the least 60 percent for the Fresnel zone in order to have acceptable RF line of sight. Maintaining a clear RF line of sight is more difficult as the distance between two points increases. There are many obstructions that can cause the Fresnel zone to be blocked enough for communications to suffer between a transmitter and receiver. These include:

- Trees
- Buildings or other structures
- Earth curvature
- Natural elements such as hills and mountains

Figure 6.25 illustrates the Fresnel zone between two highly directional antennas.

FIGURE 6.25   Visualization of Fresnel zone

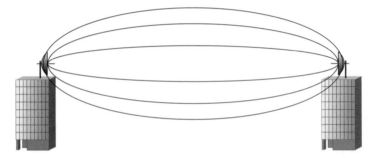

In order to stay clear of obstructions, antenna placement and antenna height will need to be carefully planned. It is important to remember that a wireless LAN link may cross public areas in which an integrator will have no control over the environment. There is a possibility depending upon the environmental conditions that an IEEE 802.11 wireless LAN link may not be a feasible solution due to the inability to maintain an RF line of sight. It is recommended to perform an outdoor site survey prior to the procurement and installation of wireless LAN hardware to ensure the installation and operation of the wireless LAN will be successful.

Summary

Antennas are a critical component in a successful operation of a wireless LAN. In this chapter, we discussed some of the RF signal characteristics and basic RF antenna concepts such as:

- Lobes
- Beamwidth
- Passive and active gain
- Horizontal and vertical polarization

By understanding these characteristics and concepts, a sales engineer, integrator, or other wireless LAN professional can help choose the best antenna to be used for a specific application.

Understanding the RF propagation patterns of various antenna types as well as the recommended use of an antenna will assist in deciding which antenna is best suited for the desired application. As discussed in this chapter, antennas are available in various types:

- Omnidirectional
- Semidirectional
  - Patch/panel
  - Sector
  - Yagi
- Highly directional
  - Parabolic dish

Omnidirectional antennas are one of the most common types of antenna used for indoor applications of wireless networking. Omnidirectional antennas provide a horizontal radiation pattern of 360°. Other antennas such as patch/panel, Yagi, or parabolic dish can be used if justified by the application. This chapter discussed the radiation patterns of each of these type of antennas as well as applications of each.

A proper mounting fixture is required to ensure safety and correct operation of the antenna and wireless network. This chapter looked at various methods for mounting antennas, including pole/mast mount, ceiling mount, and wall mount.

Finally, in this chapter we discussed other factors to be considered when choosing and installing an antenna for use with wireless LANs. The other areas of concerns are:

- Visual line of sight
- RF line of sight
- Fresnel zone

Understanding these concepts will help achieve more successful deployment, operation and use of antennas in wireless LANs.

Exam Essentials

Understand RF signal characteristics and basic RF concepts used with antennas.   Know the difference between passive and active gain. Understand that antennas use passive gain to change the RF radiation pattern. Understand the difference between beamwidth and polarization.

Know the different types of antennas used in wireless networking.   Be familiar with a different type of antennas used with wireless networking, including omnidirectional, semidirectional, and highly directional. Understand the different radiation patterns each of these antennas is capable of.

Identify various RF cables, connectors, and accessories used in wireless LANs.   Understand that, depending on the local regulatory body, proprietary connectors may be required for use with antennas. Know that cables will induce some level of loss in a wireless LAN system. Be familiar with the various types of connectors available.

Understand additional concepts regarding RF propagation.   Understand and know some of the additional concepts when choosing and installing antennas used with wireless LANs. These concepts include:

- Visual line of sight
- RF line of sight
- Fresnel zone

Key Terms

active gain	multipath
antenna diversity	omnidirectional antenna
azimuth	parabolic dish antennas
beamwidth	passive gain
earth curvature	patch/panel antenna
elevation	polarization
Fresnel zone	proprietary connectors
gain	sector antennas
grounding rods	semidirectional
impedance	signal loss
insertion loss	voltage standing wave ratio (VSWR)
lightning arrestors	wind loading
line of sight	Yagi antennas
lobe	

Review Questions

1. Omnidirectional antennas have a horizontal beamwidth of _____ degrees.

   A. 90

   B. 180

   C. 270

   D. 360

2. Antennas provide an increase in RF coverage by using _____ gain.

   A. Active

   B. Passive

   C. Positive

   D. Maximum

3. Horizontal beamwidth is _____ to the earth's surface.

   A. Parallel

   B. Perpendicular

   C. Positive

   D. Negative

4. An access point requires _____ antennas for diversity functionality.

   A. One

   B. Two

   C. Three

   D. Six

5. What device is used to shunt transient current to ground in the event of an indirect lightning strike?

   A. Lightning suppressor

   B. Lightning arrestor

   C. Lightning prevention

   D. Lightning breaker

6. Amplifiers provide an increase in signal strength by using _____ gain.

   A. Active

   B. Passive

   C. Positive

   D. Maximum

7. Highly directional antennas are typically used for _____ connectivity.

    A. Short-range

    B. Omnidirectional

    C. Long-range

    D. Dipole

8. You are a network engineer. While moving a handheld wireless LAN device, you notice that the signal strength increases when the device is moved from a horizontal to a vertical position. This is because the _____ is changing.

    A. Polarization

    B. Wavelength

    C. Frequency

    D. Phase

9. RF line of sight is required for what type of IEEE 802.11 WLAN installation? (Choose two.)

    A. Point-to-point

    B. Scattered

    C. Point-to-multipoint

    D. Reflected

    E. Refracted

10. Which can cause a loss in signal strength? (Choose two.)

    A. Antenna

    B. Amplifier

    C. Cable

    D. Connector

    E. Transmitter

11. An IEEE 802.11g access point requires a minimum of how many antennas to move data?

    A. One

    B. Two

    C. Four

    D. Six

12. 802.11a access points support which antenna technology to help reduce the effects of multipath?

    A. Adjustable gain

    B. Antenna diversity

    C. Adjustable polarization

    D. Antenna multiplexing

13. The following graphic shows what type of antenna?

A. Omnidirectional

B. Yagi

C. Patch/panel

D. Parabolic dish

14. Which weather element would commonly have an affect on a wireless LAN system?

A. Rain

B. Snow

C. Wind

D. Hail

15. Wireless network cables and devices have impedance (AC resistance) of _____ ohms.

A. 10

B. 25

C. 50

D. 75

16. The curvature of the earth will have an impact on the wireless LAN signal after how many miles?

A. 2

B. 7

C. 10

D. 25

17. A patch antenna is an example of what type of antenna?

   A. Semidirectional

   B. Omnidirectional

   C. Highly directional

   D. Dipole-directional

18. An azimuth chart shows which RF radiation pattern?

   A. Vertical

   B. Horizontal

   C. Positive

   D. Negative

19. A point-to-point wireless link requires what percent of the Fresnel zone to be clear in order to be considered to have an acceptable RF line of sight?

   A. 0

   B. 20

   C. 40

   D. 60

20. The image below shows what type of antenna?

IMAGE PROVIDED BY WWW.L-COM.COM.

   A. Highly directional

   B. Dipole-directional

   C. Omnidirectional

   D. Semidirectional

Answers to Review Questions

1.   D. Omnidirectional antennas have a horizontal beamwidth of 360°. The vertical beam-width will vary depending on the design and the gain of the antenna.

2.   B. Antennas provide an increase in RF coverage by means of passive gain. Passive gain occurs when isotropic RF energy is focused into a specific radiation pattern. Active gain requires the use of an external power source.

3.   A. Horizontal beamwidth is parallel to the earth's surface. This is based on how the E-field propagates away from the antenna element. Vertical beamwidth is perpendicular to the earth's surface.

4.   B. An access point will require two antennas for diversity. Although there are two anten-nas, a single input/single output access point will have only one radio. The access point provides additional intelligence to determine which antenna to use. Other wireless LAN technologies such as MIMO may use up to three antennas.

5.   B. A lightning arrestor is used to protect a wireless LAN system from indirect lightning strike. A lightning arrestor will direct transient or induced electrical current to earth ground as a result of lightning strike.

6.   A. Active gain requires an external power source to provide an increase in signal strength. An amplifier is an example of a device that uses active gain. Antennas provide an increase in strength by using passive gain.

7.   C. Highly directional antennas are typically used for long-range point-to-point connectiv-ity such as bridge links. Omnidirectional antennas are typically used as part of an access point system or to provide point-to-multipoint links.

8.   A. Changing the orientation of a device or antenna will change the polarization and affect the received signal strength. The signal strength may either increase or decrease depending upon how the polarization is changed from the original position. Wavelength, frequency, and phase are characteristics of radio frequency.

9.   A, C. Point-to-point and point-to-multipoint both require RF line of sight to be able to effectively communicate. Scattering, reflection, and refraction are all behaviors of radio frequency.

10. C, D. Cables and connectors can both result in a loss of signal strength. Antennas and amplifiers will add gain or increase signal strength. A transmitter outputs an absolute amount of power.

11. A. 802.11g access points require only one antenna to function. Systems that support antenna diversity will require two antennas to correctly operate.

12. B. 802.11a access points can use antenna diversity. Gain and polarization are considered RF concepts.

13. A. The image is an example of an omnidirectional antenna. This type of antenna provides a horizontal radiation pattern of 360°.

14. C. Of the answers listed, wind would have the biggest impact on a wireless LAN system. Rain, snow, and hail do not affect wireless transmission unless the weather is severe. In this case, the collection of the elements may have an impact on the wireless LAN signal transmitted or received.

15. C. Wireless LAN cables and devices are rated at 50 ohms impedance. Cable and satellite television is rated at 75 ohms.

16. B. The curvature of the earth or earth bulge will have an impact on a wireless LAN signal after seven miles. If the signal needs to travel farther than seven miles, the antenna will have to be installed in a higher location.

17. A. A patch antenna will provide semidirectional coverage. The amount of coverage depends on the design and gain of the antenna. Parabolic dishes are highly directional.

18. B. The horizontal RF radiation pattern of an antenna is displayed using an azimuth chart. The vertical radiation pattern is displayed using an elevation chart.

19. D. It is recommended that at least 60 percent of the Fresnel zone be free of obstruction in order to have acceptable RF line of sight. Up to 40 percent of the zone can be blocked by obstructions without affecting the signal.

20. D. The image shows a patch antenna. This is an example of a semidirectional antenna.

Chapter
7

WLAN Terminology and Technology

THE FOLLOWING CWTS EXAM OBJECTIVES ARE COVERED IN THIS CHAPTER:

✓ **Define basic characteristics of Wi-Fi technology**

- Active and passive scanning

- Power saving operation

- Data rates and throughput

- Dynamic rate switching

- Authentication and association

- The distribution system and roaming

- Infrastructure and ad hoc modes

- BSSID, SSID, BSS, ESS

- Protection mechanisms

This chapter will look at some of the terminology used in IEEE 802.11 wireless networks. 802.11 wireless LANs may be configured in one of two modes, either ad hoc or infrastructure mode. Both of these modes as well as how the technology is applied, advantages, and disadvantages will be discussed in addition to the some of the technical aspects such as naming the wireless LAN and identifying the devices through Layer 2 MAC addressing. We will also look at the methodology a wireless LAN device or client station uses to locate and connect to the wireless LAN (these include passive and active scanning as well as the authentication and association process).

It is important to learn how IEEE 802.11 wireless LAN infrastructure devices such as access points are connected together using a common distribution system. This distribution system allows access points to communicate with each other and give the connected wireless LAN devices the capability to roam between access points and maintain consistent connectivity across the wireless LAN.

Other wireless LAN technology factors are important to understand when studying IEEE 802.11 wireless networking. This chapter will discuss the differences between data rates and throughput. A sales or technical support specialist should be able to understand and explain why, for example, an IEEE 802.11g access point advertises a maximum data rate of 54 Mbps but in many cases the data transfers are half or less than half of this advertised data transfer rate.

Finally, this chapter will look at protection mechanisms in depth and explain why these are needed for backward compatibility and the effect they may have on the data transfer rate.

Some of the topics we will see in this chapter have been briefly touched on in earlier chapters. One of the objectives of this chapter is to tie the terminology and topics together. In wireless LAN technology education, it can be somewhat challenging to cover certain parts of the technology without touching lightly on some other topics. This chapter will put some of the loose ends together and help you to better understand how IEEE 802.11 wireless networks operate.

Wireless LAN Modes of Operation

Wireless LANs can be configured to operate in several different modes for device and user access. Two common modes for access are ad hoc and infrastructure mode. These two modes can be broken down into three different configurations:

- Independent basic service set (IBSS)

- Basic service set (BSS)

- Extended service set (ESS)

Each of these configurations will be discussed in more detail in this chapter. The application/deployment scenario for a wireless LAN is the determining factor for the best mode to use. The IBSS configuration does not require the use of an access point and unless specifically justified is not commonly used in enterprise wireless LAN deployments. In addition the IBSS can introduce security vulnerabilities if not properly implemented. The most common configuration for 802.11 wireless LANs is infrastructure mode, which uses at least one access point. Infrastructure mode requires a minimum of one access point but can consist of up to thousands of access points. The access points are connected by a common medium known as the distribution system. This chapter will look at each of these modes and the details of how they are configured.

Independent Basic Service Set (IBSS)

It is important to understand what the *independent basic service set* (IBSS) is, how it works, and potential uses, advantages, and disadvantages. This operation mode uses no access points and consists of only wireless LAN devices or client computers. Communication occurs only among devices that are part of the same IBSS. Unlike an access point, this mode has no centralized control or managed security features. Figure 7.1 shows devices in IBSS.

FIGURE 7.1   Example of an independent basic service set

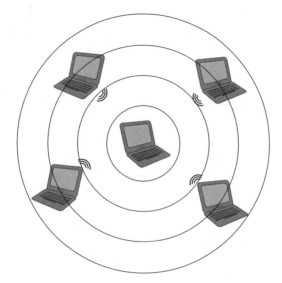

Certain parameters must be set on the devices that wish to participate in an IBSS. These parameters must be the same on all the devices in order for them to effectively communicate with one another. Three common parameters set on devices that belong to the same IBSS are

- Service set identifier (SSID)
- Radio frequency channel
- Security configuration

Service Set Identifier (SSID)

The *service set identifier* (SSID) is a common parameter used in all WLAN operation configurations. Although it is discussed here, it does pertain to the other configurations discussed later in this chapter. The SSID is the name of the service set used to identify the wireless network and for device segmentation. The SSID is used by devices to select a wireless network to join. This is accomplished through processes known as active and passive scanning, both which will be discussed later in this chapter.

In some cases, naming a wireless network can be a tough decision. Organizations that deploy a wireless network may already have a naming convention in place for such devices. If not, a decision will need to be made regarding the names (SSIDs) used for access points and other devices used to identify the wireless LAN.

Every device that wishes to be part of the same wireless LAN IBSS, BSS, or ESS will use a common SSID. (See Figure 7.2 for an IBSS example.) For infrastructure devices such as access points, the SSID parameter is manually set on the access point. From the client access side, the SSID is a user-configurable parameter that can be set manually in the client software utility or received automatically from networks that broadcast this parameter. Networks that are set to broadcast the SSID—also known as *open networks*—allow other devices to connect and use resources from the network based on the designated permissions or rights of the resource.

The SSID is case sensitive and has a maximum limit of 32 characters or, as specified in the IEEE 802.11 standard, 32 octets.

Figure 7.3 shows an example of where the SSID is entered in the Microsoft Wireless Zero Configuration client utility for an ad hoc network. First you select ad hoc (IBSS) mode, then you enter the SSID on the Wireless Network Properties page.

SSID Hiding

Most manufacturers of SOHO and enterprise-grade access points allow the SSID to be hidden from view for devices attempting to locate a wireless network. In this case a client device would need to know and specify the SSID in the client utility profile in order to connect to the network. Even though this is not an effective way to secure a wireless network, it is a practice some choose to use for various reasons. SSID hiding (also known as a *closed network*) will be discussed in more detail in Chapter 10, "WLAN Security."

FIGURE 7.2 IBSS, ad hoc, or peer-to-peer network using common configuration parameters

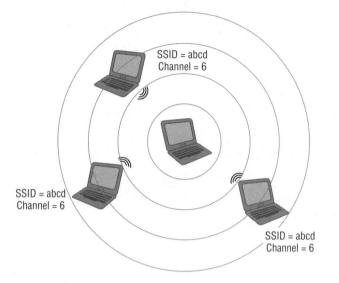

SSID = abcd
Channel = 6

SSID = abcd
Channel = 6

SSID = abcd
Channel = 6

FIGURE 7.3 Entering the SSID in the Microsoft Wireless Zero Configuration client utility

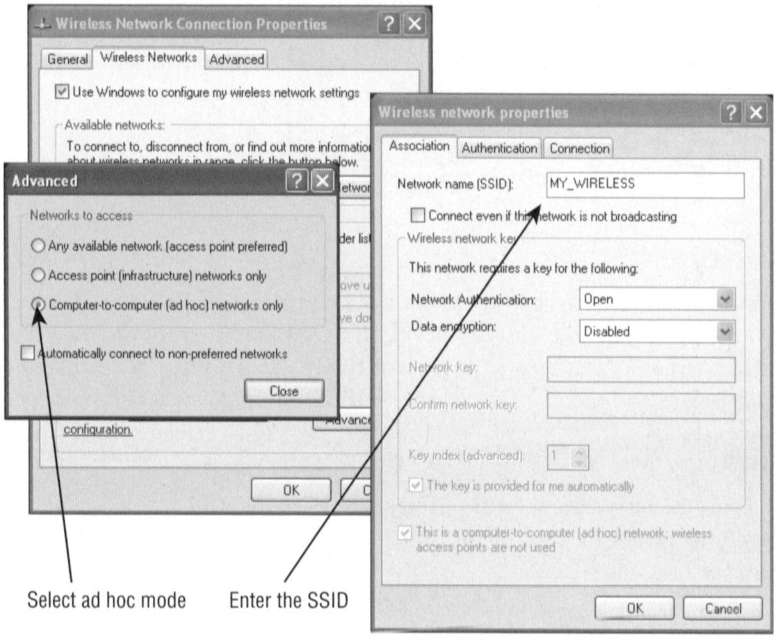

Select ad hoc mode   Enter the SSID

Radio Frequency Channel

The IBSS configuration requires a user to set the specific RF channel that will be used by all devices that are part of the same IBSS network. This is accomplished in the client utility software for the network adapter. Some client software utilities set this automatically, in which case the IBSS will use the channel automatically specified.

It is important to understand that all devices in any common IBSS must be communicating on the same channel. If the client utility does allow a channel to be set, the channel chosen is up to the user but based upon the regulatory domain in which the network is used. Figure 7.4 shows an example of setting the RF channel on a notebook computer.

FIGURE 7.4   Setting the RF channel for an IBSS in the Broadcom 802.11g wireless network adapter driver advanced settings page

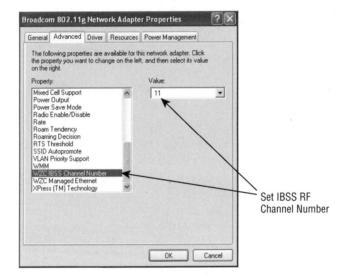

IBSS Security

With IBSS networks, there is no centralized control and no security management features. Security is left up to the individual user or device. If a user inadvertently shares a resource it could expose sensitive information and pose security threats. This can be a concern for many enterprise installations and therefore the use of an IBSS may be against corporate policy.

IBSS Terms

The wireless LAN industry uses several different terms to identify an IBSS. The term used is up to the manufacturer or a specific implementation. An IBSS is usually identified by one of three terms:

- IBSS
- Ad hoc
- Peer-to-peer

Regardless of the terminology used—*IBSS, ad hoc*, or *peer-to-peer*—it comes down to wireless LAN devices connecting to each other without the use of an access point or other wireless infrastructure device. All devices in an IBSS network work independently of one another, and there is no centralized management or administration capability. This type of connection may be useful in homes or small offices for ease of installation.

Advantages and Disadvantages of IBSS

The advantages and disadvantages of an IBSS network will vary depending upon the application.

Some of the advantages of IBSS are as follows:

- Easy to configure
- No investment in access point hardware

Some disadvantages of IBSS are as follows:

- Limited radio frequency range

  Because radio communications is two-way, all devices need to be in a mutual communication range of one another in order to effectively operate.

- No centralized administration capability

  In many large or enterprise deployments, IBSS connectivity is against corporate security policy because it is impossible to manage such networks centrally.

- Not scalable

  There is no set maximum number of devices that can be part of an IBSS network, but the capacity of such networks is low compared to other types.

- Difficult to secure

  Some computer operating systems have made the setup of an IBSS wireless network very easy for any type of user. These users may inadvertently share or allow access to sensitive or proprietary information. This security threat is worse if an IBSS user is also physically connected to a wired network and provides a bridge from an unsecured or unmanaged wireless network to a company's wired infrastructure.

WARNING   A wireless LAN device such as a notebook computer configured as an IBSS device can be a potential security threat if it is also connected to a wired infrastructure. It could provide a bridge for unsecured wireless access to the company's wired network. In this configuration, potential intruders would have access to information from a corporate network by connecting to the unsecured ad hoc network. For this reason, this type of configuration is against corporate security policies of many companies. Many organizations use wireless intrusion prevention systems to detect and shut down ad hoc networks. It is important to inform visitors and contractors who may be physically connected to the company's infrastructure when ad hoc networks are against the corporate security policy to prevent potential security issues.

Setting up an IBSS network is similar to setting up a workgroup for an operating system. All devices with the same workgroup name will be able to
communicate with each other sharing resources such as files, printers, etc.

Basic Service Set (BSS)

The *basic service set* (BSS) is the foundation of the wireless network. This mode consists of an access point connected to a network infrastructure and associated devices. This is considered the foundation because it may be one of many access points that form a wireless network. With a BSS setup, each access point is connected to a network infrastructure, also known as the distribution system (DS) and allows connected wireless LAN devices to access network resources based on the appropriate permissions the device or user has access to. The radio frequency area of coverage depends on several factors such as the antenna gain and output power settings; this area of coverage is known as the *basic service area (BSA)*. Any wireless device in radio range and part of the BSA with the correct configuration parameters, including SSID and security settings, will be able to successfully connect to the access point. Figure 7.5 shows an example of a BSS.

As mentioned earlier, an infrastructure mode consists of an access point connected to a distribution system. The BSS consisting of one access point is a common implementation in many homes, small office/home office (SOHO), or small to medium businesses (SMB). The decision to use a single access point will depend on several factors, some of which are size of the location, use of the wireless network, and how many devices will be connected.

Just as in an IBSS configuration, there are several parameters that need to be configured for a BSS. These parameters include SSID or name of the network and the radio frequency channel to be used. The access point will broadcast these and other parameters about the network to devices wanting to connect to the BSS, therefore requiring minimal configuration on the wireless client side.

Advantages and Disadvantages of BSS

A BSS has many benefits, advantages, and disadvantages. Some of the advantages are as follows:

- Uses intelligent devices with a large feature set to provide users with consistent, reliable, and secure communications to a wireless network
- Useful in a variety of situations: homes, SOHO, and small to large businesses
- Very scalable; you can increase the coverage and capacity of a BSS by adding more access points
- Centralized administration and control
- Security parameters and specific access can be set centrally

Some of the disadvantages of a BSS are as follows:

- Incurs additional hardware costs compared to IBSS
- Usually will require a site survey to determine coverage
- Must be connected to a network infrastructure
- Additional knowledge required for configuration and deployment

Figure 7.6 shows configuring the SSID on an access point.

FIGURE 7.5   Basic service set consisting of a single access point connected to a distribution system and associated devices

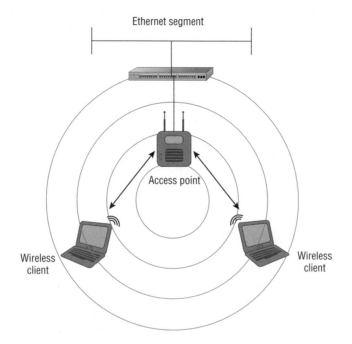

FIGURE 7.6   Graphical user interface for a Linksys access point configuring the SSID

Extended Service Set (ESS)

As stated in the IEEE 802.11-2007 standard, an *extended service set* (ESS) is defined as "a set of one or more interconnected basic service sets (BSSs) that appears as a single BSS to the logical link control (LLC) layer at any station (STA) associated with one of those BSSs." In basic terms, this can be one or more basic service sets connected to a common distribution system. An ESS is a common configuration in many wireless LAN deployments for small to medium businesses as well as large enterprise organizations. In most cases, an ESS would be used to provide consistent and complete coverage across an entire organization. An ESS can be thought of as several basic service sets (BSSs) that have matching parameters such as SSID and security settings. It is the distribution system connecting these together that makes up the ESS. In most cases, the basic service area for each BSS will overlap to allow roaming from one BSS to another. Figure 7.7 shows an example of an extended service set (ESS).

Roaming between access points is a critical component of wireless LAN technology in most modern deployments. This is because the wireless LAN is now a major part of every corporate network. Many envision a complete wireless network for all communications, including data, voice, and video.

FIGURE 7.7 Two basic service sets connected by a common distribution system, making an extended service set

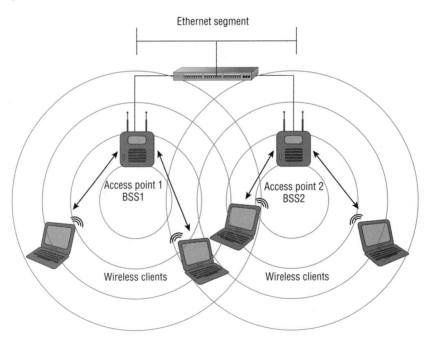

Know Your Abbreviations: SSID vs. ESSID vs. BSSID

It is easy to confuse the abbreviations for several wireless terms. This section will explain the differences.

SSID (Service Set Identifier)

SSID (service set identifier) is the name and segmentation of the wireless network.

ESSID (Extended Service Set Identifier)

Although not defined by the IEEE 802.11 standard or amendments, *extended service set identifier (ESSID)* is a term that some manufacturers use in place of SSID. For the most part, ESSID and SSID are synonymous terms for the name or segmentation of a wireless network. The term used will vary among manufacturers. The term ESSID was adopted by some manufacturers because it implies more than one access point is using the same SSID and security settings connected to a common distribution system.

BSSID (Basic Service Set Identifier)

It is sometimes easy to confuse the *basic service set identifier (BSSID)* with the SSID or name of the network. The BSSID is defined as the Media Access Control (MAC) address of the radio in an access point. It is important to note, some manufacturers may allow for several BSSIDs to be connected to a single access point radio or for a single common BSSID to be shared among many access points.

To review, the MAC address is the unique identifier of a network adapter or what is known as the hardware address. The radio in an access point is also a network adapter. The difference between a wired and a wireless network adapter is simply that no Ethernet jack is available on a wireless adapter. Instead, a radio is used for Layer 1 communications.

The MAC address is a 48-bit IEEE 802 format address that uniquely identifies the network interface adapter—or, in this case, radio card. The format of the BSSID is *XX:XX:XX:YY:YY:YY* where *X* is the number assigned to a manufacturer and *Y* is the unique hardware address of the device.

Although the BSSID uniquely identifies the access point's radio, the SSID is broadcast as the name of the network in order to allow devices to connect. Some devices allow for multiple SSIDs, which use multiple BSSIDs for a single radio. This lets a single access point connected to a wired infrastructure provide multiple WLANs.

In an ad hoc or IBSS network there is no access point for centralized communication. Instead, wireless LAN devices communicate directly with each other. Because there is no access point in this configuration, the BSSID is a randomly generated number that has the same format as the 802 MAC address and is generated by the ad hoc device at startup.

Connecting to a Wireless Network

In order for a device to connect to a wireless network, several different frame exchanges must take place. Various frame types allow for specific functions to occur. They include the authentication and association process, reserving the medium, exchanging data, and power save functions. The following section introduces various frame types and the role they play in wireless networking.

Frame Types

As discussed in Chapter 4, "Radio Frequency (RF) Fundamentals for Wireless LAN Technology," devices communicate by sending RF waves to each other through the air. These RF waves carry the data from one device to another. At this stage, the information traveling through the air is known as frames. These frames play various roles depending on the information being sent. Wireless LANs use three different frame types.

Management Frames

Management frames are used to manage the network. This includes advertising the capabilities of the WLAN and allowing connections by the authentication and association process. Some examples of management frames include

- Beacon
- Probe request
- Probe response
- Authentication
- Association request
- Association response

Control Frames

Control frames are used to control access to the wireless medium and acknowledge data. In addition, some control frames are used with protection mechanisms to allow device coexistence. Some examples of control frames include

- RTS
- CTS
- ACK

Data Frames

As the name implies, data frames are used to carry data payload between devices.

A special type of data frame is the null function frame, which helps implement power save features and is not used to carry any data payload. There is also a variant of the null frame called the QoS null frame, which is used with quality of service functions.

The details of the specific functions of each of these frame types are beyond the scope of this book and the CWTS certification, but some of these frames need to be briefly introduced in order to explain upcoming topics. This includes a wireless device "listening" for a network to join, supplying the appropriate credentials, and finally connecting to send data to the network infrastructure.

Passive Scanning

The first part of the the discovery phase in IEEE 802.11 of wireless networking is known as *passive scanning*. This process allows wireless LAN devices to "listen" for information about wireless networks in the radio receiving area of the wireless network or the BSA. During the passive scanning process, wireless LAN devices will listen for specific information to make them aware of networks in the area. An analogy to this process would be using an FM radio tuner to scan through the entire band listening for a station to tune in.

As mentioned earlier in this chapter, management frames assist wireless LAN devices in finding and connecting to a wireless network. An example of a management frame that works in the discovery phase or passive scanning is a beacon frame. This frame for the most part is an advertisement of the wireless network. It carries specific information about the basic service set such as the SSID, RF channel, available data rates, and much more. During the passive scanning phase, wireless devices listen for beacons advertising the details about the wireless networks in the area. Wireless LAN devices are constantly listening for beacon frames. Figure 7.8 shows a wireless LAN client passive scanning and listening for an access point to connect with.

FIGURE 7.8 An example of passive scanning with a wireless LAN client listening for access points in the area

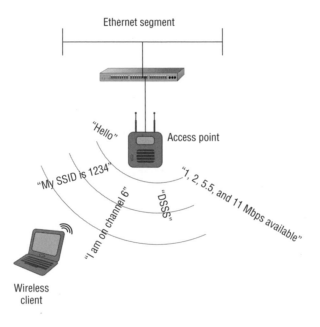

By default, beacons broadcast at 10 times a second. Although this interval can be changed, it is recommended to only do so if necessary or recommended by the manufacturer. In some cases, manufacturers may suggest specific timing intervals for such frames as beacons.

Figure 7.9 shows a packet analyzer capturing beacon frames generated from an access point.

FIGURE 7.9   Packet analyzer capture of beacon frames

00:14:A8:53:5F:C0	Ethernet Broadcast	00:14:A8:53:5F:C0	47%	802.11 Beacon
00:14:A8:53:5F:C0	Ethernet Broadcast	00:14:A8:53:5F:C0	45%	802.11 Beacon
00:14:A8:53:5F:C0	Ethernet Broadcast	00:14:A8:53:5F:C0	44%	802.11 Beacon
00:14:A8:53:5F:C0	Ethernet Broadcast	00:14:A8:53:5F:C0	44%	802.11 Beacon
00:14:A8:53:5F:C0	Ethernet Broadcast	00:14:A8:53:5F:C0	44%	802.11 Beacon
00:14:A8:53:5F:C0	Ethernet Broadcast	00:14:A8:53:5F:C0	44%	802.11 Beacon
00:14:A8:53:5F:C0	Ethernet Broadcast	00:14:A8:53:5F:C0	45%	802.11 Beacon
00:14:A8:53:5F:C0	Ethernet Broadcast	00:14:A8:53:5F:C0	47%	802.11 Beacon

Active Scanning

Active scanning is another part of the wireless LAN discovery phase. In active scanning, wireless LAN devices wishing to connect to a network send out a frame known as a probe request. The function of this management frame is to find a specific wireless access point to connect with. Depending on the client software used, if an SSID is specified in the client utility software active profile, the device will join only a network with the matching SSID.

Access points constantly listen for probe request frames. Any access point within hearing range of the wireless device and having a matching SSID sends out a probe response frame to the wireless device. If more than one access point responds, the device selects the "best" access point to connect with based on certain factors such as signal strength and signal quality. Figure 7.10 illustrates the *active scanning* process.

Frames Used for Active Scanning

During the active scanning process, two frames are exchanged between the device and the access point.

1. The wireless LAN device sends a broadcast probe request frame to all devices including access points within radio range.

2. The access point(s) send a probe response frame to the device so it can identify the parameters of the network before joining.

Figure 7.11 shows a packet analyzer capturing frames of the active scanning process.

FIGURE 7.10   Wireless device sending a probe request frame to access points in radio range

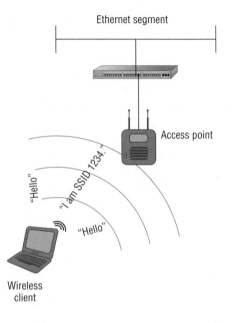

FIGURE 7.11   Packet analyzer capture of probe request and probe response frames

00:19:7E:43:4E:E8	Ethernet Broadcast	Ethernet Broadcast	74%	802.11 Probe Req
00:14:A8:53:5F:C0	00:19:7E:43:4E:E8	00:14:A8:53:5F:C0	48%	802.11 Probe Rsp
00:19:7E:43:4E:E8	00:14:A8:53:5F:C0		75%	802.11 Ack

The IEEE 802.11 standard requires access points to respond to devices that are sending a null or blank SSID. The standard refers to this as a broadcast SSID. It is important not to confuse this with disabling the SSID broadcast on an access point. Most manufacturers provide the capability to set the access point not to respond to a probe request with a null or blank SSID. If the AP is set not to respond to such probe requests, the wireless device is required to have the SSID specified in the client utility in order to connect to the BSS.

Authentication

Authentication in general is defined as verifying or confirming an identity. We use a variety of authentication mechanisms in our daily lives, such as logging onto a computer or network at home or at the office, accessing secure sites on the Internet, using an ATM machine, or showing an identification badge to get access to a building.

IEEE 802.11 devices must use an authentication process in order to access network resources. This authentication process differs from conventional authentication methods such as providing a username and password to gain access to a network. The *authentication* discussed here is device authentication, required in order for the device to become part of the wireless network and participate in exchanging data frames. (Providing a username and password or a preshared key is a different type of authentication, to be discussed in Chapter 10.) The IEEE 802.11 standard addresses two types of authentication methods: open system and shared key.

Open System Authentication

This authentication method as defined by the IEEE 802.11 standard is a two-step process. Two management frames are exchanged between the device and the access point during open system authentication. For the most part, open system authentication cannot fail unless other security measures such as MAC filtering are put in place that will prevent the device from accessing the network. This method is the only valid authentication process allowed with newer wireless LAN security amendments and interoperability certifications for the network to be considered a robust security network (RSN).

Open system authentication is a very simple process. A wireless LAN device will ask an access point, "Can I be a part of this network?" and the access point will respond, "Sure, come join the party." So there really is no validation of identity. *Open system* authentication is considered a two-way handshake because two authentication frames are exchanged during this process. It is not a request and response situation, it is authentication and success.

Figure 7.12 illustrates open system authentication.

FIGURE 7.12   A wireless client authenticating to an access point using open system authentication

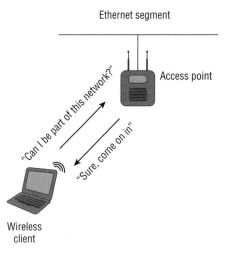

Open system authentication does not provide any type of data encryption. With open system authentication, Wired Equivalent Privacy (WEP) is *optional* and can be used for data encryption if desired. WEP will be discussed in more detail in Chapter 10.

These are the two steps used for open system authentication. One management frame is sent in each step.

1. The wireless LAN device wanting to authenticate sends an authentication frame to the access point. This frame is acknowledged by the access point.

2. The access point accepting the authentication sends a successful authentication frame back to the device. This frame is acknowledged by the authenticating device.

Figure 7.13 shows a packet capture of the two-way open system authentication frame exchange.

FIGURE 7.13 Packet capture of open system authentication

00:19:7E:43:4E:E8	00:14:A8:53:5F:C0	00:14:A8:53:5F:C0	75%	802.11 Auth
00:14:A8:53:5F:C0	00:19:7E:43:4E:E8		47%	802.11 Ack
00:14:A8:53:5F:C0	00:19:7E:43:4E:E8	00:14:A8:53:5F:C0	50%	802.11 Auth
00:19:7E:43:4E:E8	00:14:A8:53:5F:C0		75%	802.11 Ack

Shared Key Authentication

Shared key is another authentication method defined by the IEEE 802.11 standard. It is a little more complex than open system. This authentication method is a four-step process. During *shared key* authentication, four management frames are exchanged between the device wanting to join the wireless network and the access point. Shared key authentication differs from open system authentication in that shared key authentication is used for both device authentication and data encryption.

Shared key authentication is considered flawed because the encryption method used could be captured by an intruder. Shared key authentication requires the use of Wired Equivalent Privacy (WEP) for both device authentication and data encryption. Because WEP is mandatory with shared key authentication, an intruder could potentially identify the WEP key used for the network by capturing the authentication process using a wireless packet analyzer. Shared key authentication therefore should be avoided whenever possible. However, some legacy devices may not support other authentication options.

 Some manufacturers have removed the option to set shared key authentication in infrastructure devices such as access points and bridges also in client software utilities. Some legacy devices may still use shared key authentication as the only authentication option. If this is the case, steps need to be taken to protect the integrity of the network and also identify an appropriate upgrade path for the devices using shared key.

Figure 7.14 illustrates the four frames exchanged during the shared key authentication process.

FIGURE 7.14   Shared key authentication uses a four-way frame exchange

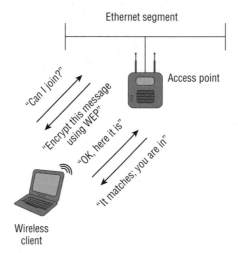

As mentioned earlier, because WEP is mandatory with shared key authentication it makes a system vulnerable to intrusion. Therefore, open system authentication is considered more secure than shared key authentication when WEP is used with open system. This is because WEP is used to encrypt the data only and not used for 802.11 authentication. WEP was designed as a way to protect those that use wireless networking from casual eavesdropping.

Frames Used for Shared Key Authentication

A device must authenticate to the wireless network prior to associating. The following steps show the four-way handshake for shared key authentication. This method should not be used but is shown to illustrate the process.

1. The wireless LAN device wanting to authenticate sends an authentication frame to the access point. This frame is acknowledged by the access point.

2. The access point sends a frame back to the WLAN device that contains a challenge text. This frame is acknowledged by the WLAN device.

3. The WLAN device sends a frame back to the access point containing an encrypted response to the challenge text. The response is encrypted using the device's WEP key. This frame is acknowledged by the access point.

4. After verifying the encrypted response the access point accepts the authentication and sends a "successful authentication" frame back to the device. This final frame is acknowledged by the device.

Figure 7.15 shows the four authentication frames used in shared key authentication.

FIGURE 7.15   Packet capture of four-way shared key authentication

00:19:7E:43:4E:E8	00:14:A8:53:5F:C0	00:14:A8:53:5F:C0	88%	802.11 Auth
00:14:A8:53:5F:C0	00:19:7E:43:4E:E8		44%	802.11 Ack
00:14:A8:53:5F:C0	00:19:7E:43:4E:E8	00:14:A8:53:5F:C0	45%	802.11 Auth
00:19:7E:43:4E:E8	00:14:A8:53:5F:C0		84%	802.11 Ack
00:19:7E:43:4E:E8	00:14:A8:53:5F:C0	00:14:A8:53:5F:C0	88%	802.11 Auth
00:14:A8:53:5F:C0	00:19:7E:43:4E:E8		42%	802.11 Ack
00:14:A8:53:5F:C0	00:19:7E:43:4E:E8	00:14:A8:53:5F:C0	44%	802.11 Auth
00:19:7E:43:4E:E8	00:14:A8:53:5F:C0		87%	802.11 Ack

Association

Association takes place after a device has been successfully authenticated either by open system or by shared key authentication. In the association state, the authenticated device can pass traffic across the access point to the network infrastructure or other associated wireless devices, allowing access to resources that the device or user has permissions to access. After a device is authenticated and associated, it is considered to be part of the basic service set. A device *must* be authenticated before it can be associated. Figure 7.16 illustrates the association process.

FIGURE 7.16   Authentication and association

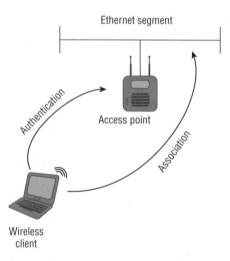

Ethernet segment

Authentication

Access point

Association

Wireless
client

Figure 7.17 shows frames used during the association process.

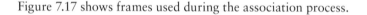

FIGURE 7.17   Packet capture of association request and association response

00:19:7E:43:4E:E8	00:14:A8:53:5F:C0	00:14:A8:53:5F:C0	78%	802.11 Assoc Req
00:14:A8:53:5F:C0	00:19:7E:43:4E:E8		44%	802.11 Ack
00:14:A8:53:5F:C0	00:19:7E:43:4E:E8	00:14:A8:53:5F:C0	50%	802.11 Assoc Rsp
00:19:7E:43:4E:E8	00:14:A8:53:5F:C0		71%	802.11 Ack

After successful association, the IEEE 802.11 authentication and association process is complete. Keep in mind that this is very basic access to the network using either open system or WEP for authentication and encryption. After this process is complete, more sophisticated authentication mechanisms such as IEEE 802.1X/EAP (which provides user-based authentication) can be used to secure the wireless network. These and other security components will be discussed in more detail in Chapter 10.

Frames Used for Association

After a successful authentication, the association process will begin. Association allows a wireless device to send information across the access point to the network infrastructure.

1. Wireless LAN device sends an association request frame to the access point. This frame is acknowledged by the access point.

2. The access point sends an association response frame to the device. This frame is acknowledged by the associating device.

Deauthentication and Disassociation

It is worthwhile to understand that the opposite of authentication and association can occur in a wireless LAN. These are known as *deauthentication* and *disassociation*. Deauthentication occurs when an existing authentication is no longer valid. This can be caused by a wireless LAN device logging off from the current connection or roaming to a different BSS. A disassociation occurs when an association to an access point is terminated. This may occur when the associated wireless LAN device roams from one BSS to another. Both deauthentication and disassociation are notifications and not requests. Since neither can be refused by either side, they are both considered automatically successful from the sender's perspective. Deauthentication can also be a security issue. Both deauthentication and disassociation frames are management frames. Figure 7.18 shows how disassociation and deauthentication frames would look on a packet analyzer.

FIGURE 7.18   Packet capture of disassociation and deauthentication frames

00:19:7E:43:4E:E8	00:14:A8:53:5F:C0	00:14:A8:53:5F:C0	77%	802.11 Disassoc
00:14:A8:53:5F:C0	00:19:7E:43:4E:E8		50%	802.11 Ack
00:14:A8:53:5F:C0	00:19:7E:43:4E:E8	00:14:A8:53:5F:C0	48%	802.11 Deauth
00:19:7E:43:4E:E8	00:14:A8:53:5F:C0		74%	802.11 Ack

Intrusion tools are available that will continuously send deauthentication frames to a device. Use of this tool is considered a denial-of-service (DoS) attack. This as well as other possible intrusion techniques will be mentioned in Chapter 10. The 802.11w amendment will provide enhancements to the IEEE 802.11 standard that will enable data integrity, data origin authenticity, replay protection, and data confidentiality for selected IEEE 802.11 management frames.

Distribution System (DS)

In wireless LAN technology, the *distribution system (DS)* is the common infrastructure to which access points are connected and can be wired or wireless. In most cases this would be Ethernet. In this capacity, the access point acts like a Layer 2 translational bridge. A *translational bridge* is defined as a device used to connect two or more dissimilar types of LANs together, such as wireless (802.11) and Ethernet (802.3). From a receiver's perspective, this allows an access point to take information from the air (the communication medium in wireless networking) and make a decision either to send it back out to the wireless radio or to forward it across to the distribution system. An access point can do this because it has enough intelligence to determine if a data frame is destined to be sent to the distribution system or if it should stay on the wireless side of the network. This is possible because the access point knows whether a device is part of the wireless LAN side through the authentication and association methods mentioned earlier. Figure 7.19 shows an example of a distribution system.

FIGURE 7.19   Two access points connected to a common distribution system, in this case Ethernet

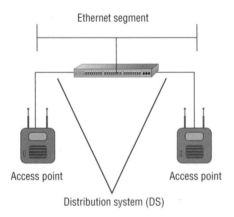

The distribution system is a network segment that consists of one or more connected basic service sets. As mentioned earlier, according to the original IEEE 802.11 standard, one or more interconnected basic service sets make up an extended service set. The distribution

system allows wireless LAN devices to communicate with resources on a wired network infrastructure or to communicate with each other through the wireless medium. Either way, all wireless frame transmissions will traverse through an access point.

In some cases it may be feasible and justified to use a *wireless distribution system (WDS)*. Unlike the wired distribution system mentioned earlier, a wireless distribution system will connect basic service sets together using WLAN technology. Typically the best way to use a WDS is to use two different radio technologies in the same access points. For example, using the 2.4 GHz band for device access and the 5 GHz band for the distribution system will limit contention and provide associated devices a better experience because one radio is used for device access and the other creates the WDS. Figure 7.20 shows an example of a wireless distribution system.

Data Rates

The speed in which wireless devices are designed to exchange information is known as the *data rate*. As mentioned in Chapter 5, "Access Methods, Architectures, and Spread Spectrum Technology," these rates will differ depending on the wireless standard, amendment, spread spectrum type or technology in use. Table 7.1 shows data rates for various WLAN technologies.

Data rates do not accurately represent the amount of information that is actually being transferred between devices and a wireless network. Figure 7.21 shows an 802.11g wireless LAN card in a notebook computer reading a data rate of 54 Mbps. To learn more about the actual amount of information transferred, see the next section, "Throughput."

FIGURE 7.20 Two dual-band access points used to create a wireless distribution system

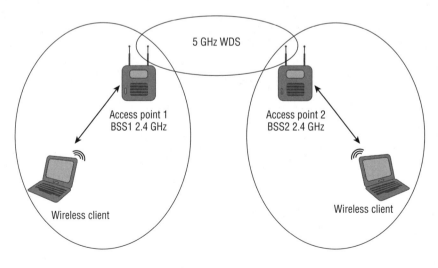

TABLE 7.1 DATA RATES BASED ON SPREAD SPECTRUM TYPE

Standard/Amendment	Technology	Data Rates
802.11	FHSS	1 and 2 Mbps
802.11	DSSS	1 and 2 Mbps
802.11b	HR/DSSS	5.5 and 11 Mbps; 1 and 2 Mbps from DSSS
802.11a	OFDM	6, 9, 12, 18, 24, 36 and 48 Mbps
802.11g	ERP-OFDM	6, 9, 12, 18, 24, 36 and 48 Mbps
802.11n	HT-OFDM	Up to 300 Mbps

FIGURE 7.21   Microsoft wireless zero configuration utility showing a data rate of 54 Mbps for an 802.11g Broadcom wireless LAN adapter

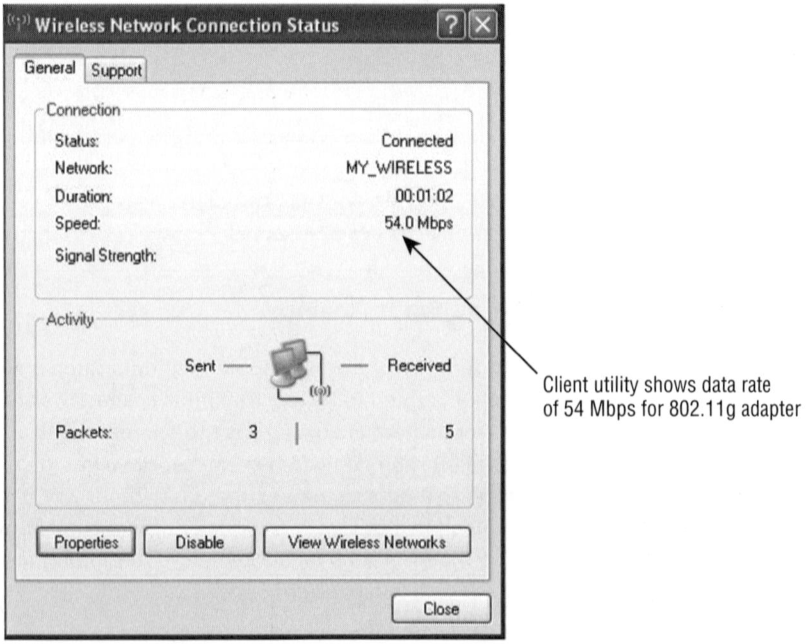

Client utility shows data rate of 54 Mbps for 802.11g adapter

Throughput

Unlike data rate (the maximum amount of information theoretically capable of being transmitted), *throughput* is the amount of information actually being transmitted or received. Many variables affect the actual throughput of information being sent. Some of these include

- Spread spectrum or technology type in use
- RF interference
- Number of users connected to an access point

For example, an 802.11b wireless access point has a maximum data rate of 11 Mbps. With one user connected to this access point, chances are the best throughput that could be expected is about 50 percent of the maximum, or 5.5 Mbps. If more users connect to the same access point, the throughput for each user would be even less, because of the contention between users sharing the same wireless medium. Figure 7.22 shows an example of actual throughput for an 802.11g wireless LAN adapter.

FIGURE 7.22   Actual throughput of an 802.11g 54 Mbps wireless LAN adapter

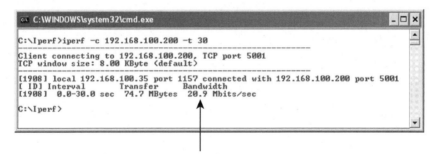

Throughput utility shows throughput of 20.9 Mbps for
an 802.11g wireless adapter with data rate of 54 Mbps.

Packing and Shipping Data: A Throughput Analogy

Packing and shipping an item in a cardboard box is a way of looking at data rate versus throughput. You have a cardboard box that is rated to have a maximum capacity of two cubic feet of space. You want to send a fragile item such as a vase to somebody else. The vase if measured would really only take about one cubic foot of space. However, this is a very fragile item, and you want to make sure it gets to the destination without any damage. So rather than just put the vase by itself in a box with a capacity of one cubic foot, you want to protect it with some packing material such as bubble wrap. Wrapping the vase in bubble wrap will take an additional one cubic foot of space.

The data rate is analogous to the box capable of holding two cubic feet of material. The one-cubic-foot vase is analogous to the actual data being sent. The packing material is analogous to the contention management and other overhead that causes the throughput to be less than the theoretical capacity of the WLAN device.

In Exercise 7.1 you will measure the throughput of your own wireless network.

How to Measure Throughput of a Wireless Network

In this activity, you will measure throughput of a wireless network. If you have the proper equipment it is not too difficult. If you already have an existing wireless network setup with a computer connected to the wired side or distribution system, you have a good part of the setup done. The following step-by-step instructions assume a wireless access point already configured with TCP/IP settings as well as SSID. In order to perform this activity you will need the following equipment:

- Two computers
- One wireless access point
- One wireless network adapter
- Iperf software available from www.sourceforge.net

Complete the following steps to measure throughput:

1. Connect the required equipment as shown in the graphic.

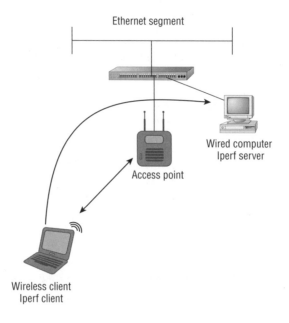

Ethernet segment

Wired computer
Iperf server

Access point

Wireless client
Iperf client

2. Create a folder named iperf on the C:\ drive on both computers and copy the Iperf program `iperf.exe` to this folder. This folder needs to be created at the root or C:\ in order for the remaining steps to work as written.

3. On the computer connected to the wired distribution system, open a command prompt. This will vary based upon the operating system in use. For example, if you are using Windows XP, click on Start, All Programs, Accessories, and Command Prompt.

4. In the command prompt window, type the command **ipconfig** at the C:\ prompt and note the IP address of this computer. An example of this is shown in the graphic.

```
C:\WINDOWS\system32\cmd.exe                                    _ □ ×

C:\>ipconfig

Windows IP Configuration

Ethernet adapter Wireless Network Connection:

        Connection-specific DNS Suffix  . :
        IP Address. . . . . . . . . . . : 192.168.100.35
        Subnet Mask . . . . . . . . . . : 255.255.255.0
        Default Gateway . . . . . . . . :

C:\>
```

5. This computer will act as the Iperf server. In the open command window, type **c:\cd\iperf**. This will put you in the proper location of the Iperf program you copied to this computer in step 2.

6. Type the following command to start the Iperf server: **iperf.exe -s**

7. The Iperf server is now ready for throughput testing.

8. On the computer with a wireless network adapter, connect to the access point using the wireless network adapter. This computer will act as the Iperf client for throughput testing.

9. On this same computer, open a command prompt.

10. In the command prompt window, type the command **ipconfig** at the C:\ prompt and verify the IP address of this computer.

11. Verify connectivity to the Iperf server by typing the following command: **ping {IP address}**

    You will need to replace {*IP address*} with the server address you recorded in step 4. You should see several replies if you are correctly connected to the server through the access point.

12. This computer will act as the Iperf client. In the open command window, type the following command: **C:\cd\iperf**

This will put you in the proper location of the Iperf program you copied to this computer in step 2.

13. In the command prompt window, type the following command to start the throughput testing: **Iperf -c {*IP address*} 30 -t**

You will need to replace {*IP address*} with the server address you recorded in step 4.

14. After 30 seconds the test will be complete and in the command prompt window you will see the actual throughput recorded using the Iperf program.

15. Close the command prompt window on both computers by typing **exit**.

When you are finished, you can delete the Iperf program and folder you created in step 2.

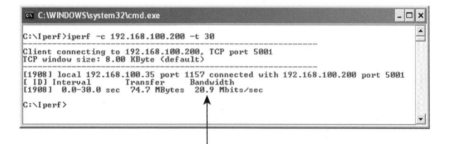

Throughput utility shows throughput of 20.9 Mbps for an 802.11g wireless adapter with data rate of 54 Mbps.

Dynamic Rate Switching (DRS)

When a wireless device moves through the BSA or as the distance from the access point increases, the data rate will decrease. This is called *dynamic rate switching (DRS)*, also known as dynamic rate selection. This process allows a device to adapt to the RF in a particular location of the BSA. DRS is typically accomplished through proprietary mechanisms set by the manufacturer of the wireless devices. The main goal of dynamic rate switching is to improve performance for the wireless device connected to an access point. Figure 7.23 illustrates how dynamic rate shifting works. As the wireless device moves away from the access point, the data rate will decrease. Keep in mind the opposite is true as well. As a wireless device moves closer to an access point, the data rate will increase.

FIGURE 7.23 A graphical representation of dynamic rate switching

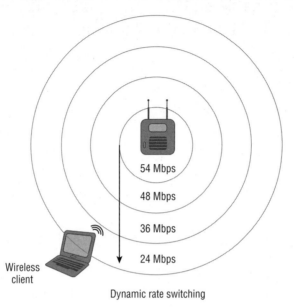

Dynamic rate switching

WLAN Roaming

In wireless LAN technology, *roaming* is the term for what happens when a device moves from one basic service set to another. Roaming is not addressed in the original IEEE 802.11 standard. This process is typically accomplished in a proprietary manner based on how the manufacturer chooses to implement it. Manufacturers use different criteria to initiate roaming from one access point to another. There was an amendment to the IEEE 802.11 standard (IEEE 802.11F, Inter-Access Point Protocol) which was ratified in June 2003 as a recommended practice intended to address multivendor access point interoperability. However, this recommended practice was not implemented by most manufacturers, and it was withdrawn by the IEEE 802 Executive Committee in February, 2006.

When a wireless LAN device moves through a BSA and receives a signal from a second access point, it needs to make a decision whether to stay associated to the current access point or to reassociate to the new access point. This decision when to roam is proprietary and based on specific manufacturer criteria. Some of these criteria are

- Signal strength
- Signal to noise ratio
- Error rate
- Number of currently associated devices

When a wireless LAN device chooses to reassociate to the new access point, the original access point will hand off the association to the new access point as requested from the new access point. This is done over the wired network or distribution system based on how the manufacturer implemented the roaming criteria. Figure 7.24 illustrates a notebook computer roaming from one access point to a new access point.

FIGURE 7.24 The roaming process for wireless LAN

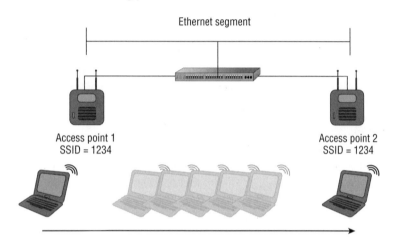

Access point 1
SSID = 1234

Access point 2
SSID = 1234

Roaming wireless client

Frames Used for Reassociation (Roaming)

When a device moves or "roams" to a new access point, it needs to associate to the new access point. Because the device is already associated, in order to connect to the new access point it must complete a reassociation process.

1. A wireless LAN device sends a reassociation request frame to the access point. This frame is acknowledged by the access point.

2. The access point sends a reassociation response frame to the device after handoff across the distribution system from the original access point has occurred. This frame is acknowledged by the reassociating device.

Figure 7.25 shows reassociation request and reassociation response frames.

FIGURE 7.25 Packet capture of the reassociation process

00:19:7E:43:4E:E8	00:14:A8:53:5F:C0	00:14:A8:53:5F:C0	77%	802.11 Reassoc Req
00:14:A8:53:5F:C0	00:19:7E:43:4E:E8		50%	802.11 Ack
00:14:A8:53:5F:C0	00:19:7E:43:4E:E8	00:14:A8:53:5F:C0	45%	802.11 Reassoc Rsp
00:19:7E:43:4E:E8	00:14:A8:53:5F:C0		74%	802.11 Ack

The 802.11r amendment to the standard was recently ratified. This amendment is for fast BSS transition (FT) and allows for fast secure roaming for devices between basic service sets. The main objective of this amendment is to support Voice over IP (VoIP) technology.

Power Saving Operation

Many wireless LAN devices are portable and utilize DC battery power to some degree. A wireless network adapter uses DC power to operate, and in some cases this could be a significant drain on the battery in the device. The original IEEE 802.11 standard addresses power saving operation. This power save operation is designed to allow a wireless LAN device to enter a doze state in order to conserve DC power and extend battery life. If the wireless LAN device is plugged into a consistent power source such as an AC outlet, there is no reason to implement power save features. However portable devices that are mobile and may not have access to an AC power source should consider using power save operations. The original IEEE 802.11 standard addressed two different power save modes: active mode (AM) and power save (PS) mode. In some cases, power save mode is considered legacy because the IEEE 802.11e amendment for quality of service addresses new more efficient power save mechanisms. Although the original PS mode may be considered legacy, it is still widely used in many devices. As mentioned earlier in this chapter in the section "Frame Types," a data frame known as a *null function frame* is used with power management and does not carry any data.

Active Mode (AM)

In *active mode* a wireless LAN device or station (STA) may receive frames at any time and is always in an "awake" state. In this case, the wireless LAN device is not relying on battery power, therefore there is no reason for the device to assume a low power state, and it will never doze. Some manufacturers refer to active mode as continuous aware mode (CAM).

Power Save (PS) Mode

In *power save* mode the wireless LAN device or station (STA) will doze or enter a low power state for very short periods of times. At specific time intervals the device will "listen" for selected beacons and determine if any data is waiting for them buffered at the access point. The beacon contains information for associated devices regarding power save. When a wireless LAN device associates to an access point, the device receives what is known as an *association ID (AID)*. The association ID is a value that will represent that device in various functions, including power save mode. The beacon frame contains an indicator for each AID to let wireless devices know whether they have data buffered at the access point. If it is determined the access point does have data buffered for a specific device, the device will send a message (PS-poll frame) to the access point to request the buffered data. Figure 7.26 shows where power save mode can be set in the advanced settings of the wireless adapter device driver.

FIGURE 7.26   The driver settings for a Broadcom wireless adapter and power save mode setting

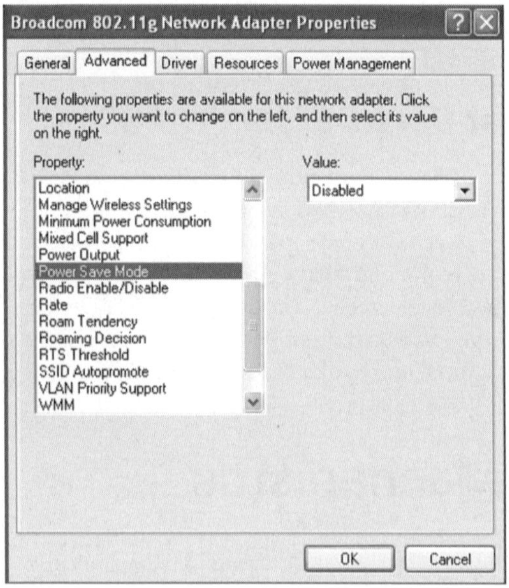

Power save mode may cause some amount of overhead for the wireless LAN device, and there is a trade-off in performance. With power save mode enabled, the battery life will be extended; however, performance will suffer to some degree because the device will not be available to continuously receive data. The device will only be able to receive buffered data during the "awake" state. Power save mode is common in applications where battery conservation is important, such as barcode scanners, voice over Wi-Fi phones, and other handheld devices.

⊕ **Real World Scenario**

Use of Power Save Mode in Barcode Scanners

Organizations such as retail, manufacturing, and warehousing have been using 802.11 wireless LAN technologies for many years. Many of these businesses use wireless LAN devices such as barcode scanners in addition to notebook computers and other portable devices. Barcode scanners are used heavily for inventory and asset tracking purposes. These devices must run for many hours at a time, typically in 8- or 10-hour shifts for individuals who may be using them. Applications such as this greatly benefit from using IEEE 802.11 power save features and extending battery life of wireless LAN devices. This minimizes downtime because batteries in these devices will not have to be changed or recharged as often during a work shift.

Automatic Power Save Delivery (APSD)

The IEEE 802.11e Quality of Service amendment to the standard fueled the need for more efficient power save mechanisms in wireless networking. Depending on the implementation and requirements, legacy power save mode may not be efficient enough to work with applications that use QoS, such as voice and video. *Automatic power save delivery (APSD)* differs from the original power save mode in that a trigger frame will wake a device in order to receive data. APSD is a more efficient way of performing power save functions. It works with time-bound applications that are subject to latency, such as voice and video.

Protection Mechanisms

In order to allow newer, faster wireless LAN technology such as 802.11g and 802.11n devices to communicate with older, slower devices, technology called protection mechanisms was designed to allow compatibility. The mechanisms available depend on which amendment to the standard is used. Protection mechanisms will provide the backward compatibility needed to allow different technologies to coexist in the same RF space.

There are two broad categories of protection mechanism:

- Extended rate physical (ERP) protection mechanism
- High throughput (HT) protection mechanism

Each category includes several modes for specific situations.

Extended Rate Physical (ERP) Protection Mechanism

In order for 802.11g and 802.11b devices to coexist in the same basic service area and be associated to the same access point, the AP must use *extended rate physical (ERP) protection.*

Most manufacturers of IEEE 802.11 wireless LAN equipment will provide options when it comes to coexistence. These options usually include the capability to set an access point to one of three modes:

- 802.11b only mode - DSSS and HR/DSSS
- 802.11g only mode - ERP-OFDM
- 802.11b/g mixed mode - DSSS, HR/DSSS and ERP-OFDM

802.11b Only Mode

This mode requires setting an access point to operate in 802.11b only mode. This requires disabling all of the ERP-OFDM data rates of 6, 9, 12, 18, 24, 36, 48, and 54 Mbps and allowing only DSSS data rates of 1, 2 and HR/DSSS rates of 5.5, and 11 Mbps. Enabling this mode limits the maximum data rate to only 11 Mbps. Setting an access point to this mode has limited applications.

802.11g Only Mode

This mode is the opposite of 802.11b only mode. All of the DSSS and HR/DSSS data rates of 1, 2, 5.5, and 11 Mbps will be disabled and the ERP-OFDM data rates of 6, 9, 12, 18, 24, 36, 48, and 54 Mbps would be allowed. This operation mode is useful in an environment where backward compatibility to 802.11b is not required. This could be useful in an environment where all devices connecting are capable of 802.11g capability, and throughput needs to be maximized.

802.11b/g Mixed Mode

Most deployments in the 2.4 GHz ISM band use this mode for communications. This allows devices that support the 802.11g amendment and 802.11b devices to operate together in the same BSA and associated to the same access point. As mentioned in Chapter 1, "Introduction to Wireless Local Area Networking," throughput will decrease when 802.11b devices and 802.11g devices are both associated to the same access point.

Mixed mode uses control frames to reserve the RF medium. Two options are available:

Request to Send/Clear to Send (RTS/CTS)   is one option of control frames that are used as a protection mechanism to reserve the RF medium.

Clear to Send (CTS) to Self   is a single frame used as a protection mechanism. This is a common implementation used by wireless LAN equipment manufacturers. A benefit of using this frame is less overhead than the RTS/CTS process.

High Throughput (HT) Protection Mechanism

802.11n devices will operate in either the 2.4GHz or 5 GHz bands. Backward compatibility for 802.11b/g and 802.11a needs to be taken into consideration. The IEEE 802.11n amendment (currently in draft) identifies several different modes for *high throughput (HT) protection* mechanisms. These mechanisms are known as HT protection modes and are a set of rules devices and access points will use for backward compatibility:

- Mode 0—Greenfield mode
- Mode 1—HT non-member protection mode
- Mode 2—HT 20 MHz protection mode
- Mode 3—HT mixed mode

Mode 0—Greenfield Mode

Mode 0 or *Greenfield mode* allows HT devices only. These HT devices must also share operational functionality; for example they must all support 20 MHz or 24/40 MHz channels. Mode 0 does not allow 802.11a/b/g devices using the same RF channel. 802.11a/b/g devices will not be able to communicate with an access point in Mode 0. Transmissions from these devices will cause collisions at the access point causing some degradation in throughput.

Mode 1—HT Non-member Protection Mode

All devices in *Mode 1* or *HT non-member protection mode* must be HT capable. When a non-HT device—e.g., a 802.11a/b/g access point or client device—is within the hearing range of the HT access point, this protection mode will be activated.

Mode 2—HT 20 MHz Protection Mode

All devices in *Mode 2* or *HT 20 MHz protection mode* must be HT capable as well. The operation of this protection mode is based on the fact that 802.11n devices can use 20 MHz or 40 MHz wide channels. Mode 2 means that at least one 20 MHz HT station is associated with the access point and that the access point provides compatibility for 20 MHz devices.

Mode 3—HT Mixed Mode

Mode 3 or *HT mixed mode* is used if one or more non-HT stations are associated in the BSS. This mode allows backward compatibility to non-802.11n devices.

Additional HT Protection Modes

Two new modes have recently become available:

- Dual CTS is a new, Layer 2 protection mechanism that is used for backward compatibility between HT and 802.11a/b/g devices.
- PCO is an optional BSS mode with alternating 20 MHz and 40 MHz phases controlled by a PCO capable access point.

As mentioned in Chapter 1, the 802.11n amendment to the standard for high throughput (HT) has yet to be ratified. Currently the Wi-Fi Alliance is certifying 802.11n draft 2.0 equipment for interoperability. Although major deployments with 802.11n equipment are in progress, they are still in the early stages.

Summary

Wireless LANs can operate in two modes, one being ad hoc mode, which means no access points are used, and the other being infrastructure mode, where an access point provides a central point of communication for the wireless LAN devices. In this chapter, we looked at these modes of operation as well as the service sets IEEE 802.11 networks use. We looked at the three configurations for wireless LANs:

- IBSS
- BSS
- ESS

This chapter discussed the configuration of each, some of the advantages and disadvantages of each configuration—from an IBSS, which uses no access points, to a BSS or ESS, which uses one or many access points. Some of the configuration parameters, such as SSID and radio frequency channel, and how these are used were also explained. Some of these acronyms are very close in spelling and sound similar when spoken. It is important to understand the differences among the following abbreviations:

- SSID
- ESSID
- BSSID
- IBSS
- BSS
- ESS

For example, SSID is the name of the wireless network, and the BSSID is the MAC address of the AP radio.

In addition to explaining the different configurations and terminology used, this chapter discussed the processes devices use to connect to and become part of a wireless LAN, including

- Passive scanning
- Active scanning
- Authentication
- Association

The processes of passive scanning (listening for beacons) and active scanning (joining a wireless LAN) are important parts of starting the connection process. This continues with 802.11 authentication—in most cases open system—and the association process. Once these processes are complete, the device finally becomes part of the wireless network, enabling it to pass traffic across to the access point.

This chapter also discussed components and technology that play a role with IEEE 802.11 wireless networks, such as:

- Distribution system
- Wireless distribution system
- Data rate
- Throughput

Both a wired distribution system, in most cases Ethernet, and a wireless distribution system using radios and access points provide connectivity for wireless infrastructure. We looked at the differences between data rate and throughput. It is important to understand that an access point may have a data rate of 54 Mbps, but throughput (the actual data transmission rate) is typically less than half of the data rate. Because wireless LANs are contention-based, data throughput will be even less when more devices connect to the network.

Dynamic rate switching—a client transferring more or less data depending on the proximity from an access point as well as roaming or moving through the basic service areas and being able to maintain connectivity—was also discussed in this chapter. Finally, the chapter covered the important topics of power save mode and protection mechanisms. With power save mode, a wireless LAN device is able to extend battery life by entering into a low-power state or "doze" for very short periods of time. This permits the device to consume less battery power, therefore allowing connectivity for longer periods of time without changing or recharging the battery. The modes discussed were

- Active mode
- Power save mode
- Automatic power save delivery (APSD)

It is beneficial to understand the differences in power save capabilities among these modes.

Lastly, this chapter discussed protection mechanisms and the importance of these methods in order to provide backward compatibility and coexistence to older technology devices.

- ERP protection
- HT protection

We looked at some highlights of both protection mechanism technologies for IEEE 802.11g and 802.11n networks.

Exam Essentials

Understand the different operation modes for IEEE 802.11 wireless networks.   Know the difference between infrastructure and ad hoc mode as well as the use of both.

Be familiar with the different service sets used with wireless networking.   Understand the differences among IBSS, BSS, and ESS.

Identify the terminology used with IEEE 802.11 wireless networking.   Understand the differences among SSID, ESSID, and BSSID. Know which one identifies the name of a network and which one identifies the physical address of an access point.

Know the process devices use to join a wireless LAN.   Understand the process and operation of passive scanning, active scanning, authentication, and association.

Understand the differences between distribution systems as well as data transfer.   Identify the differences as well as the function of a distribution system and wireless distribution system and roaming between each. Know the differences between data rate and throughput as well as dynamic rate switching.

Identify the power save capabilities of IEEE 802.11 wireless networks.   Know the various power save modes of both legacy and Wi-Fi Multimedia (WMM), including active mode, power save mode, and APSD.

Know the various protection mechanisms available for both IEEE 802.11g and 802.11n wireless networks.   Be familiar with the two protection mechanisms: ERP protection mechanisms and HT protection mechanisms. Understand these mechanisms provide coexistence for newer and legacy wireless LAN devices.

Key Terms

active mode

active scanning

ad hoc

association

association ID (AID)

authentication

automatic power save delivery (APSD)

basic service area (BSA)

basic service set

basic service set identifier (BSSID)

data rate

deauthentication

disassociation

distribution system (DS)

dynamic rate switching (DRS)

extended rate physical (ERP) protection

extended service set

extended service set identifier (ESSID)

Greenfield mode (Mode 0)

high throughput (HT) protection

HT 20 MHz protection mode (Mode 2)

HT mixed mode (Mode 3)

HT non-member protection mode (Mode 1)

independent basic service set

open system

passive scanning

peer-to-peer

power save

roaming

service set identifier

shared key

throughput

translational bridge

wireless distribution system (WDS)

Review Questions

1. When a wireless LAN device listens for beacon frames, it is participating in which phase?

   A. Power save

   B. Passive scanning

   C. Active scanning

   D. Authentication

2. You are a sales engineer connected to an IEEE 802.11a access point with a mobile computer. As you move away from the access point, the connection speed slows to the next lowest supported data rate. The change in data rate is described by which term?

   A. Dynamic frequency selection

   B. Transmit power control

   C. Dynamic rate switching

   D. Transmit save mode

3. An independent basic service set (IBSS) consists of how many access points?

   A. 0

   B. 1

   C. 2

   D. 4

4. Wireless LAN devices in an 802.11a peer-to-peer network will connect to which device(s)?

   A. An access point

   B. Other 802.11g devices

   C. Other 802.11a devices

   D. A wireless switch

5. As a device moves away from an access point, which of the following is true regarding dynamic rate switching?

   A. Data rate decreases

   B. Output power decreases

   C. Data rate increases

   D. Output power increases

6. A service set identifier (SSID) has a maximum limit of how many characters?

   A. 8

   B. 16

   C. 32

   D. 128

7.   You are a technical support engineer and receive a call from a customer regarding a problem with their wireless network connection. The building has an ESS network with five 802.11g access points. The customer claims that when they move from their office to a conference room using the 802.11g network they lose their connection and cannot connect to the access point in the conference room. Which is the most likely cause for this user to lose their connection when they roam on the wireless network?

A.   Different RF channel

B.   Mismatched SSID

C.   Different BSSID

D.   Mismatched association

8.   A beacon frame advertises information about the wireless network. A beacon frame is what type of frame?

A.   Data

B.   Control

C.   Management

D.   Detail

9.   In order for a wireless client to become completely part of the basic service set it must first _____ then _____.

A.   Associate, authenticate

B.   Authenticate, associate

C.   Deauthenticate, authenticate

D.   Disassociate, authenticate

10.   The process in which a wireless LAN clients connection moves from one access point to another is called _____.

A.   Reauthentication

B.   Roaming

C.   Rebuilding

D.   Roving

11.   In order to set up an ad hoc network a user must know which two parameters? (Choose two.)

A.   SSID

B.   BSSID

C.   Channel

D.   MAC address

E.   Protection mode

12. The open system authentication process uses how many frames?

   A. One

   B. Two

   C. Three

   D. Four

13. You are a help desk support technician at a retail department store and you receive a call from a manager in the administrative offices. He complains the performance of his 802.11g notebook computer decreases several times throughout the day. Upon visiting the customer, you realize several people are performing inventory using 802.11b barcode scanners in the adjacent room. What is most likely the cause of the poor performance for the manager's notebook computer?

   A. Association

   B. Authentication

   C. ERP protection

   D. HT protection

14. Which items are unique to a service set identifier (SSID)? (Choose two.)

   A. 32 characters maximum

   B. 64 characters maximum

   C. Is case sensitive

   D. Is not case sensitive

15. A basic service set identifier (BSSID) is the MAC address of the _____.

   A. AP radio

   B. AP Ethernet port

   C. Router

   D. Client

16. When an IEEE 802.11g wireless LAN consists only of wireless client stations, the network is operating as what type of basic service set?

   A. Active

   B. Independent

   C. Passive

   D. Infrastructure

17. You are a technical support engineer and provide help desk support for the network in a manufacturing company. You receive a call from the sales manager, who wants to know how power save operations should be set up on her notebook computer to optimize the system performance. The notebook computer is plugged into an AC power source and rarely used on battery. Which mode would you recommend her to set on the wireless adapter?

    A. Power save mode

    B. Association mode

    C. Active mode

    D. Passive mode

18. According to the IEEE 802.11 standard, an extended service set (ESS) consists of how many interconnected basic service sets?

    A. One or more

    B. Two or more

    C. Three or more

    D. Four or more

19. The association process happens after which phase?

    A. Authentication

    B. Distribution

    C. Deauthentication

    D. Reauthentication

20. A basic service set (BSS) consists of how many access points?

    A. 0

    B. 1

    C. 2

    D. 4

Answers to Review Questions

1. B. When a wireless client device listens for beacons it is performing passive scanning. Active scanning is sending a probe request. Authentication occurs after the probe phase. Power save puts the device into a low power state.

2. C. Dynamic rate switching (also called dynamic rate selection) allows a wireless LAN device to adjust data rates based on received signal. Dynamic frequency selection allows an access point to pick the best frequency to operate on based on the environment. Transmit power control automatically adjusts output power. Transmit save mode does not exist.

3. A. An IBSS uses no access points and is also known as peer-to-peer or ad hoc networking. A BSS uses one access point.

4. C. If a device is part of a peer-to-peer network it will connect to other like devices. An access point and a wireless switch are both infrastructure networking devices and will be part of either a BSS or ESS.

5. A. The data rate decreases as a wireless LAN device moves away from an access point. The data rates increase as a wireless LAN device moves closer to one access point. The output power does not change based upon the location of the wireless device in the radio range of the access point.

6. C. An SSID can be a maximum of 32 characters or octets and is also case-sensitive.

7. B. If access points on the same distribution system are set with different SSIDs, the client will lose the connection while roaming unless all SSIDs are set in the client utility. The channel is set by the access point and the BSSID is the MAC address of the AP radio.

8. C. Beacons are management frames and are used in the passive scanning process. Data frames carry data payload. Control frames reserve the medium and acknowledgement frames. Detail frames do not exist.

9. B. The client must authenticate to an access point before it can associate. After both authentication and association have been completed, the client is considered to be part of the BSS.

10. B. Moving throughout a location will cause a wireless client to roam from one access point to another. As part of the roaming process a client sometimes, but not always, needs to reauthenticate.

11. A, C. To successfully set up an ad hoc network, a user must know two parameters, the SSID and the RF channel it will be operating on. The BSSID is automatically generated in an ad hoc network. The BSSID is the MAC address of an AP radio; APs are not used in ad hoc networks. Protection mode does not apply to the situation.

12. B. Open system authentication uses two frames. The first frame is from the client to the access point and the second frame is from the access point back to the client. Shared key authentication uses four frames.

13. C. In 802.11b/g and mixed mode environments, throughput will be affected because of ERP protection mechanisms. Association and authentication are normal frames exchanged and do not affect throughput. HT protection mode is for 802.11n.

14. A, C. An SSID has a maximum of 32 characters or octets. SSIDs are case-sensitive.

15. A. The BSSID is the MAC address of the AP radio network adapter. This abbreviation is sometimes confused with SSID, which is a network name. The other MAC addresses are used in networking but are not representative of the BSSID.

16. B. A network consisting only of wireless client stations is an independent basic service set (IBSS). Other terms for this type of network are ad hoc and peer-to-peer. Infrastructure mode is a term used with a basic service set that consists of a single access point. Active and passive are scanning modes in which wireless devices to connect to a wireless network.

17. C. Because the computer is almost always plugged into an AC power source, it is unnecessary to have the device perform power save functions. Therefore active mode (sometimes referred to as continuous aware mode) is the best solution. Power save mode would work well for device that is on battery power and will help extend the battery life. Association and passive mode do not pertain to power save.

18. A. An ESS as stated in the IEEE 802.11 standard is one or more interconnected basic service sets.

19. A. In order for a wireless client to become part of a basic service set it must first authenticate, then associate. The distribution system is the network in which the access point is physically connected. Deauthentication and reauthentication occur when a client either logs off the wireless network or roams from one access point to another.

20. B. A BSS consists of only one access point. An IBSS has zero access points. A network with more than one access point would be considered an ESS.

Chapter

8

Planning a WLAN Site Survey

THE FOLLOWING CWTS EXAM OBJECTIVES ARE COVERED IN THIS CHAPTER:

✓ **Understand and describe the requirements to gather information prior to the site survey and do reporting after the site survey**

- Gathering business requirements

- Interviewing managers and users

- Defining physical and data security requirements

- Gathering site-specific documentation

- Documenting existing network characteristics

- Identifying infrastructure connectivity and power requirements

- Understanding RF coverage requirements

- Client connectivity requirements

- Antenna use considerations

This is the first of two chapters discussing wireless LAN site surveys. This chapter covers site survey planning and the business aspects related to a wireless LAN site survey, including gathering business requirements, interviewing the appropriate people, and gathering additional information regarding the site in which the network will be installed. Chapter 9, "Performing a WLAN Site Survey," will discuss the technical aspects of performing a site survey.

Early deployments for wireless LANs in many cases required a one-time site survey. This is because wireless LANs were fairly static and the radio frequency dynamics of the locations in which these networks were installed did not change much. However, due to the rapid pace at which wireless LAN technology and deployments are growing and the increasing use of other devices that use unlicensed radio frequency, site surveys can be an ongoing process for the areas where these wireless networks are installed. Although there are no set rules as to when or how wireless site surveys should be performed, there are guidelines that many manufacturers suggest based upon deployment scenarios for wireless networks that use their equipment. This chapter will look at requirements such as understanding the business requirements for the intended use of the wireless LAN and asking plenty of questions by interviewing department managers and users to help determine the applications and security requirements for the proposed network. Gathering information is a major part of a site survey to ensure a successful deployment. This chapter will also look at the importance of documentation of every step, from the design to the installation, and the validation of the wireless network.

Wireless LAN Site Surveys

The main objectives of a wireless LAN *site survey* are to find areas of *RF coverage* and interference sources as well as installation locations for hardware infrastructure devices such as access points, bridges, antennas, and any other devices that will be used with the wireless LAN. This will help ensure that applications to be used—both hardware and software—will be supported by the wireless network. Site surveys vary in complexity, depending on the organization or location in which a wireless network will be used.

As mentioned earlier, there is not a specific set of rules that must be followed, but many manufacturers of wireless LAN equipment have guidelines and suggestions when it comes to a site survey and where this survey fits into the process of design and implementation of the wireless network.

Knowing the expectations of the client or business in regard to the wireless LAN is a critical part of a successful deployment. To understand these client expectations, it is necessary to gather much information. This includes interviews and meetings with all those who will be affected by the deployment of the wireless LAN, which is nearly all departments of the company in most deployments.

The scope of the wireless LAN site survey is dependent on many factors, some of which include:

- Size of physical location
- Intended use of the network
- Number of users
- Performance expectations

Size of Physical Location

Depending on the size of the physical location in which the wireless network will be installed, a complete wireless LAN site survey may not be necessary. For example, a small sandwich shop wishes to offer free wireless Internet access as a convenience for its patrons who choose to have a meal there. This sandwich shop is approximately 1,200 square feet, has seating for about 15 people, and is located in a small street retail mall. In this case, a single access point would more than likely be sufficient for the number of users who access the wireless network at any one time and the type of data being sent across the access point. Although a full-blown site survey determining areas of RF interference coverage and interference would more than likely not be required, it would still be beneficial to visit the location and determine the best place for the access point. In a situation like this, a "site survey lite" may be all that is necessary. This would include testing the area to determine the best RF channel to use as well as access point mounting, consideration of aesthetics, and connecting to the wired network for access to the Internet. A larger deployment would require a more extensive site survey.

Intended Use of the Network

Looking at the sandwich shop scenario again, chances are the intended use of this wireless network will consist of patrons staying online for short periods of time and browsing the Internet or checking e-mail. It is unlikely many users would be performing any high-end or bandwidth intensive applications on this type of connection. Therefore, the one access point model would be sufficient for this deployment.

Number of Users

The number of users or devices that will be accessing a wireless network is a factor in determining the number of access points required, which in turn will determine the scope of a site survey. It has already been established that in our sandwich shop example a single access point would be sufficient based on the size of the location and the intended use of the network. However, as the number of actual users grows, the need for additional access points will also increase. In a case where more than one access point is required, a more extensive wireless site survey is also required.

Performance Expectations

Keeping in mind that wireless networks are half-duplex and contention-based, many factors will affect the performance of a wireless LAN, including the number of users, types of applications used, location, and number of infrastructure devices providing access. These infrastructure devices include access points and bridges. Part of a wireless LAN site survey includes defining what the customer expects for performance of the network. A mutual understanding of the factors that affect performance as well as how they will be dealt with is imperative from the beginning of the wireless LAN site survey process.

Gathering Business Requirements

Gathering information is typically the first step of a wireless LAN design and implementation. As mentioned, the business model or type of business where the wireless LAN will be deployed is a major part of deciding the level of a wireless LAN site survey. The type of business will determine the needs and use of a wireless network. Knowing the applications used—both hardware and software—is a critical part of a wireless LAN deployment as this will affect recommendations such as the number and locations of access points. Expectations can make or break a wireless LAN deployment. The expectations of the wireless network must be discussed, evaluated, and documented up front. To completely understand what the customer expects, you will need to gather information from various areas of the business. A high-quality site survey is going to require many questions to be asked and answered, including the following:

Bandwidth needs   How much bandwidth will be required for users of the wireless network?

Coverage area   In what rooms or areas of the buildings is wireless coverage expected?

Applications used   What type of applications—either hardware or software—are used at the facility?

Wireless devices used   What type of wireless devices will be used? These include notebook computers, handheld scanners, wireless phones, PDAs and tablet PCs.

Desired 802.11 technologies   What type of IEEE 802.11 technology would be the best suited to the specific environment? 802.11g, 802.11a or 802.11n?

Wireless networks were once considered extensions to wired networks providing access to a few users in areas exceeding the physical distance of Ethernet or other wired networks in place. Wireless LAN technology has grown tremendously over the past several years and is now a major part of every business, corporation, or company's computer network infrastructure. It is difficult to find any business that does not provide some type of wireless network access. Fully understanding the *business requirements* is part of a successful wireless LAN site survey and deployment.

General Office/Enterprise

Office buildings and other enterprise installation locations may consist of walled offices or open spaces with many cubicles. This type of installation usually will require infrastructure devices to aesthetically fit the environment and may require antennas to be mounted to drop ceilings with the access points located out of sight. Figure 8.1 shows an example of a floor plan for an office deployment.

FIGURE 8.1   A small office deployment using omnidirectional antennas

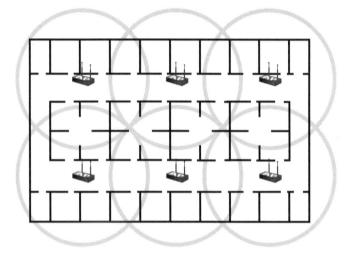

These deployments may have a high density of users and therefore require more access points to handle the load. The software and hardware applications used in these environments will need to be closely evaluated to ensure optimal performance for the user base. Chances are interference sources in this type of deployment would be limited mostly to computer networking. Radio frequency challenges may be limited.

Case study—Enterprise

A case study by Aruba Networks discusses a wireless LAN deployment for Ariba, a provider of enterprise commerce software systems.

Customer

- Ariba
- Commerce software
- Sunnyvale, California

Requirements

- Integrate a seamless 802.11 wireless solution without disrupting wired network
- Provide VPN support for a diverse OS environment, including Mac, Linux, and Windows clients
- Add centralized wireless management and RF spectrum management
- Scale to support hundreds of simultaneous users
- Ensure multilayered wireless security that addresses authentication, encryption, rogue AP detection, and policy management

Solution

- One Aruba MMC-5000 Mobility Controller
- 44 Aruba 52 dual-purpose 802.11a+b/g access points
- Three Aruba 800 Mobility Controllers
- ArubaOS Mobility Software

Benefits

- Enhanced user experience
- Centralized security and control for entire WLAN
- Remote RF visibility and monitoring
- Seamless integration with existing wired network

Read the complete case study, "ariba_case_study.pdf," on the CD included with this book.

Manufacturing

Deploying a wireless network in a manufacturing environment will not be as straightforward as general office/enterprise or other deployment types. Manufacturing environments have a completely different set of challenges, including equipment that operates in the 2.4 GHz ISM band, which means RF interference can be a major issue. In addition to interference, aspects of the structure itself such as high ceilings and large manufacturing facilities create mounting, accessibility, and RF signal concerns. Equipment installed in manufacturing facilities may have to withstand harsh environmental conditions such as extreme temperature, grease, and dirt.

Case study—Manufacturing

A case study by Trapeze Networks details a manufacturing deployment for Dutch firm Thomassen Compression Systems (TCS). A Trapeze wireless LAN solution was selected by this firm.

Customer

- Thomassen Compression Systems
- Manufacturing compression solutions
- The Netherlands

Objective

- Implement a wireless LAN solution that combines barcode scanning and wireless synchronization with the back office
- Provide real-time information to the company's enterprise resource planning (ERP) system
- Increase accuracy of data being entered into engineering and document management applications
- Improve level of automation in company's factory

Solution

- Trapeze wireless LAN Mobility System consists of 17 Trapeze Mobility Point access points and a central MX-200 Mobility Exchange controller.
- Trapeze RingMaster provides centralized wireless LAN planning, management, monitoring, and performance optimization without requiring RF expertise.
- Barcode scanners provide wireless synchronization with TCS's Isah ERP system.

Result

- Employees are making fewer errors and working more efficiently.
- All compression system parts are immediately registered using the Trapeze wireless LAN.
- The Trapeze wireless LAN helps integrate applications and monitor business processes based on real-time information.
- TCS is better able to manage the assembly and delivery process, and systems are now monitored in real time.
- Future plans for the wireless LAN include voice-over-wireless to further improve customer response times and reduce management costs.

Warehousing

Warehousing presents unique challenges for wireless networking. Like manufacturing environments, warehouses are typically large facilities with high ceilings, making for a potentially difficult site survey and deployment. In addition, one of the biggest concerns with warehousing deployments is the storage of products and materials. Certain types of product in large quantities, such as paint and other liquids, can cause RF behaviors such as refraction, absorption, and reflection, thereby affecting performance of the wireless network. Liquids, especially in large quantities, will have an absorbing effect on RF. Other products, such as those made of paper, will also have an impact. These issues should be evaluated closely as part of the site survey process for a warehouse implementation.

Case Study—Warehousing

Cellynne Corporation/STEFCO Industries selected Xirrus to deploy 802.11abg+n Wi-Fi Arrays across their Florida headquarters and manufacturing facility. A case study describes the details of this solution.

Customer

- Cellynne Corporation/STEFCO Industries
- Fully integrated paper manufacturer capable of processing pulp into a wide variety of premium paper and towel products
- Corporate Headquarters—Haines City, FL 33844

Objective

- Wireless network to deliver pervasive connectivity for wireless scanners on forklifts, handheld scanners, and notebook computers.
- Reliable Wi-Fi coverage throughout the offices, manufacturing, and distribution warehousing
- Easy to deploy and manage network
- Upgradeable infrastructure as business and technology needs change

Solution

- A Xirrus 802.11abg+n Wi-Fi Arrays across the Florida headquarters and manufacturing facility.

- The Xirrus Wi-Fi Array integrates up to 24 802.11abg+n radios coupled with a high-gain directional antenna system into a single device along with an onboard multi-gigabit switch, Wi-Fi controller, firewall, dedicated Wi-Fi threat sensor, and an embedded spectrum analyzer.
- Provides more than enough bandwidth, security, and control to replace switched Ethernet to the desktop as the primary network connection and results in 75% fewer devices, power, cabling, switch ports, and installation time than a traditional "thin" AP architecture.

Result

Using an array architecture with directional antennas eliminated the need for an additional 18 access points, cable runs, and switch ports. It also saved Cellynne Corporation/STEFCO Industries over 8600 kWh of energy each year.

- Reliable Wi-Fi platform for critical business applications
- Flexible Wi-Fi infrastructure as performance needs increase
- Secure Wi-Fi connection to protect against internal/external threats

Read the complete Cellynne Corporation/STEFCO Industries case study online by clicking the hyperlink on the CD included with this book.

Retail/Point of Sale (POS)

Retail and point of sale deployments may have some characteristics similar to those of the warehousing environment. In addition to a large quantity of products such as paper and liquids, there may be RF interference sources in businesses that sell appliances and electronics. The use or demonstration of items such as microwave ovens, two-way radios, consumer grade IEEE 802.11 access points, and computers may cause interference issues that need to be evaluated. Security is another major concern for this type of business in order to protect information such as credit card numbers and personal identification numbers (PINs).

Health Care/Medical

Health care deployments such as hospitals can be a challenging installation for many reasons. These environments will have both WLAN and non-WLAN devices that operate in the 2.4 GHz ISM band; therefore interference may be a critical factor for both the wireless LAN deployment and the other medical devices that use the same RF range. Some areas in hospitals—such as the intensive care unit, emergency room, or operating rooms—may have limitations on the type of wireless that may be installed, while others may require coverage throughout the entire hospital.

IEEE 802.11 wireless LAN technology has greatly improved the way hospitals function by allowing doctors, nurses, and lab technicians to use notebook computers as well as other portable devices while working with patients and staff members. In addition to aiding the hospital infrastructure, wireless LANs are used by patients and visitors quite extensively. This gives patients recovering at a hospital and their visitors the capability to use the Internet to access information.

Case study—Healthcare

A case study by Cisco Systems for Hennepin County Medical Center describes a wireless LAN deployment for the health care industry.

Customer

- Hennepin County Medical Center
- Health care
- Minneapolis, Minnesota

Challenge

- Improve hospital-wide communication, productivity, and patient care
- Increase bandwidth and RF coverage to support next-generation mobile applications and communication systems that improve clinical workflow
- Implement a unified wireless network supporting the needs of an integrated biomedical and IT department

Solution

- Unified wireless network simplified management and facilitated 802.11n upgrade.
- 802.11n access points support a wide range of bandwidth-intensive mobile devices and services over one secure unified wireless infrastructure.
- Wireless control system enables easy location of RF equipment throughout the hospital.

Results

- Improved staff communication, as well as accuracy, efficiency, and safety of patient care through increased bandwidth and coverage from 802.11n deployment
- Increased responsiveness of mobile clinicians and helped ensure business continuity by enhancing network reliability
- Improved management efficiency of the wireless network, maximizing biomedical and IT resources

Read and download the complete Hennepin County Medical Center case study online by clicking the hyperlink on the CD included with this book.

Government/Military

Government agencies and military installations also need to be taken into consideration for wireless networking. One of the biggest concerns for wireless LAN deployments in these environments is security. Some government or military agencies do not allow any wireless LAN access and have what is known as a "No Wi-Fi" policy. In a situation like this, a site survey is still required because the wireless LAN deployment, instead of allowing access to network resources, will keep all wireless access out.

For government and military agencies that do allow wireless access to resources and the Internet, security is of the utmost concern. Government and military installations may span large campuses similar to those in educational deployments such as universities and may require outdoor point-to-point or point-to-multipoint connections. In this case, an outdoor site survey will be required.

Case study—Government

A case study for the city of Gilroy, California, discusses an outdoor wireless deployment by Cisco Systems for public safety.

Customer

- City of Gilroy
- Municipal government
- Gilroy, California

Business Challenge

- Support real-time traffic monitoring system to improve traffic flow. Find more efficient way for mobile public safety vehicles to share information in the field.
- Enhance public image of the city's downtown.
- Provide broadband service capability for citizens in downtown.

Network Solution

- Deployed secure, flexible outdoor wireless network to support a variety of governmental and public-facing applications.

Business Results

- Improved traffic flow through busy intersections and overall driving experience in the city

- Improved the ability of public safety officers to take full advantage of mobile computing capabilities

- Helped enhance the city's reputation as a forward-thinking technological community

- Provided Wi-Fi public access for citizens

 Read and download the complete City of Gilroy case study online by clicking the hyperlink on the CD included with this book.

Education

Education deployments will vary in size and complexity. Some of the factors that play a role in educational wireless deployments include density and coverage. For example, a large university campus may have tens of thousands of students and thousands of access points covering many acres of land and many buildings.

Case study—Education

Motorola cites a case study of a deployment for education for the San Marino Unified School District, located in central Los Angeles County. In this deployment, indoor and outdoor coverage was required for the K–12 school district.

Customer

- San Marino Unified School District:
- K–12
- Schools: two elementary, one middle, one high school
- 3,200 students
- 300 staff members

Solution

- Motorola 802.11n WLAN
- AP-7131 Access Points
- AP-5181 Access Points for outdoor coverage
- Mesh football stadium coverage

Results

- High-speed campus-wide coverage
- Savings of $100 per Ethernet drop
- Streaming video

 NOTE   Read and download the complete San Marino Unified School District case study online by clicking the hyperlink on the CD included with this book.

Public Access, Hotspots, Hospitality

Public access, hotspots, and hospitality may need to accept connections from a wide variety of client devices, including IEEE 802.11b/g and 802.11a devices. In many cases, consumer brand notebook computers will be limited to 802.11b or 802.11b/g technology. Backward compatibility to these technologies is essential because the infrastructure will have no control over the type of client device that may connect. If backward compatibility is not taken into consideration, some devices may not be able to connect and use the wireless network.

Although many WLAN deployments should take these factors into consideration it is especially important in environments in which the infrastructure has little or no control over the client device population that may be connecting to the WLAN. This type of network includes public access installations such as hotels or resorts, restaurants, airports, arenas, and other small to large service businesses.

Case study—Hospitality

A case study for the American Airlines Center in Dallas, Texas, by Aruba Networks discusses an example of a wireless LAN deployment for the hospitality industry.

Customer

- American Airlines Center
- Sports and entertainment venue
- Dallas, Texas

Requirements

- Secure in-seat wireless concession application
- Provide on-demand 802.11 a/b/g service to media and visitors
- Use a single wireless network to provide different access and security rights to different users
- Provide centralized policy management for wired and wireless users

- Provide high-speed VPN termination of IPSec and PPTP tunnels
- Allow plug-and-play installation and automated configuration
- Support existing third-party APs already in use

Solution

- Aruba MMC-5000 Mobility Controller
- More than 50 Aruba AP-60/61 dual-purpose 802.11a/b/g APs
- ArubaOS Mobility Software, VPN Server, Adaptive Radio Management, and Wireless IDS

Benefits

- Reduced operational management and capital expense
- Plug-and-play deployment
- Per user roles and policies automatically enforced upon authentication
- Remote troubleshooting
- Secures third-party "thick" APs

Read the complete case study, "aa_center_case_study.pdf," on the CD included with this book.

Interviewing Managers and Users

Understanding the intended use of a wireless LAN is a critical part of a successful deployment. Who better to explain what the wireless network will be used for than those who will be using it? Those performing a site survey may not necessarily understand the functional aspects of a certain type of business, therefore it is critical to get input from all who will be using the wireless network. Department managers, team leads, and business unit managers usually know the function of their specific areas of the organization the best. Therefore they will also know the needs and requirements of users of the wireless network and how a successful deployment will help increase job productivity.

It is recommended to create some type of checklist or formal site survey questionnaire to use during the interview process. This will ensure specific details about the business and proposed wireless deployment are not missed. The use of such forms helps ensure uniform, repeatable interviews. These forms can also become part of the documentation and final deliverable that will be presented to the customer. Although there are some general questions that can be asked, there will be more specific questions based upon the business model of the organization or the wireless LAN to be installed.

A sample sensor placement site survey form is included on the CD that comes with this book.

Some generic interview questions that will pertain to most installations are as follows:

Has a site survey ever been performed in the past?   It is good to know if a site survey has previously been performed at a location. Although the previous site survey is only as good as the person who performed it, it may be beneficial and a timesaver to have some information available. Depending on when it was performed, a previous site survey report may not be accurate—physical changes to the location may have taken place—for example, additions of rooms or walls or changes to the interior design.

Are any blueprints, floor plans, or any other site-specific documentation available? Blueprints, floor plans, or other documentation about the location are very helpful in performing a site survey. If this information is not available it may have to be created, which in turn would create an additional expense for the customer. The accuracy of these documents needs to be considered in order to provide ideal site survey results.

How many users anticipate using the wireless network?   The number of expected users of the wireless network is valuable information to have. Knowing the number of users will help determine the amount of infrastructure equipment, such as access points and bridges, which will be required for the deployment. Discussing with department managers the number of users on the network as well as the number of working shifts will help provide adequate planning.

Will public access be required?   If public access to the network is required, that will potentially affect the number of infrastructure devices such as access points required for the deployment. In addition to the equipment, security and backward compatibility also need to be taken in consideration in this situation.

Is there any preference for a specific manufacturer's equipment?   It is a recommend practice for a site survey to be performed with the same manufacturer's equipment that will be used in the deployment. So understanding the customer's preference of manufacturer must be determined at the initial phases of the site survey. This will ensure good results based on the design of the wireless network.

What is the coverage area?   The intended coverage area of the facility also needs to be addressed. This helps provide a surveyor with information to accurately estimate how long a physical site survey may take and roughly estimate the amount of hardware required. Knowing the coverage area will also help determine any unexpected obstacles that may occur as part of the site survey process.

Is an existing wireless network in place?   If an existing wireless network is in place, it needs to be addressed as part of the site survey process. Questions need to be asked such as:

- What technology is in use?
- How many users?

- Where the access points?
- What is it used for?

Knowing the answers to these and other questions will help determine the role, if any, that the existing wireless network will play in the new deployment. Keep in mind some organizations may have a quite extensive existing wireless network and may be in the process of upgrading to newer technology. If this is the case, it will need to be determined if any of the existing network components can or will be used with the new deployment.

Are there any known areas of RF interference?   Information regarding known areas of RF interference is very useful in a site survey. It will save time if previous knowledge of RF interference is made available as part of the site survey process.

Are there any known areas that may lack RF coverage?   Just as previous knowledge of areas affected by RF interference is valuable, the lack of RF coverage in specific areas is also very good to know. This will help a surveyor determine any special situations that may be addressed during the site survey process. This may require testing of various types of antennas to help provide RF coverage in areas that are currently lacking.

What type of applications will be used?   It is important to know the types of applications that will be used. Applications—either software or hardware—will affect the load and number of access points or other infrastructure devices required. The surveyor should also become familiar with any special circumstances that may be required to support these applications.

Will voice or other applications that require quality of service (QoS) be used?   If applications (such as voice handsets) are planned for the location, this will have an impact on the site survey and design of the wireless network. Because these types of applications have greater requirements for signal quality and signal strength as well as roaming, this will need to be taken into consideration during the site survey. Additional density and more access points may be required.

Video over wireless LAN is another application that may require quality of service. Like voice, video is subject to latency and may involve special design requirements. Video over wireless LAN is used in applications ranging from sports venues to security surveillance and monitoring.

Is roaming required?   In most cases, the answer to this question is yes. This is especially true with networks that will be using voice handsets. Voice handsets are one of the most commonly used wireless LAN devices that require seamless roaming capabilities. Although notebook computers and PDAs may require roaming, voice and video applications are time bounded and subject to latency issues. Fast secure roaming may also be required. If roaming is required, the amount of overlap between RF cells would need to be closely looked at to ensure reliable sessions for the devices connected to the network.

Is Power over Ethernet (PoE) required?   Understanding the Power over Ethernet requirements is another essential part of the wireless LAN site survey. Knowing the capabilities as well as the number of devices expected to use PoE will play a role in the design and types of equipment used in the wireless network.

What are the wireless security requirements?   As much information as possible on the security requirements is very helpful with a site survey and design of the network. Some security solutions may require additional hardware or software that would have to be taken into account for the network design.

Will an escort be required?   In many cases, people are not allowed to roam freely throughout a business. An escort might be needed to walk through a location with a site surveyor. In addition, the escort and surveyor will need access to areas that may be locked or secure, such as wiring closets and computer rooms.

Are there any legislative compliance requirements?   Depending on the type of business in which the wireless network will be installed, there may be legislative or other compliance requirements. For example, medical institutions may need to meet HIPAA requirements, and retail establishments may require PCI compliance. These need to be taken into consideration as part of a wireless LAN site survey and deployment.

Manufacturer Guidelines and Deployment Guides

The information just presented includes some types of questions that need to be addressed during the site survey process. Keep in mind that the actual questions and details are dependent upon the business model and the implementation of the wireless network. Check with the specific manufacturer of the equipment to be used for site survey guidelines and deployment guides. These will provide additional information that is helpful in generating a list of questions and concerns that will need to be addressed.

Defining Physical and Data Security Requirements

Understanding the security requirements of both the physical environment and the user data is another design aspect of a wireless network. Because wireless LANs use RF to send and receive information such as computer data, wireless LANs are vulnerable to something known as *RF jamming*, which is caused by RF interference and can be either intentional or unintentional. As the name implies, RF jamming disrupts RF communications. If an intruder wants to wreak havoc in a wireless network, they can use an RF signal jammer to cause interference on the same RF bands used by the wireless network. The only way to protect against this kind of activity is through physical security. *Physical security* includes blocking RF signals from either entering or leaving a location. This could be done in a variety of ways—shielding materials can include metal, paint, or even wallpaper. If physical security is a concern where the wireless network will be installed, this needs to be taken into consideration during a site survey and design stages.

Due to situations beyond their control, some organizations may still require the use of legacy IEEE 802.11 security solutions for *data security*—ensuring that information such as computer data is received by the intended recipients without tampering during transit. This may include legacy hardware or software devices that have limited security capabilities. If legacy security solutions are used, special considerations may need to be taken into account from an infrastructure design perspective. This could mean using more access points or potentially using virtual local area network (VLAN) technology, which involves defining broadcast domains in a Layer 2 network. Other more advanced security solutions may require additional hardware or software for both the infrastructure and devices accessing the network.

Security solutions will be discussed in more detail in Chapter 10, "WLAN Security."

Gathering Site-Specific Documentation

Documentation for the location where a wireless network will be installed will make a surveyor's job much easier and result in a better overall deployment. Drawings and other documentation pertaining to the following list can provide valuable information:

- Floor plans
- Blueprints
- Proposed location of furnishings
- Electrical specifications

Floor Plans and Blueprints

Gathering any site-specific documentation that exists, such as floor plans or blueprints, is very helpful for a site survey. This documentation is useful to a variety of individuals who will be participating in a wireless LAN design and deployment. The documentation can be used during a physical or predictive RF site survey and spectrum analysis to note areas of importance. Having floor plans and blueprints available allows a surveyor to document specific parts of a site survey such as location of access points and other wireless devices. If a predictive modeling site survey is used, an electronic version of a floor plan can be imported into the software program to help streamline the surveyor's job. Blueprints or floor plans will also help those who install cable and mount hardware and if necessary can be provided to electricians for AC power installation.

Furnishings

The proposed types and location of furnishings or other items that may affect RF signal propagation or penetration are also good to know if the information is available. This will help during the design and site survey phase to determine access point locations and pinpoint other things that may affect RF signals, such as reflection, refraction, diffraction, and absorption.

Be sure to gather information about the following:

- In an office or enterprise environment, furnishings may consist of desks, cabinets, chairs, and other items.

- In warehousing and retail environments, furnishings will include storage racks and shelving as well as product inventories.

- In manufacturing environments, information should be gathered about the location of industrial equipment used in the manufacturing process and about equipment used to move product throughout the factory.

- In medical environments, furnishings or equipment will include devices that may cause interference and operate in the same frequency range as the proposed wireless network. Storage of items used within the hospital or medical environment for patients and employees may also affect RF coverage.

These are just some examples of the types of furnishings and other items that may affect a wireless LAN deployment and should be taken into consideration.

Electrical Specifications

Documentation of the electrical specifications of the environment is helpful in determining whether the current electrical implementation will be sufficient to handle the proposed wireless network deployment. This will allow the site survey process to determine if any upgrades need to be made in order to support devices that may be using Power over Ethernet or if the existing infrastructure is sufficient. It is best to gather information regarding electrical power sources, electrical panel information, existing wiring, and location of electrical outlets.

Documenting Existing Network Characteristics

Documentation is a major part of any business, and computer networks are no exception. In order to have a successful deployment of a wireless network, it is critical to know the details of the *existing network infrastructure* as well as future implementations, upgrades, and modifications. These existing infrastructures may include a wired or wireless network already in place and functioning that may be upgraded or in a new deployment.

Documentation of networks is usually the responsibility of the IT department. Some organizations may lack good documentation of the existing network infrastructure. If this is the case, additional work may be required prior to starting a wireless site survey.

Existing wireless networks   One of the questions that must be asked during the interview process is to determine the scope of any existing wireless networks. If a wireless network does exist (as it often does) it will need to be dealt with during the site survey and design procedure. The questions that are asked regarding the existing wireless network will help determine the role it is going to play. If the existing network is going to remain in place, understanding its technical details and how to work it into the design of the new or upgraded deployment will help create a successful and productive wireless LAN deployment.

Existing wired networks   In addition to knowing of any existing wireless networks, it is also important to know about the wired network infrastructure. Any existing documentation on the wired network infrastructure will help streamline the process for connecting in the wireless components of the network. The wired infrastructure is discussed in more detail in the next section of this chapter.

Identifying Infrastructure Connectivity and Power Requirements

Why are there so many wires in wireless networking? From data connectivity to providing electrical power, wireless networks require some type of wired infrastructure for many reasons, including connecting access points together, allowing user access to network resources, providing access to a wide area network, Internet connectivity, and to supply electrical power.

Network infrastructure connectivity plays a big role in wireless networking. A wireless LAN site survey will require additional information about the network infrastructure and power requirements. In a sense, a wireless site survey also requires a wired or infrastructure survey. Some of the information regarding the wired network includes:

- Location of wiring closets
- Wired infrastructure network devices in use
- Connection speed between sites
- Electrical power requirements

Location of wiring closets   A *wiring closet* is a room (usually secured) containing electrical power and cabling for voice and data that is terminated and connected to infrastructure devices such as switches and routers. Knowing not only the physical locations of wiring closets but also the capacity of existing infrastructure devices is good information to have when it comes to deploying a wireless network. This is because wired connections such as

IEEE 802.3 Ethernet have limitations for cable lengths, and infrastructure devices such as access points and bridges will have to be placed within the physical limitations of infrastructure connectivity. For example, the IEEE 802.3 Ethernet standard has a physical maximum of 328 feet (or 100 meters) cable length for unshielded twisted pair wiring.

In addition to cable length, feasibility of running the Ethernet cable from the wiring closet to the desired location must also be taken into consideration. For example, the intended location for an access point may be on a ceiling without any access from above. In this case, lack of accessibility could pose a problem for installation of the Ethernet cabling from the wiring closet and or AC power to the devices.

Wired infrastructure network devices in use   The wired infrastructure devices in use may have an impact on a successful deployment of a wireless LAN. An evaluation of the infrastructure devices by a wireless LAN site surveyor or a network infrastructure professional may be required to determine if any additional hardware or changes must be made prior to deploying a wireless LAN. If the infrastructure devices, such as Layer 2 switches and routers, are not adequate to support a new wireless deployment, additional hardware may need to be purchased.

Connection speed between sites   The connection speeds and type of connections between sites should be evaluated to determine any bottlenecks that could affect the overall network performance. Placement of authentication servers and other network resources may be affected by the speed of these links.

Electrical power   Since all wireless LAN infrastructure devices including access points, bridges and wireless switches require an AC power source and these devices may be supplying Power over Ethernet to the infrastructure devices, verification of an adequate AC power supply must be performed. The AC power sources are sometimes taken for granted or not taken into consideration, which could pose a problem during the installation phase.

Because PoE is used not only in infrastructure devices, but also with IP telephones, cameras, and other user devices, it may be necessary to perform calculations and verify that the power supply to the wiring closet will be adequate to support the powered infrastructure (including the PoE devices). Electrical components of a wiring closet may need to be upgraded to support a new wireless LAN deployment. Newer wireless LAN technologies such as 802.11n MIMO systems may require more DC power than is currently available with standardized PoE, based on the IEEE 802.3af amendment to the Ethernet standard. If these technologies will be used, the power requirements will need to be carefully considered to verify enough DC power will be available to the end powered devices. Some manufacturers are currently providing IEEE 802.3at draft (providing new PoE capabilities) endpoint or midspan devices to provide the necessary amount of DC voltage. Others are providing 802.11n access points that are single band and 802.3af compliant. Some manufacturers claim the capability to power dual band 802.11n access points with standard 802.3af power. This will likely result in decreased performance or limited functionality of the AP.

Understanding RF Coverage and Capacity Requirements

A major aspect of a wireless LAN site survey is to understand and verify the RF coverage and capacity requirements based on the network design. In Chapter 4, "Radio Frequency (RF) Fundamentals for Wireless LAN Technology," we discussed coverage versus capacity and the differences between them. A wireless LAN site surveyor will need to verify these requirements as part of the site survey. This can be accomplished either manually or automatically through a predictive process, both to be discussed in more detail in Chapter 9.

To review, the wireless coverage and capacity requirements are going to depend on several factors such as:

- Physical size of the area to be covered
- Number of users or devices accessing the wireless network
- Software or hardware applications in use
- Obstacles and propagation factors based on the environment
- Radio frequency range of the network to be installed
- Wireless LAN hardware to be used
- Output power of the transmitters
- Receive sensitivity of the receivers

In addition to an RF coverage analysis, an *RF spectrum analysis* will also be beneficial. An RF spectrum analysis allows a site surveyor to view areas of RF coverage as well as interference sources. This will be discussed further in Chapter 9. Although a spectrum analysis is not required, it does allow a site surveyor to view sources of RF in the locations where a wireless LAN will be deployed.

Client Connectivity Requirements

Client devices that will be connecting to the wireless LAN also need to be considered as part of a site survey. This includes knowing the radio type, antenna type, gain, orientation, portability, and mobility of the device. Understanding the type and function of client devices will have an impact on the design of the wireless network. Common wireless client devices include:

- Notebook computers
- PDAs
- Pocket computers
- Barcode scanners

- Point of sale devices
- Voice handsets

Other wireless devices used in various wireless LAN applications include but are not limited to:

- Desktop computers
- Print servers
- Manufacturing equipment
- Security cameras

Many environments have both desktop and notebook computers as client devices. These devices may or may not require roaming capability. Office and enterprise deployments commonly use handsets for voice communications. Although it is fairly difficult to take all potential client devices into consideration, it is best to understand the type of devices that will be used. This information can be obtained through the interview process and the gathering information stage of the site survey.

Antenna Use Consideration

In Chapter 6, "WLAN Antennas and Accessories," we discussed various types of antennas and accessories. The antenna used in any deployment will depend on the specific scenario. As part of the site survey various antenna types may need be used for testing purposes to determine the best antenna for a specific application. In some cases, the customer may want a specific type of antenna, such as omnidirectional mounted directly to the access points. Others may be using lightweight access points without external antenna capabilities. Some businesses are concerned about aesthetics and are particular about the appearance of an antenna and the mounting location. The proper antenna selection will ensure correct coverage as intended by the design and site survey of the wireless LAN. The antenna type used will determine the propagation pattern of the radio frequency and is a significant part of a successful wireless LAN deployment. The antenna used in various deployments will depend on the business model in which the network is installed. Listed are some examples of the business models discussed earlier in this chapter and the type of antennas and may be used in these implementations:

General office/enterprise   General office/enterprise solutions usually require complete coverage throughout the entire location. In many cases, this type of installation will require access points mounted out of sight and aesthetically pleasing antennas. This could be an omnidirectional antenna mounted to a ceiling tile or integrated within a lightweight access point.

Manufacturing   Manufacturing environments are usually industrial facilities with high ceilings and various types of manufacturing and industrial equipment. These environments may use a combination of omnidirectional and semidirectional antennas due to the physical architecture of the buildings. The antennas also may need to withstand harsh environmental conditions such as extreme temperature fluctuations and dirt.

Warehousing Warehousing implementations have some characteristics in common with manufacturing. The buildings that house this type of business are in many cases large open areas with high ceilings allowing the storage of large volumes of product and equipment. Antenna mounting needs to be looked at very closely to ensure equipment such as forklifts used to move product do not come in contact with antennas. Warehousing also may use a combination of omnidirectional and semi-directional antennas for proper coverage. Figure 8.2 shows a sample floor plan for a combination small office/warehouse deployment using a combination of omnidirectional and semidirectional antennas.

FIGURE 8.2   Small office/warehouse floor plan showing RF coverage using various antenna types

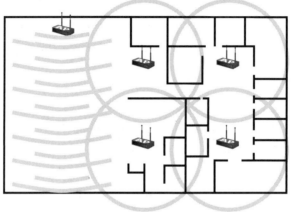

Retail/point of sale (POS)   Retail/point of sale installations may have to accommodate publicly accessible areas as well as warehousing and storage in the back of the buildings. In this type of installation, antennas are going be a combination of omnidirectional and semi-directional. The devices may consist of computers as well as other handhelds such as barcode scanners or portable devices. Appropriate antenna selection and gain need to be considered to ensure the devices have good signal connectivity to the infrastructure. In many cases, the public areas will require aesthetics to be taken into account when it comes to antenna selection. In the storage part of the building, antennas are similar to those described in warehousing.

Health care and medical   Many health care and medical deployments are publicly accessible, therefore aesthetics and security are both important. Antenna types that fit the environment and are not accessible to the public are commonly used. Some health care facilities, such as hospitals, may require the use of only omnidirectional antennas mounted to the autonomous access point or integrated in a lightweight access point. Others may allow semidirectional antennas such as Yagis to cover long hallways and corridors.

Government and military   Government and military wireless environments are usually not publicly accessible and in many cases are campus-based and require outdoor solutions as well as indoor. In these installations, antennas mounted directly to an access point or semidirectional antennas may well fit the environment. For outdoor point-to-point or point-to-multipoint, highly directional antennas such as parabolic dish may be required.

Education   Education deployments are typically campus-based and may require the use of outdoor antennas to link buildings together. However, for indoor solutions, ensuring the antennas will fit the environment and not be tampered with need to be evaluated. These deployments may use a combination of omnidirectional and semidirectional antenna types. Some locations may require the use of enclosures for the infrastructure devices to ensure security of the physical devices. In these cases special connectors and antenna adapters may be required.

Public access, hotspot, hospitality   Public access, hotspot, and hospitality sites are publicly accessible locations that will require aesthetics and security when it comes to antenna selection, as with some of the previous examples. These deployments may use a combination of omnidirectional, semidirectional, and highly directional antennas.

🌐 Real World Scenario

Typical Steps Used in a Wireless LAN Site Survey

Listed are some basic common steps to provide an overview of the wireless LAN site survey process.

1. **Gathering information and discussing business requirements**

    Determine the need and intended use of the wireless LAN and interview appropriate individuals. Explain the site survey process and provide an overview of wireless networking.

2. **Project timeline and planning**

    Understand and document the extent and estimated timeline of the survey process and deployment.

3. **Wireless LAN design**

    Determine areas of RF coverage and interference as well as potential placement of access points and other infrastructure devices.

4. **RF spectrum analysis and RF testing**

    Perform testing of the proposed design and verify RF sources of interference. Also verify coverage and lack of coverage.

5. **Deployment of infrastructure devices**

    Install infrastructure devices as described by the design.

6. **Verification of RF coverage**

    Perform verification testing and spot checks of RF coverage per the design. Make necessary adjustments based on the results of RF testing.

7. **Support**

    Provide technical support for wireless LAN deployment.

Summary

In this chapter, we discussed the business aspects of wireless LAN site surveys. We looked at the objective of a site survey, which is to find areas of RF coverage, interference, and hardware installation locations. We considered the factors determining the complexity of a site survey. These factors include:

- Size of physical location
- Intended use of network
- Number of users
- Performance expectations

This chapter also discussed the importance of gathering information as well as the type of information required to successfully perform a wireless LAN site survey and design of a wireless network. We looked at several examples of deployment scenarios and case studies from different manufacturers of wireless LAN equipment as to the benefits and solutions of a wireless LAN deployment, which is the result of a successful site survey.

It is necessary to completely understand the expectations of how the network will perform in the environment prior to a wireless LAN deployment. These expectations will be met by asking the correct questions of the right people—managers and users of the wireless network—since they are the ones who will be using it. This chapter discussed the types of questions that may be asked to provide information that will allow for a successful wireless LAN site survey and deployment.

This chapter also discussed taking into consideration the physical and data security requirements of the wireless network. This is part of a site survey because it will have an impact on the final design, including the number of access points and the physical and data security solutions. Having the appropriate documentation is a key element to a successful deployment. If documents such as floor plans and blueprints are not available they may need to be created as part of the site survey and design process and may require additional cost for the customer. Accurate documentation will also help streamline some of the site survey process and deployment of a wireless LAN hardware. Accurate documentation will help with the installation of cabling and access points and minimize questions about the installation.

It is essential to know the location and type of existing networks, both wired and wireless. If existing wireless networks are in place, it will need to be determined what role, if any, they will play in the new deployment or upgrade. Identifying the location of wiring closets and determining power requirements are two other important tasks in a site survey.

This chapter discussed RF coverage requirements and the factors to be taken into consideration to ensure proper coverage throughout the location where the wireless network is installed. Finally, client connectivity requirements and other considerations were discussed. The types of client devices that will be used, such as notebook computer, PDA, or barcode scanner, must be evaluated. Antenna orientation to ensure correct polarization will need to be considered during the site survey process. We also looked at the type of antennas commonly used in particular deployment scenario.

Exam Essentials

Understand the business requirements of a WLAN. Be familiar with the necessary business information required for successful wireless LAN site survey. These business requirements include bandwidth needs, expected coverage area, and hardware and software applications used in devices and technologies.

Know various types of business models. Understand that the site survey process will vary based upon the business model in which a wireless LAN is deployed. These will include enterprise, manufacturing, health care, and public access, to name a few.

Understand the interview process. Know whom to interview and the type of questions to ask during the site survey and design process. This will help ensure a more successful wireless LAN deployment.

Identify the importance of site-specific documentation. Know the different types of documentation required based on the business model for the wireless LAN site survey. This includes blueprints and floor plans as well as other important documentation.

Know the importance of identifying existing networks. Understand the details of existing wired and wireless networks and be able to define the characteristics of both, such as wiring closet location and power requirements.

Be familiar with RF coverage requirements. Know the factors involved with providing adequate RF coverage within a wireless LAN deployment.

Understand client connectivity requirements. Know the various types of clients or devices that will use the wireless LAN based on a specific business model.

Identify proper antenna use. Know the different types of antennas that may be used based on site survey results within a specific deployment. Understand that the type of antenna used will depend on the implementation in which the network is installed.

Key Terms

business requirements

data security

existing network infrastructure

physical security

RF coverage

RF jamming

RF spectrum analysis

site survey

wiring closet

Review Questions

1. The main objectives of a wireless site survey are to determine _____ and
   _____. (Choose two.)

   A. RF coverage

   B. Cost of equipment

   C. RF interference

   D. Manufacturer's equipment

   E. Which client devices to purchase

2. What factor determines whether a site survey is required?

   A. Number of access points

   B. Geographic location of business

   C. Number of wiring closets

   D. Number of servers on site

3. The first step of a wireless LAN site survey is typically _____.

   A. Determining the RF coverage

   B. Installing access points

   C. Gathering business requirements

   D. Documenting existing networks

   E. Interviewing managers and users

4. Enterprise wireless LAN deployments commonly use _____ antennas for most
   installations.

   A. Omnidirectional

   B. Semidirectional

   C. Yagi

   D. Parabolic dish

5. You are a wireless network engineer contracted to perform a site survey for a company that
   manufactures widgets. The site survey will require a physical walk-through of the area. One
   concern in this implementation is interference from existing _____.

   A. Wireless 3G internet devices

   B. Cellular telephones

   C. 900 MHz two-way radios

   D. 2.4 GHz ISM band devices

   E. CB radios

6. Implementations that may have existing non-WLAN devices that will potentially interfere with a 2.4 GHz wireless LAN deployment most likely fall under what business model?

   A. Office

   B. Government

   C. Health care

   D. Education

7. You are hired to perform a wireless LAN site survey for a large enterprise company with over a thousand employees. You need to come up with a list of questions to ask users of the wireless network. Which question would be the most relevant for the user community?

   A. Where are the wiring closets?

   B. Do you have any floor plans available?

   C. What applications do you use?

   D. Do you have an equipment manufacturer preference?

   E. What is the RF coverage area?

8. A wireless LAN site survey and design includes defining _____ and _____ security requirements to help protect against RF jamming and protect the integrity of information. (Choose two.)

   A. Physical

   B. Access point

   C. Data

   D. Device

   E. Infrastructure

9. Which device is the best candidate to use the roaming features of an IEEE 802.11g wireless computer network?

   A. Notebook computer

   B. PDA

   C. Voice handset

   D. Wireless camera

10. Which is a main factor in determining the number of access points required for an IEEE 802.11g wireless LAN deployment?

   A. Type of client devices in use

   B. Number of client devices

   C. Manufacturer of client devices

   D. Antennas in client devices

11. Interviewing managers and users will help determine which part of the site survey process?

   A. Performance expectations

   B. Locations of UNII band interference

   C. Creating floor plans

   D. Locations of access points

12. Which of the following can be imported into a commercial site survey program to assist in predicting the RF coverage of access points?

   A. Electrical specifications

   B. Access point models

   C. Bandwidth requirements

   D. Floor plans

   E. Cost estimates

13. Warehouse inventory such as paint and other liquids in large quantities can cause which RF behavior?

   A. Reflection

   B. Refraction

   C. Diffraction

   D. Absorption

   E. Scattering

14. You are a wireless LAN consultant contracted to assist in a site survey for a retail outlet that will deploy an 802.11g WLAN. You've been asked to participate in an initial meeting with top management to determine the details of a site survey. What topics would most likely be discussed at this meeting? (Choose two.)

   A. Business requirements

   B. Available antenna types

   C. Recommended manufacturer hardware

   D. Bill of materials

   E. Applications in use

   F. Purpose of WLAN

15. A wireless LAN will be deployed in a hospital. Which criteria would be addressed when discussing a potential RF jamming attack?

   A. Data security

   B. Access point security

   C. Physical security

   D. Infrastructure security

   E. Wiring closet security

16. You are a wireless LAN consultant hired to perform a site survey for a hotel. You need to interview the management and staff regarding the proposed installation of the wireless network. Which is an appropriate question to ask the hotel manager?

    A. Is PoE used in the hotel?

    B. What are the aesthetic requirements?

    C. Which areas lack RF coverage?

    D. Which areas have RF interference?

17. Which of the following will be the most likely reason in determining the number of access points required for a wireless LAN deployment?

    A. Applications used

    B. Security requirements

    C. Equipment manufacturer

    D. Ceiling height

18. RF coverage of access points depends on which factor?

    A. Wiring closet location

    B. Access point output power

    C. Electrical power requirements

    D. Floor plans and blueprints

19. Which of the following is *not* a requirement for the initial gathering of technical information for a wireless LAN site survey in a new deployment scenario?

    A. Number of users

    B. Applications in use

    C. Other wireless networks

    D. Cost of equipment

20. Which wireless LAN deployment scenario uses mostly omnidirectional antennas mounted directly to an access point?

    A. Manufacturing

    B. Warehousing

    C. Office building

    D. Sports arena

Answers to Review Questions

1.   A, C. The purpose of a wireless site survey is to find areas of RF coverage and interference and to determine placement of equipment such as access points and bridges. The cost of equipment and selection of manufacturer also play a role but are not part of the site survey objective.

2.   A. The number of required access points is a good gauge whether a site survey is required. The geographic location of the business, number of wiring closets, and the number of servers do not determine if a site survey is required.

3.   C. Typically the first step of a wireless LAN site survey is to gather the necessary business requirements. Interviewing managers and users is the next step, followed by determining RF coverage and documenting existing networks. Installing access points is one of the final steps.

4.   A. Enterprise wireless LAN deployments typically use omnidirectional antennas connected directly to an access point. Other antenna types may be used but are not as common in this type of deployment.

5.   D. Manufacturing environments typically use equipment that interferes with devices in the 2.4 GHz ISM band. Wireless 3G and cellular telephones work in other frequency ranges and do not affect wireless LANs. 900 MHz is not used by IEEE 802.11 wireless networks. CB radios work at a different frequency range.

6.   C. Health care locations typically have equipment that works in the 2.4 GHz ISM band. These devices could potentially cause interference with a wireless network that operates in this band. Office, government, and education installations will not have as much ISM equipment.

7.   C. The type of applications—either hardware or software—that will be used on the wireless network will have a large impact on the final deployment. This is an important question to ask end users. The other questions also need to be answered, but should be asked of managers and IT staff.

8.   A, C. Physical and data security requirements are part of a wireless LAN site survey. These requirements may have an impact on the number of access points or other devices required for the network. Access point, device, and infrastructure security also plays a role but is typically not considered part of an initial site survey.

9.   C. Of all the devices listed, the voice handset would be the best candidate that would use roaming features of a wireless network, mostly because of mobility and features. Notebook computers and PDAs may have roaming capabilities, but these devices are not as sensitive to latency. Wireless cameras are usually stationary devices.

10.   B. The number of devices is an important determining factor in the number of access points required for a wireless LAN deployment. The type and manufacturer of devices are not concerns. The antenna in a client device will help with providing and maintaining device connectivity.

11. A. Interviewing managers and users will help determine the performance expectations of the wireless LAN because they are the ones who will be using it and they have the best understanding of the needs of an organization. Locations of RF interference and access points are part of the network design stage, which takes place after the gathering of information stage. In most cases, creating floor plans is not a primary responsibility of a site survey; however, obtaining floor plans is significant.

12. D. Floor plans of facilities can sometimes be imported into site survey software programs. This helps in determining the RF propagation by placing access points in a simulated environment. Access point models as well as cost estimates are required at a later time in a site survey.

13. D. Storage of paint and other liquids in large quantities can cause RF to be absorbed.

14. A, F. The business requirements and purpose of the wireless LAN are two areas that would be discussed at an initial meeting regarding a site survey. The other topics will be discussed at a later time.

15. C. An RF jamming attack would fall under physical security. Access point security, infrastructure security, and wiring closet security do not involve RF jamming. Data security is a separate issue.

16. B. The aesthetic requirements are usually discussed with hotel management since they are the ones responsible for the appearance of the hotel. PoE requirements and RF coverage and interference would be questions for a different group, which in some cases may be an outside provider.

17. A. The applications used will determine the number of access points in a wireless LAN deployment. Bandwidth-intensive applications may require more access points. Security requirements are important but typically do not strongly affect the number of access points required. Ceiling height is a factor when determining the RF coverage, not necessarily the number of infrastructure devices.

18. B. Access point output power is a determining factor in what type of coverage the AP will provide. Wiring closet locations and electrical power requirements are more related to wired infrastructure connectivity. Floor plans and blueprints will be used to note access point locations.

19. D. The initial gathering of information includes number of users, applications and their use, and other wireless networks in the area. The cost of the proposed equipment is not usually addressed at this point.

20. C. Office building deployments commonly use omnidirectional antennas that are mounted directly to an access point. Manufacturing, warehousing, and sports arenas deployments more often use a combination of omnidirectional, semidirectional, and sometimes highly directional antennas.

Chapter

9

Performing a WLAN Site Survey

THE FOLLOWING CWTS EXAM OBJECTIVES ARE COVERED IN THIS CHAPTER:

✓ **Define the need for and use of a spectrum analyzer in a manual site survey**

- Identification and location of interference sources
- Differentiation of Wi-Fi and non-Wi-Fi interference sources

✓ **Define the need for and the use of a manual site survey tool and differentiate between the following manual site survey types**

- Active surveys
- Passive surveys

✓ **Differentiate between manual and predictive site surveys**

- Advantages and disadvantages of each site survey methodology

✓ **Define the need for and use of a protocol analyzer in a manual site survey as it relates to the following**

- Identifying, locating, and assessing nearby WLANs

✓ **Differentiate between site surveys involving networks with and without a mesh access layer**

✓ **Define and differentiate between the following WLAN system architectures and understand site survey concepts related to each architecture. Identify and explain best practices for access point placement and density.**

- Multiple channel architecture (MCA)
- Single channel architecture (SCA)

✓ **Identify limitations on hardware placement**

- Areas where APs or antennas cannot be placed

- Areas beyond Ethernet distance limitations

✓ **Understand industry best practices for optimal use of directional and omnidirectional antennas in site surveys**

This is the second of two chapters on the subject of wireless LAN site surveys.

In Chapter 8, "Planning a WLAN Site Survey," we looked at the business aspects of a site survey, which included gathering of information such as the business requirements for the wireless network, interviewing managers and users, and gathering site-specific documentation. It is important to have all the necessary groundwork prior to starting a physical site survey. Having all the correct information in hand will allow for a complete and thorough site survey, which in turn will result in a successful wireless LAN deployment.

In this chapter, we will look at some of the components of performing a site survey, including determining areas of RF interference by using a spectrum analyzer. Taking into consideration both Wi-Fi and non-Wi-Fi interference sources and understanding how this interference will affect the deployment are also important parts of performing a site survey. This chapter will take a look at different types of site surveys, both manual and predictive. We will discuss the two types of manual site surveys, passive and active, and show the advantages and disadvantages of both manual and predictive site surveys. Understanding the steps involved and the details of each site survey type will help a wireless LAN engineer determine the best methodology to use. This chapter will look at some of the tools that may be used in a site survey, including wireless protocol analyzers and scanners. Finally, we will look at the two different types of channel architectures and best practices for hardware placement, including access points and antennas, as well as some of the limitations you may encounter during the physical site survey process.

The Physical Site Survey Process

After all the up-front work is completed, such as gathering of information, including the business requirements and site-specific documentation, defining physical and data security requirements, and interviewing managers and users, it is time to start the physical site survey process. This is one of the most important parts of a successful wireless LAN deployment. This process includes locating areas and sources of RF interference, RF coverage areas (or lack thereof) and determining the locations of access points, bridges, sensors, and other infrastructure devices that will be used in the network. The following sections detail the entire physical site survey process and guidelines. The physical site survey is very subjective and people have different opinions on how the entire process works. In many cases, this process can be tailored based on the individual needs or requirements of the location where the wireless LAN will be installed. The following steps should be viewed as recommendations or guidelines:

1. Arrange a walkthrough of the entire location

2. Take thorough notes

3. Perform RF spectrum analysis

4. Determine preliminary placement of infrastructure devices

5. Perform on-site testing

6. Determine actual placement of infrastructure devices

7. Install infrastructure hardware as specified

8. Perform on-site verification testing and make adjustments

9. Deliver final report

In today's wireless world, an RF site survey can be considered an ongoing process. Just a few years ago, not nearly as many wireless networks existed as do today, so the interference factor was not as significant. With the RF dynamics constantly changing and more devices using RF for communications, it is up to the network engineer to take into consideration that site requirements may also be constantly changing. Therefore the RF site survey may need to be updated periodically.

RF Spectrum Analysis

The wireless LAN site survey includes finding areas of RF coverage and RF interference as well as locations for hardware such as access points, bridges, and other infrastructure devices. Although radio frequency is not visible to the human eye, some tools are available to "see" a visual representation of the RF. A common tool is the RF *spectrum analyzer.* Figure 9.1 shows a spectrum analyzer view of the 2.4 GHz ISM band with the access point set to channel 6. Spectrum analyzers will vary in cost and complexity depending on the frequency ranges they are designed to work with.

Some spectrum analyzers are available that are designed specifically for the wireless LAN market. These usually will work only in the license-free radio bands and are typically less expensive because of spectrum limitations. Spectrum analyzers allow us to view the physical layer of communication between devices used in wireless networking. WLAN spectrum analyzers are available in PC card models, devices that attach to a USB port on the computer, and instrumentation style devices that can be used for applications other than wireless networking. Figure 9.2 shows an example of a WLAN spectrum analyzer that connects to a USB port on a computer.

FIGURE 9.1   Chanalyzer v3.2 shows RF capture of access point on channel 6

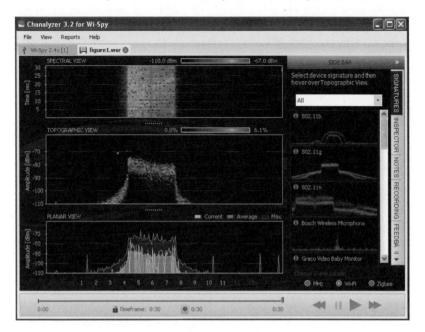

FIGURE 9.2   Wi-Spy DBx spectrum analyzer by MetaGeek for 802.11a/b/g/n networks operating in the 2.4 GHz and 5 GHz frequency ranges

Some manufacturers of wireless LAN equipment integrate spectrum analyzer tools into devices such as wireless LAN switches/controllers for constant monitoring of the radio frequency. Others offer stand-alone products that can be used to monitor more specific areas. Listed are some manufacturers of WLAN spectrum analyzers:

Product	Website
AirMagnet Spectrum Analyzer	www.airmagnet.com
Cisco Spectrum Expert	www.cisco.com
Fluke Networks AnalyzeAir	www.flukenetworks.com
Motorola AirDefense	www.airdefense.net
Wi-Spy by MetaGeek	www.metageek.net

The ability to analyze the RF allows a site surveyor to find areas that lack coverage, also known as *dead spots*, as well as interference caused by other devices and other wireless networks that operate in the same radio frequency range. Although a spectrum analysis is not a requirement, it is beneficial in most medium to large-scale deployments of wireless networks. Due to the vast number of devices that use unlicensed radio bands, spectrum analysis can be considered an ongoing process. Performing regular spectrum analysis gives wireless LAN engineers the capability to monitor the area in which wireless LAN devices are located for RF interference and other issues. Figure 9.3 shows an example of a PC card spectrum analyzer designed for wireless networks.

FIGURE 9.3   AirMagnet Spectrum Analyzer

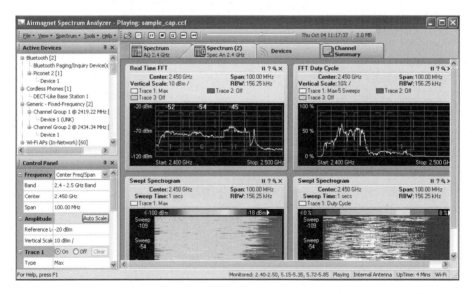

Wi-Fi and Non-Wi-Fi Interference Sources

The performance of wireless networks can be significantly affected by various types of interference sources. Interference may be either intentional or unintentional and caused both by wireless networks and by other devices that also operate in the 2.4 GHz ISM or 5 GHz UNII band. The use of portable and mobile devices that employ radio frequency for communication is on the rise, so interference from these devices is also more prevalent. As mentioned in previous chapters of this book, these interfering devices typically operate in the unlicensed radio spectrum 2.4 GHz ISM band. Other sources of interference from the industrial, medical, and scientific communities will also affect the amount of interference. *Non-Wi-Fi interference* in the ISM band can be caused from devices such as:

- Microwave ovens

- Cordless telephones

- Bluetooth devices

- Medical equipment

- Manufacturing or industrial equipment

- Wireless security cameras

- Radar systems (5 GHz bands)

This is by no means a complete list, but it does contain some of the devices used daily that may cause some level of interference in the world of wireless networking. Figure 9.4 shows an example of interference caused by a microwave oven. This screenshot shows a capture that ran for approximately two minutes. Microwave ovens operate in the 2.4 GHz frequency range.

FIGURE 9.4   Microwave oven operating at maximum power for two minutes

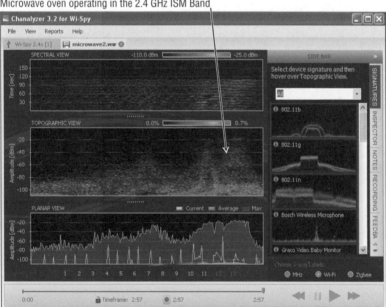

In Exercise 9.1, you will use the Chanalyzer spectrum analysis software to look at some sample captures.

Spectrum Analysis Demonstration

In this exercise, you will install the Chanalyzer software program by MetaGeek. This software will allow you to view some predefined RF captures available as part of the program. In order to perform actual captures, you will need to purchase one of the Wi-Spy analyzers available at www.metageek.net. The Chanalyzer program is included on the CD that comes with this book.

1. Locate the Chanalyzer software package named `Chanalyzer_Installer.3.2.msi` on the book CD and execute the program. The setup wizard will appear.

2. Click Next to start the installation process. The license agreement will appear.

3. Read the license agreement, then select the I Agree button and click Next. The Select Installation Folder dialog box will appear.

4. Click Next to accept the default installation folder.

EXERCISE 9.1   *(continued)*

5. Click Next on the Confirm Installation dialog box to start the installation process. The Chanalyzer program will now be installed on your computer. The Installation Complete dialog box will appear.

6. Click Close to complete the installation process and exit the installer program. The Chanalyzer program is now installed on your computer.

7. Start the Chanalyzer program by clicking on the Windows Start, All Programs, Meta-Geek, Chanalyzer 3.2 icon. The Chanalyzer 3.2 for Wi-Spy will appear on your screen.

Select 802.11b Sample Recording Hyperlink

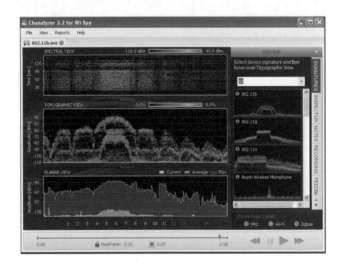

8. Locate the Sample Recordings section in the Your Options screen and click on the 802.11b hyperlink. The sample recording for an 802.11b capture will appear on the screen.

9.   While observing the screen, let the sample recording run for approximately 2 min-
      utes and notice the capture change as the program displays the recorded session.
      This sample recording runs for 2 minutes and 36 seconds. If desired you can pause
      the capture or rewind by using the controls on the bottom right corner of the Wi-Spy
      window.

10.   Close the 802.11b capture by clicking on the X next to the file name 802.11b.wsr. The
      Your Options screen will appear.

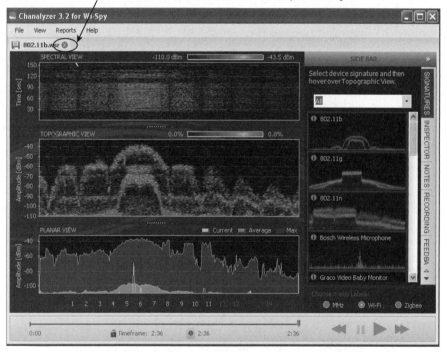

11.   Locate the Sample Recordings section in the Your Options screen and click on the
      Cordless Phone hyperlink. The sample recording for a cordless phone capture will
      appear on the screen.

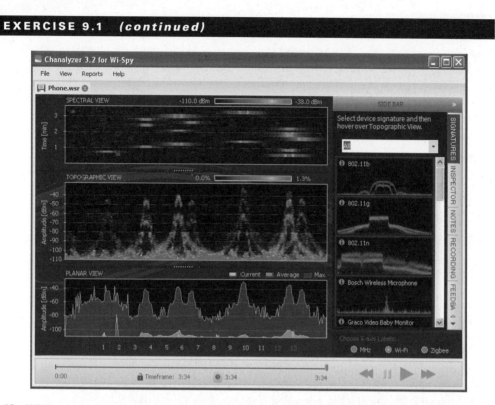

12. While observing the screen, let the sample recording run for approximately 3 minutes and notice the capture change as the program displays the recorded session. This sample recording runs for 3 minutes and 34 seconds. As with all the sample captures, you can pause the capture or rewind by using the controls on the bottom right corner of the Wi-Spy window.

13. Close the Phone.wsr capture by clicking on the X next to the file name Phone.wsr.

14. Continue to view the other sample recordings by clicking on the 802.11n, 802.11g, Microwave, and Baby Monitor sample recordings and repeating steps 9–10.

After you have completed this exercise, you can remove the Chanalyzer program from your computer.

The Wi-Spy spectrum analyzer device is available in several different models. This device will plug into an available USB port on your computer. The Chanalyzer program we used in this exercise is the same you would use to perform actual captures with the Wi-Spy device.

Wi-Fi Interference

Wi-Fi interference is caused by wireless LAN devices that operate in the 2.4 GHz ISM or 5 GHz UNII band. In some cases, this is the largest source of interference for wireless LANs. There are two types of Wi-Fi interference: co-channel interference (other devices on the same channel) or adjacent channel interference (other devices on overlapping channels). The following network types will cause Wi-Fi interference:

- FHSS networks: 2.4 GHz
- DSSS networks: 2.4 GHz
- ERP-OFDM networks: 2.4 GHz
- OFDM: 5 GHz
- HT-OFDM: 2.4 GHz and 5 GHz (802.11n)

Wi-Fi devices that cause interference can be operating in either infrastructure mode or ad hoc mode. The number of devices that are part of the wireless network will also determine the extent of the interference. In Chapter 5, "Access Methods, Architectures and Spread Spectrum Technology," we discussed different types of spread spectrum technologies that wireless networks use to communicate. FHSS, DSSS, ERP-OFDM, OFDM, and HT-OFDM are technologies used for IEEE 802.11 wireless networking in the 2.4 GHz and 5 GHz bands. However, some of these technologies are used in non-wireless LAN devices as well. For example, Bluetooth devices operating in the 2.4 GHz ISM band also use FHSS technology for communication. Zigbee devices operate in the 2.4 GHz band and use DSSS technology for communication. 2.4 GHz cordless phones may use either FHSS or DSSS depending on the manufacturer. Performing an RF spectrum analysis is one way you can determine the source of this type of interference. If an instrumentation spectrum analyzer (a calibrated device that has the capability to view entire radio spectrums) is used, it will be necessary to understand how to interpret the data collected as well as how to operate the device.

In Exercise 9.2, you will explore the AirMagnet Spectrum Analyzer program.

EXERCISE 9.2

PC Card Spectrum Analyzer Demonstration

In this exercise, you will install the AirMagnet Spectrum Analyzer Demo software program by AirMagnet. This software will allow you to view some predefined RF captures available as part of the program. In order to perform actual captures, you will need to purchase the complete product from AirMagnet, which includes a PCMCIA adapter. The AirMagnet Spectrum Analyzer Demo program can be downloaded from AirMagnet at www.airmagnet.com/cwts/wiley.

1. Locate the software package you downloaded from AirMagnet and execute the program. The following installation dialog box will appear:

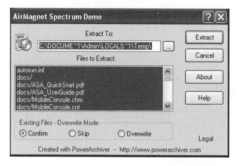

2. Click the Extract button to start the installation process. This will extract the files in a temporary folder necessary to install the program. If files by the same name already exist in this temporary folder, you will be prompted to overwrite. Click the box labeled "Don't ask again" and then click Yes. The program will now be installed on your computer.

3. The AirMagnet Spectrum Analyzer – InstallShield Wizard will appear. Click on Next to start the installation process.

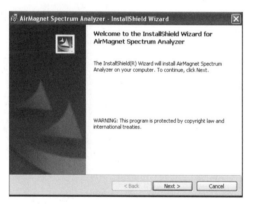

4. The License Agreement dialog box will appear.

5. Read the license agreement, then select the "I accept the terms in the license agreement" button and click Next. The Customer Information dialog box will appear. Fill in the blank fields, then click Next.

6. The Destination Folder dialog box will appear. Accept the default destination folder and click Next.

7. The Ready to Install the Program dialog box will appear. Click Install to finalize the installation process.

8. The InstallShield Wizard Completed dialog box will appear. If you wish to register, leave the Register Product check box selected. Click Finish to complete the installation process.

9. Click the Windows Start button, All Programs, AirMagnet, AirMagnet Spectrum Analyzer Demo icon to start the AirMagnet Spectrum Analyzer Demo.

10. The AirMagnet Spectrum Analyzer program will appear on the screen and the sample_cap.ccf file will run.

EXERCISE 9.2   (continued)

11. Click the Spectrum (2) tab near the top center of the screen. This will display the RF spectrum analysis capture from the sample file.

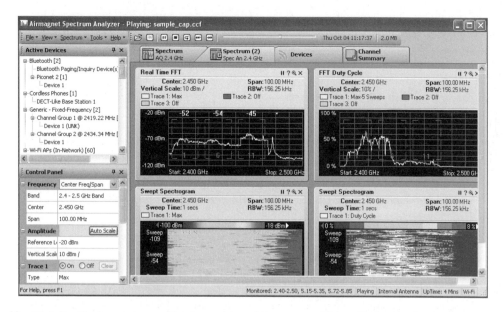

12. Click the Devices tab near the top center of the screen. This will display the devices that were identified during the capture process.

13. Continue to explore the program by selecting various tabs and dropdown menus to see many of the features of the product.

14. When you are finished, click the File dropdown menu and then click Exit to close the program.

You may uninstall the demonstration software after you have completed viewing the features of the AirMagnet Spectrum Analyzer program.

Standards vs. Industry Definitions

The following information is from the "Exam Terms" document available from www.cwnp.com and was added here for clarification. It is recommended to read the entire document prior to attempting any CWNP certification exam.

The 802.11-2007 standard loosely defines an adjacent channel as any channel with non-overlapping frequencies for the DSSS and HR/DSSS PHYs. With ERP and OFDM PHYs, the standard loosely defines an adjacent channel as the first channel with a non-overlapping frequency space.

This contradicts how the term "adjacent channel interference" is typically used in the marketplace. Most Wi-Fi vendors use this term to loosely mean both interference resulting from overlapping cells, and interference resulting from the use of overlapping frequency space. For example, vendors typically use this terminology in a case where AP-1 (channel 1) is located near AP-2 (channel 2).

The CWNP Program has decided to define two separate terms for clarity: Adjacent Overlapping Channel (e.g. channels 1 and 2 that are overlapping, and are directly next to each other in the band) and Adjacent Non-overlapping Channel (e.g. channels 1 and 6, which are the first immediately side-by-side channels that do not overlap). Channels 1 and 7, 1 and 8, etc., are simply considered Non-overlapping channels and are not adjacent.

Adjacent Channel Interference is a performance condition that occurs when two or more access point radios are providing RF coverage to the same physical area using overlapping frequencies. Simultaneous RF transmissions by two or more of these access point radios in the same physical area can result in corrupted 802.11 frames due to the frequency overlap. Corrupted 802.11 frames cause retransmissions, which results in both throughput degradation and latency.

Co-channel Interference is a performance condition that occurs when two or more independently coordinated access point radios are providing RF coverage to the same physical area using the same 802.11 channel. Additional RF medium contention overhead occurs for all radios using this channel in this physical area resulting in throughput degradation and latency.

Performing a Manual Site Survey

Although some in the industry feel the manual site survey process is "old school," it provides some of the most accurate results. A manual site survey requires a physical walkthrough of the area, recording information to determine the performance of clients and devices that will be connected to the wireless network. This type of site survey can be very accurate because the surveyor is recording actual statistics such as:

- Signal strength
- Signal-to-noise ratio (SNR)
- Data rate of connected devices

These measurements are recorded while physically moving through the facility or location. Recommended received signal strength and signal-to-noise ratio (SNR) values are discussed later in this chapter. Small-scale manual site surveys can be performed very inexpensively by using either a wireless client adapter with site survey functionality, one of several freeware/shareware utilities, or commercial software designed specifically for this type of application. Figure 9.5 shows an example of a site survey utility as part of the client utility software.

FIGURE 9.5 Cisco Systems Aironet Site Survey Utility included with the client utility as an optional install

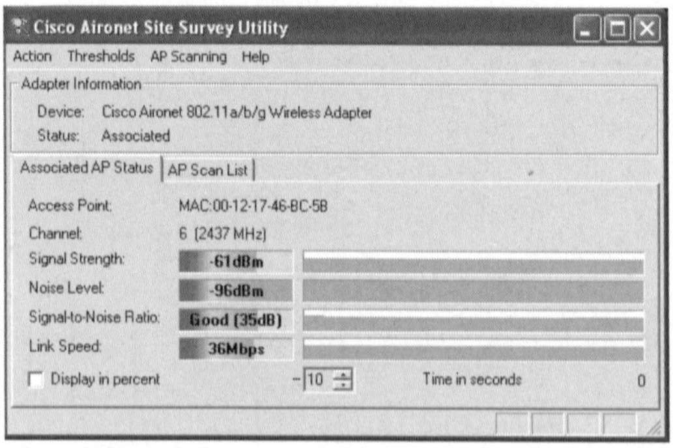

The manual site survey process can be used for recording measurements to determine the actual placement of hardware infrastructure devices and for spot checking or verification after a predictive site survey has determined the placement of these devices. Just a few years ago this manual process was the only way to perform a wireless site survey. The main advantage to the manual process is accuracy. One disadvantage is that it can be very time consuming depending on the extent of the installation. Some of the basic steps may include:

1. Obtaining a floor plan or blueprint of the location to be surveyed
2. Performing RF spectrum analysis
3. Testing access point placement
4. Analyzing the results

Obtaining a Floor Plan or Blueprint

The first step in a manual site survey is to review a floor plan or blueprint of the location. This could be a simple sketch and is required to note access point placement as well as readings. The readings to note on the floor plan include signal strength and signal-to-noise ratio values from client devices. Figure 9.6 shows a basic floor plan of a small office building. The floor plan should be marked with approximate access point locations. In some cases, a floor plan or CAD drawing of the location may not be available. Depending on the size of the location, a fire evacuation plan could be scanned in and used as a starting point to create a drawing and may be adequate for the site survey.

FIGURE 9.6   Approximate access point locations

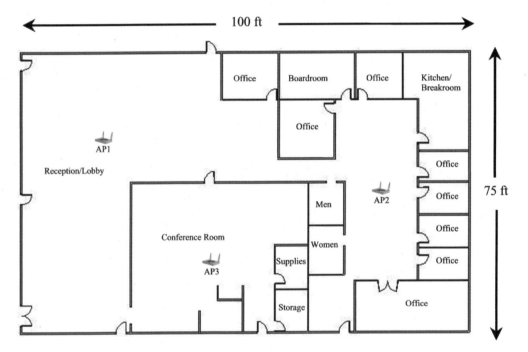

The floor plan and approximate access point locations used in these examples are for illustration purposes only.

Identifying Existing Wireless Networks

As part of a manual site survey, you should identify existing WLANs in the area noting locations that include possible sources of RF interference and may have an impact on the wireless LAN that will be installed. Using a device or software program designed specifically for wireless networks would be ideal. However, freeware or shareware programs may be satisfactory. Figure 9.7 shows an example of a software program that can be used to find existing wireless networks.

FIGURE 9.7 NetStumbler can be used to view wireless networks

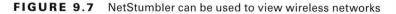

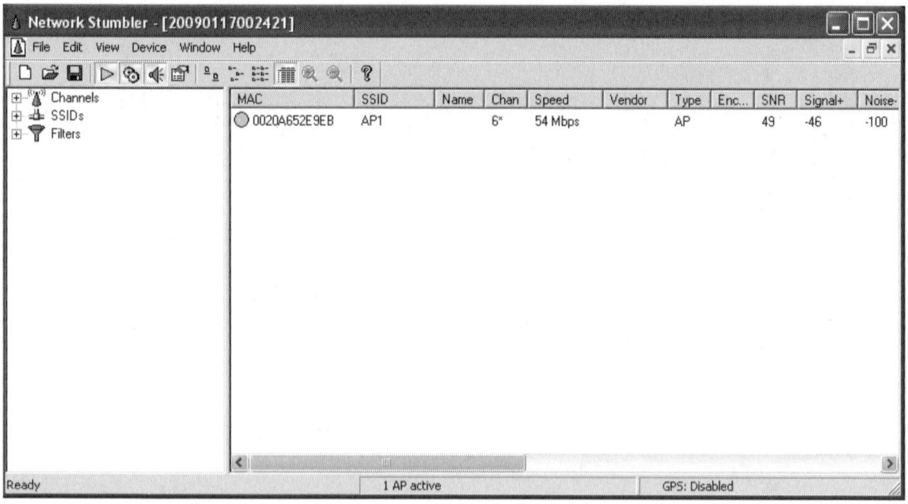

Testing Access Point Placement

Once you have identified potential locations for access points, you can start testing the proposed access point placement. This can be done by temporarily mounting an access point at the desired location to get the most accurate results. In some cases, a tool or fixture made specifically for wireless LAN site surveys or even a tall ladder could be used as a temporary mounting solution. Refer to the documentation that was created prior to going on-site for mounting locations. Figure 9.8 shows an example of a potential temporary mounting solution.

Using one or two temporarily mounted access points, document the results of the testing while moving around the facility. One testing method is to associate to the test access points using the site survey computer. A passive process (listening to all access points in the area) may also be used for this type of site survey. The area to be tested should include a reasonable proximity around the temporarily mounted access point. The information documented will depend on the surveyor but commonly includes signal strength and signal-to-noise ratio. Figure 9.9 shows the floor plan with the proposed access point locations as well as readings taken during the manual walkthrough. It may be necessary to make adjustments of access point mounting during the testing process based on the results of the testing process. It could be beneficial to test an actual device and software application that will be used with the network in order to see if the performance meets expectations. Figure 9.9 shows a true manual process for a very small site survey commonly used in early WLAN site surveys and would not be adequate for a survey of any large size. More elaborate and cost effective software assisted programs as described later in this chapter are commonly used for a site survey of any size in todays WLAN deployments.

FIGURE 9.8 Access point temporarily mounted using an expandable light pole

FIGURE 9.9 Floor plan with signal readings taken during a manual walkthrough using a client adapter site survey utility. This is an example of a true manual process. The software assisted tools described later in this chapter is the recommended solution for a manual site survey.

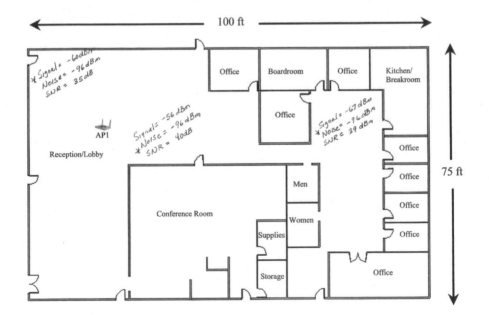

Analyzing the Results

Once all the testing is complete, it is necessary to perform an offline analysis to determine the final placement of access points or other infrastructure devices that may be used in the deployment. This may include making adjustments from the original plan prior to testing or possibly adding and removing access points. The use of various antennas may also need to be analyzed and documented.

Advantages and Disadvantages of Manual Site Survey

Listed are some of the advantages and disadvantages of the manual site survey process.

- Advantages
  - Very accurate because it is based on actual readings
  - Physical characteristics of building are physically tested (attenuation values)
  - Allows verification of actual RF signal coverage
  - Allows marking exact installation locations of hardware while on-site
- Disadvantages
  - Can be very time consuming
  - Usually only one access point is used for testing so readings will need to be merged
  - Requires a physical walkthrough of entire location
  - Some areas may require an escort for access

WLAN equipment used in a manual site survey should be from the same manufacturer as the hardware that will be installed in the actual deployment. This will minimize any potential issues from variations between manufacturers' devices.

Software Assisted Manual Site Survey

The manual site survey technique discussed earlier in this section may be adequate for smaller deployments or for organizations that have limited resources and budget. Manual site surveys can also be accomplished with the aid of commercial software programs designed specifically for this process. These programs vary in cost, complexity, and features and contain many advanced features including:

- Capability to perform both passive and active surveys
- Capability to import floor plans with support for many graphic formats, i.e., CAD, JPG, BMP
- Capability to record critical data such as signal and signal-to-noise ratio

- Visual representation of RF signal propagation of surveyed areas
- Post-survey offline analysis of collected data

Passive Site Survey

A *passive site survey* consists of monitoring the air and recording RF data from all access points and wireless client stations or devices in the "hearing range" of the surveying station and includes information from your own and neighboring devices. This type of site survey does not require an association to an access point, and no traffic is passed between the survey station and the access point. A passive survey will provide an overall snapshot of the RF in use in or around the location, including RF noise and other wireless networks in the area. It is used to get an overall picture of the wireless LAN access points that are transmitting within the area being surveyed. Figure 9.10 shows an example of a commercial site survey application in passive mode.

FIGURE 9.10 AirMagnet survey showing passive survey

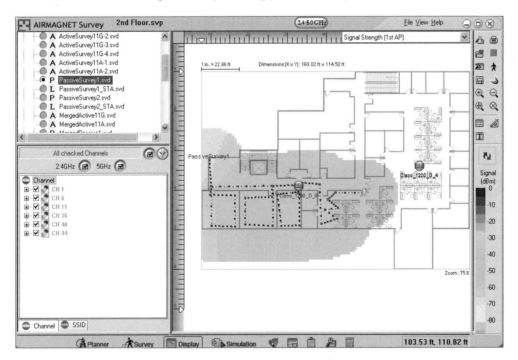

Since passive site surveys do not require an association to an access point, all RF will be detected, displayed, and recorded. Most commercial software applications with this functionality will have the capability to filter on specific access points from the information that was recorded.

Active Site Survey

An *active site survey* consists of a survey device such as a notebook computer associating to an access point prior to taking readings and collecting the data. Some claim this type of manual survey will provide more accurate results because of this direct association to an access point. The association of the survey device to an access point will actively send and receive some basic RF information to and from the access point, allowing for the information regarding signal strength and noise levels to be recorded. Figure 9.11 shows a commercial site survey performing an active site survey.

FIGURE 9.11 AirMagnet survey showing an active site survey

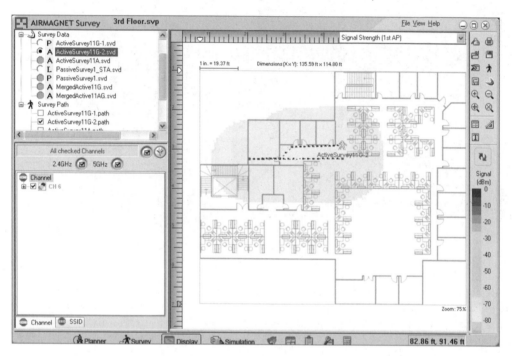

Performing either a passive or active site survey using software involves many of the same steps discussed in "Performing a Manual Site Survey" earlier in this chapter. The main difference is the features and capabilities that are available in these commercial software packages. These elaborate features will eliminate the need to manually document and record all the information obtained while walking the area because the program handles this task for the surveyor.

Manual Site Survey Toolkit

To perform a manual site survey, a toolkit containing essential components is recommended. A floor plan or blueprint is required to record data collected during a manual site survey. If an assisted software program is used, both an electronic version of the floor plan and a paper printout are necessary. Site survey toolkits will vary in complexity and cost. Figure 9.12 shows a wireless LAN 802.11n MIMO site survey kit from TerraWave Solutions.

FIGURE 9.12 802.11n MIMO site survey kit from TerraWave Solutions contained in a durable and airline-approved transportable carrying case

IMAGE PROVIDED BY WWW.TERRAWAVE.COM.

Spectrum Analyzer (Optional) A spectrum analyzer is an optional item that may be used in a site survey. This device will sweep the area to look for devices that may cause interference with the deployment. Spectrum analyzers vary in cost and features, as discussed earlier in this chapter.

Access Points One or two access points are needed to take signal measurements during the manual site survey process. It is important to use access points from the same manufacturer and if possible the same model that will be installed, to simulate what will be used in the actual installation.

It is recommended to set the test access points' output power level at about 50 percent or less during the site survey. This usually requires lowering the default power, which in many cases is set at maximum. This will allow for adjustments after installation to help compensate for potential differences from when the space was originally surveyed. The output power settings used will be determined by the individual performing the site survey.

Client Device Such as a Notebook Computer   A device to take measurements from the client side is an important component of the site survey kit. This can be a notebook computer or Pocket PC with appropriate software to take signal measurements. Size and weight should be considered as well. A Wi-Fi, VoIP handset may also be used for locations that are considering WLAN Voice over Internet Protocol capabilities.

Battery Packs or Extension Cords   Battery packs to temporarily power access points are recommended. However, if these are not available, extension cords are a good substitute. The disadvantage of extension cords is that they require accessible AC power outlets, which might not be available at all sites. An extra battery pack for the survey device is also recommended.

Various Antennas (If Required)   If antennas other than those mounted directly to an access point will be used in the deployment, a variety of these antennas should be on hand for testing during the site survey process. If 802.11n technology will be tested during the site survey, appropriate 802.11n antennas will be required as part of the site survey kit.

Temporary Mounting Hardware   Mounting hardware for temporarily mounting access points and antennas should also be considered, including expandable poles, brackets, tape, and nylon tie straps.

Measuring Device, Either Tape or Wheel   A measuring tape or wheel is recommended for measuring distance to wiring closets and distance between access points and any other areas where distance is of importance.

Digital Camera   As they say, a picture is worth a thousand words. Using a digital camera to take photographs of situations that may be difficult to explain in writing is a great help. This also adds quality to site survey reports.

Pens, Pencils, and Paper   Documentation is a critical part of wireless site surveys as well as all other areas of the network. Keeping clean and accurate notes will allow the surveyor to document areas of importance.

Ladder   Ladders or lifts are required for mounting temporary access points and antennas. The height of the ladder or lift will depend on the mounting locations for the access points.

Cart   A cart or dolly to move all equipment used for the site survey will ease the burden of getting the equipment around the facility.

Performing a Predictive Site Survey

A *predictive site survey* can be an accurate way to design a wireless LAN without having to spend time on-site performing a physical walkthrough and testing of the entire location. This type of site survey can be performed a couple of different ways depending on the equipment used. You can use a commercial software program designed specifically for this purpose or, in some cases, manufacturers build this site survey functionality directly into a wireless LAN controller/switch.

This type of site survey requires the wireless engineer or surveyor to input a floor plan drawing of the facility, such as a CAD, JPEG, BMP, or other format file, directly into the software program or the controller/switch. Then information and details such as the attenuation values of the facility is added. This information includes:

- Type of walls: for example, drywall, brick, or poured concrete

- Thickness of walls

- Types of windows, including glass, thickness, and coating

- Type of doors, such as hollow core, solid core, fire doors, wood, steel

- Location of certain types of furnishings, such as cubicle offices

- Height of ceiling

One thing to keep in mind about a predictive site survey is that the accuracy and final results are only as good as the information that was input into the program. It is essential for the surveyor to use accurate information about the location, including the attenuation value of all the building materials. Figure 9.13 shows a predictive analysis site survey tool.

FIGURE 9.13 Motorola LANPlanner showing a predictive modeling site survey

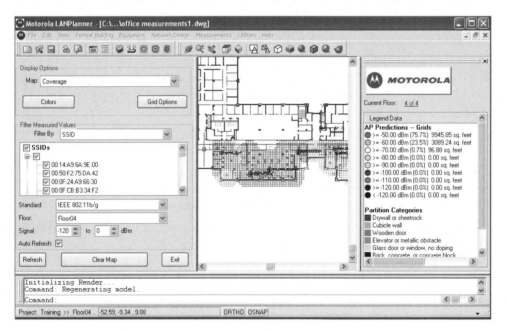

Listed are some the advantages and disadvantages of using the predictive site survey process:

- Advantages

  - Limited time on-site

  - Does not require a complete physical walkthrough for testing

- Allows for easy adjustment of access point locations and settings
- Can model different scenarios
- Disadvantages
  - Surveyor may be unfamiliar with the location's physical characteristics
  - Accuracy limited to data input within program
  - Requires extensive knowledge of physical properties of the installation area including attenuation values

In Exercise 9.3, you will explore a predictive site survey program.

EXERCISE 9.3

Predictive Site Survey Demonstration

In this exercise, you will install the Motorola LANPlanner program. This site survey demo program can be requested by contacting the Motorola Enterprise Mobility Group at www .motorola.com.

1. Start the installation by executing the LANPlanner setup program.

2. The LANPlanner Setup dialog box will appear. Click Next to start the installation wizard.

3. The License Agreement dialog box will appear. Read the license agreement; if you agree, select the "I accept" radio button and click Next. The serial number dialog box will appear. Fill in the blank fields, then click Next.

4. The Destination Folder dialog box will appear. Accept the default location by clicking Next.

5. The Start Installation dialog box will appear. Click Next to start the installation.

6. The LANPlanner Program Has Been Successfully Installed dialog box will appear. Click Finish to complete the installation.

7. Click on the LANPlanner icon on your desktop. The LANPlanner program will start
    and the Activation Code Not Found dialog box will appear on the screen. Click OK to
    start the evaluation process.

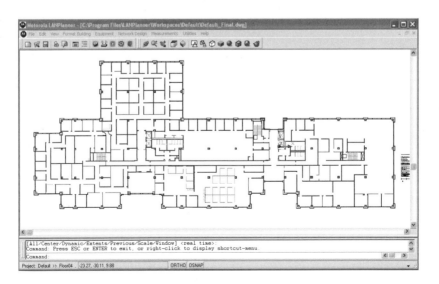

8. The License Maintenance dialog box will appear. Click Exit Update Dialog to continue
    the evaluation. This product can be evaluated for two days.

9. Click the File dropdown box and New/Open Project. The Building Wizard Setup dia-
    log box will appear; click Next. Click No in the Save Changes dialog box.

10. The default sample drawing will appear on the screen. You can resize the drawing by
    left-clicking and dragging on the magnifying glass icon. Place an access point on the
    drawing by selecting the Equipment dropdown box and Place Access Point.

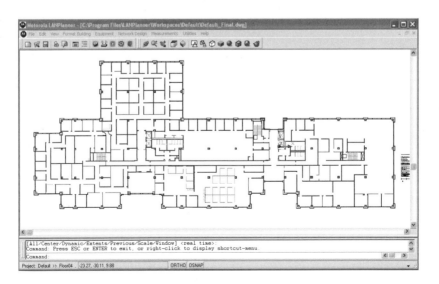

11. Select an access point from the list with your mouse. Double-click on the desired access point and drag it to an area on the floor plan. Click your left mouse button to place the access point.

12. Hit the ESC button on your keyboard and click Exit in the Place Access Point dialog box.

13. Click on the Network Design dropdown box and Quick Predict. The quick Predict dialog box will appear; click Next to continue.

14. The Select Access Point dialog box will appear. Select an access point and click OK.

15. Move your mouse around throughout the floor plan to see the predicted signal readings based on the characteristics of the building.

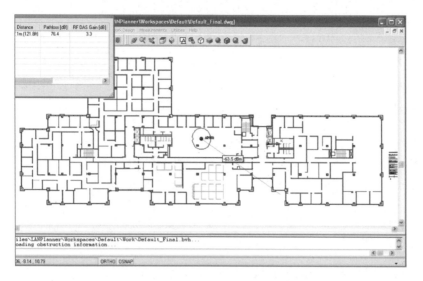

16. Press the ESC button on your keyboard to return to the floor plan screen. Click on various buttons and menus to explore the features associated with this program. When finished with the demonstration, exit the program by clicking on the File drop down menu and Exit. Click No in the Save Changes dialog box.

After you have completed the exercise and evaluation process, you can remove the software from your computer.

There are many different site survey programs to choose from, both commercial and freeware or shareware. You should compare the programs and determine which would be best suited for your environment based on features, cost, and capabilities. Listed are many common programs for predictive modeling or manual site surveys that are available on the market today.

Site Survey Program	Web site
AirMagnet Survey/Planner	www.airmagnet.com
Airtight Networks	www.airtightnetworks.com
Berkeley Varitronics Systems (BV Systems) Swarm	www.bvsystems.com
Ekahau Site Survey	www.ekahau.com
Fluke Networks InterpretAir	www.flukenetworks.com
Helium Networks Wireless Recon	www.heliumnetworks.com
Motorola LANPlanner	www.motorola.com
Motorola SiteScanner	www.motorola.com
Psiber RF3D WiFiPlanner	www.psiber.com
VisiWave – AZO Technologies	www.visiwave.com
InSSIDer (freeware)	www.metageek.net
NetStumbler (donationware)	www.netstumbler.com

Some wireless client adapter utilities can also be used in site surveys.

Protocol Analysis

Wireless LAN protocol analyzers are becoming a common tool, and many network administrators will have one as part of their wireless LAN toolkit. A *protocol analyzer* will allow a network administrator or engineer to view all wireless frames that are traversing across the air in the hearing range of the analysis device. At one time protocol analysis was a specialty role, and without extensive training few people had the skills to perform this task. Along with the evolution of wireless LAN technology in recent years, protocol analyzers are becoming more mainstream, affordable, and easier to use. Many variations of analyzers are available in the market today. Listed are some of the manufacturers and their products:

Manufacturer	Product	Web Site
AirMagnet	WiFi Analyzer	www.airmagnet.com
BV Systems	Yellowjacket	www.bvsystems.com
Motorola	AirDefense Mobile	www.airdefense.net
NetScout	Sniffer	www.netscout.com
Network Instruments	Observer	www.networkinstruments.com
TamoSoft	CommView for WiFi	www.tamos.com
WildPackets	OmniPeek	www.wildpackets.com

 Most wireless protocol analyzers require the use of certain network adapters and in many cases use a special device driver. It is recommended to verify you have access to an adapter that is supported by the protocol analyzer's manufacturer.

Protocol analyzers are available in software programs that can be installed on a notebook computer or Pocket PC and are also available in specialty dedicated handheld devices. In addition to performing protocol analysis or frame decoding, many analyzers are feature rich with the capability to view security information, perform legislative compliance analysis and reporting, and generate a variety of different reports. Figure 9.14 shows an example of a wireless LAN protocol analyzer.

The main goals of a wireless LAN analyzer or any protocol analyzer are to troubleshoot network problems, gather information about security issues, and optimize the network's performance. When it comes to wireless LAN site surveys, a protocol analyzer is a valuable tool for evaluating which wireless LAN devices are currently in the same RF space where the proposed wireless LAN will be deployed. They can also be used to view the signal strength, security implementations, the network name or SSID, and which channels access points and other devices are currently operating on. An analyzer will show not only access points but any wireless LAN device that may have an impact on the site survey and deployment. Some of the devices an analyzer is able to locate and identify include:

- Access points
- Ad hoc networks
- Wireless bridges
- Mesh networks
- Client devices

FIGURE 9.14   OmniPeek by WildPackets identifies nearby wireless networks

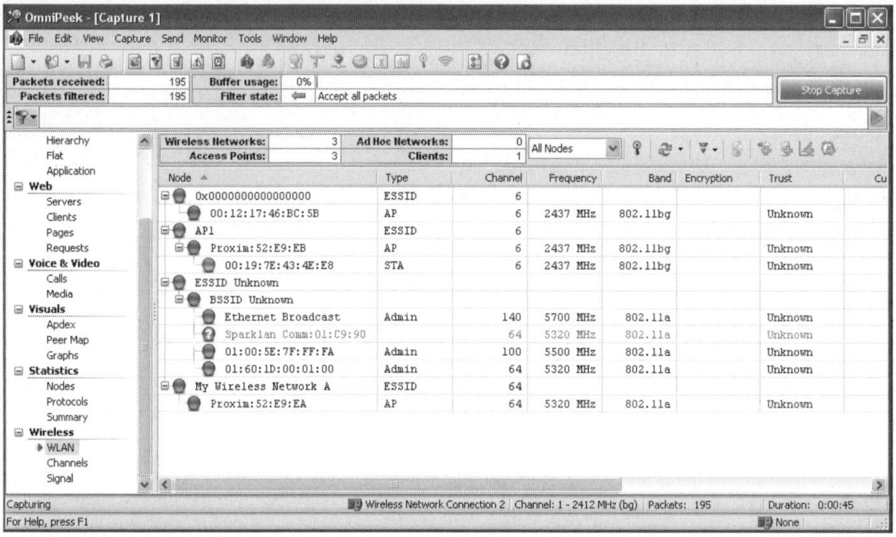

In Exercise 9.4, you will explore a protocol analyzer.

EXERCISE 9.4

Protocol Analyzer Demonstration

In this exercise you will install the CommView for WiFi protocol analyzer by TamoSoft. This protocol analyzer demo program is included on the CD that comes with this book.

1. Locate the CommView for WiFi setup program located on the CD that is included with this book.

2. Start the setup process by executing the setup.exe program

3. The CommView for WiFi setup wizard will appear on the screen. Click Next to start the installation process.

4. The license agreement will appear. Read the license agreement; click Yes. The Select Installation Folder dialog box will appear.

5. A second license agreement will appear applicable to Intel adapters only. If this pertains to you, read the agreement and click Yes to agree. If this does not pertain to you, click N/A.

6. The License Type dialog box will appear. For this demonstration, select the radio button next to Standard Mode and click Next.

EXERCISE 9.4 *(continued)*

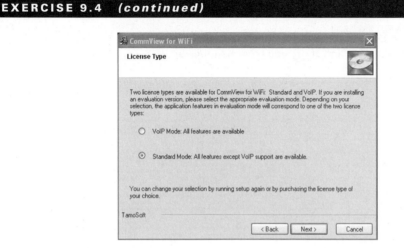

7. The Destination Location dialog box will appear. Click Next to accept the default location.

8. The Select Program Manager Group dialog box will appear. Select Next to accept the default Program Manager Group.

9. The Additional Settings Dialog box will appear. Select the appropriate language and deselect the checkbox next to "Launch CommView for WiFi once the installation has been completed."

10. The Start Installation dialog box will appear. Click Next to start the installation.

11. After the installation is complete, the CommView for WiFi dialog box will appear. Click Finish to complete the installation.

12. Click on the CommView for WiFi icon on your desktop to start the program.

EXERCISE 9.4 *(continued)*

13. The program will attempt to start and the Driver Installation Guide dialog box will appear. Read this guide and verify you have a supported wireless adapter.

14. At the bottom of the Driver Installation Guide dialog box, click Next to start the installation wizard.

15. The Driver Installation dialog box will appear. Select the appropriate radio button and click Next.

16. A second Driver Installation dialog box will appear. Select the "I want the program to install the driver automatically" radio button and click Next.

17. A third Driver Installation dialog box will appear. Select the supported adapter from the list and click Install Driver.

18. Click the Restart Windows Now button in the Driver Installation dialog box. The device driver has been updated and your computer will restart.

19. After your computer restarts, log in and start the CommView for WiFi program by double-clicking on the icon on your desktop. The evaluation version of the program will start.

20. Click on the arrow in the upper left corner of the program window or click on the File dropdown box and Start Capture to start a capture with the program. The Scanner dialog box will appear.

21. Select the channel you wish to view or click on the Start Scanning button. Then click Capture.

22. The screen will show all devices captured on the channel scanning.

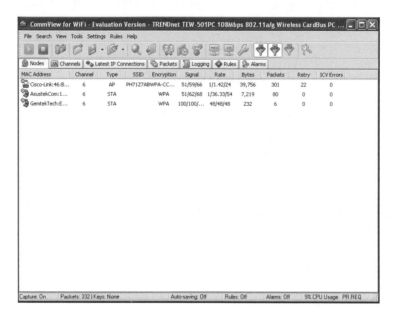

22. Click on various buttons to see the features associated with this program. When finished with the demonstration, exit the program by clicking on the File dropdown menu and Exit.

23. A "Thank you for trying this evaluation version" dialog box will appear. Click OK to close the program.

24. Using Device Manager, restore the original device driver for the wireless network adapter used with this demonstration.

After you have completed the exercise and evaluation process, you can remove the software from your computer.

Surveying Networks with a Mesh Access Layer

As discussed in Chapter 2, "Wireless LAN Infrastructure Devices," mesh technology is becoming more prevalent in the wireless LAN industry. This technology was originally popular for outdoor implementations but is becoming more common indoors as well. Newer mesh access points or routers typically are dual-band, supporting both the 2.4 GHz ISM and 5 GHz UNII bands. In many cases, different RF bands will be used for different functions. The 2.4 GHz ISM band is popular for client access. This is because many client devices only support the 2.4 GHz ISM band. The 5 GHz UNII band is sometimes used for infrastructure device connectivity only. This will limit contention with client devices accessing the network. The number of client devices that currently utilize the 5 GHz UNII band is still limited. Therefore the amount of potential interference is less than with the 2.4 GHz band.

When performing a site survey, either indoors or outdoors, in which mesh technology will be used, it is important to survey for both RF bands. Keep in mind that the propagation characteristics of the two frequencies will be different as well as the amount of interference.

Documenting Existing Network Characteristics

Existing wireless networks can play a big role in a new wireless LAN deployment. Understanding the current location of infrastructure and other wireless LAN devices is an important part of a site survey. One way to see devices that are part of a wireless network is to use a protocol analyzer. Other programs will also be able to view existing wireless networks, such as NetStumbler and InSSIDer, and in some cases these programs may be adequate based on the complexity and size of the site survey. But these typically do not have the extensive feature set that many protocol analyzer packages have.

Some of the questions that need to be taken into consideration when performing a wireless LAN site survey are:

- What frequency range will the new wireless LAN operate in?

- Are there any existing wireless LANs in the same RF space?

- Will all or part of the existing wireless LAN be utilized in the new deployment?

- What effect will the neighboring wireless networks have on this deployment?

Ignoring existing wireless networks may have a significant impact on how the wireless LAN will operate and result in poor performance for the clients or devices that will be connecting.

Figure 9.15 shows an example of a software tool that will identify existing wireless networks.

FIGURE 9.15   InSSIDer by MetaGeek can identify wireless networks

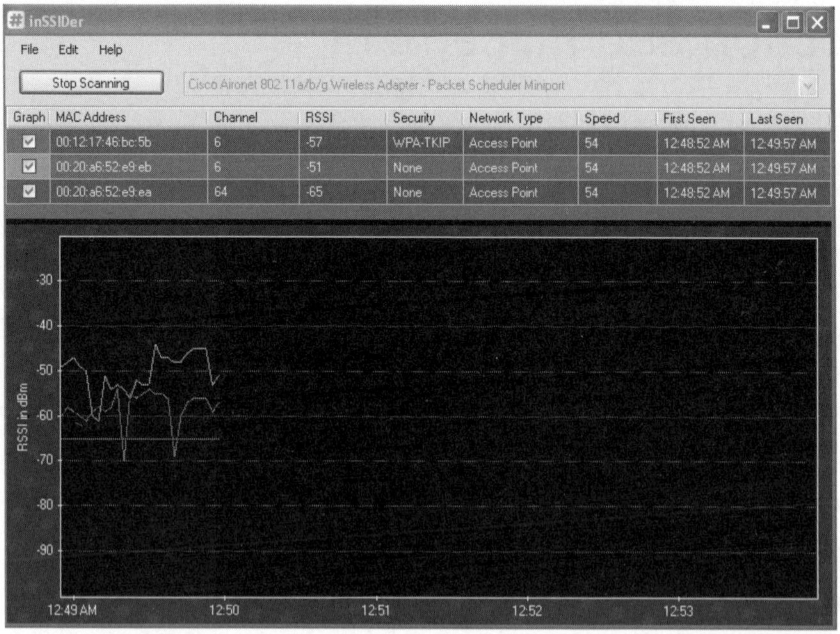

RF Coverage Requirements

As mentioned previously, one of the main goals of a wireless LAN site survey is to determine areas of RF interference and RF coverage. The details of the required coverage and capacity in any wireless network are part of the wireless LAN design, which involves determining the need, use, and business requirements of the network. This was discussed in Chapter 8. Some of the factors that need to be taken into consideration during a physical site survey are:

- Size of area
- Number of users
- Obstacles
- Signal propagation
- Radio frequency range
- Bandwidth requirements of applications to be used
- Frequency of WLAN hardware

The planning process will provide some of the answers while a visit and on-site testing will determine others, such as obstacles, signal propagation, and RF range.

Infrastructure Hardware Selection and Placement

In addition to identifying areas of RF coverage and interference, a site survey will also determine the best locations for wireless access points and other infrastructure devices. The correct placement of these devices is important in order to allow clients and devices to benefit fully from the deployment of wireless LAN. The location of these devices is traditionally partly based on the following criteria:

- RF coverage
- Bandwidth
- Aesthetics
- Applications
- Cell overlap
- Channel reuse

Mapping out the infrastructure device placement is considered part of the planning process. Manual, software assisted, or predictive site survey processes will help identify the proper locations based on the items mentioned above. In most cases, a preliminary visit to the location is highly recommended regardless of the site survey method that will be used. Knowing the physical location will benefit the entire site survey process because it will help identify areas of concern.

Infrastructure Connectivity and Power Requirements

Even though the main objectives of this book are all about wireless networking, it is still important to understand that infrastructure devices require some sort of wired connectivity for data and electrical power. Data access will usually come by way of an Ethernet connection from a wired network infrastructure or backbone. As stated in the IEEE 802.3 Ethernet standard, the maximum length for unshielded twisted-pair Ethernet cable is 328 feet or 100 meters. This limitation may have an impact on how and where access points and other infrastructure devices are placed.

During the site survey process, the surveyor will likely need access to wiring closets.

Another consideration is power requirements. Infrastructure devices need electrical power as well as data connectivity to operate. If the electrical power is decentralized and located at each device, an electrician will need to evaluate and determine the requirements.

Another option for supplying electrical power to infrastructure devices is Power over Ethernet (PoE). This technology is now very common and is supported by all enterprise device manufacturers. A survey of the wired infrastructure and devices is almost always required to determine if the infrastructure will be capable of handling the new PoE devices that will be installed. Keep in mind that zoning and building regulations, electrical contractors, and union requirements may add to the overall cost of WLAN deployment. PoE was discussed in Chapter 2, "Wireless LAN Infrastructure Devices."

Received Signal Strength

The main objective of a wireless network is to provide access to resources and services for devices that are connected to the network. This means it is essential for client devices to have reliable connectivity to the wireless network infrastructure. In order to provide this connectivity, the site survey process should include testing to verify that the received signal is adequate for the application of the device.

Devices that communicate wirelessly require two-way communications in order to operate correctly. This means the receiver must be able to receive enough of the signal in order to determine the data that was sent from the transmitter. Wireless LAN devices use what is known as the *received signal strength* to show the amount of power received from a transmission. Figure 9.16 shows a client utility that displays specifics regarding the received signal.

FIGURE 9.16   Broadcom wireless utility shows signal, noise, and data rate

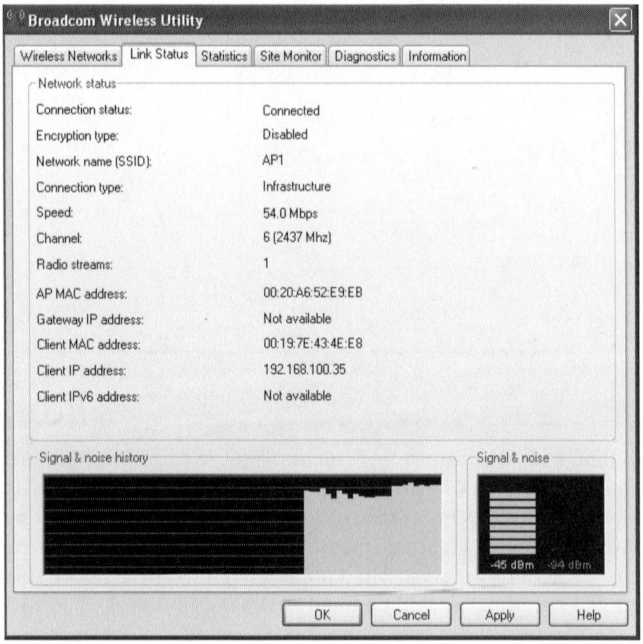

The amount of received signal strength required will be determined by the type or application of the device as well as the amount of RF noise in the area. RF noise is extraneous undesired radio signals in the area emitted by a variety of devices other than the transmitter. You should check with the device manufacturer to determine the minimum amount of received signal that is acceptable for a specific application. Some applications will require more received signal than others. For example, the manufacturer of a voice handset may recommend a minimum of –65 dBm whereas a computer network card may require a minimum of –70 dBm.

The *signal-to-noise ratio (SNR)* is the difference between the received signal and the noise floor. For example, if the received signal is –65 dBm and the noise floor is –95 dBm, then the signal-to-noise ratio will be 30 dB. This value is calculated by subtracting the received signal from the noise. In this case –65 dBm – (–95 dBm) = 30 dB.

The recommended signal-to-noise ratio (SNR) for most wireless LAN systems is a minimum of 20 to 25 dB.

Table 9.1 shows received signal minimums for specific data rates. These values will vary by manufacturer.

TABLE 9.1 Examples of Minimum Received Signal Strengths Required for Specific Data Rates

Data Rate (mbps)	2.4 GHz (dBm)	2.4 GHz (dBm) Voice	5 GHz (dBm)
54	–61	–56	–58
36	–63	–58	–63
24	–67	–62	–67
12/11	–72	–67	–72
6/5.5	–79	–74	–75
2	–81	–76	N/A
1	–84	–79	N/A

Source: Certified Wireless Network Administrator (CWNA)

In IEEE 802.11 wireless LAN technology, the received signal strength indicator (RSSI) value is an arbitrary number assigned by the device manufacturer. There is no standard for this value and it will not be comparable between devices from different manufacturers. When performing a site survey, whenever possible it is beneficial to survey with the same network adapter model that will be used in the deployment. This will provide more accurate results for the client devices using the network.

Antenna Use Considerations

In Chapter 6, "WLAN Antennas and Accessories," we looked at various types of antennas, including omnidirectional, semidirectional, and highly directional models. The characteristics and features of these antennas were discussed as well as the best use for each based on a specific scenario. As part of a site survey, it may be necessary to test different antennas to determine the best RF coverage. This usually involves the surveyor connecting and temporarily mounting various types of antennas to access points in order to determine the proper radiation pattern and to verify RF coverage within the desired area. A temporary antenna mounting example is shown in Figure 9.17.

FIGURE 9.17   Expandable light pole used for temporary mounting and testing of a Yagi and Patch antennas

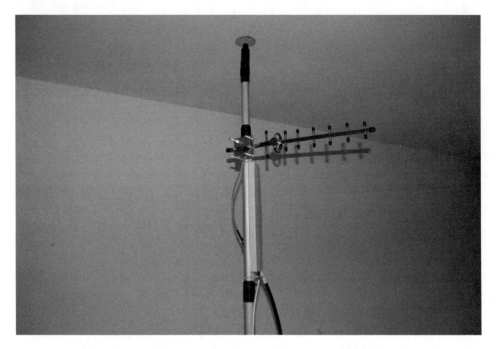

Testing Multiple Antenna Types

If different antennas will be used in the deployment, it is important for the surveyor to have several different types of antennas as part of the site survey kit. Some organizations that deploy wireless networks are extremely concerned about aesthetics, therefore they will allow only specific types of antennas to be used. For example, if access points with removable antennas are used, in many cases the only type allowed will be omnidirectional antennas that are attached directly to the access point with a gain of about 2 or 3 dBi. Other deployments may use lightweight access points in which antennas are permanently part of the access point and cannot be removed or changed.

> **TIP**   Keep in mind that polarization of antennas must be taken into consideration during a manual site survey. Polarization of antennas for infrastructure devices is critical and tests should mimic as closely as possible what will actually be installed. With the variety of client devices that may be used in a wireless network, it is a challenge to predict the polarization of all the devices that might be used. However, it is advisable for the surveyor to take this into consideration during the site survey.

Choosing the Correct Antennas

Choosing the correct antenna to be used in a specific deployment is part of the wireless design and site survey process. Many factors play a role in determining which antenna will be best for the application. Some locations have strict requirements about the type of antenna that may be used. Therefore the surveyor may have to work with specific antennas to ensure proper RF coverage. The following factors should to be taken into consideration when choosing antennas.

Manufacturer's recommendations   The manufacturer of an access point may recommend only a specific type of antenna. If this is the case, it is important to perform the site survey with the same type of antenna.

Customer requirements   A customer may require only specific types of antennas to be used. In this case, the survey should be performed with the type of antenna required by the customer. For example, a deployment consisting of walled offices may require the use of thin access points. Usually this type of access point uses an omnidirectional internal antenna.

Environmental conditions   The environment where the wireless network is installed may also determine the type of antenna to be used. If the location is a factory with harsh environmental conditions, that could have an impact on the type of antenna and may also call for an enclosure for the access point.

Aesthetics   Many organizations are sensitive to the type of devices that are visibly seen by customers and clients. Therefore aesthetically pleasing antennas may be required by the customer in order to be a good fit for the location in which they will be used. Figure 9.18 shows an example of this type of antenna.

FIGURE 9.18   Ceiling mount antenna from L-com

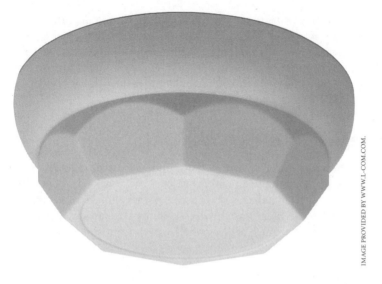

IMAGE PROVIDED BY WWW.L-COM.COM.

Required coverage   The required RF coverage will also affect the choice of antenna as well as the gain of the antenna. For example, a large office area may require the use of omnidirectional antennas that are physically attached to access points. A manufacturing facility may require semidirectional antennas to cover areas of the manufacturing floor.

Number of access points   The number of access points to be installed in a location will also be a determining factor in the type of antenna to be used. An office building with a combination of walled offices and cubicles may have a dense deployment of access points with a limited number of users connecting to any particular access point. Omnidirectional antennas connected directly to the access point may be an adequate solution for this type of deployment.

Physical geometry of location   The attributes of the physical location will have an affect on the type of antenna to be installed and therefore should be tested during the site survey. This includes propagation of the signal and attenuation of obstacles. In the case where a building has long hallways or corridors, a Yagi antenna would be a good candidate for a solution.

Channel Architectures

There are two common types of channel architectures available today that pertain to wireless LAN technology. In wireless LAN technology, channel architecture is the design, layout, or channel plan in use. In the 2.4 GHz band, for example, using channels 1, 6, and 11 non-overlapping channels is a channel architecture. The CWNP program defines these two architectures and coined the terms known as multiple channel architecture (MCA) and single channel architecture (SCA).

Multiple Channel Architecture (MCA)

Most wireless LAN deployments today use *multiple channel architecture (MCA)*. This type of installation will use access points set to different RF channels in order to avoid overlapping channel interference, as shown in Figure 9.19. A channel plan may be used with access points set to specific channels, or in many cases automatic channel selection allows the devices to choose the best channel to operate on. Until recently this is how all wireless LAN access points were deployed.

Single Channel Architecture (SCA)

Single channel architecture (SCA) is a fairly new wireless networking technology. SCA allows all access points to communicate on the same RF channel. The controller that the access points are connected to manages these access points and avoids co-channel interference. In single channel deployments, not all access points are transmitting at the same time. The controller will determine which access points can transmit simultaneously based on the wireless devices that are in a specific area.

FIGURE 9.19   Example of multiple channel architecture deployment

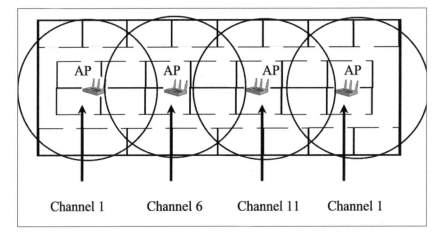

Channel 1   Channel 6   Channel 11   Channel 1

There are a few terms you should know with respect to single channel architecture: stacking, spanning, and blanketing. They all refer to a means of managing coverage in a single channel architecture. The term used will depend on the manufacturer.

For example, let's look at a three-story building. Each floor in the building may be assigned a channel to use; this is known as *stacking*. The first floor would be set to channel 1, the second floor would be set to channel 6, and the third floor would be set to channel 11. Since all access points on the same floor are set to the same RF channel, co-channel interference or overlapping channel interference is not a significant issue because of how the technology works.

Using single channel architecture may help save some time when it comes to the site survey. It is best to follow the manufacturer's recommendations for deployment for this type of system. Figure 9.20 shows an example of single channel architecture.

FIGURE 9.20   Example of single channel architecture deployment

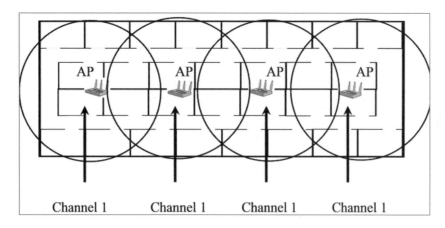

Installation Limitations

The installation limitations of any device that will be installed and used on the wireless network need to be taken into consideration. Sometimes things looks great on paper, but when it comes time to actually perform the task it may be a little different. The following sections discuss the installation limitations of various wireless devices.

Access Points   An installer may run into limitations when it comes to mounting access points or other infrastructure devices. For this reason the surveyor must pay close attention to the intended location where these devices will be mounted. The type of ceiling and mounting hardware need to be considered. A site survey should include a physical walkthrough evaluation of the proposed mounting locations to observe any issues that may affect where access points, bridges, or repeaters can be mounted.

Antennas   If antennas other than those that are designed to be connected directly to an access point are used, special circumstances may need to be taken into consideration, including:

- Mounting issues
- Cabling issues
- Aesthetics
- Height restrictions

Ethernet/PoE   As mentioned earlier in this chapter, the maximum distance an Ethernet unshielded twisted pair cable can run is 328 feet or 100 meters, per the IEEE 802.3 standard. Part of the site survey process includes verification of the distance infrastructure devices will be mounted from the wiring closet to be certain they do not exceed the maximum. The capabilities of the Ethernet system must also be evaluated to verify the capacity of the wiring system. This will ensure there is adequate connectivity for the new wireless infrastructure devices.

If Power over Ethernet will be used, it is important to verify that the infrastructure will be able to support the number of devices that require DC power from the PoE infrastructure devices. If the current wired infrastructure is not PoE compliant, the infrastructure may need to be upgraded prior to wireless deployment. If an upgrade is not feasible, an alternate solution such as single port power injectors or patch panels may be required.

Site Survey Report

The survey report should be a complete document itemizing all components of the site survey. This includes the business aspects of the site survey as discussed in Chapter 8 as well as the physical aspects of the site survey as discussed in this chapter. This report should include but not be limited to notes, charts, graphs, photos, test results, and any other pertinent data that will have an effect on the wireless LAN deployment. Most reports will be of a custom nature based on the individual needs and requirements of the customer. Most commercial site survey application programs have reporting features that can be included in the site survey report.

Summary

In this chapter, we looked at the site survey process. The site survey process is one of the most important components of a successful wireless LAN deployment. Many areas need to be considered, including an RF spectrum analysis to determine RF interference sources that may affect the wireless deployment. Although a spectrum analysis can be considered optional, it is advisable to complete one whenever possible. Keep in mind the spectrum analysis is based on a walkthrough of a facility and recording data at an instant in time. The results of this type of spectrum analysis can change once the surveyor has left the area. Spectrum analyzers are available in various types consisting of instrumentation devices, PC card–based, and USB adapters.

This chapter discussed Wi-Fi and non-Wi-Fi sources of interference, both which can have an effect on the performance of a wireless LAN installation. It is important to understand the various types of interference, such as:

- Microwave ovens
- Bluetooth devices
- Radar systems
- Devices that operate in the ISM band
- Devices that operate in the UNII band
- Other wireless LANs

This chapter looked at the different types of site surveys that can be performed, including manual and predictive. We also looked at the two types of manual site surveys, passive and active. Passive surveys see all RF from access points in the hearing range of the survey device. An active survey requires an association to a specific access point. Manual site surveys typically require a walkthrough of the entire area. Predictive site surveys perform a simulated analysis of the proposed space where the wireless LAN will be deployed. The accuracy of a predictive survey is dependent on the information input to the program. Both manual and predictive site surveys can be simplified by using a variety of software programs made specifically for this function.

In this chapter, we discussed some of the items that may be included in a survey toolkit as well as temporary mounting examples for access points and antennas. We also discussed the use of a protocol analyzer in a site survey and how one could be used to identify existing wireless networks in the area of concern.

Finally, we looked at both multiple channel architecture (MCA) and single channel architecture (SCA) and the differences between them. Best practices for hardware placement were also reviewed, including access points and antennas as well as some of the limitations that may be encountered during the site survey process.

Exam Essentials

Understand the need for an RF spectrum analysis and how to locate sources of interference. Know that an RF spectrum analysis will allow you to "see" RF in an area proposed for a wireless LAN. Identify different types of RF interference that can have an effect on a wireless network.

Know the differences between manual and predictive site surveys.   Know that a manual site survey typically requires a complete walkthrough and testing throughout the proposed area where a wireless LAN will be deployed. A predictive site survey may require minimal time on-site and is a software-based analysis solution.

Identify two different types of manual site surveys.   Know that manual site surveys can be passive or active and the differences between each.

Know how a protocol analyzer can be used as part of wireless LAN site survey.   Explain how a wireless protocol analyzer can be used to help identify existing wireless networks and how they may have an impact on the site survey.

Understand the importance of identifying existing wireless networks.   Know the importance of existing wireless networks and how they may have an effect on a new wireless LAN deployment.

Be familiar with the limitations of placement regarding wireless infrastructure devices.   Explain some of the limitations regarding placement of wireless LAN devices, including access points, bridges, and antennas.

Understand the factors regarding proper antenna use.   Identify the different uses of antennas based on the customer requirements and characteristics of the environment.

Key Terms

active site survey	received signal strength
dead spot	signal-to-noise ratio (SNR)
multiple channel architecture (MCA)	single channel architecture (SCA)
non-Wi-Fi interference	spectrum analyzer
passive site survey	stacking
predictive site survey	Wi-Fi interference
protocol analyzer	

Review Questions

1. A main objective of a wireless LAN site survey is to determine _____ and _____. (Choose the best two options.)

   A. Areas of RF interference

   B. Applications to be used

   C. Access point locations

   D. Wiring closet locations

   E. Security implementations

2. You are a network engineer tasked with performing a site survey for a multiple channel architecture (MCA) system in a three-story building. Which characteristic must be considered while performing a site survey?

   A. All omnidirectional antennas should be vertically polarized.

   B. Multiple floors require the same channel.

   C. Each floor should be treated as an individual site survey.

   D. The channel plan should take all three floors into consideration.

3. What devices, tools, or programs can be used in a manual site survey? (Choose two.)

   A. Spectrum analyzer

   B. Passive scanning utility

   C. Predictive site analyzer

   D. Association analyzer

   E. Authentication analyzer

4. The manual site survey consists of which possible methods? (Choose two.)

   A. Passive

   B. Scanning

   C. Active

   D. Spectrum

   E. Packet

5. Non-Wi-Fi interference for an 802.11g network can be caused by _____ and _____. (Choose two.)

   A. AM radios

   B. Microwave ovens

   C. 802.11b networks

   D. Cordless phones

   E. Radar systems

   F. Digital TV systems

6. You are a network consultant hired to perform a manual site survey for a small office build-ing. The wireless network to be installed will use data and voice. For backward compat-ibility the customer needs to support 2.4 GHz equipment. In order to provide the highest quality of service for the voice application, you recommend that the received signal strength be a minimum of _____ for a data rate of 54 mbps.

   A. –20 dBm

   B. –25 dBm

   C. –56 dBm

   D. –76 dBm

7. A type of site survey that is software-based, requires minimum time on-site, and takes into consideration the attenuation value of materials such as the type of walls and doors is _____ .

   A. Active

   B. Passive

   C. Predictive

   D. Optional

8. You are performing a protocol analysis in order to determine potential interference from other wireless LANs in the immediate area of the site survey. You discover several wireless LANs that can potentially cause interference with the proposed installation. Which technol-ogy in use would *not* have an impact on the 802.11g wireless network you are surveying for?

   A. FHSS

   B. OFDM

   C. DSSS

   D. ERP-OFDM

   E. PBCC

9. You are using a wireless client adapter with a site survey utility and a notebook computer to perform a manual site survey in a very small office building. Which values are important to record to verify proper RF coverage for the location?

   A. Signal strength

   B. SNR

   C. Packet retries

   D. Signal loss

   E. Propagation loss

10. You have been hired by a company to perform a manual site survey. When explaining the difference between a manual and predictive survey, you let the customer know the advantages and disadvantages of each. A manual site survey has which advantage?

   A. Fast

   B. No hardware required

   C. Accurate

   D. Facility access not required

11. A spectrum analyzer can be used to view what?

   A. Radio frequency

   B. Wireless packets

   C. Data rates

   D. Association frames

12. You have been hired by a company to perform a wireless LAN site survey in a multi-tenant building. You discover numerous access points on channels 1, 6, and 11. In order to optimize the new deployment, what recommendation could you make to the customer? Assume that all new hardware will be purchased and backward compatibility is not required.

   A. Configure the access points to automatic channel selection for the 2.4 GHz ISM band

   B. Configure the access points to operate in the 5 GHz band

   C. Perform a spectrum analysis to find space in the 2.4 GHz band

   D. Perform a predictive site survey to determine which channels to use

13. Which of the following is true of a predictive modeling survey?

   A. It takes more time than a passive survey to get accurate results.

   B. It takes less time than a passive survey to get accurate results.

   C. It finds areas of interference from neighboring wireless LANs.

   D. It helps you choose the manufacturer's equipment to be used for the wireless LAN.

14. When using a predictive site survey approach, which of the following is true about manual verification?

   A. Manual verification never has to be performed.

   B. Manual verification is always required.

   C. Manual verification should be performed only at the customer's request.

   D. Manual verification should be performed, but it is not required.

15. When performing a manual site survey, choose the best way to identify areas that lack RF coverage.

   A. Mark them with tape so they can be located at a later time

   B. Use a camera to take a photograph and document it in the report

   C. Show the site manager the areas that lack coverage

   D. Document on the floor plans or blueprints

16. When a device associates to an access point during a site survey, it is performing what type of survey?

    A. Predictive

    B. Active

    C. Passive

    D. Required

17. When considering the use of antennas for wireless LAN deployment during a site survey, which antenna could be tested to verify proper coverage for a long hallway or corridor?

    A. High gain omnidirectional

    B. Low gain omnidirectional

    C. Parabolic dish

    D. Yagi

18. You need to perform a site survey for a small real estate office that currently has no wireless network. Which factors must be considered as part of the site survey?

    A. Spectrum analysis

    B. Packet analysis

    C. Environmental conditions

    D. Correct antenna selection

19. Co-channel interference is caused by access points on _____ .

    A. Channels 1 and 1

    B. Channels 1 and 2

    C. Channels 1 and 6

    D. Channels 1, 6, and 11

20. Which guidelines are recommended when performing a manual site survey? (Choose two.)

    A. Walkthrough of location

    B. Predictive analysis

    C. Equipment purchase

    D. Client device configuration

    E. Spectrum analysis

Answers to Review Questions

1. **A, C.** The main objectives of a wireless site survey are to determine areas of RF interference and RF coverage as well as locations of access points and other infrastructure devices. The applications used have more to do with capacity planning. Wiring closet locations and security implantations are factors that need to be taken into consideration but are not the main objectives.

2. **D.** Because of RF propagation, site surveys are really three-dimensional. Therefore in a three-story building all floors need to be taken into consideration. Omnidirectional antennas may be polarized either vertically or horizontally. Single channel architectures use the same channel for multiple floors.

3. **A, B.** A spectrum analyzer and a tool that passively scans for wireless networks such as NetStumbler can be used for a manual site survey. The other options' association and authentication can be viewed using a protocol analyzer and are not "stand-alone" tools.

4. **A, C.** Manual site surveys can be either passive or active. Scanning is a method of locating wireless LANs. A spectrum analyzer will allow you to see the RF. A packet is information that carries computer data from one device to another.

5. **B, D.** Non-Wi-Fi interference is interference by anything other than wireless LANs that operates in the same frequency range. AM radios and digital TV systems do not operate in the license-free bands. 802.11b interference is wireless LAN interference. Radar systems operate in the 5 GHz UNII band.

6. **C.** Recommended received signal strength for voice applications in the 2.4 GHz ISM band at a data rate of 54 mbps is about –56 dBm. A recommended signal-to-noise ratio is less than 20 to 25 dB. –76 dBm is good for data at 54 mbps.

7. **C.** A predictive site survey is software based and takes the attenuation values of the building and other materials into consideration. Active and passive are forms of manual site surveys and record actual information about the site.

8. **B.** OFDM networks operate in the 5 GHz UNII band and would not affect a 802.11g network that operates in the 2.4 GHz ISM band. FHSS, DSSS, and ERP-OFDM all operate in the 2.4 GHz ISM band and could cause interference with an 802.11g network.

9. **A, B.** The signal strength and SNR are two important values to record during the manual site survey process. Signal loss and propagation loss have different effects, and packet retries are more of an issue with dynamic rate selection.

10. **C.** Manual site surveys can be very accurate because actual readings are taken at the site using test access points and a wireless client. This can take quite some time to complete depending on the size of the location. Wireless hardware is required to perform the site survey, and access to the whole facility is required.

11. **A.** A spectrum analyzer can be used to view radio frequency. Wireless packets, data rates, and association frames can be viewed with a protocol analyzer.

12. B. Since new hardware will be purchased and backward compatibility is not required, you could recommend using wireless network hardware that works in the 5 GHz band. This will eliminate interference from the other tenants that are using the 2.4 GHz ISM band. Automatic channel selection, spectrum analysis, and predictive site survey will not help because surrounding access points already use the entire band.

13. B. A predictive modeling site survey will take less time than a passive survey because a passive survey requires a manual analysis. On-site protocol analysis or scanning utility will determine areas of RF interference from wireless LANs. The predictive modeling survey does not help you choose manufacturer's equipment to be used in a deployment.

14. D. A verification of the predictive survey should be performed to verify that the survey meets the customer's requirements. Although is not required, it should be considered.

15. D. Dead spots (areas that lack RF coverage) should be identified on floor plans or blueprints. This is part of standard documentation practices. Marking them with tape, taking a photograph, and showing the site manager in person are not the best ways to document dead spots.

16. B. An active site survey requires the survey device to associate to an access point. A passive site survey monitors all access points in the area. A predictive site survey does not involve associating to an access point. Associating to an access point is not a required part of manual testing.

17. D. A semidirectional antenna such as a Yagi is a good choice for an application requiring coverage down a long hallway or corridor. Low or high gain omnidirectional antennas will provide 360-degree horizontal coverage. Parabolic dish antennas are typically used for outdoor long-range bridging.

18. D. In this situation, correct antenna selection is important to provide optimal coverage as well as proper aesthetics. In this example, a spectrum analysis or protocol analysis could be performed but are not required. Environmental conditions are typically not an issue in a small office deployment.

19. A. Co-channel interference is caused by two access points operating on the same radio frequency channel. Access points operating on channels 1 and 2 may cause adjacent channel interference. Channels 1, 6, and 11 are non-overlapping channels and will not interfere with one another.

20. A, E. A walkthrough of the location and spectrum analysis are both recommended guidelines when performing a manual site survey. Equipment purchase and client device configuration are additional factors to consider but are not part of the manual site survey. A predictive analysis is a software-based site survey solution that does not require manual testing.

Chapter

10

WLAN Security

THE FOLLOWING CWTS EXAM OBJECTIVES ARE COVERED IN THIS CHAPTER:

✓ **Identify and describe the following WLAN security techniques**

- SSID hiding

- Legacy security mechanisms: WEP and MAC filtering

- User-based security 802.1X/EAP and RADIUS authentication

- Passphrase-based security

- Push-button or PIN-based wireless security

- Encryption: TKIP/CCMP

- Role-based access control (RBAC)

- Virtual private networking (VPN)

- Wireless intrusion prevention systems (WIPS)

✓ **Regulatory compliance**

- PCI compliance

- HIPAA compliance

- Enforcing compliance with WIPS

Security is an important part of wireless networking just as it is in any other type of computer networking or information technology. When the IEEE 802.11 standard was first ratified, it addressed some types of basic security. However, the security solutions were considered weak and were easily compromised early on. In this chapter, we will look at some of the WLAN security techniques used for standards-based wireless networking, including:

- Service set identifier (SSID) hiding

- Media access control (MAC) filtering

- Wired equivalent privacy (WEP)

We will also take a look at some of the vulnerabilities of these solutions and see why they should not be used, if possible. This chapter will also discuss some of the newer security solutions available based on the IEEE 802.11i amendment to the standard and available from WPA or WPA 2.0. We will take a look at both SOHO security solutions and enterprise-level security solutions. They include:

- Preshared key

- Passphrase

- User-based authentication

- IEEE 802.1X/EAP

- Remote Access Dial In User Service (RADIUS)

In Chapter 1, "Introduction to Wireless Local Area Networking," we discussed some of the certifications available from the Wi-Fi Alliance that pertain to security. This chapter will explore further some of the concepts of push-button, PIN-based wireless security, passphrase, and 802.1X/EAP. We will also discuss encryption methods, ways to scramble computer data that are useful for wireless LANs. One thing that is often overlooked is security from a remote location, such as a wireless hotspot. In this chapter, we will take a look at virtual private network (VPN) solutions and how they can be used to secure wireless connections for users connecting to the corporate network. Wireless intrusion prevention systems (WIPS) are also becoming very popular in today's wireless LAN world. If WIPS is implemented correctly, these solutions can provide a wealth of information as well as protection for your network infrastructure and wireless devices. Finally, this chapter will look at legislative regulatory compliance that is currently in effect for a variety of industries, such as medical, retail, and financial.

Introduction to Wireless Security

The importance of network security is often underestimated, and wireless LAN security is no different. "Why do I need to secure my access point?" "I don't have anything on my computer that would be of interest to anybody other than me." "I tried to enable security on my wireless, but I could not get it to work so I just turned it off." These are some of the common phrases many technical support engineers or consultants used to hear from people when it came to wireless security. In the early days of wireless networking, security was weak. This led to much vulnerability, which in turn made wireless networking not a very attractive solution for many enterprise deployments, especially those concerned about security. With the improvements in wireless LAN security, partly due to the Wi-Fi Alliance certifications as well as the IEEE 802.11i amendment to the standard, wireless LANs have become part of many enterprise networks in various industries and businesses. Due to the unbounded nature of wireless networks, it is possible to have more security protecting wireless communication than what is used to secure most wired LANs. This is the case in many wireless LAN implementations.

Wireless LAN Threats and Intrusion

Computer networks have always been the target of various types of intrusion techniques. Wireless networks are no different—in fact, wireless networks are more vulnerable to intrusion because the communication is not bounded by any physical media such as an Ethernet cable. The level of security applied to a wireless network will depend on a couple of things:

- What are you trying to protect?
- What are you trying to prevent?

There are many security concerns related to wireless networking. Some of these concerns are because wireless LANs use radio frequency and the air to communicate. Others are a threat to either wired or wireless networks. The following list identifies some of these concerns and threats:

- Eavesdropping
- RF denial of service (DoS)
- MAC spoofing
- Hijacking
- Man-in-the-middle attacks
- Peer-to-peer attacks
- Encryption cracking

Although many of these threats or methods of intrusion are common, advanced security solutions are available to help discover and mitigate them. Figure 10.1 illustrates some of these vulnerabilities.

FIGURE 10.1 Wireless LANs are subject to many potential security threats

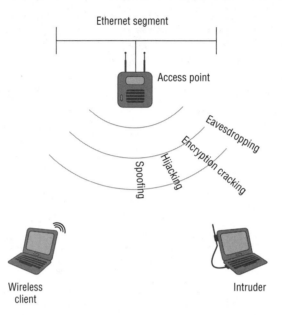

Real World Scenario

Locking the Door of Your Automobile

Let's take a quick look at an analogy that may make network security easier to understand. You need to run some errands on a Saturday afternoon and decide to go to the market to pick up some supplies. When you arrive at your destination, you leave your automobile but do not lock the door. Who could potentially enter your vehicle? The answer is anybody who attempts to open the door. Locking the door of your vehicle will prevent the casual intruder from being able to enter through the door. Therefore the lock on your door is one layer of security that could be used to prevent a potential intruder from entering your vehicle.

So, with the door locked, now who could potentially get into your vehicle? The answer is two different individuals: first, you (because you have the key to the door); second, a potential intruder who could compromise the lock on the door. As you can see, locking the door provides a layer of security and will prevent the casual intruder from entering your vehicle, but it will not prevent a determined intruder.

Now let's add a second layer of security. In addition to locking the door you set an alarm on your vehicle. You now have two layers of security: the door lock and the alarm. For an intruder to gain access to your vehicle, they would now need to have the knowledge and the ability to overcome two layers of security. First, they would need the ability to compromise the lock on the door, and then they would need the knowledge to disable the alarm, both without being noticed. The number of potential intruders has decreased significantly, from those who can just open the unlocked door, to those that have the knowledge to not only compromise the door lock but also disable the alarm.

IEEE 802.11 Standards Security

Even though wireless LAN security has greatly increased over the past decade, it is important to look at the original IEEE 802.11 standard as it relates to security. It is important to understand some of the basics or building blocks prior to getting into more sophisticated areas of security. From a security viewpoint, the original standard addressed two areas of security: authentication and privacy. Both of these are common components of computer network security. In regards to computer networking, *authentication* is defined as a way of confirming an identity; basically, it determines that you are who you say you are. Privacy is ensuring that information or data is understandable only by the individuals or groups it is intended for, the sender and the intended receiver.

One way many people may think of authentication is to supply a username and password in order to log onto a computer. Another would be to supply the appropriate logon before performing an activity like Internet banking. To review from Chapter 7, "WLAN Terminology and Technology," the original IEEE 802.11 standard addresses two types of authentication: open system authentication and shared key authentication. These authentication types are different from the examples described above, which most people are familiar with. 802.11 authentication is performed by the wireless LAN technology and, except for shared key authentication, does not require user intervention.

Open System Authentication

To review from Chapter 7, this type of authentication is a two-step process, also known as a two-way handshake, and is one of the simplest ways to provide an authentication process. Open system authentication cannot fail. This authentication is what is known as a *null authentication*, which for the most part means it doesn't really authenticate anything at all. For example, if a wireless client device such as a notebook computer wants to join the wireless network, it will ask the access point if it can authenticate, and the access point will always accept.

Shared Key Authentication

Also discussed in Chapter 7, shared key authentication is a four-step process, also known as four-way handshake, not to be confused with the four-way handshake in the 802.11i amendment and WPA 2.0. The main difference between open system and shared key authentication is, with shared key authentication, Wired Equivalent Privacy (WEP) is required in order for it to function correctly. But WEP is not very secure, so it makes shared key authentication weak and vulnerable to intrusion. WEP was intended only to protect wireless network users against casual eavesdropping and for authentication with shared key. Figure 10.2 shows how to set either open system or shared key authentication on an enterprise-grade access point.

FIGURE 10.2 Cisco 1200 access point security settings

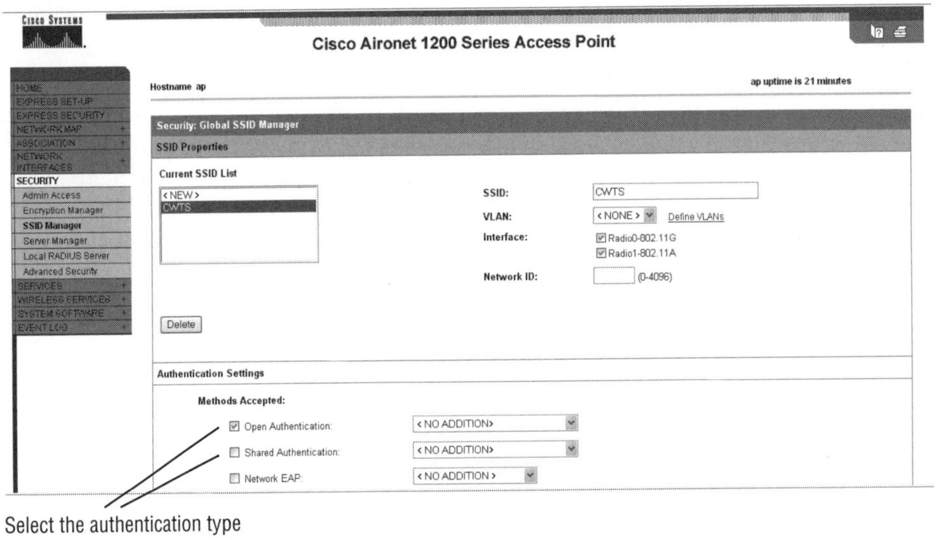

Select the authentication type

Early WLAN Security Mechanisms

Because of the way security was defined in the original IEEE 802.11 standard, manufacturers of wireless LAN equipment were able to design several ways a user could secure wireless LAN. But even though they look good on paper they did not do much to provide a good security solution. Some of these common WLAN security methods and legacy security solutions discussed in this chapter are:

- Service Set Identifier (SSID) hiding (closed network)
- Media Access Control (MAC) filtering
- Wired Equivalent Privacy (WEP)

If some of these are considered WLAN security solutions and are considered legacy, why is it important to discuss them? These solutions need to be discussed because there are still a large number of implementations that may use some or all of them as part of wireless security. Because standards-based wireless LAN technology has been around for about a decade now, many early adopters had no choice but to use these security techniques. Over the years, wireless LAN security has improved tremendously; however, it is a fact that many of these early adopters still have a large amount of equipment that will not support the latest and greatest security technology. Therefore these solutions may still currently play a role in the wireless infrastructure.

Service Set Identifier (SSID)

Looking back to Chapter 7, SSID is a name for the wireless network and was designed to be used for device segmentation. The SSID will allow wireless devices such as notebook computers to identify and connect to a wireless LAN. There are a couple of ways this can be accomplished. One is to specify the SSID of the wireless LAN to be joined in the wireless client utility of the connecting device. In this case, a wireless client sends a probe request frame with the intent of joining that particular network. The SSID is specified in a beacon frame. (A beacon is an advertisement of the wireless network. The beacon frame by default is sent at 10 times a second.)

The IEEE 802.11 standard requires access points to respond to what is known as a wild-card SSID (an SSID with a value of 0). This is when a client device does not specify the SSID in the client utility software. If a client is scanning or looking for a wireless network to join, they will see the wireless network because the beacon frame is broadcasting the SSID. Most manufacturers of SOHO and enterprise access points provide the capability to not broadcast the SSID in beacon frames. This is commonly known as disabling the SSID broadcast, SSID hiding, or a closed network.

SSID Hiding

Most manufacturers of wireless LAN equipment provide the capability to disable SSID broadcasting, as shown in Figure 10.3. Another term for this process is *SSID hiding*. SSID hiding allows a user to remove the SSID that would normally appear in broadcast beacon frames. If the SSID is not being broadcast, the network is invisible to the client devices that do not have that network's SSID specified in their client utility. If somebody knows the SSID, they would be able to enter it into their client device software and then be able to connect to the network.

In the early days of wireless networking, people would hide the SSID, believing it would secure the network because it was no longer visible to devices passively scanning for a network to join. This was a misconception, because even though the SSID is not being broadcast in these beacon frames, it is still identified in other frames. This means anyone with a scanning utility such as a packet analyzer would be able to determine the SSID by monitoring the frames that are sent through the air. Therefore hiding the SSID should not be used as a way to secure a wireless network.

FIGURE 10.3 Motorola WS2000 wireless LAN switch allows you to disable SSID broadcast

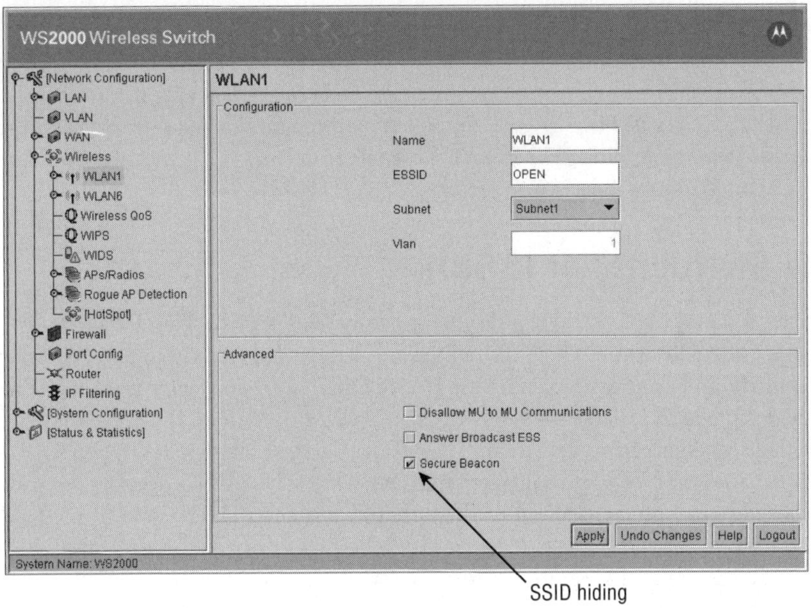

SSID hiding

Media Access Control (MAC) Address

To review, the Media Access Control (MAC) address is a unique hardware identifier of a network device. This 6-byte address is the Layer 2 address that allows frames to be sent and received to and from a device. Figure 10.4 shows the MAC address of a wireless network adapter. An important point here is that the MAC address is unique and no two devices should ever have the same MAC address. In a wireless network, MAC addresses are easily visible using a packet analyzer. These addresses are required for a device to send and receive information; therefore, they cannot be encrypted and are visible to anyone with the knowledge to view them.

FIGURE 10.4 Microsoft Windows command-line utility ipconfig.exe will display MAC address

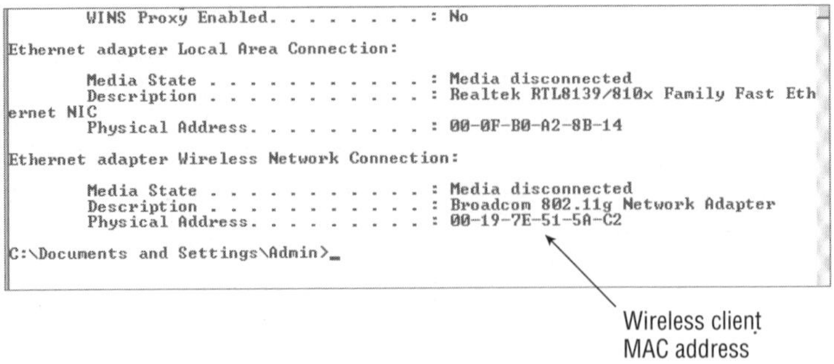

Wireless client
MAC address

MAC Address Filtering

Since wireless LAN device technology operates at the lowest two layers of the OSI model, the MAC address plays a big role in wireless networking. Manufacturers of wireless LAN equipment provided a level of security known as *MAC address filtering*. The objective of this legacy security implementation is to either allow or disallow access to the network by restricting which MAC addresses can authenticate and associate to a network. Figure 10.5 is an example of how to apply a MAC filter on an access point.

FIGURE 10.5 Linksys WRT54G MAC filter setup

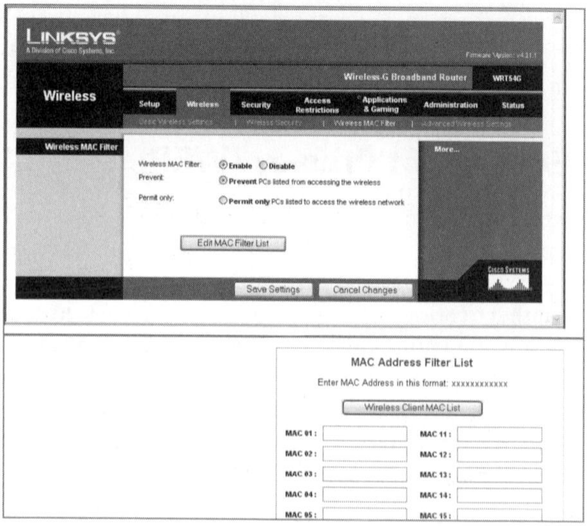

This looks great on paper but is a weak security solution because it can be compromised. Remember, wireless networks use the air as their access medium to communicate, and radio frequency is what exchanges the information between devices. So if an intruder were to monitor the air with a tool such as a packet analyzer, they would be able to see all the wireless traffic within hearing range. Because wireless LAN devices communicate with each other using MAC addressing, all of these addresses would be visible to whoever wants to see them.

MAC Spoofing

Since MAC addresses are visible to anyone who wants to take the time to see them by using the correct tool, they create a potential problem for those who implemented MAC address filtering. An intruder can easily perform a task called *MAC spoofing*. This involves tricking the wireless device into thinking its MAC address is something other than what is encoded in the actual network card. There are several ways for an intruder to accomplish MAC spoofing. It can be done with software programs such as SMAC or within the computer operating system (for example, in the Microsoft Windows registry).

Authentication and Encryption

As discussed earlier in this chapter, authentication is defined as validating an identity. Authentication also gives the capability to control access to a system. In the original IEEE 802.11 standard, this is accomplished by using either open system or shared key authentication. Since open system authentication is a null authentication method, it cannot fail and the device will always authenticate. Shared key, on the other hand, uses Wired Equivalent Privacy (WEP) for authentication as well as for data encryption. Encryption is the process of modifying information from its original form to make it unreadable except by those who know the technique or the method in which the data was modified. In the original 802.11 standard, data encryption was accomplished by using WEP. In order for a device to pass information across an access point, it must first authenticate, and then associate.

About Wired Equivalent Privacy (WEP)

From a security perspective, one major drawback with wireless networking is the fact that the information travels through the air from one device to another. This makes wireless LANs vulnerable to eavesdropping and inherently less secure than bounded networking. With open system authentication, all information is broadcast through the air in clear text. What this means is anyone with knowledge of how to use a packet analyzer or other software tool can easily see all the information that is passing between devices.

WEP was designed as a way to protect wireless networking from casual eavesdropping. The original 802.11 standard states that the use of WEP is optional. The manufacturer supplies the capability, but it is up to the user to implement it.

In wireless LANs, WEP can be used in one of two ways: with open system authentication to encrypt the data or with shared key authentication, which is used for device authentication and data encryption. The original standard specified only 64-bit WEP (40-bit key + 24-bit WEP IV).

How to Use WEP

WEP is fairly simple to implement. It requires all devices to have the same key. The WEP key can be either 64-bit or 128-bit; however, the standard required only 64-bit WEP. One disadvantage to WEP is that it is static, which means all wireless devices—access points, bridges, and client stations—must have the key manually entered into them.

As part of Payment Card Industry (PCI) compliance, if anyone knowing the shared key leaves an organization or if the key is compromised, the key must be changed on all devices to maintain compliance. WEP will no longer be allowed within PCI compliance by the end of 2010. Legislative compliance is discussed later in this chapter.

Figure 10.6 shows configuring an enterprise-grade access point for WEP.

FIGURE 10.6   Cisco 1200 WEP key settings

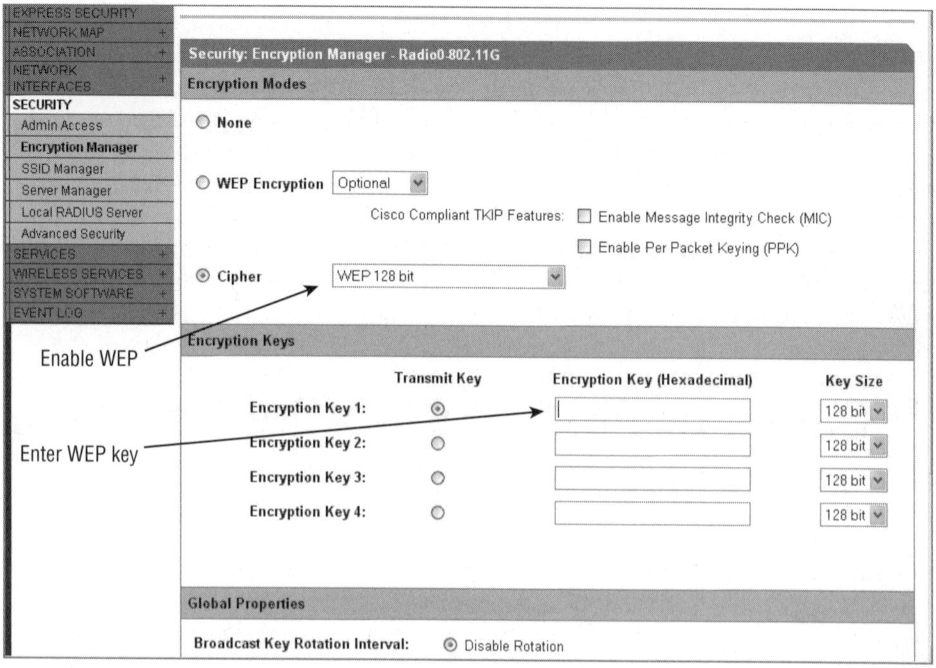

Table 10.1 describes the features of the two types of WEP keys.

TABLE 10.1   Features of the Two Types of WEP Keys

Key Length	# of ASCII Characters	# of Hex Characters
64 bit	5	13
128 bit	10	26

One major disadvantage of using WEP is that it was compromised early on and therefore not secure. A few years back, someone could capture data using a packet analyzer and with a little knowledge and correct software utilities would be able to crack the WEP key fairly easily. This made WEP a weak security solution, but it was pretty much the only solution available at the time.

With today's technology, WEP can be cracked very easily and very quickly. WEP will be discussed in more detail in the section "Encryption: WEP/TKIP/CCMP" later in this chapter.

SOHO and Enterprise Security Solutions

The IEEE 802.11i amendment to the standard provided much improvement in the ways wireless LANs can be secured. Enterprise-based wireless LANs are now capable of the most up-to-date security solutions available in the industry. This amendment to the standard introduced what is known as the Robust Secure Network Association (RSNA). In order for wireless LAN equipment to create an RSNA, it must be RSNA capable or 802.11i compliant, which means it will support Temporal Key Integrity Protocol (TKIP) and it must also support Counter mode with Cipher-block chaining Message authentication code Protocol (CCMP). The Wi-Fi Alliance has released several certifications that pertain to wireless networking: WPA, WPA 2.0, and WPS.

PIN-Based or Push-Button Configuration (PBC) Wireless Security

Many manufacturers of SOHO-grade wireless equipment have adopted either PIN-based or push-button wireless security. Both of these solutions simplify the process of securing a wireless network either for the SOHO environment or for home-based users. As discussed in Chapter 1, the Wi-Fi Alliance has branded a certification for push-button and PIN-based security called Wi-Fi Protected Setup. The Wi-Fi Protected Setup certification (WPS) addresses both of these solutions.

PIN-Based Security

Personal identification number (PIN) functionality is required in order for a wireless device to be Wi-Fi Protected Setup (WPS) certified. *PIN-based security* requires a unique PIN to be entered on all devices that will be part of the same secure wireless network. A PIN will come as either a fixed label or sticker on a device, or it can be dynamically generated in the setup utility and shown on the computer screen. The registrar device in the case of a wireless LAN is the access point. The access point will detect when a new wireless device that supports WPS is in radio range. When this device tries to join the network, the registrar will prompt the user to enter the unique PIN. Once the PIN is entered, the process authenticates the device and encrypts the network data sent to and from the device. Figure 10.7 shows an example of PIN-based wireless security.

Push-Button Configuration (PBC) Security

Push-button security or push-button configuration (PBC) allows users to configure wireless LAN security with "the push of a button," making setting up wireless security a one-step process. When a user pushes a hardware button on the wireless residential gateway (wireless router) and clicks a software button in the utility for the network adapter installed in the client device wanting to associate, push-button security creates a connection between the devices, configures the network's SSID, and turns on security. This allows a secure connection among all devices that are part of the wireless network. Figure 10.8 shows an example of push-button security. The Linksys version of push-button security is called SecureEasySetup (SES).

In order to use SES, all devices, including the wireless residential gateway/router and the wireless client adapters, must support the feature. First a button is pushed on the wireless residential gateway/router, then a button (a software setting in the client utility) is clicked on the wireless device(s). Usually in less than a minute the process is complete and all devices have a secure connection. Only those devices within RF hearing range that are participating in the process will become part of the secure network.

FIGURE 10.7   D-Link access point with PIN-based security

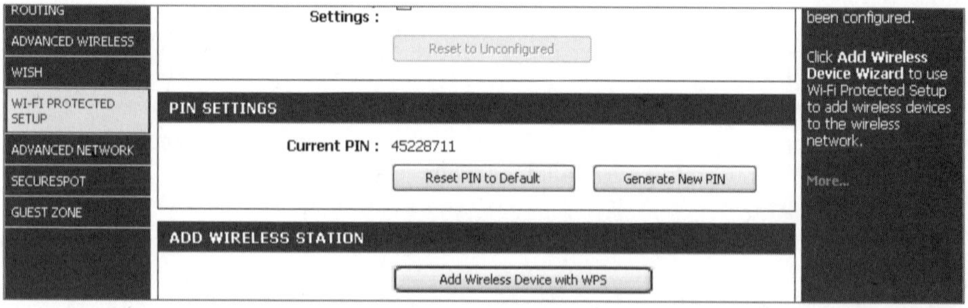

FIGURE 10.8   Linksys WRT54G wireless residential gateway/router with push-button security (SES)

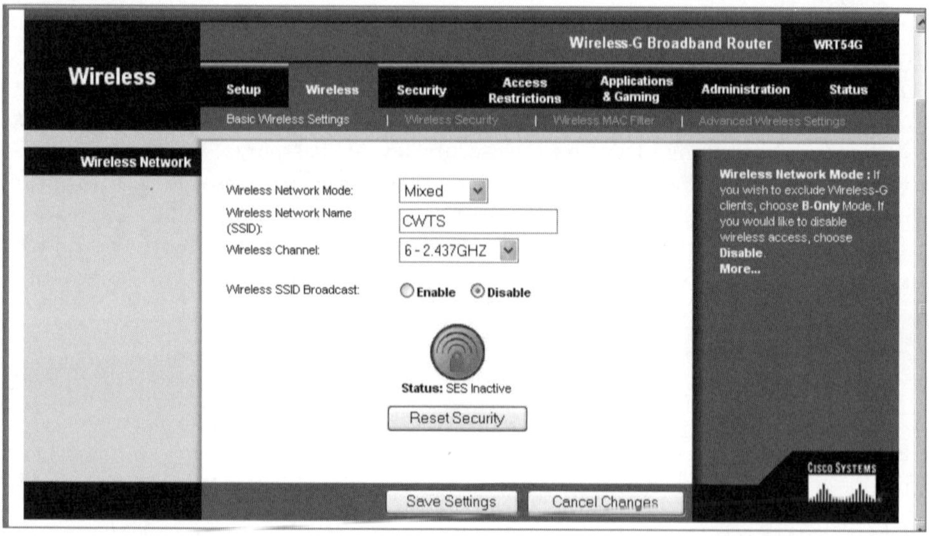

Support for both PIN and PBC configurations is required for access points; client devices at a minimum must support PIN. A third, optional method, near field communication (NFC) tokens, is also supported. A USB flash drive (memory card or solid-state storage drive with a USB interface) may be used to store and transfer credentials. There are many SOHO equipment manufacturers that have Wi-Fi Protected Setup certified devices on the market today. Some include:

- Belkin
- Broadcom
- D-Link
- Linksys
- Netgear
- TRENDnet
- ZyXEL

For these and other manufacturers that support Wi-Fi Protected Setup (WPS), visit the Wi-Fi Alliance website at www.wi-fi.org.

Passphrase-Based Security

Passphrase-based security was designed with the SOHO user or home-based user in mind. This type of security allows a user to create a very secure wireless LAN solution without the experience or knowledge necessary to configure enterprise-level components such as an 802.1X/EAP and a RADIUS server. Passphrase-based security requires all devices that are part of the same wireless network to have the same 256-bit preshared key (PSK) in order to communicate. The capability to derive a secure key of this length would be a daunting task; to ease the burden of having to create a long secure key, the passphrase was introduced. This works by requiring the user to enter a strong passphrase on all devices that are part of the same wireless LAN to be secured. The benefit of a passphrase is it can be a sequence of words or other text that is memorable only to the user who created it. After the passphrase is entered into the device, with the help of an electronic algorithm it will create a 256-bit preshared key.

Passphrase Features

The features of the passphrase are as follows:

- 8 to 63 ASCII or 64 hexadecimal characters
- Creates a 256-bit preshared key
- The longer the passphrase, the more secure
- Weak passphrases can be compromised

Figure 10.9 shows how to configure a passphrase on a SOHO access point.

FIGURE 10.9   D-Link access point passphrase settings

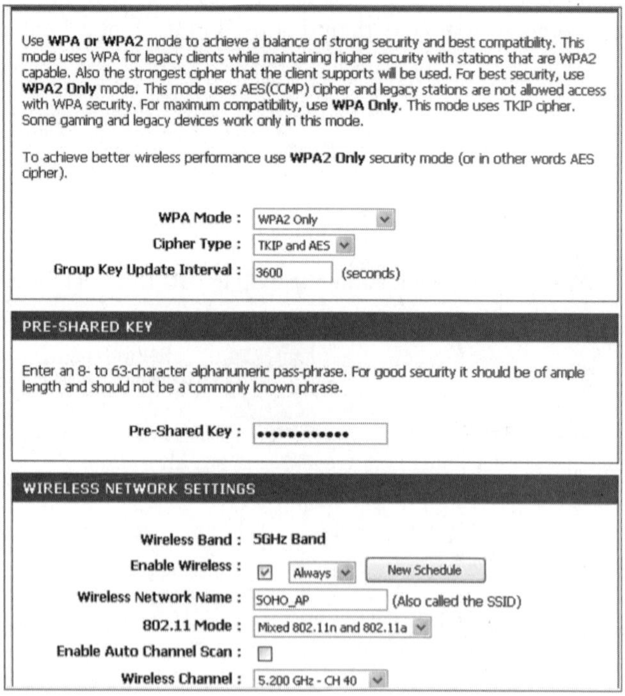

User-Based Security

Concerned about problems connected with MAC filtering and WEP, the industry drove the development of additional, improved wireless security solutions. One of these solutions also operates at Layer 2 and is an IEEE standard. This advanced enterprise-level solution is known as IEEE 802.1X, also called user-based security. User-based security allows an administrator to restrict access to a wireless network and its resources by creating users in a database. Anyone trying to join the network will be required to authenticate as one of the users by supplying a username and password. After successful authentication, the user will be able to gain access to resources for which they have permissions. This type of mutual authentication is more secure than the previously mentioned security measures.

802.1X

IEEE 802.1X is a port-based access control method and was designed to work with wired networks. However, this standard was adapted into the wireless world as an alternate, more powerful solution to legacy 802.11 security. Devices that use 802.1X technology are identified using different terminology than that used in IEEE 802.11 standards-based networking:

- Supplicant
- Authenticator
- Authentication server

Figure 10.10 illustrates the 802.1X/EAP process for a wireless LAN.

FIGURE 10.10   Wireless LAN client authenticating to a RADIUS server using 802.1X/EAP

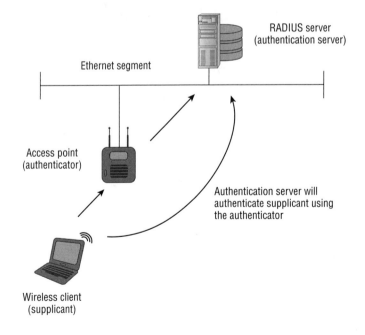

Supplicant   The supplicant is another name for the client device wanting to connect to the wireless network. This typically is the software security component of the client device and the 802.1X terminology.

Authenticator   The authenticator is the 802.1X term for the access point or wireless LAN controllers/switch. The authenticator acts as a middleman between the supplicant and the authentication server. When the supplicant requests to join the wireless network, the authenticator will pass the authentication information between the two devices.

Authentication server   The term authentication server is used by the 802.1X standard to identify the server that will authenticate the supplicant. The authentication server receives all information from the authenticator.

EAP

802.1X is a framework that allows for an authentication process. The authentication process used with 802.1X is *Extensible Authentication Protocol (EAP)*. The 802.1X standard will employ some EAP type to complete this process. There are many types of EAP available in the industry that can be used with wireless networking. These vary from proprietary solutions to very secure standard solutions. Examples of some popular EAP types include:

- EAP-TLS
- TTLS (EAP-MSCHAPv2)
- PEAP (EAP-MSCHAPv2)
- EAP-FAST

These and other EAP types allow a user to authenticate to a wireless network several different ways, including credentials such as username/password or certificate-based authentication.

 The details of EAP and how it works are beyond the scope of the CWTS certification and exam objectives. For more information, refer to other CWNP materials.

802.1X/EAP

Now it is time to put these two parts together to form the 802.1X/EAP authentication process. This authentication process is typically used for enterprise-level security. As mentioned earlier, there are a variety of EAP types available in the industry that work very well with wireless LAN solutions. The EAP type chosen will depend on the environment in which the wireless LAN is deployed. EAP types vary in specifications, costs, and complexity. Figure 10.11 shows 802.1X/EAP configuration on a wireless LAN switch.

FIGURE 10.11   Motorola WS2000 wireless LAN switch 802.1X/EAP configuration screen

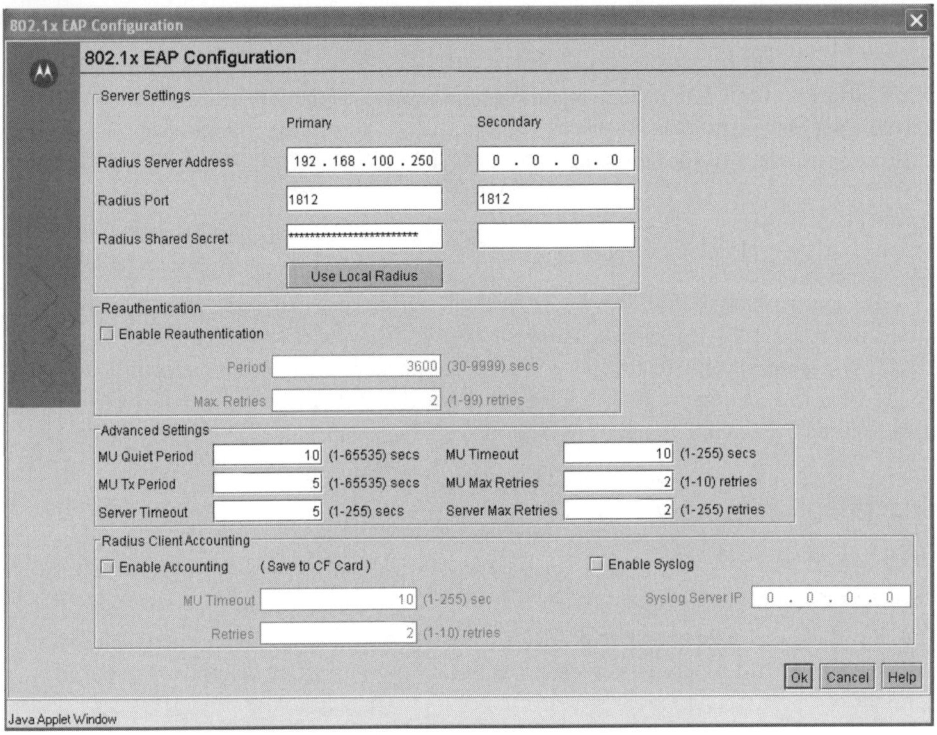

Remote Authentication Dial In User Service

Remote Authentication Dial In User Service (RADIUS) is a networking service that provides centralized authentication and administration of users. RADIUS started as a way to authenticate and authorize dial-up networking users. A remote user would dial up to a network using the public switched telephone network (PSTN) and a modem. A modem from a modem pool on the receiver side would answer the call. The user would then be prompted by a remote access server to enter a username and password in order to authenticate. Once the credentials were validated, the user would then have access to any resources for which he or she had permissions. Figure 10.12 illustrates the remote access service authentication mechanism.

FIGURE 10.12   Remote user authenticating to a RAS

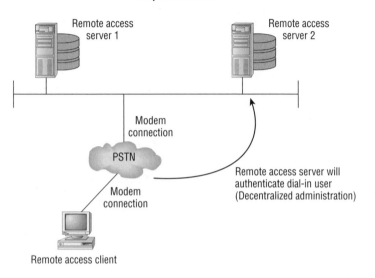

In this example, the remote access client would be the computer dialing into the network and the remote access server would be the one performing the authentication for the dial-up user. As networks grew in size and complexity and remote access technology improved, there was a need to optimize the process on the remote access server side. This is where RADIUS provides a solution. RADIUS took decentralized remote access services databases and combined them into one location, allowing for centralized administration and centralized management. It eased the burden of having to manage several databases and optimized administration of remote access services.

A company does not need a large number of RADIUS servers. For a small to medium-sized company, one RADIUS server should be sufficient (with a backup if possible). Larger enterprise organizations may need several RADIUS servers across the wide area network. In wireless networking, the wireless access point can act as a RADIUS client, which means it will have the capability to accept requests from wireless client devices and forward them to the RADIUS server for authentication. Figure 10.13 shows this configuration.

As illustrated, the remote access client is now the wireless access point. The wireless client device is authorized as a user in the database of the RADIUS server. The RADIUS server is the authenticating server or database. A RADIUS server may also be known as an authentication, authorization, and accounting (AAA) server. In this configuration, it will authenticate users and provide access to the resources for which they have permissions. In addition, it will keep track of all transactions by accounting.

FIGURE 10.13   Wireless access point as a RADIUS client device

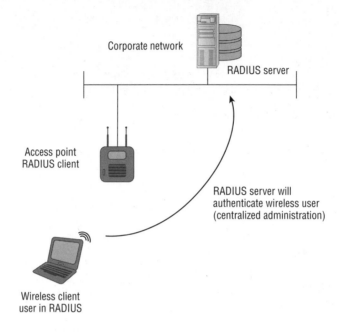

Encryption: WEP/TKIP/CCMP

In the most basic sense, encryption is taking information and scrambling it so only the sender and intended recipient that know the method are able to decipher the information. In addition to authenticating and verifying an identity, encryption also needs to be considered for wireless networking. In the IEEE 802.11 standard, there are three different encryption mechanisms that can be used on a wireless network to protect data traffic:

- Wired Equivalent Privacy (WEP)
- Temporal Key Integrity Protocol (TKIP)
- Counter Mode with Cipher Block Chaining Message Authentication Code Protocol (CCMP)

WEP

As discussed earlier in this chapter, WEP was an optional encryption method specified in the original IEEE 802.11 standard. WEP was intended to protect wireless network users against casual eavesdropping. As discussed, this encryption mechanism is considered legacy and was compromised early on, making it a weak solution to use with modern wireless networks. With early deployments of standards-based wireless networking, WEP was the only solution available, thereby making it very popular. At that time, the capability to crack WEP was available but that did not mean anyone could do it. Initially, cracking WEP required a large amount of data, some knowledge of the process, and usually a software program to extract the WEP key. Newer technology has made cracking WEP a very simple process. WEP can be cracked in minutes rather than hours, days, or weeks. The fact that WEP is available in two key lengths—64-bit or 128-bit—makes no difference to the experienced intruder. WEP uses the RC4 stream cipher for bit-level encryption. The problem with WEP does not lie in RC4 but in how it was used in the encryption process. One reason WEP is vulnerable to intrusion because of something called an initialization vector (IV). The 24-bit IV is broadcast in the clear or unencrypted. This being the case, it exposes a weakness in the way WEP was designed, thereby allowing it to be compromised.

Is WEP Still Used?

As a general rule, it is best not to use WEP as a security measure for protection of a wireless network and its users. However, there are still many large-scale deployments that use devices with wireless networking that have limited capabilities when it comes to security. WEP may be the only security option they have. If upgrading the devices to something that supports higher-level security is not an option, the organization may have no choice but to use WEP. If this is the case, it is important for the network administrator to use appropriate device segmentation for the WEP-enabled devices in order to not compromise the entire network infrastructure. One way to do this is to consider the use of a virtual local area network (VLAN). This gives the administrator the ability to separate wireless devices that may be potentially compromised because of WEP from other devices that are capable of more advanced security solutions.

There are many tools available to allow someone with limited knowledge to be able to crack WEP. As mentioned earlier, newer, more sophisticated tools allow WEP to be cracked in minutes. If a wireless network has the capability of more advanced security such as 802.11i, WPA, or WPA 2.0, one of those should be used instead of WEP. An appropriate device upgrade path should be evaluated in order to eliminate the use of WEP on any wireless network.

TKIP

Temporal Key Integrity Protocol (TKIP) was designed as a firmware (software instructions for the hardware) upgrade to WEP. TKIP added several enhancements to the WEP algorithm and was the foundation for the Wi-Fi Protected Access (WPA) certification from the Wi-Fi Alliance. These enhancements include:

- Per-packet key mixing of the IV to separate IVs from weak keys
- A dynamic re-keying mechanism to change encryption and integrity keys
- Use of the RC4 stream cipher, thereby allowing backward compatibility to WEP

Configuring a wireless network to use TKIP is a fairly straightforward process. It can be accomplished either by using the web interface available on most SOHO access points or by using the web interface or command-line interface for enterprise-level access points. For the client devices, TKIP will be configured through the client utility. Some older wireless hardware devices may not support TKIP. If this is the case, replacement of the hardware will be necessary in order to take advantage of newer security solutions. Figure 10.14 shows how to configure TKIP using WPA on an access point.

 TKIP uses a 48-bit IV and can be compromised in the same way as WEP if a weak key is used. Using a stronger solution such as Advanced Encryption Standard (AES) is a better solution.

FIGURE 10.14   Proxim AP4000 access point security configuration screen

Security Profile 1

☐ *Non Secure Station*		
	Authentication Mode	None
	Cipher	None
☐ *WEP Station*		
	Authentication Mode	None
	Cipher	WEP
	Encryption Key 0	●●●●●●●●
	Encryption Key 1	●●●●●●●●
	Encryption Key 2	●●●●●●●●
	Encryption Key 3	●●●●●●●●
	Encryption Transmit Key	Key 0
☐ *802.1x Station*		
	Authentication Mode	802.1x
	Cipher	WEP
	Encryption Key Length	64 Bits
☐ *WPA Station*		
	Authentication Mode	802.1x
	Cipher	TKIP
☑ *WPA-PSK Station*		
	Authentication Mode	PSK
	Cipher	TKIP
	PSK Passphrase	●●●●●●●●
☐ *802.11i Station*		
	Authentication Mode	802.1x
	Cipher	AES
☐ *802.11i-PSK Station*		
	Authentication Mode	PSK
	Cipher	AES
	PSK Passphrase	●●●●●●●●

OK   Cancel

Select TKIP cipher

CCMP

Counter Mode with Cipher Block Chaining Message Authentication Code Protocol (CCMP) is a mandatory part of the IEEE 801.11i amendment and part of Wi-Fi Protected Access 2.0 (WPA2) certification from the Wi-Fi Alliance. CCMP uses the *Advanced Encryption Standard (AES)* algorithm. AES apparently has been cracked using extraordinary measures. However, it is extremely hard to defeat and most intruders would not be able to crack it. CCMP is also intended as a replacement to TKIP. Because of the strong encryption CCMP provides, it may require replacement of legacy hardware. In some cases, it uses a separate chip to perform computation-intensive AES ciphering.

Configuration of CCMP is similar to that of TKIP, discussed above. The main difference with CCMP is that older hardware may not support it.

Figure 10.15 shows configuring the CCMP cipher using WPA2.

FIGURE 10.15 Cisco 1200 access point security configuration selection

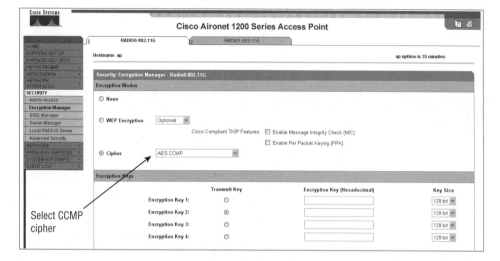

Upgrading the Firmware on Wireless LAN Hardware

In some cases, it may be necessary to upgrade the firmware (software instructions for the hardware) in order to get either TKIP or CCMP capability. It is important to follow the manufacturer's instructions when upgrading firmware to prevent damage to the device. Improper firmware upgrades or a loss of power during the upgrade process may render the device unusable or require the device to be sent back to the manufacturer for repair.

Some of the above-mentioned security technologies are part of the Wi-Fi Alliance interoperability testing for standards based wireless LAN equipment. As mentioned in Chapter 1, equipment certified for both WPA and WPA2.0 can function in either personal or enterprise modes. Table 10.2 shows the details of both WPA and WPA 2.0 certifications.

TABLE 10.2   Details of the WPA and WPA 2.0 Certifications

Wi-Fi Alliance Security Mechanism	Authentication Mechanism	Cipher Suite/ Encryption Mechanism
WPA – Personal	Passphrase	TKIP/RC4
WPA – Enterprise	802.1X/EAP	TKIP/RC4
WPA 2.0 – Personal	Passphrase	CCMP/AES or TKIP/RC4
WPA 2.0 – Enterprise	802.1X/EAP	CCMP/AES or TKIP/RC4

Role-Based Access Control (RBAC)

Role-based access control (RBAC) is a way of restricting access to only authorized users. It was designed to ease the task of security administration on large networks. RBAC has characteristics similar to those of a common network administration practice—the creation of users and groups.

In order to give a user on a network access to a network resource, best practices recommend creating a group object, assigning the group permissions to the resource, and then adding the user object to the group. This method allows any user who is a member of the group to be granted access to the resource. Role-based access control can be used for various activities users may perform while connected to a wireless LAN, including limiting the amount of throughput or controlling access to specific resources such as the Internet.

Virtual Private Networking (VPN)

Virtual private networking (VPN) is the capability to create private communications over a public network infrastructure such as the Internet. The security solutions discussed earlier in this chapter are Layer 2 security solutions; that is, all such solutions work at Layer 2 of the OSI model. By contrast, VPNs are Internet Protocol–based—they typically operate at Layer 3 of the OSI model. Figure 10.16 illustrates VPN technology in relationship to the OSI model.

FIGURE 10.16   Representation of a Layer 3 VPN security solution

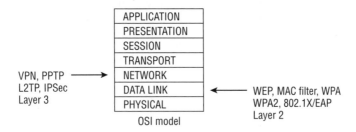

```
VPN, PPTP  ─────▶
L2TP, IPSec
Layer 3
```

| APPLICATION |
| PRESENTATION |
| SESSION |
| TRANSPORT |
| NETWORK |
| DATA LINK |
| PHYSICAL |

OSI model

```
◀───── WEP, MAC filter, WPA
       WPA2, 802.1X/EAP
       Layer 2
```

Prior to the ratification of the 802.11i amendment to the standard, VPN technology was prevalent in enterprise deployments as well as in remote access security. Since Layer 2 security solutions have become stronger (partly due to the 802.11i amendment and the Wi-Fi Alliance certifications), VPN technology is not as widely used within enterprise LANs. However, VPN still remains a very powerful security solution for remote access on both wired and wireless networking.

VPNs consist of two parts—tunneling and encryption. Figure 10.17 illustrates a VPN tunnel using the Internet. A stand-alone VPN tunnel does not provide data encryption, and VPN tunnels are created across Internet Protocol networks. In a very basic sense, VPNs use encapsulation methods where one IP frame is encapsulated within a second IP frame. The encryption of VPNs is performed as a separate function.

FIGURE 10.17   Representation of a VPN tunnel

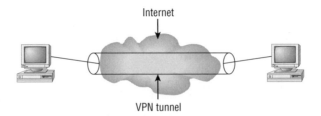

Internet

VPN tunnel

🌐 Real World Scenario

Shipping a Crate Using VPN Technology

An example of the VPN process is shipping a locked crate from one location to another. You are a technical support engineer for the headquarters office of a company that has five offices in different locations around the world. You get a telephone call from a co-worker at one of the remote offices. She needs to replace an access point with a newer model at the remote office. You need to ship the preconfigured replacement access point to her using a common carrier. You want to ensure that the access point arrives at the destination location without coming into physical contact with anybody other than the intended recipient.

The access point is analogous to the *IP frame*. You put the access point into a crate that has a combination lock to secure it. This crate containing the access point is analogous to the *second IP frame,* or the one that *encapsulates* the original IP frame.

You ship the crate to the destination using a common carrier, which would be analogous to the *public infrastructure* over which the encrypted data is sent. Many other packages are shipped by this common carrier, but no one will be able to see the contents of the crate because they do not know the combination to the lock (the encryption method).

When the access point arrives at the destination, the recipient (the technical support engineer for the remote office) must know the combination of the lock on the crate in order to open it to retrieve the access point. So you tell her the combination over the telephone. This is analogous to the *encryption method*. Over a secure telephone line, only you (the sender) and she (the recipient) know the combination to the lock. The tech support engineer will be able to unlock the crate using the combination you supplied her, and she will be able to retrieve the access point.

The two most common types of VPN protocols are:

- *Point-to-Point Tunneling Protocol (PPTP)*
- *Layer 2 Tunneling Protocol (L2TP)*

PPTP

Developed by a vendor consortium that included Microsoft, Point-to-Point Tunneling Protocol (PPTP) was very popular because of its ease of configuration and was included in all Microsoft Windows operating systems starting with Windows 95. PPTP uses Microsoft Point-to-Point Encryption (MPPE) Protocol for encryption. This process provides both tunneling and encryption capabilities for the users and data.

WARNING   If the PPTP configuration is configured to use MS-CHAP version 2 for user authentication, it can be a security issue. This authentication process can be captured using a protocol analyzer or other software tool and potentially allow someone to perform a *dictionary attack* allowing them to acquire a user's credentials and eventually giving them the capability to log on to the network. A dictionary attack is performed by software that challenges the encrypted password against common words or phrases in a text file (dictionary).

L2TP

Layer 2 Tunneling Protocol (L2TP) is the combination of two different tunneling protocols: Cisco's Layer 2 Forwarding (L2F) and Microsoft's Point-to-Point Tunneling Protocol (PPTP). L2TP is the tunneling process and requires some level of encryption in order to function. With L2TP, a popular choice of encryption is Internet Protocol Security (IPSec), which provides authentication and encryption for each IP packet in a data stream. Since it was published in 1999 as a proposed standard and because it is more secure than PPTP, L2TP has gained much popularity and for the most part is a replacement for PPTP.

Components of a VPN Solution

A VPN solution consists of three components:

- Client side
- Network infrastructure
- Server side

In many cases, both client side and server side are known as endpoints. The infrastructure in many cases is a public access network such as the Internet. The client side typically consists of software allowing it to be configured for the VPN. This software is available at a nominal cost from a variety of manufacturers. Newer Microsoft Windows operating systems include VPN client software for both PPTP and L2TP. Figure 10.18 shows a VPN client configuration.

FIGURE 10.18 Microsoft Windows built-in VPN client utility

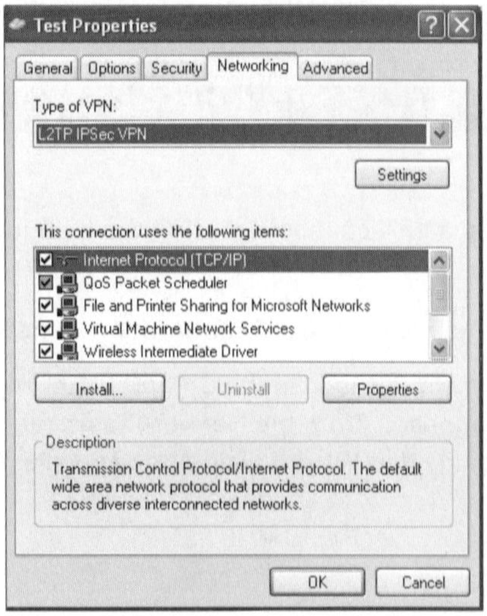

Wireless LAN devices have the capability to be a VPN client. The VPN can terminate either at an access point or across the Internet to the corporate network. Figure 10.19 shows a common example of a wireless client device connecting to a wireless hotspot to access the corporate network.

FIGURE 10.19   Wireless LAN client using hotspot to connect to corporate office using VPN technology

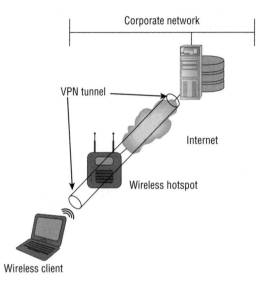

In Exercise 10.1, you will explore the built-in VPN client utility in Windows XP.

EXERCISE 10.1

VPN Setup

In this exercise, you will set up a VPN connection using the built-in VPN client utility in Microsoft Windows XP.

1. Click on Start, Control Panel. The Control Panel window appears.

2. Click on the Network Connections icon in the Control Panel window. The Network Connections dialog box appears. From the Network Tasks menu, click Create a New Connection. The New Connection Wizard dialog box appears. Click Next.

3. The New Connection Wizard Network Connection Type dialog box appears. Select the radio button next to "Connect to the network at my workplace" and click Next

4. The New Connection Wizard Network Connection dialog box appears. Click on the radio button next to "Virtual Private Network connection" and click Next.

5. The New Connection Wizard Connection Name dialog box appears. Enter your company name and click Next.

6. The New Connection Wizard VPN Server Selection dialog box appears. Type the IP address or host name of the remote VPN server you wish to connect to. Click Next.

7. The New Connection Wizard Completing the New Connection Wizard dialog box appears. Click Finish to complete the setup.

8. The Connect dialog box appears, prompting for a username and password. Enter a valid username and password and click Connect to connect to the VPN server.

9. After your credentials have been validated by the VPN server, you will have access to the network.

Wireless Intrusion Prevention Systems (WIPS)

In wireless networking, a *wireless intrusion prevention system (WIPS)* is a software/hardware solution that monitors the radio waves and, using a hardware sensor, can report captured information to software to be recorded in a server database. The WIPS solution will then be able to take the appropriate countermeasures to prevent intrusion. These countermeasures are based on identifying the intrusion by comparing the captured information to an intrusion signature database within the WIPS. There are many advantages to using a WIPS. Some of them include:

- Captures information by 24/7 monitoring
- Detects threats to the wireless infrastructure such as denial-of-service (DoS) attacks and rogue access points
- Notifies of threats through a variety of mechanisms
- Supports integrated spectrum analysis
- Includes elaborate reporting systems
- Ensures compliance with regulatory policies
- Retains data for forensic investigation
- Uses hardware sensors for monitoring

24/7/365 monitoring   With WIPS, monitoring of the wireless network can be accomplished 24 hours a day, seven days a week, to help identify potential attacks, including denial of service, either from RF or from software such as a deauthentication storm. WIPS also finds rogue (unauthorized) access points and misconfigured wireless devices.

Detection and mitigation   Unlike many wireless intrusion detection systems (WIDS), WIPS has the capability to detect and react. WIPS solutions will automatically respond to threats against a wireless LAN by stopping the device or process that contains the threat before it has a chance to cause any damage to the wireless network.

Notification of threats   WIPS solutions have the capability to provide notifications to network administrators based on alerts and alarms of potential threats that the WIPS encounters during monitoring. These notifications can be provided in a variety of ways, such as e-mail or pager.

Integrated spectrum analysis   This feature allows an administrator to view the state of a remote radio environment at a branch office or remote location. This allows the accurate diagnosis of radio spectrum problems, including Layer 1 denial-of-service (DoS) attacks.

Elaborate reporting systems   In addition to standard reports, most WIPS solutions allow network administrators to create their own customized reports in a very short period of time. These reports will enable an organization to meet the specific requirements of audit groups, either internal or external, to the organization.

Regulatory policy compliance   A WIPS will have the capability to help ensure that an organization maintains the necessary legislative compliance. Compliance requirements include Health Insurance Portability and Accountability Act (HIPAA) and Payment Card Industry (PCI).

Retains data for forensics   Many WIPS solutions can retain data that may be used in forensics investigations. The WIPS will provide the documented proof an organization may require to take the appropriate action based on events recorded. WIPS solutions will require fine-tuning to some degree to eliminate misrepresentation of the threat signatures the system will detect. This starts with a baseline of the environment, allowing the administrator to gauge the levels of detection and reaction.

Uses hardware sensors for monitoring   WIPS solutions will use either dedicated hardware sensors or share the sensor functionality with access points. These sensors will collect data by monitoring the air 24/7 and allowing information to be reported to a server database.

⊕ Real World Scenario

Preventing WEP from Being Cracked with a Patented Technology Called *WEP Cloaking*

As discussed earlier in this chapter, Wired Equivalent Privacy (WEP) is weak and because of vulnerabilities it is able to be cracked. Therefore using WEP is not a recommended solution to secure wireless computer data.

You are a network consultant and have been assigned the task to evaluate a wireless network in a retail establishment that currently uses wireless barcode scanners for a variety of applications. You determine these devices currently have no security solution enabled. After evaluating the system, you come to the conclusion that the only possible wireless security solution that can be applied to these devices is WEP.

You know from experience that WEP is not secure and can be compromised. Therefore you make a recommendation to the IT manager to upgrade all of the wireless barcode scanners to support a higher level security such as WPA 2.0 to adequately secure the data. You are told by the IT manager that unfortunately the budget for the current year will not allow hardware upgrade of the devices. This being the case, you have an alternate solution. This organization currently is considering a WIPS solution.

The capability to crack WEP has been available for many years through a variety of free-ware WEP cracking tools. There are 23 known attacks against the original 802.11 encryption standard for either 64-bit or 128-bit WEP. Through the use of sophisticated utilities, WEP can be cracked in minutes regardless of the key strength. One solution known as WEP Cloaking allows organizations to operate WEP-encrypted networks securely and preserve their existing investment in mobile devices such as barcode scanners. This patented WEP Cloaking technology will make these popular freeware cracking tools useless. This solution would allow the company to maintain the current barcode scanner technology and still provide a secure wireless solution for the organization. Keep in mind that WEP Cloaking is one manufacturer's method to protect legacy devices forced to use WEP until they can be replaced with newer, more secure devices.

Regulatory Compliance

It is very important for companies, organizations, and businesses that collect private or personal information of individuals to secure that information appropriately. In recent years, there have been several legislative compliances that various businesses are required to conform to. These legislative compliances regulate how data is handled for businesses such as health care, retail, financial, and others. When using wireless networks it is imperative for companies to verify any additional requirements from a security perspective that may be needed when dealing with regulatory compliance. The next couple of sections briefly describe some of these legislative compliances.

PCI Compliance

PCI stands for *Payment Card Industry* and is a regulation requiring companies to adhere to security standards created to protect card information pertaining to financial transactions. According to the PCI Standards Council, in order to be PCI compliant a company must meet the following six requirements:

- Build and maintain a secure network
- Protect cardholder data
- Maintain a vulnerability management program
- Implement strong access control measures
- Regularly monitor and test networks
- Maintain an information security policy

For more information on PCI, visit the PCI Security Standards Council website at www.pcisecuritystandards.org

HIPAA Compliance

HIPAA is the abbreviation for the United States *Health Insurance Portability and Accountability Act* of 1996. The goal of HIPAA is to provide standardized mechanisms for electronic data exchange, security, and confidentiality of all health care related computer information and data. HIPAA consists of two parts:

▪ HIPAA, Title I

▪ HIPAA, Title II

If someone loses or changes their job, Title I of HIPAA protects their health insurance coverage.

In the information technology industries, Title II is what most people mean when they refer to HIPAA. HIPAA establishes mandatory regulations that require extensive changes to the way that health care providers conduct business by securing computer information and data.

For more information on HIPAA, visit the U.S. Department of Health and Human Services website at www.hhs.gov/ocr/hipaa

Other Regulatory Compliances

Regulatory compliances for other industries may also need to be considered. The Sarbanes-Oxley Act of 2002 (SOX), also known as the Public Company Accounting Reform and Investor Protection Act of 2002, is based on accounting reform. The Gramm-Leach-Bliley Act, also known as the Gramm-Leach-Bliley Financial Services Modernization Act, deals with financial institutions.

Summary

In this chapter, we briefly discussed network intrusion and the impact it can have on a wireless LAN. We also took a look at IEEE 802.11 security methods and a quick review from Chapter 7 of the authentication types defined in the standard, open system and shared key. We explored some of the 802.11 WLAN security techniques, including:

- SSID hiding
- MAC address filtering
- Wired Equivalent Privacy (WEP)

We discussed the vulnerabilities in each of these solutions. We showed an example of how the SSID could be hidden from view and also discussed why this is not a good security solution because other wireless frames contain the SSID and it can be found even though it is removed from a beacon frame. We looked at how MAC address filtering can be spoofed using freeware utilities downloadable from the Internet or though the operating system. The last of three security solutions, WEP, was also discussed and illustrated how it could be compromised; therefore showing it is a weak wireless security solution.

In addition to the legacy security solutions, we explored some of the more modern solutions:

SOHO and home-based solutions

- Passphrase/preshared key
- Push-button or PIN-based configuration

Enterprise-based solutions

- 802.1X/EAP
- RADIUS

We learned that encryption is taking information and scrambling it so only the sender and the intended recipient, who know the algorithm, will be able to decipher the data. We looked at various types of encryption used in wireless networking, including:

- WEP
- TKIP
- CCMP

Role-based access control (RBAC) is a component for administration of wireless networks to allow access and authorization based on individual groups and users and other parameters.

We also discussed virtual private networking (VPN), a Layer 3 solution that provides a secure connection over a public infrastructure such as the Internet. This chapter discussed how VPN technology could be a solution for wireless network users from a remote location to access corporate or other networks from a hotspot or other unsecured wireless LAN. We also compared PPTP and L2TP and discussed the differences between them. It was mentioned that PPTP using MS-CHAP version 2 is not a good security solution for wireless LANs because the authentication can be captured and potentially compromised through a dictionary attack.

Products are available for enterprise wireless LANs that will monitor the airwaves 24/7 and record all activity detected by the wireless sensors. We discussed these solutions, known as wireless intrusion prevention systems (WIPS), which have the capability to detect and react to a potential intrusion on the wireless network. We also addressed the functionality and features of these solutions. Finally, we discussed regulatory compliances such as the Health Insurance Portability and Accountability Act (HIPAA) and Payment Card Industry (PCI), and the importance of securing computer data for industries such as health care, retail, and financial.

Exam Essentials

Be familiar with 802.11 legacy security solutions Know the characteristics and features of security mechanisms, including Service Set Identifier (SSID), Media Access Control (MAC) filtering, and Wired Equivalent Privacy (WEP), and the weaknesses or vulnerabilities of each.

Understand passphrase-based security Identify the components of passphrase-based security that are commonly used for SOHO and home wireless networks.

Identify user-based security components Know the features and use of 802.1X port-based access control, Extensible Authentication Protocol (EAP), and Remote Authentication Dial In User Service (RADIUS).

Understand Layer 3 wireless security solutions Know how a virtual private network (VPN) operates as well as the components of the VPN solution. Understand the differences between Point-to-Point Tunneling Protocol (PPTP) and Layer 2 Tunneling Protocol (L2TP).

Be familiar with wireless intrusion prevention systems (WIPS) Know what a WIPS solution is and the benefits it can provide an organization to help manage wireless LAN security.

Understand the purpose of regulatory compliance Be familiar with regulatory compliances such as the Health Insurance Portability and Accountability Act of 1996 (HIPAA) and Payment Card Industry (PCI) and the important role these play in wireless LAN security.

Key Terms

802.1X

Advanced Encryption Standard (AES)

authentication

Counter Mode with Cipher Block Chaining Message Authentication Code Protocol (CCMP)

dictionary attack

encryption method

Extensible Authentication Protocol (EAP)

Health Insurance Portability and Accountability Act (HIPAA)

Layer 2 Tunneling Protocol (L2TP)

Media Access Control (MAC) address filtering

Media Access Control (MAC) spoofing

null authentication

passphrase-based security

Payment Card Industry (PCI)

PIN-based security

Point-to-Point Tunneling Protocol (PPTP)

push-button security

Remote Authentication Dial In User Service (RADIUS)

role-based access control (RBAC)

SSID hiding

Temporal Key Integrity Protocol (TKIP)

virtual private networking (VPN)

Wired Equivalent Privacy (WEP)

wireless intrusion prevention system (WIPS)

Review Questions

1. Which security methods do 802.11g access points support? (Choose three.)

    A. WPA Enterprise

    B. WEP

    C. PPTP

    D. RBAC

    E. MAC filters

    F. IPSec

2. Both _____ and _____ are wireless LAN security methods that support shared key security. (Choose two.)

    A. WPA2 Personal

    B. WPA2 Enterprise

    C. 802.1X/EAP

    D. WEP

    E. WPA Enterprise

3. Which security feature provides the strongest security for a home-based wireless network?

    A. SSID hiding

    B. Passphrase

    C. MAC filters

    D. 128-bit WEP

4. You need to attend a business meeting out of town that requires air travel. You are at the airport and have some extra time. While waiting to board your plane you decide to check your office e-mail using an 802.11g hotspot access point at the airport. In order to provide a secure connection, you would enable your notebook computer to use _____.

    A. Passphrase security

    B. WEP

    C. A VPN to the office network

    D. 802.1X/EAP to the office network

5. A _____ filter is used to allow or deny wireless barcode scanners access to an 802.11b/g network.

   A. WEP

   B. IPSec

   C. SSID

   D. RF

   E. MAC

6. The security amendment to the IEEE 802.11 standard requires _____.

   A. WEP

   B. CCMP

   C. TKIP

   D. PPTP

   E. VPN

7. Which process is a VPN solution intended to provide for users connecting to a network?

   A. Secure Layer 3 transmissions over a public network infrastructure

   B. Secure Layer 2 transmissions over a public network infrastructure

   C. Secure Layer 3 transmissions over a corporate network infrastructure

   D. Secure Layer 2 transmissions over a corporate network infrastructure

8. Which function does RBAC provide?

   A. Restricts access to authorized users

   B. Provides access to only network administrators

   C. Streamlines hardware installation

   D. Allows users to install software

9. Hiding the Service Set Identifier of a wireless LAN will require a user to _____ in order to gain access to the wireless network.

   A. Enter a username and password when prompted

   B. Call the help desk and ask for a new password

   C. Enable the SSID broadcast on the client device

   D. Know the SSID and enter it manually

10. The Remote Authentication Dial In User Service (RADIUS) service requires users on a wireless network to perform what function?

   A. Access the corporate network using only the PSTN and a modem

   B. Call in to the help desk service and request a username and password

   C. Enter a username and password that will be centrally administered

   D. Request remote assistance to help solve a software problem on a computer

11. The IEEE 802.1X standard identifies the authenticator as another term for the
_____ in wireless networking.

    A. Client device

    B. Access point

    C. RADIUS server

    D. EAP server

12. Which data encryption/authentication method is identified in the IEEE 802.11 standard?

    A. TKIP

    B. AES

    C. CCMP

    D. WEP

    E. EAP

13. You are a wireless network administrator monitoring the reports for a recently installed
wireless intrusion prevention system. You receive an alert notifying you of high levels of RF
detected from an access point operating as a sensor and currently set to channel 6. Which
problem could be causing the alert? (Choose two.)

    A. Interference from a neighboring access point

    B. RF deauthentication storm

    C. RF denial-of-service (DoS) attack

    D. Misconfigured client workstation

    E. RF encryption attack

14. The length of a WEP key is typically _____ or _____.

    A. 5-bit, 10-bit

    B. 13-bit, 26-bit

    C. 64-bit, 128-bit

    D. 128-bit, 256-bit

    E. 192-bit, 256-bit

15. Which security solution is mandatory for client devices in order to be considered Wi-Fi Protected Setup certified?

    A. WEP

    B. PIN

    C. WPA

    D. PBC

    E. TKIP

16. A newly configured wireless intrusion prevention system will _____.

    A. Require a network administrator to monitor for intrusions

    B. Automatically monitor the network for potential attacks

    C. Require an administrator to manually shut down a rogue access point

    D. Automatically notify a network administrator regarding a firmware upgrade

17. You are a network administrator and are asked for a security recommendation regarding older wireless 802.11-compliant VoIP handsets. The company does not have the budget to upgrade the equipment at this time. Which would be the best recommendation you could provide?

    A. Don't worry about securing the handsets because voice transmissions cannot be deciphered

    B. Carefully plan a strategy using WEP and VLANs

    C. Use a VPN solution with L2TP/IPSec

    D. Use a CCMP/AES Layer 2 solution

18. A weakness with MAC filtering is that it allows an intruder to _____.

    A. Crack the encryption

    B. Spoof an address

    C. Cause an RF DoS attack

    D. Steal user authentication

19. What type of wireless network device is PIN-based security most commonly used with?

    A. SOHO brands that support WPA 2.0

    B. Enterprise brands that support WPA 2.0

    C. SOHO brands that support WPS

    D. Enterprise brands that support WPS

20. Layer 2 Tunneling Protocol commonly uses which encryption method?

    A. IPSec

    B. PPTP

    C. AES

    D. WEP

    E. MPPE

Answers to Review Questions

1. **A, B, E.** WPA Enterprise, WEP, and MAC filtering can all be used to secure 802.11g access points. PPTP is a Layer 3 security solution that consists of both tunneling and encryption. IPSec is a Layer3 VPN encryption mechanism. RBAC stands for role-based access control and is a way of restricting access to only authorized users.

2. **A, D.** Both WPA2 Personal and WEP support shared key security. The WPA2 Personal algorithm creates a 256-bit preshared key. WEP can be used with either a 64-bit or 128-bit key. WPA Enterprise, 802.1X/EAP, and WPA2 Enterprise all use the 802.1X process to create a key.

3. **B.** Passphrases are available for use with WPA Personal or WPA2 Personal and are capable of providing strong security for the home user or small office. SSID hiding should not be used for security because the SSID can be found in frames other than beacons. MAC filters are considered legacy solutions and can be easily spoofed using software downloadable from the Internet. 128-bit WEP can be cracked very quickly using software tools and is therefore not a secure solution.

4. **C.** In order to provide a secure connection between your laptop and the office network, a Layer 3 VPN solution would be the best choice. Passphrase security and WEP require the access point to be configured and this typically is not the case in public hotspots. 802.1X/EAP is enterprise security and usually does not apply to public hotspots.

5. **E.** A MAC filter is used to allow or deny wireless LAN devices access to wireless access point. WEP is a shared key security mechanism. IPSec encryption is used in Layer 3 VPNs. SSIDs are used as a network name and for segmentation. RF is radio frequency and cannot be filtered.

6. **B.** The IEEE 802.11i amendment to the standard requires CCMP. WEP is an optional authentication/encryption method defined in the original 802.11 standard. TKIP is an enhancement to WEP that usually was accomplished as a firmware upgrade for older equipment. PPTP and VPN are both Layer 3 solutions and not defined in any IEEE wireless amendment.

7. **A.** A virtual private network (VPN) is a Layer 3 security solution that provides secure data transmissions over a public network infrastructure such as the Internet. WEP, WPA, 802.1X/EAP, and WPA 2.0 are examples of Layer 2 security solutions.

8. **A.** Role-based access control (RBAC) is a method used to restrict access only to authorized users. RBAC assigns permissions or access to roles to which users can be added.

9. **D.** If the SSID of the wireless network is hidden, the user will need knowledge of the SSID in order to connect to the wireless network. The SSID broadcast is only enabled on an access point or wireless LAN controller/switch. Getting a new password from the help desk will not provide the SSID of the wireless network. Entering a username and password is user-based authentication.

10. C. RADIUS is a centralized authentication method that is used to authenticate users on a wireless network. Accessing a corporate network using a modem is a function of remote access services. Making a call to the help desk and requesting a username and password is not a function of RADIUS; however, the help desk may be able to assist with username and password issues. Requesting remote assistance to help solve a software problem is more related to troubleshooting and not a function of RADIUS.

11. B. In 802.1X networking, the access point is also known as the authenticator. The supplicant is another term for the client device, and the authentication server can be a RADIUS or AAA authentication source.

12. D. The original IEEE 802.11 standard identifies WEP as an optional authentication/ encryption method. AES and CCMP are addressed in the 802.11i amendment to the standard. TKIP is an enhancement to WEP and not identified in the original standard. EAP provides an authentication process and is used with 802.1X networks.

13. A, C. Higher levels of RF reported by an intrusion prevention system could mean an RF denial-of-service attack is underway or could be misrepresented as interference from a neighboring access point. A deauthentication storm or encryption attack would be identified differently in a wireless intrusion prevention system. A misconfigured client workstation would not cause this type of alert.

14. C. WEP is typically 64-bit or 128-bt encryption. The numbers 5, 10, 13, and 26 are related to the number of characters the WEP key can be in either in ASCII or hexadecimal.

15. B. PIN-based security is mandatory for both access points and client devices in order to be considered Wi-Fi Protected Setup certified. PBC or push-button security is optional for client devices in this certification. WPA is a pre-802.11i certification that addresses TKIP and is used in either SOHO or enterprise-based wireless networks. Wi-Fi Protected Setup is not intended for enterprise WLAN deployments.

16. B. A wireless intrusion prevention system will automatically monitor the network for signatures that match potential intrusion techniques. An intrusion prevention system has the capability to automatically shut down a rogue access point. An intrusion detection system requires a manual shutdown. A WIPS will not notify a network administrator of a recent firmware upgrade.

17. B. If WEP must be used on a wireless network, the devices that use WEP should be separated using VLANs. This will protect the rest of the network from being compromised. Voice transmissions can be seen with the correct tools. CCMP/AES is available in newer devices that support the latest wireless security methods but is not available in older devices.

18. B. An intruder can spoof a MAC address in order to circumvent the MAC filter and gain access to the wireless network. Encryption cracking is a different form of intrusion that also could possibly allow an intruder to steal a user's authentication credentials. An RF denial-of-service attack is caused by transmitting high energy RF to prevent access to the wireless network.

19. C. PIN-based security is usually used with SOHO brand wireless devices that support Wi-Fi Protected Setup certification (WPS). The devices are typically used in small office/home office installations or by home-based users. WPA 2.0 solutions can use either passphrase or 802.1X/EAP.

20. A. Layer 2 Tunneling Protocol (L2TP) commonly uses IPSec for encryption. PPTP is another VPN method that uses MPPE 128-bit encryption. AES and WEP are used with Layer 2 802.11-based wireless networks.

Chapter

11

Troubleshooting and Maintaining Wireless Networks

THE FOLLOWING CWTS EXAM OBJECTIVES ARE COVERED IN THIS CHAPTER:

✓ Recognize common problems associated with wireless networks and their symptoms, and identify steps to isolate and troubleshoot the problem. Given a problem situation, interpret the symptoms and the most likely cause. Problems may include:

- Decreased throughput

- Intermittent or no connectivity

- Weak signal strength

- Device upgrades

✓ **Identify procedures to optimize wireless networks in specific situations**

- Infrastructure hardware selection and placement

- Identifying, locating, and removing sources of interference

- Client load balancing

- Analyzing infrastructure capacity and utilization

- Multipath and hidden node

In addition to a wireless LAN site survey, troubleshooting and maintenance are very important parts of a successful wireless LAN deployment. Wireless networks, like most areas of technology, do require support and maintenance. The extent of this will depend on the size and complexity of the network. Troubleshooting problems is a key component in the maintenance, reliability, and operation of a wireless network. A wireless LAN technical support engineer will have all the same problems that come about with regular networking plus more because this technology uses radio frequency for communication. In this chapter, we will look at some of the common problems associated with wireless networking, how to identify the problems based on the symptoms, and how to determine if they are global or isolated issues. These problems range in complexity and magnitude and many times are associated with the following:

- Connectivity

- Signal strength

- Throughput

- Upgrades

Troubleshooting is not something that can be learned overnight or from reading a book. Troubleshooting is an acquired skill that requires many hours of hard work and the "school of hard knocks." This is true with any type of troubleshooting, not just computer networking. To be a good mechanic, for example, it takes years of working with automobiles to learn how to diagnose and perform the necessary repairs.

The steps involved in troubleshooting a wireless networking problem will vary and depend on the complexity of the network and the environment. In this chapter, in we will discuss some of the causes and solutions associated with throughput, connectivity, signal strength, and upgrades. We will also discuss some of the procedures used for optimizing a wireless network. Some of these topics may sound familiar because they are also related to site surveys; however, changes may need to be made to accommodate physical environment conditions that have an impact on a wireless LAN installation. Finally, we will review multipath and the effect it has on a wireless LAN, and look at different types of hidden node problems.

Identifying Wireless LAN Problems

A first step in troubleshooting wireless LAN problems is to identify whether it is a global issue or an isolated problem. Global issues often include infrastructure devices and components. A global problem usually involves many users or groups of users. Some of the wireless devices that can be related to a global problem include:

- Access points
- Bridges
- Wireless controllers/switches

In addition to wireless infrastructure devices, wired infrastructure components can also be a potential source for global problems. Keep in mind that wireless devices usually require a wired infrastructure in order to pass information between infrastructure devices or outside the wireless network. Devices and components that can contribute to wired infrastructure problems include:

- Cabling
- Switches
- Routers
- WAN connectivity

As shown in Figure 11.1, there are many components that can be the source of problems associated with wireless networking.

FIGURE 11.1 Any components, whether wired or wireless, can be the source of or contribute to wireless LAN problems.

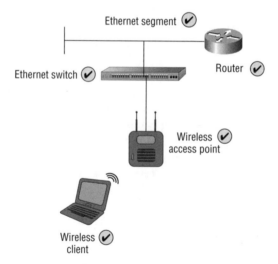

Once it has been determined whether the problem is global or isolated, appropriate steps are necessary to determine the solution. But before we look at some of the common problems associated with wireless networking, it is important to understand a little more detail about how wireless LAN technology functions. This includes understanding the components used to send and receive RF information. This is accomplished by two main components:

- Transmitter
- Receiver

Transmitters and Receivers

As discussed in previous chapters, wireless networks use radio frequency to send and receive data. This is possible because all wireless devices have transmitter and/or receiver capability. Unlike a television or FM radio you may have in your home, both of which are only receivers, all wireless LAN devices have the capability to act as either a transmitter or a receiver (also known as a transceiver). The following sections explain transmitter and receiver functionality in order to provide the groundwork necessary to diagnose and resolve wireless networking problems.

Transmitter

In wireless networking, a *transmitter* combines digital computer data with high frequency alternating current (AC) to prepare it to be sent across the air. This is known as *modulation*. The connected antenna then transforms this signal into radio waves and propagates them through the air. The frequency of the signal depends on the technology in use. With IEEE standards-based wireless networking, this is a few select frequency ranges.

Receiver

A *receiver* collects the propagated signal from the air using an antenna and reverses the process by transforming the received signal back into an alternating current signal. Through the use of a demodulation process, the digital data is recovered. The modulation/demodulation technology used depends on the wireless standard or amendment with which the device is compliant. For example, an IEEE 802.11g wireless LAN will use 64QAM (quadrature amplitude modulation) when transmitting data at 54 Mbps. Figure 11.2 illustrates this entire process. Keep in mind that wireless LAN devices are transceivers, so they have the capability of performing either task. In this figure, the access point is the transmitter and the client device is the receiver. The detail of modulation technologies is beyond the scope of the CWTS exam objectives and is not covered in this book.

Figure 11.2 sums up the entire process of wireless LAN communications discussed throughout this book and is an introduction to understanding the process of troubleshooting.

No Connectivity

There are several components of a network that can cause connectivity issues with wireless networking. Keep in mind that wireless networks are not bound by a physical medium such as Ethernet cable; therefore, issues other than wiring may result in either no connectivity or intermittent connection problems.

Let's review some of the OSI model information discussed in Chapter 2, "Wireless LAN Infrastructure Devices." The Physical layer provides the medium for connectivity (the air) in a wireless network and is used to carry RF information. This layer also includes network adapter cards, which provide an interface to the wireless computer or device. Layer 1 connectivity provides the capability to transfer information that is sent between devices. Figure 11.3 illustrates the Physical layer and wireless connectivity.

FIGURE 11.2   Wireless access point (transmitter) and wireless client device (receiver) with data traversing the air using radio frequency

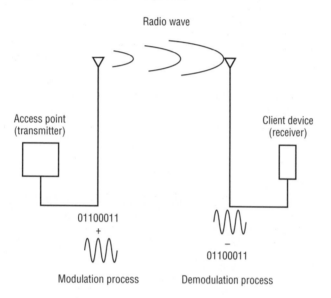

FIGURE 11.3   The lower two layers of the OSI model are responsible for the operation of wireless networks. The Physical layer provides a connection between devices.

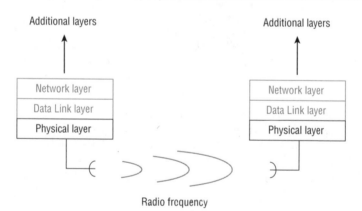

No Connectivity on the Client Side

Wireless networks require Physical layer connectivity in order to provide successful communications. This section describes some potential connectivity issues associated with client-side wireless devices. In many cases, no connectivity on the client side is an isolated issue that will not affect a large number of users. Problems that can cause client-side lack of connectivity include:

- Disabled radio or wireless adapter

- Misconfigured client utility

- Microsoft Wireless Zero Configuration (WZC) not running or not configured

- Protective supplicants can disable the radio in response to specific policy violations

A disabled radio or client adapter in a wireless client device can cause lack of connectivity. Many devices such as notebook computers have physical switches or a combination of keys that can disable a radio. A disabled radio cannot provide RF communication between the client device and the wireless infrastructure, such as an access point. Figure 11.4 shows the icon for a disabled wireless adapter and the window explaining that Microsoft Wireless Zero Configuration (WZC) service is not started.

FIGURE 11.4   Disabled wireless LAN adapter and WZC service not running

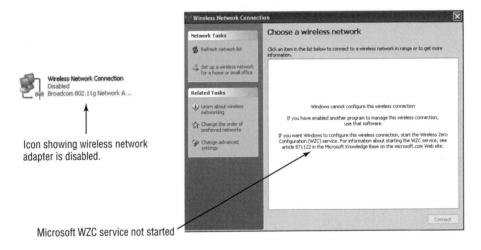

Icon showing wireless network adapter is disabled.

Microsoft WZC service not started

If a client utility is misconfigured—for example, an incorrect SSID is specified—it would potentially cause a lack of connectivity for the wireless client device. Client utilities have the capability to specify the SSID as a parameter. If the client does not see an access point with the specified SSID, it will not be able to connect to the wireless LAN. This feature in a client device is often set by a selection to connect to a preferred SSID only.

Remember that the Service Set Identifier (SSID) is case sensitive and has a maximum length of 32 characters or 32 octets as defined in the IEEE 802.11 standard. Incorrect use of case in the SSID can lead to lack of connectivity.

Microsoft Wireless Zero Configuration (WZC) is a very popular client utility for connecting to wireless networks. WZC runs as a service or background process in some Microsoft Windows operating systems. If this service is not running or if the client device is not configured correctly to use WZC, the client will not be able to connect to the wireless network unless a different client utility is used. Figure 11.5 illustrates some of these potential issues from a wireless client device that may cause a lack of connectivity to the wireless infrastructure.

FIGURE 11.5 Devices and components that make up a wireless LAN showing potential client-side issues

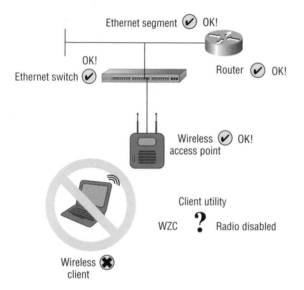

Other Connectivity Issues

Connectivity issues can also arise if a misconfigured client utility has incorrect security settings or client IP address issues. Both will prevent a wireless client device from successfully completing the connection process and will prevent the transfer of data. Even though the Physical layer (Layer 1) and Data Link layer (Layer 2) connection may have been successful, the Layer 3 process would not be complete.

Before we discuss incorrect security settings further, it is important to have a better understanding of how an *IP address* (a logical address for a network interface) may have an impact on a successful connection and some of the issues associated with TCP/IP.

IP Address Connectivity Issues

Although wireless networks operate at Layer 1 and Layer 2 of the OSI model, Layer 3 and IP addressing also play a role because TCP/IP is used in most of today's computer networks. Not long ago computer networks used various proprietary protocols to communicate with one another, such as Novell's IPX/SPX or Microsoft's NetBEUI. (A *protocol* is a set of rules that defines data communication between devices.) With the growth of local area networks, expanding to wide area networks and the World Wide Web (WWW) service, TCP/IP has become the standard protocol used in most computer networks. Layer 3 and Layer 4 of the OSI model are responsible for addressing and routing both information and the session connection using the TCP/IP protocol. Figure 11.6 illustrates the two layers responsible for the TCP/IP protocol and the function of each.

FIGURE 11.6   Layers 3 and 4 of the OSI model are responsible for the addressing and routing of information as well as the session connection between devices.

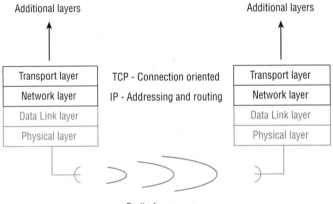

Radio frequency

Misconfigured IP address information can cause connectivity issues in a wireless LAN. Most wireless networks, both SOHO and enterprise, have the capability to use *Dynamic Host Configuration Protocol (DHCP)*. DHCP is a service that issues IP addresses and other TCP/IP parameters to connected client devices. This service eliminates the need to manually assign logical IP addresses to all devices on the network. In wireless networking, this DHCP service is provided directly from an access point, a wireless router, or from a server running DHCP services on the wired LAN. Many issues related to Layer 3 or above can cause failure to obtain a valid IP address. But this problem is often blamed on the wireless network even though a successful authentication and association have occurred. Figure 11.7 shows an example of DHCP services using a wireless residential gateway/router.

A cable or DSL modem device connected to the ISP service will receive a DHCP address from the ISP. This modem will then issue IP addresses to client devices or intermediary devices such as the wireless router. If DHCP services are not running or are not operating correctly on the wireless router, the connected wireless client devices will not be able to obtain a valid IP address.

FIGURE 11.7   DHCP and IP address information from the ISP to the wireless client device

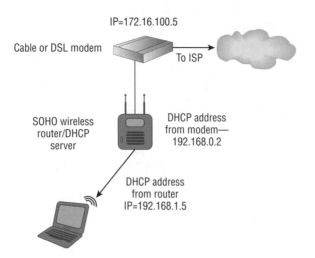

The computer operating system in use will determine what action the client device takes if an IP address cannot be obtained from a DHCP server. Microsoft Windows uses a service that became available starting with Windows 98 and is now available in all versions of Microsoft Windows, called *Automatic Private IP Addressing (APIPA)*. APIPA is designed to provide an IP address automatically to any device requesting one that is connected to a common LAN. APIPA does not require the use of a DHCP server. It also eliminates the need for users to manually set up IP addressing on all the devices. An APIPA address will be in the 169.254.*X.X* range. For example, a device such as a notebook computer may have an APIPA such as 169.254.100.20. If DHCP services are running on the LAN and a device cannot obtain an address from the server, or if DHCP services are not available, an APIPA will be issued. Figure 11.8 shows the ipconfig utility displaying an IP address from Microsoft's Automatic Private IP Addressing.

FIGURE 11.8   Microsoft Windows APIPA

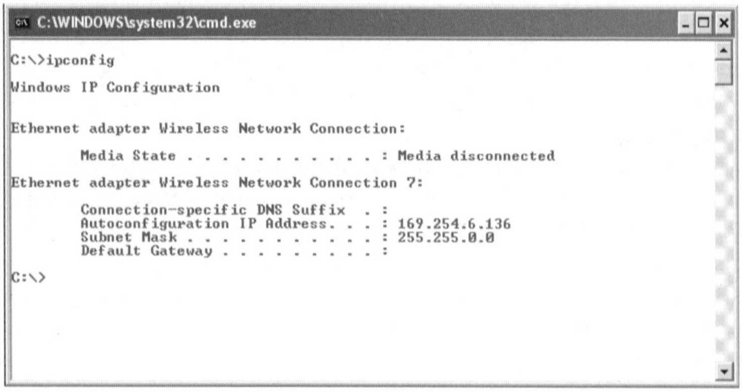

```
C:\WINDOWS\system32\cmd.exe                                          _ □ x

C:\>ipconfig

Windows IP Configuration


Ethernet adapter Wireless Network Connection:

        Media State . . . . . . . . . . . : Media disconnected

Ethernet adapter Wireless Network Connection 7:

        Connection-specific DNS Suffix  . :
        Autoconfiguration IP Address. . . : 169.254.6.136
        Subnet Mask . . . . . . . . . . . : 255.255.0.0
        Default Gateway . . . . . . . . . :

C:\>
```

If an access point or wireless router is connected to an IP subnet other than the one that uses automatic addresses, the wireless client device will require a valid IP address from the DHCP service in order to complete a connection. If a valid IP address cannot be obtained from the DHCP service, the client will not have a valid TCP/IP connection to the access point or wireless router and instead will obtain an IP address from the 169.254.*X.X* range. If this is the case, the wireless connection icon will show a "Limited or no connectivity" message and exclamation point, as shown in Figure 11.9.

FIGURE 11.9 Limited or no connectivity as the result of an IP address not being obtained from a DHCP server

Wireless Network Connection
Limited or no connectivity
Broadcom 802.11g Network A...

No valid IP address received
from a DHCP server

Security Settings

Incorrect security settings can also cause connectivity issues. Although you may get a physical connection to the access point you will not get a valid Layer 3 TCP/IP address from the DHCP server with incorrect security settings on a client device. For example, assume an access point is using WPA 2.0 personal mode for security. If a wireless client device has the wrong passphrase or preshared key entered, it will not complete the authentication process and will not have a valid Layer 3 TCP/IP address. In this case, the network adapter would stay in the "Acquiring network address" state; it would not be able to complete the Layer 2 connection process and would not receive a valid IP address. Figure 11.10 shows an example of a wireless network adapter with the wrong passphrase set using the Microsoft Wireless Zero Configuration (WZC) service client utility.

Intermittent Connectivity

Intermittent problems are some of the most difficult to diagnose and repair. You may have had the experience of an intermittent problem with your car. For example, at a stoplight the car may start to idle rough and stall. There is not really any rhyme or reason as to when this happens—it could be in the morning; it could be in the afternoon. You take your car to the mechanic for repair and of course the problem does not occur. Therefore the mechanic may have to keep your car for a period of time to try to duplicate the problem.

Intermittent problems with computers and networking are no different—they are difficult to diagnose if they can't be reliably reproduced.

Most intermittent connectivity issues in wireless LANs are associated with signal strength. If nothing else has changed (for example, a security setting or any type of device upgrade) and the device was working before, there is a good possibility the problem is associated with signal strength.

FIGURE 11.10 Microsoft Windows WZC with incorrect passphrase

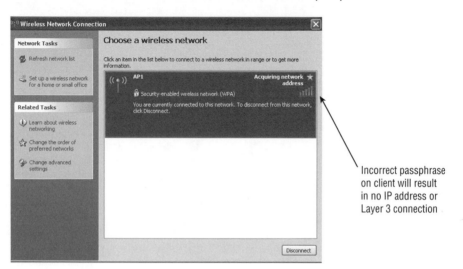

Incorrect passphrase on client will result in no IP address or Layer 3 connection

Understanding Received Signal Strength

One of the main concerns associated with wireless networking is how much of the transmitted signal is identified by the receiver as usable signal. As mentioned in Chapter 9, "Performing a WLAN Site Survey," this is known as the received signal strength indicator (RSSI) value. RSSI is an arbitrary number assigned by the device manufacturer. There is no standard for this value and it will not be comparable between devices from different manufacturers. The calculation of the RSSI value is done in a proprietary manner and a wireless device from one manufacturer may indicate a different signal strength than that indicated by another, even though they both are receiving the exact same signal and at the same actual signal strength. This value is a key determinant of how well the wireless LAN device will perform. How the device is used with the network will determine the required levels of signal for optimal connectivity. The actual recommended signal strength will vary based on the manufacturer, but some general numbers do exist. For example, in the 2.4 GHz ISM band, in order to get 54 Mbps of data, and depending on the application either voice or data, some manufacturers recommend between −61 dBm to −67 dBm of received signal strength. Keep in mind, the closer the number is to zero, the better the received signal and −61 dBm is closer to zero than −67 dBm. Figure 11.11 shows an example of an access point with an output power of 100 mW and the wireless client receiving a fraction of that amount or 0.000001 mW. Although the wireless client device is receiving only a fraction of the amount of the transmitted power output, it is still able to move data at 54 Mbps. Amazing!

FIGURE 11.11   Wireless client device receiving a fraction of the amount of power output by the access point

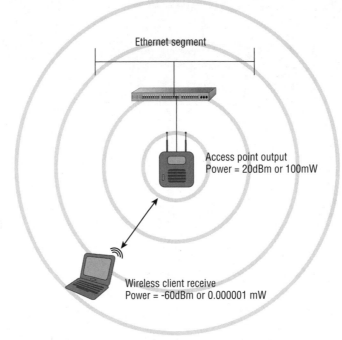

Ethernet segment

Access point output
Power = 20dBm or 100mW

Wireless client receive
Power = -60dBm or 0.000001 mW

Testing Received Signal Strength

So what does this mean? It means the lower the amount of signal received by the receiver, the lower the data rate will be. As mentioned in Chapter 9, several tools are available that will allow a technical support specialist to see the received signal strength. These tools include:

- InSSIDer
- NetStumbler
- Wireless network adapter client utilities
- Spectrum analyzer

Any of these tools can be used to check the received signal strength at an end user's location to determine how much signal is actually being received, which will relate to the rate they should be transferring data.

Figure 11.12 shows the Microsoft WZC utility with bars representing the amount of received signal strength and the current data transfer rate.

> The Microsoft Wireless Zero Configuration (WZC) client does not contain any specialized utilities that show signal strength or signal-to-noise ratio values. However, this utility will display bar values representing the received signal strength.

FIGURE 11.12   Representation of received signal strength and data rate using the Microsoft WZC client utility

```
Wireless Network Connection Status                    [?][X]
 General | Support

  Connection
    Status:                              Connected
    Network:                                   AP1
    Duration:                             00:03:20
    Speed:                              48.0 Mbps
    Signal Strength:                      ••••••        ←── WZC shows received
                                                             signal strength and
                                                             data transfer rate
  Activity
                    Sent  ──  [computer]  ── Received

    Packets:              72    |           10


  [Properties]  [Disable]  [View Wireless Networks]

                                    [Close]
```

Weak Signal or No Signal

Weak, low, or no signal is typically an indication that the wireless LAN client device is too far away from an access point or it is experiencing some level of RF interference. In order for a client device to operate correctly, the signal will need to be strong enough to connect to an access point and maintain the connection. A device will have a difficult time distinguishing between signal and noise if the signal level is too close to the noise floor.

To review, the signal-to-noise ratio is the difference between the amount of received signal and the noise floor level in the area where the device is located. Chapter 9 discussed the noise floor and signal-to-noise ratio in more detail. Figure 11.13 shows the Microsoft WZC utility and two access points in the vicinity. Notice the client device is associated to AP1 with a good signal level, and AP2 shows only one bar, which represents low signal strength.

Other client utilities may show a more elaborate view of the signal strength and the noise level in an area. These are represented by dBm values rather than bar levels. In addition to client utilities, third-party utilities such as NetStumbler or InSSIDer will show received signal strength or noise levels, or possibly both.

FIGURE 11.13 Microsoft WZC displays signal strength difference between two different access points.

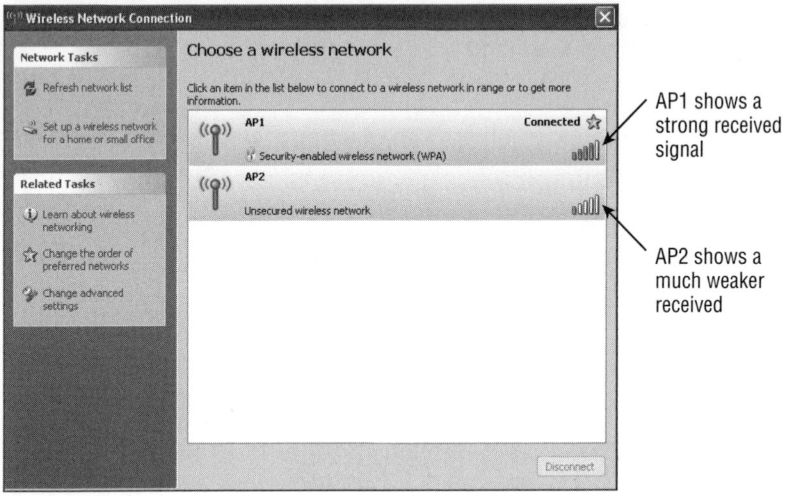

AP1 shows a strong received signal

AP2 shows a much weaker received

Throughput

Papa User says, "Someone's been taking my throughput!" Mama User says, "Someone's been taking my throughput!" Baby User says, "Someone's been taking my throughput and that someone still is!" Sound familiar? Receiving and maintaining enough throughput can be a tough chore in today's world of wireless networking.

It is important to understand the difference between data rate and throughput. *Throughput* is the rate at which data is actually being transferred. It seems there is never enough to go around. When it comes to throughput, expectations are a key factor. It is important for users to realize that the actual throughput will always be lower than the advertised data rate. For example, in an 802.11g network the maximum data rate is 54 Mbps, but the actual throughput will be at best 18 to 22 Mbps, less than half of the advertised data rate.

Maximizing throughput is part of overall network design. A well-designed wireless LAN and site survey will yield excellent results. However, several factors may affect the throughput the users are receiving, including:

- Distance from access point
- Output power of access point
- Number of users associated

Distance from Access Point

As we discussed earlier, as the distance from an access point increases, the signal strength will decrease, thereby providing less average throughput. The type of device in use—computer, VoIP handset, handheld device, or barcode scanner—will determine the acceptable levels of throughput. Most client utilities will show that the expected data rate is based upon the received signal strength. It is important to remember that the expected data rate is not actual throughput. Figure 11.14 illustrates this point by showing two different throughput sessions, both connected to the same access point. Session 1 is in close proximity, about 15 to 20 feet from the access point. Session 2 shows the throughput at a greater distance, about 45 feet from the access point.

Output Power of Access Point

The amount of output power being transmitted from the access point will also determine signal strength for the connected clients. This is because the higher the power, the farther an RF signal will propagate. If a client is receiving a low signal, and adding an additional access point is not an option, increasing the output power of the access point may do the trick.

If a physical RF site survey is performed, it is recommended to have the access points set to less than the full available output power. What the output power level is set to during a site survey will depend on the engineer who performs the survey or the manufacturer recommendations. If an access point is not set to full power, it will be possible to make adjustments to compensate and potentially correct problems such as a user's experiencing low throughput because of low received signal strength value.

Number of Users Associated

Because wireless LANs use the air as a shared medium, the more users who associate to the access point, the less throughput each user will be able to receive. The type of hardware can also affect the throughput based on the number of associated users. For example, if 25 users are associated to an access point using barcode scanners that typically transfer small amounts of information, they may have better performance than 5 users using bandwidth-intensive applications such as CAD/CAM on notebook computers. Load balancing of devices between access points can help limit the number of associated users. Co-channel interference can cause the same issue, because wireless devices on the same or close channel, associated or not, are part of the same contention domain.

FIGURE 11.14 Two FTP file transfer sessions showing the difference in throughput based on distance from an access point

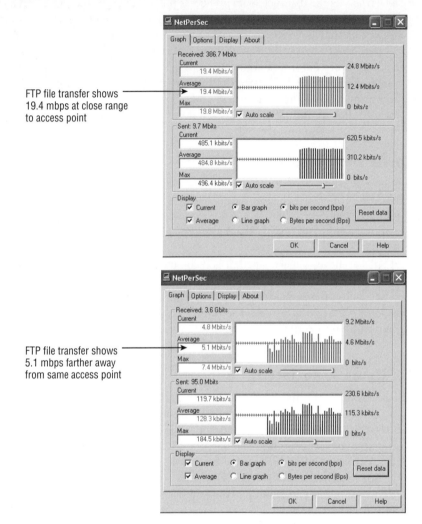

FTP file transfer shows 19.4 mbps at close range to access point

FTP file transfer shows 5.1 mbps farther away from same access point

Solutions to Low Throughput

There are several possible solutions to solve low throughput problems clients may be experiencing. The appropriate solution will depend on the specific situation. If an RF site survey was performed correctly and thoroughly, additional access points should not be needed unless there have been environmental changes in the area since the original survey was performed. Solutions to low throughput problems include the following:

- Adding more access points
- Increasing output power of access points

- Increasing antenna gain
- Enabling load-balancing solutions on access points

One or more of these solutions may help increase the throughput for users connected to a wireless network. Figure 11.15 shows a before and after scenario based on output power of an access point.

FIGURE 11.15 Increasing the output power of an access point will provide higher received signal strength for the client, parlaying into better overall throughput.

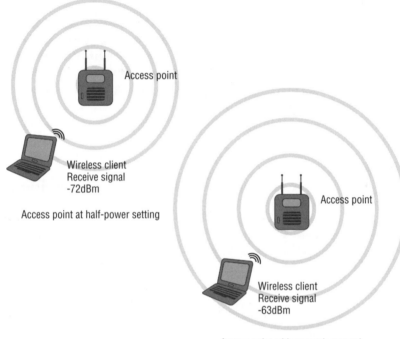

Access point

Wireless client
Receive signal
-72dBm

Access point at half-power setting

Access point

Wireless client
Receive signal
-63dBm

Access point with power increased

Of the solutions listed above, none is better than the others. Which solution you choose is going to depend on several factors, including the number of users, the number of access points, budget constraints, and potential interference issues.

Keep in mind that increasing the output power of an access point will also increase the cell size and potentially allow for more wireless client devices to associate. This will in turn increase the load or number of associated devices on the access point and may contribute to interference in other areas.

Software and Hardware Upgrades

Software and hardware upgrades play a role in the maintenance and support of any wireless LAN deployment. Having the latest device drivers or software client utilities will help increase performance and help to solve problems associated with software-related issues. Firmware also needs to be updated periodically to ensure the latest and greatest fixes, and new features are applied to the devices such as access points or wireless LAN switches/controllers.

Software Upgrades

Upgrading the software related to wireless LAN technology has many benefits that may help resolve performance or operation issues. It is recommended that technical support or network engineers find time to stay up-to-date with the latest software versions available for the hardware in their network. This can be done by looking at the manufacturer's website or subscribing to a service that will announce changes and updates. Software upgrades for wireless networks commonly fall under three areas:

- Device drivers
- Client adapter utilities
- Firmware

Software upgrades on any of these components will help enhance the performance of the device. These upgrades can come as a fix for a problem with the software or potentially provide new features for a device. In Chapter 3, "Wireless LAN Client Devices," we discussed some of the software components required that will enable a client device to connect to a wireless network. This section focuses on the process of upgrading the software associated with these devices.

Device Drivers

Device drivers are the software components that allow a hardware device to function with a computer operating system. This is accomplished by the software providing an instruction set for all devices that connect to a computer, handheld, or any other device that runs with an operating system. The following list is a small sampling of the devices that will require a software device driver:

- Hard drive
- Video card
- Keyboard
- Mouse
- USB ports
- Network adapters

With wireless networking, the device driver that is of most concern is the one used for the network adapter. The wireless network adapter is what allows a computer or other client device to connect to a wireless network in either infrastructure or ad hoc mode. Figure 11.16 shows an example of viewing the device driver properties in the Microsoft Windows XP operating system.

FIGURE 11.16   Device driver information for an integrated Broadcom wireless network adapter

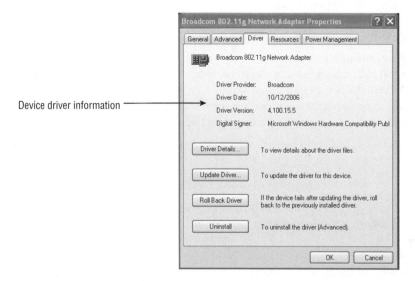

Device driver information

In addition to causing intermittent connectivity problems, device drivers may become corrupt and prevent the device from starting up. They can even cause operating system startup problems. With today's sophisticated computer operating systems and features, such as plug-and-play, having to worry about physical settings of a device is less common than it was a few years ago. Upgrading or replacing a device driver in the Microsoft Windows operating systems is a fairly straightforward process. Exercise 11.1 will step you through upgrading a device driver for your wireless network adapter.

EXERCISE 11.1

Upgrading a Device Driver

In this exercise, we will look at the process of upgrading a device driver for a wireless network adapter. This process is based on using the Broadcom 802.11g Network Adapter.

Downloading a Driver Package from a Website

1.   With the help of a web browser, connect to the appropriate website to search for the latest version of the device driver, in this case www.broadcom.com.

2. In most cases, you will look for either a support or downloads link to find the location for software such as drivers. The current link on this site is Downloads & Support. Click on the appropriate link.

3. You should be able to search by model number for the driver you will need. Download the correct device driver. This may come in the form of an individual file or possibly an entire software client utility program.

4. In this case, an update for this wireless adapter is not available from the adapter manufacturer, and because it is integrated into a notebook computer it will be necessary to visit the website for the computer in which this adapter is installed. It is important to note that for client devices with integrated adapters it is best to visit the website of the manufacturer for the device. In this case, the website is www.lenovo.com.

5. This website has links for support and downloads. Click the support and downloads links.

6. Browse for the correct driver based on the installed adapter.

7. In this case, it will be necessary to download an entire package. This one is approximately 78 Mb. Run the downloaded program to install the latest device driver file.

Manually Upgrading a Driver

These next steps are going to show how you would manually upgrade a device driver using an individual file.

1. Click Start and the Control Panel icon. Double-click the System icon and the System Properties dialog box will appear.

2. Click the Hardware tab and the Device Manager button. The Device Manager dialog box will appear.

3. Expand the Network Adapters menu and double-click on the correct network adapter. The Adapter Properties dialog box will appear.

4. Click the Driver tab and the Update Driver button. The Hardware Update Wizard dialog box will appear. Select the radio button next to "Install from a list or specific location (Advanced)." A new dialog box will appear.

5. Click the radio button next to "Don't search, I will choose the driver to install." Then click Next.

6. Click on the Have Disk button and browse to the folder where the driver is located. Select the driver, then click Open. The Install From Disk dialog box will appear. Click OK. The Select Network Adapter dialog box will appear.

7. Click Next to continue. The update will process. Click Finish to complete the device driver upgrade.

Client Utilities

Client adapter utilities may need to be upgraded occasionally. By upgrading the client adapter utility you will usually add new features or settings to enhance the performance and function of the utility.

The Microsoft Wireless Zero Configuration (WZC) utility is usually upgraded either from a service pack or a hot fix available from the Microsoft website.

Firmware

In basic terms, *firmware* is software for hardware. Firmware is the instruction set that allows hardware to operate based on its design. Firmware upgrades are common support tasks that need to be done periodically either to fix issues with the way the hardware is operating or to provide new features for the hardware. All infrastructure devices, either SOHO-grade or enterprise-grade, allow you to upgrade the firmware. In enterprise environments, firmware upgrades can be performed either manually or automatically with the aid of a wireless LAN management system software or appliance.

Many manufacturers of enterprise-grade equipment require you to purchase a support contact or service agreement in order to download firmware for wireless infrastructure devices.

Most infrastructure devices have several options for performing upgrades. These upgrade options include:

- Hypertext Transfer Protocol (HTTP)
- Trivial File Transfer Protocol (TFTP)
- File Transfer Protocol (FTP)

Figure 11.17 shows an example of a graphical user interface (GUI) screen where a firmware update is being processed.

🌐 Real World Scenario

Upgrading Firmware Warning

It is imperative to follow the manufacturer's instructions when performing a firmware upgrade. Failure to do so may result in the device becoming unusable or needing to be returned to the manufacturer for repair. Several items are very important when performing a firmware upgrade on any device.

- Always verify you have the correct firmware file for the device to be upgraded prior to performing the upgrade.
- Always read the release notes that come with the firmware.
- Never upgrade firmware on a device that is running on battery power.
- Never power down the device while the firmware upgrade is in process.

FIGURE 11.17   Motorola WS2000 Wireless Switch firmware update screen

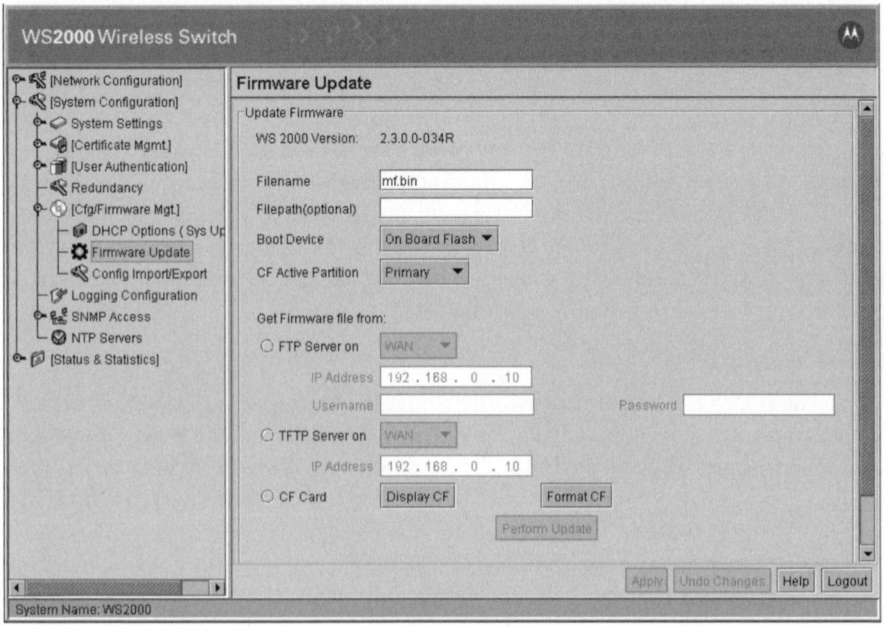

The firmware in enterprise-grade access points and wireless switches/controllers can usually be upgraded using the command-line interface instead of the graphical user interface if desired.

Infrastructure and Client Device Hardware Upgrades

There could be various reasons to upgrade hardware for both infrastructure and client-side devices. Hardware upgrades are a part of the ongoing maintenance process with all networking devices, including wireless LAN.

Infrastructure Devices

Upgrading infrastructure devices can be an expensive and time-consuming task. Justifying infrastructure device upgrades may require preparing reports that include performance of the wireless LAN infrastructure and client devices, ones that show how an upgrade will enhance the end-user performance and make users more productive in their job functions.

Upgrading infrastructure devices such as access points may give an organization the ability to enhance the performance of the wireless network by increasing the speed or reliability of the wireless LAN. The hardware currently in use will help determine the extent of an upgrade. Some upgrades may only require the installation of a new or additional radio.

One example is switching from 802.11b to 802.11g. Some access points are modular and provide this capability.

Another reason to upgrade infrastructure devices is to allow for advancements in technology such as 802.11n and MIMO.

Antennas

Unless the physical characteristics of the area where the wireless LAN is deployed have changed since the site survey, chances are that antennas will not need to be upgraded. If characteristics such as additional walls or types of furnishings or other physical attributes have changed, antennas with different propagation patterns or higher gain may be required. Another situation where antennas may need to be upgraded or changed is if the initial site survey was not performed thoroughly or correctly.

Client Device Upgrades

Client device upgrades can be automatic if the technology refresh for devices has taken place. For example, if a company replaces 50 notebook computers with newer models, the new notebooks will probably have wireless LAN adapters that are capable of 802.11a/g/n. The capabilities of these new notebooks may be more advanced than the actual infrastructure that is currently deployed.

Another situation where wireless client devices may need upgrading is one in which the infrastructure changes to different hardware or technology. If a company upgrades access points from 802.11b to 802.11g and the clients only support 802.11b, the client devices may need to be upgraded in order to take full advantage of the new wireless infrastructure.

Optimizing Wireless Networks

Making necessary changes to a wireless LAN installation may be required in order to provide optimal performance for the devices that will be connecting. In some cases, a site survey is considered an ongoing process due to the dynamics of radio frequency and changes in technology. This being the case, an existing wireless LAN deployment may need to be resurveyed to provide optimal performance for the users. Listed are some of the things that need to be taken into consideration when *optimizing* a wireless LAN:

- Hardware selection and placement
- Interference sources
- Load balancing
- Capacity and utilization
- Minimizing multipath
- Understanding hidden node

Infrastructure Hardware Selection and Placement

Infrastructure hardware selection and placement are typically part of the wireless LAN site survey process. However, occasionally you may need to reevaluate after the wireless LAN has been installed. Although the objective of a site survey is to design the network, find locations and sources of interference, and decide on locations for infrastructure devices, it may be necessary to make some adjustments to allow for optimal performance. This may include minor relocation of access points as well as radio frequency adjustments, including channel and output power settings. These adjustments would ensure clients have maximum signal strength, throughput, and roaming capabilities. Applications—both hardware and software—and user requirements could also change, requiring an optimization or resurvey of the wireless network.

Identifying, Locating, and Removing Sources of Interference

In Chapter 9, we discussed how to identify areas of RF coverage and interference. This usually is part of the site survey process. Probably the best way to identify sources of interference is with a spectrum analyzer. This could be in the form of an instrumentation device or a PC card–based spectrum analyzer designed specifically for wireless networking.

During this site survey process, interference sources should be identified. However, changes to the environment may introduce new sources of RF interference. Also, keep in mind that a walkthrough spectrum analysis of an area will only record the RF it sees at that instant in time. If a new piece of equipment is introduced into an area, it may cause interference with the wireless network that would not have been present during the RF site survey spectrum analysis process. Some businesses or organizations where this could be a factor include:

- Health care
- Warehouse/retail
- Manufacturing
- Industrial

Therefore an ongoing spectrum analysis may be required to identify and if possible remove the sources of interference. If these new sources of interference are there to stay, it will be necessary to make appropriate adjustments for the network to operate as designed. The number one source of interference in a wireless network is other wireless devices.

Figure 11.18 shows an example of a PC card spectrum analyzer that can be used to perform a spectrum analysis to help locate new sources of RF interference after a wireless LAN has been deployed.

FIGURE 11.18   AirMagnet Spectrum Analyzer showing devices that may cause RF interference

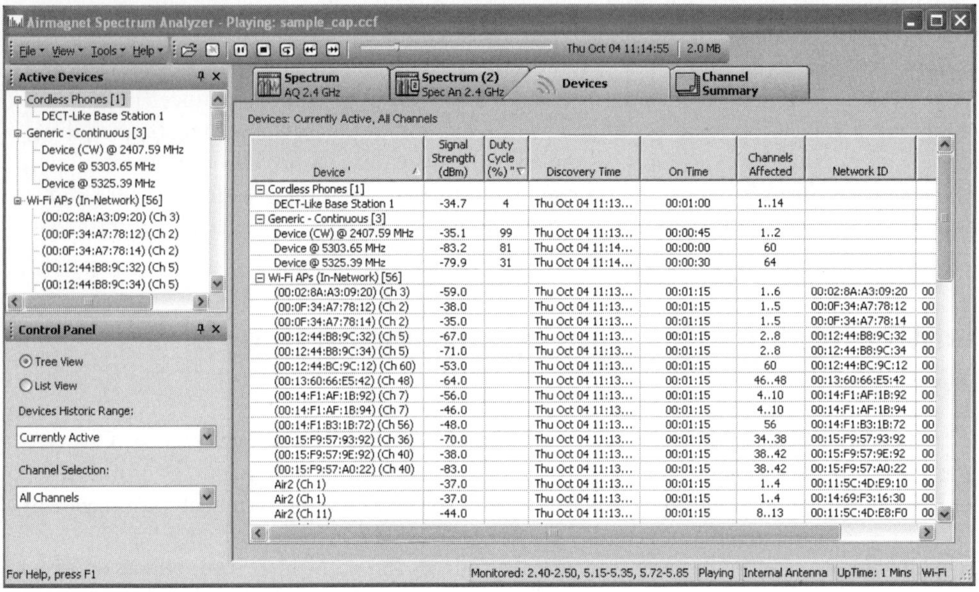

Airmagnet Spectrum Analyzer - Playing: sample_cap.ccf

File ▼ View ▼ Tools ▼ Help ▼   Thu Oct 04 11:14:55   2.0 MB

Active Devices

- Cordless Phones [1]
  - DECT-Like Base Station 1
- Generic - Continuous [3]
  - Device (CW) @ 2407.59 MHz
  - Device @ 5303.65 MHz
  - Device @ 5325.39 MHz
- Wi-Fi APs (In-Network) [56]
  - (00:02:8A:A3:09:20) (Ch 3)
  - (00:0F:34:A7:78:12) (Ch 2)
  - (00:0F:34:A7:78:14) (Ch 2)
  - (00:12:44:B8:9C:32) (Ch 5)
  - (00:12:44:B8:9C:34) (Ch 5)

Control Panel

- ⦿ Tree View
- ◯ List View

Devices Historic Range:

Currently Active

Channel Selection:

All Channels

Spectrum AQ 2.4 GHz | Spectrum (2) Spec An 2.4 GHz | Devices | Channel Summary

Devices: Currently Active, All Channels

Device	Signal Strength (dBm)	Duty Cycle (%)	Discovery Time	On Time	Channels Affected	Network ID	
Cordless Phones [1]							
DECT-Like Base Station 1	-34.7	4	Thu Oct 04 11:13...	00:01:00	1..14		
Generic - Continuous [3]							
Device (CW) @ 2407.59 MHz	-35.1	99	Thu Oct 04 11:13...	00:00:45	1..2		
Device @ 5303.65 MHz	-83.2	81	Thu Oct 04 11:14...	00:00:00	60		
Device @ 5325.39 MHz	-79.9	31	Thu Oct 04 11:14...	00:00:30	64		
Wi-Fi APs (In-Network) [56]							
(00:02:8A:A3:09:20) (Ch 3)	-59.0		Thu Oct 04 11:13...	00:01:15	1..6	00:02:8A:A3:09:20	00
(00:0F:34:A7:78:12) (Ch 2)	-64.0		Thu Oct 04 11:13...	00:01:15	1..5	00:0F:34:A7:78:12	00
(00:0F:34:A7:78:14) (Ch 2)	-35.0		Thu Oct 04 11:13...	00:01:15	1..5	00:0F:34:A7:78:14	00
(00:12:44:B8:9C:32) (Ch 5)	-67.0		Thu Oct 04 11:13...	00:01:15	2..8	00:12:44:B8:9C:32	00
(00:12:44:B8:9C:34) (Ch 5)	-71.0		Thu Oct 04 11:13...	00:01:15	2..8	00:12:44:B8:9C:34	00
(00:12:44:BC:9C:12) (Ch 60)	-53.0		Thu Oct 04 11:13...	00:01:15	60	00:12:44:BC:9C:12	00
(00:13:60:66:E5:42) (Ch 48)	-64.0		Thu Oct 04 11:13...	00:01:15	46..48	00:13:60:66:E5:42	00
(00:14:F1:AF:1B:92) (Ch 7)	-56.0		Thu Oct 04 11:13...	00:01:15	4..10	00:14:F1:AF:1B:92	00
(00:14:F1:AF:1B:94) (Ch 7)	-46.0		Thu Oct 04 11:13...	00:01:15	4..10	00:14:F1:AF:1B:94	00
(00:14:F1:B3:1B:72) (Ch 56)	-48.0		Thu Oct 04 11:13...	00:01:15	56	00:14:F1:B3:1B:72	00
(00:15:F9:57:93:92) (Ch 36)	-70.0		Thu Oct 04 11:13...	00:01:15	34..38	00:15:F9:57:93:92	00
(00:15:F9:57:9E:92) (Ch 40)	-38.0		Thu Oct 04 11:13...	00:01:15	38..42	00:15:F9:57:9E:92	00
(00:15:F9:57:A0:22) (Ch 40)	-83.0		Thu Oct 04 11:13...	00:01:15	38..42	00:15:F9:57:A0:22	00
Air2 (Ch 1)	-37.0		Thu Oct 04 11:13...	00:01:15	1..4	00:11:5C:4D:E9:10	00
Air2 (Ch 1)	-37.0		Thu Oct 04 11:13...	00:01:15	1..4	00:14:69:F3:16:30	00
Air2 (Ch 11)	-44.0		Thu Oct 04 11:13...	00:01:15	8..13	00:11:5C:4D:E8:F0	00

For Help, press F1   Monitored: 2.40-2.50, 5.15-5.35, 5.72-5.85   Playing   Internal Antenna   UpTime: 1 Mins   Wi-Fi

Client Load Balancing

Client *load balancing* is a mechanism that prevents wireless client devices from associating to an access point that has already reached the maximum number of client devices for optimal performance. There are a variety of ways this can be accomplished, typically vendor specific. Parameters for load balancing can be set on either the access points or the wireless LAN switch/controllers. Load balancing will allow for optimal use of all access points in a specific area by preventing too many devices from connecting to a single access point. Figure 11.19 illustrates the load-balancing process for wireless LAN access points.

The way in which load balancing is implemented depends on the manufacturer of the wireless LAN equipment. One solution is a settable parameter in an access point specifying a maximum number of devices allowed to connect at any one time. Once the access point has reached its capacity, a client device wanting to associate will be presented with an error message and will not be allowed to complete the process.

FIGURE 11.19   Load balancing ensures optimal performance for connected wireless client devices.

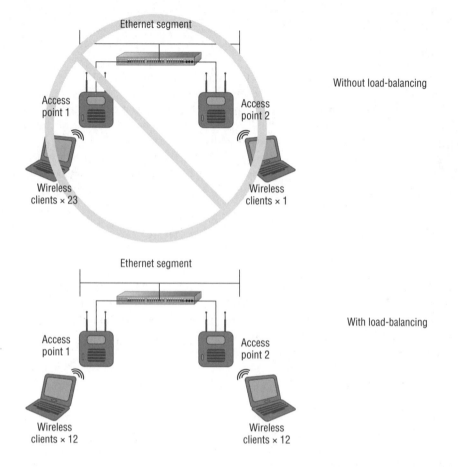

Analyzing Infrastructure Capacity and Utilization

It is important to have a baseline for the performance of your wireless LAN. This baseline will show the average utilization and capacity of the connected infrastructure devices at various times during the company's business hours. Continuous monitoring of the wireless network is similar to that of a wired network. Performance metrics will be needed to gauge the use of the wireless LAN and infrastructure devices and show how well the system performs. These metrics will also show areas that are lacking in performance, including bottlenecks or over-utilized access points. Using these performance metrics will show which infrastructure devices need attention. This may include moving or adding access points for additional capacity or to allow for higher utilization. Changes to the environment, such as the addition of users, may justify the need for additional access points.

Multipath

Poor throughput can be the result of corrupted data, which may be caused by multipath. Multipath is various RF wavefronts of the same signal being received at slightly different times. Multipath is caused by RF reflections based on the physical attributes where an access point is placed. As discussed in Chapter 6, "WLAN Antennas and Accessories," antenna diversity will help minimize the problems caused by multipath.

Although multipath is a hindrance in most wireless LAN implementations, it is beneficial for 802.11n systems. MIMO technology used with 802.11n is designed to take advantage of multipath and increase throughput by using the effects of multipath as an advantage.

Hidden Node

Hidden node is the result of client devices connected to an access point and not able to "hear" each other prior to starting a transmission. This will result in collisions at the access point and lost data. As discussed in Chapter 5, "Access Methods, Architectures, and Spread Spectrum Technology," the CSMA/CA process is designed to avoid collisions between devices sharing the same medium. This process includes the use of a mechanism called *clear channel assessment (CCA)*. CCA detects RF energy from other client devices in the same RF space and understands that the medium is busy.

Three causes of hidden node are:

- Hidden node obstacle (obstructions)
- Hidden node distance (signal strength)
- Hidden node technology (signaling methods)

Hidden Node Obstacle

Hidden node obstacle is caused by two or more client devices connecting to an access point in which access-point-to-client-device RF communication is clear, but client-device-to-client-device RF communication is blocked. Figure 11.20 illustrates an example of hidden node obstacle.

There are several physical solutions to the hidden node obstacle problem. Any of these solutions should allow for the correct RF communication between access points and wireless client devices. Some of the physical solutions to hidden node obstacle include the following:

Removing the obstacle   Removing any obstacles that do not allow for clear RF communications between client devices will solve the hidden node problem. However, in most cases removing obstacles is not a conducive solution. If this type of hidden node problem does exist, a good reason could be poor network design or an inadequate site survey.

Adding access points   Adding additional access points will help resolve issues caused by hidden node where obstacles are a factor. This will allow for clear RF communication between access points and clients as well as clear RF communications between client devices connected to the same access point.

FIGURE 11.20   Hidden node caused by an obstacle or obstruction

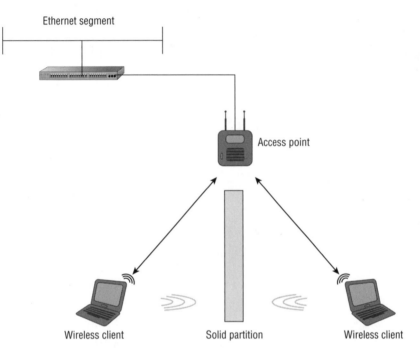

Hidden Node Distance

With hidden node distance, client-device-to-client-device RF communication cannot occur because the client devices are too far apart and not in radio range of each other. However, access-point-to-client-device RF communication does take place because these devices are within radio range. Figure 11.21 shows an example of hidden node distance.

FIGURE 11.21   Hidden node as a result of distance between wireless client devices

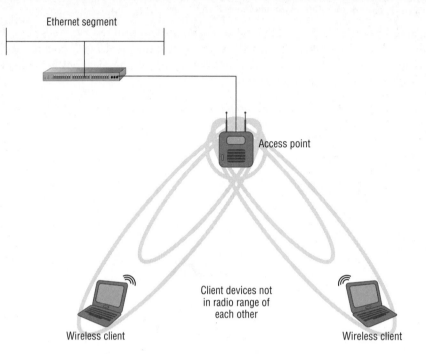

Just as in hidden node obstacle, physical solutions exist for the hidden node distance problem. These physical solutions provide adequate RF communication for access-point-to-wireless-client-device and for client-device-to-client-device. Following are examples of some of the solutions for hidden node distance.

Increasing the output power of client devices   Increasing the RF output power of client devices allows them a larger radio range. This enables wireless client devices to hear each other and therefore know whether the medium is clear prior to starting a transmission.

Moving the client devices closer together   Moving the wireless client devices closer together allows the devices to hear the RF communications between each other. In this situation they are able to detect whether the RF medium is clear prior to starting a transmission to the access point.

Adding more access points   Another solution would be to add more access points. This would allow wireless client devices to detect a clear RF medium. More access points mean a smaller basic service area for each access point on the network. This allows client devices to associate with an access point in close range, and they will not be required to contend for the same access point with other wireless devices at a distance.

Hidden Node Technology

Hidden node technology occurs when access points experience excessive collisions because of different spread spectrum or communication technologies that are sharing the same RF medium. This can happen when, for example, an access point has to share transmissions between 802.11b (HR/DSSS) and 802.11g (ERP-OFDM) client devices. Figure 11.22 illustrates the hidden node problem due to different technologies in use.

FIGURE 11.22   Hidden node based on technology types such as HR/DSSS and ERP-OFDM

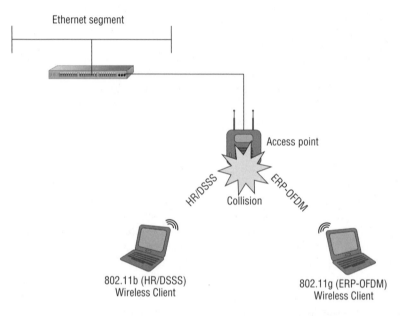

The only physical solution to the hidden node technology problem is to allow either 802.11b or 802.11g devices to communicate with the access point but not both. In most cases, this is not a realistic solution because allowing only one of the technologies to communicate with an access point prevents devices using the other technology from using the network. In other words, giving only 802.11g (ERP-OFDM) devices the capability to use the network would prevent 802.11b (HR/DSSS) devices from using the network resources or vice versa.

Software Solution to Hidden Node Problems

There is a software configuration solution for all of the above-mentioned hidden node problems. This software configuration solution is known as a process called request to send (RTS), clear to send (CTS), or RTS/CTS. The RTS/CTS process allows devices to reserve the medium for a specified period of time, enabling a device to complete a frame exchange and avoid collisions. The RTS/CTS process is beyond the scope of the CWTS exam objectives and therefore is not discussed in detail in this book.

Summary

In this chapter, we discussed some troubleshooting and maintenance concerns that may involve wireless networking. This included identifying wireless LAN problems as both global and isolated and the process for troubleshooting these problems. Global problems may include infrastructure devices such as:

- Access points
- Bridges
- Wireless controllers/switches

Isolated problems usually include a single wireless LAN client device or computer that could be experiencing connectivity or data transfer issues. We also looked at basic RF communications using a transmitter and receiver and how these devices operate in a wireless LAN. This chapter discussed connectivity issues, including no connectivity or weak connectivity, and the problems that could be associated with connectivity issues. No connectivity on the client side could be something as simple as a network adapter not enabled or could be related to something more in depth, including:

- TCP/IP
- Security configurations

In this chapter, we discussed received signal strength and the difference between a strong signal and a weak signal, as well as some of the potential reasons why a wireless client device may experience weak or no signal. Throughput is another area we looked at that involves client-side performance. We discussed some of the factors that could cause low throughput and how to solve these issues. Upgrading software is another area that needs be taken into consideration with wireless LANs from the client side, upgrading device drivers or client software utilities, as well as the infrastructure side, which includes upgrading firmware. All these areas are important parts of wireless LAN maintenance and support. Finally, we looked at optimizing wireless networks and some of the areas that should be considered for this optimization, which may include making the necessary adjustments from the original wireless site survey. These adjustments could be a result of changes to the environment such as walls, doors, windows, or other physical attributes of the location. Other factors that should be considered include client load balancing, multipath, and hidden node issues.

Exam Essentials

Identify the symptoms of common problems associated with wireless networks   Know what may cause poor throughput or connectivity issues with wireless LAN infrastructure and client devices.

Understand common troubleshooting techniques and procedures to help resolve issues associated with wireless networking   Know how to isolate problems based on symptoms and be able to correct using a suitable resolution.

Be familiar with the effects radio frequency issues may have on a wireless network   Understand received signal strength and how a weak signal could affect the performance of a wireless client device.

Know the process for device upgrades   Understand the importance of device upgrades, both software and hardware, in order to provide optimal performance of devices on a wireless network. Be familiar with the concept of firmware upgrades.

Understand the importance of correct placement of wireless infrastructure devices   Know that load balancing prevents infrastructure devices from becoming overloaded by allowing too many client associations. Understand the hidden node problems, what can cause them, and their solutions. Be familiar with what causes multipath, the solution for it, and where it can be beneficial.

Key Terms

Automatic Private IP Addressing (APIPA)

clear channel assessment (CCA)

Dynamic Host Configuration Protocol (DHCP)

firmware

hidden node

IP address

load balancing

modulation

optimizing

protocol

receiver

throughput

transmitter

Review Questions

1. In wireless networking, multipath is the result of what RF behavior?

    A. Refraction

    B. Diffraction

    C. Absorption

    D. Reflection

2. A wireless client device is showing a low receive signal strength value. What option could improve this situation?

    A. Upgrade the client device

    B. Add another access point

    C. Upgrade firmware on devices

    D. Eliminate multipath

3. You recently installed an 802.11g wireless network in a small office. One of the employees has been complaining of poor performance and mentioned her notebook computer runs very slowly because of the access point it connects to. What could cause this notebook computer to be performing poorly?

    A. The new 5 GHz phone in her office is interfering with the wireless LAN.

    B. The access point is located at the opposite side of the building from the user's office.

    C. A MAC filter is enabled on the notebook computer.

    D. The firmware was recently upgraded on the access point.

4. The RF signal strength seen by a wireless client device from an 802.11g access point can be improved by _____.

    A. Increasing the output power on the access point

    B. Enabling load balancing

    C. Upgrading the ISP service

    D. Enabling WPA 2.0 on both the access point and the client

5. You are a help desk technician providing support for a wireless network. A user calls and complains he cannot access the Internet. The user tells you he has good signal strength, but the network connection states "acquiring network address" and the IP address is all zeros. What could cause this problem?

    A. The client device has a static IP address.

    B. The client has an 802.11a network adapter.

    C. There is an incorrect WPA passphrase on the client device.

    D. A computer virus has infected the client device.

6. You provide consulting services for various companies and receive a call from one of your clients that their notebook computers suddenly started experiencing slow data transfers from the wireless LAN. This company is located in a multi-tenant building. What could cause a sudden change in performance for the notebook computers?

   A. A firmware upgrade was recently performed on the access point.

   B. The access point for a new tenant in the building is set to the same RF channel.

   C. The access point shows a low received signal strength.

   D. Someone activated the diversity antennas on the access point.

7. What can solve a hidden node problem caused by an obstacle or obstruction on an 802.11g wireless network?

   A. Adding another access point

   B. Setting the access point to mixed mode

   C. Increasing the distance between the access point and the clients

   D. Adjusting the received signal strength on the client

8. Weak signal strength would have an impact on what device?

   A. Infrastructure device

   B. Client device

   C. Multipath device

   D. Transmitter device

9. An incorrect passphrase set on a client device will result in a different preshared key that is generated for a device using WPA 2.0 as a security solution. What will be the result of a mismatched passphrase between the client device and an access point?

   A. Association is established and terminated and no valid IP address

   B. Invalid association and valid IP address

   C. A deauthentication

   D. A disassociation

10. The throughput of a wireless LAN can be affected by _____ or _____.

   A. Distance from access point, IP address

   B. Distance from access point, MAC address

   C. Distance from access point, output power of access point

   D. Distance from access point, output power of client device

11. The device driver of a wireless network adapter card is _____.

   A. Required

   B. Optional

   C. Used with security

   D. Another name for SSID

12. What is a valid solution to a hidden node problem caused by different technology types?

    A. Mixed mode technology

    B. Additional access point

    C. Increasing output power

    D. Removing an obstacle

13. You are a network administrator and receive a call from a user stating he cannot access the wireless LAN. The office contains 50 other users and nobody else is complaining about the network. What could be a potential problem that would keep this user from connecting to the access point?

    A. The connection to the Internet has been terminated.

    B. The access point needs to be upgraded.

    C. Incorrect firmware was installed on the access point.

    D. The wireless client device has a corrupt device driver.

14. Lack of RF connectivity on a wireless client could be caused by which layer of the OSI model?

    A. Layer 1

    B. Layer 3

    C. Layer 4

    D. Layer 7

15. What address would be considered a Microsoft Windows Automatic Private IP Address, assigned when no DHCP server is available on the LAN?

    A. 192.168.0.1

    B. 172.168.0.1

    C. 169.254.0.1

    D. 10.1.0.1

16. Weak or no signal at a wireless client device can be the result of _____.

    A. Distance from an access point

    B. Distance from other client devices

    C. Distance from the wiring closet

    D. Distance from Ethernet switch

17. What does the signal-to-noise ratio represent?

    A. The difference between output power and noise floor

    B. The difference between received signal and noise floor

    C. The difference between access point output power and received client power

    D. The difference between client output power and noise generated by the access point

18. What can 802.11n use to provide higher throughput to wireless client devices that 802.11g cannot?

    A. Hidden node

    B. Received signal strength

    C. DHCP

    D. Multipath

19. The throughput of a wireless LAN client device can be increased by performing which task?

    A. Adding access points

    B. Upgrade the client software to full-duplex mode

    C. Increasing the RF noise

    D. Hiding the SSID

20. The received signal strength of a wireless client could be increased by _____ .

    A. Upgrading the wireless client device

    B. Enabling load-balancing features on the access point

    C. Increasing the gain of the antenna on the access point

    D. Installing the Microsoft Wireless Zero Configuration utility

Answers to Review Questions

1. D. Multipath is caused by reflected signals arriving at the receiver at slightly different times (delay spread). Refraction is an RF behavior caused by passing through an object of different density, resulting in a change of the signal strength. Absorption is the result of a signal not reflecting or bending or passing around an obstacle.

2. B. A wireless client device showing a low received signal strength value could be too far away from an access point. Of the answers listed, an additional access point would be the best solution. Upgrading the client device or the firmware would not help the situation. Multipath is caused by reflections and cannot be eliminated.

3. B. A user experiencing a slow connection could be too far away from an access point to get a strong enough signal to move data at the highest rate. A 5 GHz phone is operating at a different frequency and would not cause interference with an 802.11g wireless LAN. A MAC filter is set on an access point and will either allow or disallow a client connection. If a firmware upgrade was causing a problem for an access point, it would affect all users.

4. A. Increasing the output power of the access point will result in a higher received signal at the wireless client device. Enabling load balancing will not improve signal strength but will limit the number of devices that associate an access point and may improve throughput. Upgrading the ISP service to faster data rates will not improve signal strength for the wireless client. Enabling security such as WPA 2.0 will not increase the signal strength seen by the client but is recommended to secure the transmission.

5. C. Incorrect security parameters such as a WPA passphrase will prevent a wireless client device from completing a Layer 2 connection and obtaining an IP address from a DHCP service. If the client device is different technology like 802.11a the device would not have been able to connect. If a static IP address is used, it will not display all zeros. Although a computer virus can create problems for the client device, it would not prevent the device from obtaining an IP address after connecting to the wireless network.

6. B. A sudden change in performance might occur if an access point for a new tenant is set to the same RF channel as your client's access point. This could cause interference, which would degrade performance. A firmware upgrade on the access point usually fixes problems or provides enhancements. Received signal strength is typically an issue based on distance from an access point. Diversity antennas would help minimize the problems associated with multipath and in most cases would improve performance rather than degrade it.

7. A. A hidden node problem caused by obstacles or obstructions could be resolved by adding another access point so wireless client devices would not be subject to clear channel assessment issues. Setting an access point to mixed mode will allow both 802.11b and 802.11g clients to connect to the network. Increasing the distance between the access point and the clients will not improve the situation but will actually make it worse. Adjusting the received signal strength on the client would improve performance for that client but would not necessarily solve the hidden node problem.

8. B. The wireless LAN client device would be mostly affected by weak signal strength. An infrastructure device such as an access point generates the signal received by the client. Multipath is a phenomenon that is a result of several wavefronts of the same signal reaching a receiver at different times. A transmitter device is responsible for sending an RF signal.

9. A. A passphrase or preshared key will be validated after an 802.11 authentication and association. In order for the client device to get a valid IP address, a successful authentication, association, and passphrase would have to occur. A deauthentication will end the authentication state, and a disassociation will no longer allow a device to pass traffic across the access point.

10. C. Two factors that may have an impact on throughput in a wireless LAN are distance from the access point or the output power level of an access point. The IP address or MAC address identify the device on the network and would not affect throughput. The output power of the client device has more to do with its transmitting capabilities than the receiver's capabilities.

11. A. The device driver is a required component that allows the wireless network adapter card to interface with the operating system. A device driver does not provide security nor does it identify the network.

12. A. Hidden node caused by different technology types is the result of the access point not being able to differentiate between spread spectrum technologies. An access point set to mixed mode will understand both HR/DSSS and ERP-OFDM, which will solve the problem. Adding another access point or increasing output power would not solve the problem although that would be a solution for other hidden node scenarios. Removing an obstacle is a valid solution for a different hidden node problem.

13. D. A corrupt device driver may cause the network adapter card in a wireless client device to operate incorrectly or to malfunction. A terminated Internet connection would be a global problem and would affect all users. An upgrade or incorrect firmware would not cause the problem only for a single user.

14. A. Layer 1 provides the physical connectivity between devices, which use the air as the medium to carry the radio frequency. Layers 3 and 4 are responsible for TCP/IP. Layer 7 is the interface to the user, also known as the Application layer.

15. C. Microsoft Windows 98 and later are designed to use the Automatic Private IP Address service. This service will provide an IP address to client devices in the range of 169.254.X.X. This will allow local connectivity for any devices that are connected to a common LAN.

16. A. The distance from an access point could affect the received signal strength for a wireless client device. The distance from other clients has no impact on devices that are connected to an access point. The distance from an Ethernet switch or from the wiring closet has no impact on a wireless client.

17. B. The signal-to-noise ratio represents the difference between the received signal strength and the level of the noise floor. A good signal-to-noise ratio will give a client the ability to distinguish between signal and noise and allow it to recover data that was transmitted.

18. D. 802.11n takes advantage of multipath, which is typically a problem for other wireless LAN technologies. By using multipath, 802.11n devices will have better throughput than 802.11g devices. Received signal strength means the same thing across technologies. DHCP is a service that provides IP addresses automatically. Hidden node is a problem that may degrade throughput for connected devices.

19. A. Adding additional access points could help increase the throughput for a wireless LAN client device. This is possible because additional access points would allow for load-balancing features and therefore provide less contention at that access point. Upgrading the client software to full-duplex mode is not an option and if the RF noise was increased throughput would be less. Hiding the SSID has no impact on throughput.

20. C. Increasing the gain of an antenna will provide a larger RF coverage cell, thereby providing more received signal at the same distance for a wireless client device. Upgrading the wireless client will not improve the received signal strength. Load balancing will help with throughput, and Microsoft WZC is a example of a built-in client utility.

Appendix

About the Companion CD

- What You'll Find on the CD
- System Requirements
- Using the CD
- Troubleshooting

What You'll Find on the CD

The following sections are arranged by category and summarize the software and other goodies you'll find on the CD. If you need help with installing the items provided on the CD, refer to the installation instructions in the "Using the CD" section of this appendix. Some programs on the CD might fall into one of these categories:

Shareware programs are fully functional, free, trial versions of copyrighted programs. If you like particular programs, register with their authors for a nominal fee and receive licenses, enhanced versions, and technical support.

Freeware programs are free, copyrighted games, applications, and utilities. You can copy them to as many computers as you like—for free—but they offer no technical support.

Trial, demo, or *evaluation* versions of software are usually limited either by time or by functionality (such as not letting you save a project after you create it). Only some are available for download.

Case studies included or for download from various manufacturers of wireless LAN equipment detail specific deployments and can also serve as additional reference material.

Demonstration Software Programs

CommView for WiFi—TamoSoft   A powerful wireless network monitor and analyzer for 802.11 a/b/g/n networks. Loaded with many user-friendly features, CommView for WiFi combines performance and flexibility with an ease of use unmatched in the industry. This program captures every packet on the air to display important information such as the list of access points and stations, per-node and per-channel statistics, signal strength, a list of packets and network connections, protocol distribution charts, and so on. By providing this information, CommView for WiFi can help you view and examine packets, pinpoint network problems, perform site surveys, and troubleshoot software and hardware.

MetaGeek Chanalyzer   This program turns data collected from a Wi-Spy into highly interactive charts and graphs, allowing users to "visualize" their wireless landscape. Together, Wi-Spy and Chanalyzer enable both enterprise and small business users to visualize, troubleshoot, and optimize their Wi-Fi (wireless fidelity) networks.

MetaGeek inSSIDer   inSSIDer is a free Wi-Fi network scanner for Windows Vista and Windows XP. inSSIDer an open-source Wi-Fi network scanner designed for the current generation of Windows operating systems.

RF3D WiFiPlanner   This program enables wireless-network professionals to accurately create WLAN plans in even the most complex building environments. Users can import single- or multi-level floor plans in various formats as well as use built-in libraries or custom design walls and floors to precisely match the building characteristics. This tool will also visualize network coverage and capacity by placing and adjusting access points, and will identify the number, location, and configuration of access points needed to provide optimum network performance before installing a single AP.

Network Stumbler   NetStumbler is a free tool for Microsoft Windows that allows users to view wireless LANs that comply with 802.11b, 802.11a, and 802.11g WLAN standards. A version called MiniStumbler is available for the handheld Windows CE operating system.

Demonstration Software Programs Available for Download

AirMagnet Survey   WLAN design and deployment verification solution, ideal for planning and designing a wireless LAN for optimal performance, security, and compliance. Enables enterprises to collect live signal, packet, and spectrum data during their site surveys. This allows enterprises to simulate and measure network performance in the most scientific way possible. This program can be used to perform both active and passive site surveys.

A demonstration copy of this program is available from AirMagnet at www.airmagnet.com/cwts/wiley. Complete the product demo request form and click the Survey link under WLAN Design to access the "Demo" download button.

AirMagnet WiFi Analyzer Express   The Express version provides the core building blocks of WiFi troubleshooting and auditing with the ability to see devices, automatically identify common problems, and physically locate specific devices.

A demonstration copy of this program is available from AirMagnet at www.airmagnet.com/cwts/wiley. Complete the product demo request form and click the Wi-Fi Analyzer link under WLAN Management Tools to access the "Demo" download button.

AirMagnet AirMedic   AirMedic is a fast and simple approach to dealing with the periodic performance and reliability problems that all wireless LANs experience. AirMedic does this by bringing together the two most essential perspectives of WLAN performance, combining lab-quality spectrum analysis and basic WiFi traffic analysis into one simple view.

A demonstration copy of this program is available from AirMagnet at www.airmagnet.com/cwts/wiley. Complete the product demo request form and click the AirMedic link under WLAN Management Tools to access the "Demo" download button.

Case Studies

- Aruba Networks: American Airlines Center Flys High with Centralized Wi-Fi from Aruba
- Aruba Networks: Centralized Management and RF Security Moves Ariba to Aruba

Case Studies Available for Download

- Motorola: Motorola Installs a Wireless LAN to Improve Communications at Kilkenny Castle
- Cisco Systems: Growing City Uses Wireless Communications to Improve Public Safety and Services
- Xirrus: Cellynne Chooses Xirrus Wi-Fi for Paper Manufacturing Plant
- Motorola: Empowering Students and Teachers with Streamlined Access and Opportunity
- Aerohive: Acuity Brands Lighting Upgrade from Autonomous APs to Support Next Generation Wireless LAN Services
- Trapeze Networks: Thomassen Compression Systems
- Cisco Systems: Minneapolis Medical Center Prepares for Next-Generation Mobility

Generic Floor Plan

Site_survey_floor_plan.jpg   This is a generic floor plan used in the text of this book that covers the site survey exam objectives. You can use this floor plan to simulate an office environment with any of the demonstration site survey software programs included on this CD.

Applications

Adobe Reader 9   Adobe Reader v9 is a freeware application from Adobe Systems for viewing files in the Adobe Portable Document Format (PDF).

Sensor Placement Site Survey Form

This form shows the type of information that can be used to document specifics about WLAN sensors used in Wireless Intrusion Prevention Systems (WIPS) and other WLAN monitoring applications. This sample form can be used as is or as a template for customization for your own WLAN site survey.

Sybex Test Engine

For Windows

   The CD contains the Sybex test engine, which includes all of the assessment test and chapter review questions in electronic format, as well as two bonus exams located only on the CD.

Electronic Flashcards

For PC

These handy electronic flashcards are just what they sound like. One side contains a question or fill-in-the-blank question, and the other side shows the answer.

System Requirements

Make sure your computer meets the minimum system requirements shown in the following list. If your computer doesn't match up to most of these requirements, you may have problems using the software and files on the companion CD. For the latest and greatest information, please refer to the ReadMe file located at the root of the CD-ROM.

- A PC running Microsoft Windows Vista or Windows XP with SP3, Intel Pentium 1.5 GHz or faster or an equivalent processor, 1 GB RAM recommended, 800 MB free hard disk space. Some demo programs will require either a Cardbus, ExpressCard slot, USB port, or Mini-PCI slot and supported wireless network adapter.

- An Internet connection.

- A CD-ROM drive.

Using the CD

To install the items from the CD to your hard drive, follow these steps:

1. Insert the CD into your computer's CD-ROM drive. The license agreement appears.

> ***Windows users***: The interface won't launch if you have autorun disabled. In that case, click Start ➢ Run (for Windows Vista, Start ➢ All Programs ➢ Accessories ➢ Run). In the dialog box that appears, type **D:\Start.exe**. (Replace *D* with the proper letter if your CD drive uses a different letter. If you don't know the letter, see how your CD drive is listed under My Computer.) Click OK.

2. Read the license agreement, and click the Accept button if you want to use the CD.

The CD interface appears. The interface allows you to access the content with just one or two clicks.

Troubleshooting

Wiley has attempted to provide programs that work on most computers with the minimum system requirements. Alas, your computer may differ, and some programs may not work properly for some reason.

The two likeliest problems are that you don't have enough memory (RAM) for the programs you want to use or you have other programs running that are affecting installation or running of a program. If you get an error message such as "Not enough memory" or "Setup cannot continue," try one or more of the following suggestions and then try using the software again:

Turn off any antivirus software running on your computer. Installation programs sometimes mimic virus activity and may make your computer incorrectly believe that it's being infected by a virus.

Close all running programs. The more programs you have running, the less memory is available to other programs. Installation programs typically update files and programs; so if you keep other programs running, installation may not work properly.

Have your local computer store add more RAM to your computer. This is, admittedly, a drastic and somewhat expensive step. However, adding more memory can really help the speed of your computer and allow more programs to run at the same time.

Customer Care

If you have trouble with the book's companion CD-ROM, please call the Wiley Product Technical Support phone number at (800) 762-2974. Outside the United States, call +1 (317) 572-3994. You can also contact Wiley Product Technical Support at `http://sybex.custhelp.com`. John Wiley & Sons will provide technical support only for installation and other general quality-control items. For technical support on the applications themselves, consult the program's vendor or author.

To place additional orders or to request information about other Wiley products, please call (877) 762-2974.

Glossary

A

absolute measure of power Actual power measurement, not a ratio or a relative value, is Watt (W), milliwatt (mW), decibel relative to one milliwatt (dBm).

absorption Occurs when material absorbs an RF signal. None of the signal penetrates through the material.

access point A wireless infrastructure device connected to a distribution system allowing wireless LAN devices to access computer network resources. Contains at least two network interfaces, 10/100/1000 BaseT/Tx Ethernet (usually) and RF (wireless).

active gain An increase in signal strength from devices such as amplifiers. Devices that provide active gain require an external power source.

active mode Part of the original IEEE 802.11 standard defining power-save features for wireless LAN devices. In this mode no power-save features are enabled and the wireless LAN device does not suspend to a low-power or doze state.

active scanning Part of the discovery phase of a wireless LAN. Allows for probe request and probe response frames to be sent and received. Takes place prior to authentication.

active site survey A type of manual site survey that requires an association to an access point.

ad hoc Another term for independent basic service set (IBSS), a wireless network in which no access points are used and only device-to-device communication takes place. This type of network is also called peer-to-peer.

Advanced Encryption Standard (AES) An encryption algorithm providing up to 256-bits of encryption, uses the Rijndael algorithm and required in IEEE 802.11i/WPA 2.0 wireless networking.

antenna diversity A technology designed to mitigate the problems associated with multi-path in a wireless LAN system.

association The final step to becoming part of a basic service set; allows wireless LAN devices to pass traffic across an access point. Allows for association requests and association response frames to be sent and received.

association ID (AID) A value assigned to a wireless device by the access point to identify the associated device.

authentication A way to validate or confirm the identity or credentials of a user, client, or device. Can be user based or hardware based.

automatic power save delivery (APSD) Newer technology used with wireless LAN devices to extend battery life by using a trigger frame for wireless devices to receive data buffered from an access point during low-power or doze state.

Automatic Private IP Addressing (APIPA)   APIPA is a feature used by Microsoft and integrated in the Windows operating systems to provide IP addresses automatically to any device requesting one that is connected to a common LAN and without the use of a DHCP server. If a network device is unable to locate a DHCP server, APIPA is used to automatically configure an IP address from a reserved range. This reserved IP address range is 169.254.0.1 through 169.254.255.254.

autonomous access point   A self-contained intelligent access point that can function as an independent wireless network device.

azimuth   In RF terminology, the angle of measurement for the horizontal radiation pattern of an antenna element.

B

basic service area (BSA)   The area of radio frequency coverage surrounding an access point or other wireless infrastructure device and the associated wireless LAN client devices.

basic service set   One access point connected to a distribution system (DS).

Basic Service Set Identifier (BSSID)   The MAC address or physical address of an access point radio card. Should not to be confused with Service Set Identifier (SSID).

beamwidth   The angle of measurement in degrees of the horizontal and vertical radiation patterns of an antenna element.

business requirements   Expectations within a certain type of business model such as manufacturing, enterprise, retail, or education.

C

captive portal   Authentication web page for a wireless hotspot or other type of wireless LAN application. The web page is a redirection and might ask users to enter authentication information and to agree to terms and conditions of use of the wireless network.

Carrier Sense Multiple Access/Collision Avoidance (CSMA/CA)   An access method used in wireless networking that attempts to avoid collisions on a network.

Carrier Sense Multiple Access/Collision Detection (CSMA/CD)   An access method used in Ethernet designed to detect collisions on a network.

cell   Area of RF coverage extending from an antenna in wireless infrastructure and client devices.

centralized administration   Configuration of many devices such as access points from one central device, software application, or location.

channel   Radio frequency range assignment varying in frequency based on the use of the device.

channel planning   A method used in the design of wireless networks so that overlapping cells are on different or non-overlapping channels and minimize interference.

clear channel assessment (CCA)   The Physical carrier sensing performed constantly by all stations which are not currently transmitting or receiving data and used to determine if the medium is available for transmission.

co-location   In wireless networking, multiple devices or access points in the same RF space and usually on different channels.

CompactFlash (CF)   Originally designed as a mass storage device format used in portable electronic devices. Now used for a variety of devices and technologies, including Ethernet networks, Bluetooth, digital cameras, RFID, and Wi-Fi networks.

contention   In wireless networking, multiple devices competing for a chance to send data on the network using an access method.

Counter Mode with Cipher Block Chaining Message Authentication Code Protocol (CCMP)   A security protocol that is a mandatory part of the IEEE 801.11i amendment to the standard and part of Wi-Fi Protected Access 2.0 (WPA2) certification from the Wi-Fi Alliance, providing strong security.

D

data bus   Carries data between components such as the CPU, memory, and expansion boards or slots within a computer.

Data Link layer   Layer 2 of the Open Systems Interconnection (OSI) model. Consists of two sublayers: Media Access Control (MAC) and Logical Link Control (LLC).

data rate   The theoretical rate at which data can be transferred based on design of the system. Actual throughput is less than the data rate because of overhead and access method used.

data security   Measures taken to ensure that information transmitted from one device to another is not seen or tampered with in transit and that the same information that is sent is what is received.

dead spot   Area that lacks RF coverage.

deauthentication   The process of no longer being authenticated to a system. In IEEE 802.11 wireless LAN technology, logging off or roaming from a basic service set will deauthenticate. It is a notification, not a request, and can be sent from either an access point or an associated wireless device.

device driver   Software allowing components such as a network adapter, keyboard, mouse video card, and all other attached devices to communicate with a computer operating system.

dictionary attack   An attack performed by software that challenges the encrypted password against common words or phrases in a text file (dictionary).

diffraction   Occurs when an RF signal passes an obstacle, such as a building. The RF wave changes direction by bending around the obstacle.

Direct-Sequence Spread Spectrum (DSSS)   A spread spectrum technology used in IEEE 802.11 and 802.11b/g with data rates of 1 and 2 Mbps set on a specific radio frequency channel.

disassociation   No longer being associated or able to pass traffic across an access point. It is a notification, not a request, and can be sent from either an access point or an associated wireless device.

distributed coordinated function (DCF)   A method that allows devices to compete for the time to transmit frames across the medium. In wireless networking this medium is the air.

Distribution System (DS)   An infrastructure, wired or wireless, connecting to an access point that allows data to be sent from wireless devices to resources on a network.

Dynamic Host Configuration Protocol (DHCP)   A protocol used to automatically distribute Internet Protocol (IP) addresses and other TCP/IP information to devices connected to a local area network.

dynamic rate switching (DRS)   The ability to change data rates based on signal quality and strength within a basic service area. Also known as dynamic rate selection or adaptive rate selection.

E

802.1X   An IEEE standard for port-based access control. Allows for an authentication process. Originally designed to work with wired networks and adapted to wireless networking. Used with extensible authentication protocol (EAP).

802.3-2005 Clause33   Formerly 802.3af, an amendment to the Ethernet standard for Power over Ethernet (PoE). Addresses supplying both data and DC power over a single Ethernet cable.

earth curvature   Has an effect after seven miles in distance; additional height needs to be added to the antenna in order to lessen the impact. Also known as earth bulge.

elevation
In RF terminology, the angle of measurement for the vertical radiation pattern of an antenna element.

encryption   A way to scramble computer data. Useful in computer networking, including wireless LANs.

endpoint device   A wireless LAN controller/switch or an Ethernet switch that delivers DC voltage directly to connected devices.

existing network infrastructure   A wired or wireless network already in place and functioning that may be used as part of an upgrade or a new deployment.

ExpressCard   The next generation of a PC card. Lower in cost, smaller in size, and higher in performance.

Extended Rate Physical (ERP) protection   Protection mechanism used with IEEE 802.11g wireless LAN systems to allow backward compatibility and coexistence between ERP, DSSS, and HR/DSSS wireless devices.

Extended Rate Physical Orthogonal Frequency Division Multiplexing (ERP-OFDM)
Required ERP modulation specified by the 802.11g amendment.

extended service set   One or more interconnected basic service sets connected to a common distribution system.

Extended Service Set Identifier (ESSID)   Another term for Service Set Identifier (SSID) used by manufacturers to identify the name of a wireless network. This term is not defined by the IEEE 802.11 standard.

Extensible Authentication Protocol (EAP)   Used in wireless networks as an authentication process to allow access to network resources. EAP is available in various types, which include user and certificate authentication.

F

Federal Communications Commission (FCC)   The regulatory body that manages RF spectrum for the United States of America.

firewall   Security hardware or software solutions to allow or disallow access to specific networking services, protocols, or ports.

firmware   An instruction set that allows hardware to operate based on the design—essentially, software for hardware.

48 VDC   The nominal amount of voltage supplied to 802.3af Power over Ethernet (PoE) devices.

Frequency-Hopping Spread Spectrum (FHSS)   A spread spectrum technology used in IEEE 802.11 with data rates of 1 and 2 Mbps and hops across the ISM band from 2.402 to 2.480 GHz. Used in other wireless technologies including Bluetooth and cordless phones.

Fresnel zone   The area of usable RF coverage between a transmitter and receiver. Must be clear of obstacles by at least 60 percent.

G

gain   An increase in signal strength of an RF signal, caused by an increase in amplitude. See also *active gain*, *passive gain*.

Greenfield mode (Mode 0)   HT protection mode that allows only high throughput (HT) functionality. 802.11a/b/g stations on the same channel are not allowed to connect. These devices will not communicate with a Greenfield access point and transmissions will collide, resulting in errors.

grounding rod   A metal rod driven into the earth eight feet or more and used to direct electrical currents to earth ground that are caused by lightning strikes.

H

half-duplex   Allows for two-way communication but in only one direction at a time.

Health Insurance Portability and Accountability Act (HIPAA)   Legislation that provides standardized mechanisms for electronic data exchange, security, and confidentiality of all health care-related computer information.

hidden node   In wireless networking, hidden node is the result of client devices connected to an access point and not able to "hear" each other prior to starting a RF transmission. Hidden node results in excessive collisions at the access point.

High Rate/Direct-Sequence Spread Spectrum (HR/DSSS)   A spread spectrum technology used in IEEE 802.11b and 802.11b/g with data rates of 5.5 and 11 Mbps set on a specific radio frequency channel.

high throughput (HT) protection   Protection mechanism that allows for IEEE 802.11n devices to be backward compatible and coexist with 802.11a/b/g devices. There are four HT protection modes.

HT mixed mode (Mode 3)   HT protection mode used in 802.11n networks if one or more non-HT stations are associated in the BSS.

HT non-member protection mode (Mode 1)   HT protection mode used in 802.11n networks if there are non-HT stations or access points using the primary or secondary channels.

HT 20 MHz protection mode (Mode 2)   HT protection mode used in 802.11n networks only if HT stations are associated in the BSS and at least one 20 MHz HT station is associated.

HTTP (Hypertext Transfer Protocol)   A Layer 7 protocol used by a server and a client using request/response architecture. By default works at port 80.

HTTPS (Hypertext Transfer Protocol Secure)   Works with HTTP to provide a Secure Sockets Layer (SSL) mechanism and to provide secure transactions across public networks such as the Internet. By default works at port 443.

hot-plug   Allows for replacement of computer system components and devices without powering down the system.

I

IEEE (formally the Institute of Electrical and Electronics Engineers)   A nonprofit organization responsible for generating a variety of technology standards, including those related to information technology.

impedance   The measurement of alternating current AC resistance, measured in Ohms.

independent basic service set (IBSS)   A wireless network in which no access points are used and only device-to-device communication takes place. Other terms for this type of network are ad hoc and peer-to-peer.

Industry Standard Architecture (ISA)   Architecture, developed by IBM, which allowed for expansion cards in early models of personal computers.

infrastructure mode   An operation mode that allows wireless LAN devices to connect to resources on the wired network or to other wireless devices by using an access point.

insertion loss   A form of signal loss caused by RF connectors. It is minor but can contribute to overall loss in a system, thereby resulting in less signal and less throughput.

interference   Two or more RF signals interacting with each other and causing a degradation of performance.

IP address   A logical Layer 3 address that identifies a device on a network. This address must be unique for devices on a common subnet.

isotropic radiator
Theoretical concept used in reference and calculations. Assumes that RF energy is broadcast equally in all directions in a spherical manner. An isotropic radiator is an imaginary, perfect antenna.

L

last-mile data delivery   A common term used in telecommunications to describe the connection from a provider to an endpoint such as home or business. Not necessarily a mile in distance.

Layer 2 tunneling protocol (L2TP)   A Layer 3 VPN security solution. L2TP is the combination of two different tunneling protocols: Cisco's Layer 2 Forwarding (L2F) and Microsoft's Point-to-Point Tunneling Protocol (PPTP). Usually works with IPSec to provide encryption.

lightning arrestor   Device used to shunt electrical currents from indirect lightning strikes to the ground. Protects electronic devices connected to the system from damage.

lightweight access points   Work with wireless LAN controllers/switches to provide network access for wireless LAN devices. Also known as thin access points.

line of sight   The ability of a transmitter and receiver to "see" each other (visual line of sight) or to transmit RF energy (RF line of site). RF line of sight is the area of coverage around the visual line of sight.

load balancing   In wireless networking, a mechanism that prevents wireless client devices from associating to an access point that has already reached the maximum number of client devices to allow for optimal performance.

lobe   In radio frequency technology terms, the shape of the RF energy emitted from an antenna element and is in the form of main, side, and rear.

M

MAC address filtering   Allows or denies access to a device based on its Layer 2 Media Access Control (MAC) unique hardware address.

MAC spoofing   A way of changing (through software) the assigned Layer 2 Media Access Control (MAC) address to something other than what it was intended to be. This may allow gaining access to restricted systems.

Media Access Control (MAC) address   A 6-byte unique number to identify a device (network interface adapter) connected to a computer network.

midspan device   Usually a single port or multiple port injector, injects DC power into Ethernet cable over the unused pairs of wires to allow power and data at the end (powered) 802.3af device.

Mini-PCI   Variation of the PCI standard designed for laptops and other small-footprint computer systems.

Mini-PCI Express (Mini-PCIe)   Replacement for the Mini-PCI card based on PCI Express and available in three types; Type I, Type II, and Type III.

Mode 0   See *Greenfield mode (Mode 0)*.

Mode 1   See *HT non-member protection mode (Mode 1)*.

Mode 2   See *HT 20 MHz protection mode (Mode 2)*.

Mode 3   See *HT mixed mode (Mode 3)*.

modulation   In wireless networking, combining digital computer data with high frequency alternating current (AC) in order to prepare it to be transmitted across the wireless meduim.

multipath   A phenomenon resulting from various wavefronts of reflected signals arriving at a receiver at slightly different times. Multipath causes corruption of the received signal, resulting in less overall throughput.

multiple channel architecture (MCA)   A wireless network design in which access points are set to different non-overlapping channels to minimize interference.

multiple input/multiple output (MIMO)   A technology using multiple radio chains and multiple antennas, allowing for high throughput currently up to 300 Mbps in wireless networks.

N

narrowband communication   High-power radio frequency within a very narrow frequency range. Some applications include radio and TV broadcasting.

network access method   Allows devices connected to a common infrastructure the opportunity to communicate and transmit data across a network medium from one device to another, as in CSMA/CD and CSMA/CA.

Network layer   Layer 3 of the Open Systems Interconnection (OSI) model where the IP protocol resides and is responsible for addressing and routing functions of data.

non-Wi-Fi interference   Interference that is not related to wireless LANs. It can be caused by devices that operate in the 2.4 GHz ISM band or the 5 GHz UNII band, such as microwave ovens, cordless phones, and ground radar.

null authentication   No means of being authenticated to an external source. Any station that requests authentication may become authenticated.

O

omnidirectional antenna   An antenna connected to an access point and commonly used indoors to provide 360-degree horizontal coverage. Can also be used with outdoor installations for point-to-multipoint connections.

open system   An automatic authentication process defined by the IEEE 802.11 standard to give wireless LAN devices the capability to connect to an access point. Consists of two wireless frames.

Open Systems Interconnection (OSI) model   Consists of seven layers and describes the basic concept of computer communications in computer network environment.

optimizing   In wireless networking, modifying or changing a system to make it work more efficiently and increase system performance.

Orthogonal Frequency Division Multiplexing (OFDM)   A technology designed to transmit many signals simultaneously over one transmission path in a shared medium and is used in wireless networking with 802.11a and 802.11g networks. See also Extended Rate Physical Orthogonal Frequency Division Multiplexing (ERP-OFDM).

P

parabolic dish antenna   A highly directional (high gain) antenna typically used outdoors for long-range point-to-point links.

parallel communication   Sending computer data simultaneously over several paths.

passive gain   The result of focusing isotopic energy into a specific radiation pattern. Using an antenna to achieve passive gain results in an increase or change in RF coverage.

passive scanning   The process in which wireless LAN devices "listen" to the RF medium for beacons that advertise the presence of an IEEE 802.11 wireless network.

passive site survey   A type of manual site survey that monitors all access points in an RF coverage area. No association to an access point is involved.

passphrase-based security   In IEEE 802.11 wireless LANs, a passphrase is a series of characters or words, 8 to 63 ASCII or 64 hexadecimal characters in length used to create a 256 bit preshared key. Designed to verify an identity and allow access to network resources.

patch/panel antenna   Antenna providing semidirectional coverage and a more specific radiation pattern than an omnidirectional antenna (but less specific than a highly directional antenna). Can be used either indoors or outdoors.

Payment Card Industry (PCI)   A regulation requiring companies to adhere to security standards created to protect card information in accordance with financial transactions.

PCMCIA   Personal Computer Memory Card International Association, a standards organization that defines and promotes PC card technology. Also used as the name of the card.

peer-to-peer   Another term for independent basic service set (IBSS), a wireless network in which no access points are used and only device-to-device communication takes place. This type of network is also called ad hoc.

Peripheral Component Interconnect (PCI)   A standard for computer interface cards developed by Intel. Cards are inserted into an available slot in a desktop computer, allowing for the attachment of peripheral devices.

personal digital assistant (PDA)   Handheld computer.

Physical layer   Layer 1 of the Open Systems Interconnection (OSI) model. Consists of bit-level data streams and computer network hardware connecting the devices together.

physical security   Measures taken to ensure that a specific type of information such as radio waves remains contained within a physical location, or to prevent the same from entering a physical location.

PIN-based security   In wireless networking, a security solution in which a unique identification number is entered on all devices that will be part of the same secure wireless network. This PIN will come with the device on a label, or it can be dynamically generated in the setup utility.

Pocket PC   A hardware specification for a handheld computer that uses the Microsoft Windows Mobile operating system. It has many of the features of notebook and desktop computers.

point-to-multipoint link   Connects three or more LANs together using a wireless bridge or access point in bridge mode depending on the antenna used. In some regulatory domains if an omni-directional antenna is used two or more LANs are considered a point-to-multipoint link.

point-to-point link   Connects two LANs together using a wireless bridge or access point in bridge mode.

Point-to-Point tunneling protocol (PPTP)   A Layer 3 VPN solution that uses the Microsoft Point-to-Point Encryption (MPPE) protocol and provides both tunneling and encryption capabilities.

polarization   The horizontal or vertical orientation of the E-field propagated from an antenna element.

powered device (PD)   Access point, VoIP phone, camera, or other network device that receives Power over Ethernet.

Power over Ethernet (PoE)   A method for supplying DC voltage and computer data together over a single Ethernet cable.

power save   The capability of a wireless LAN device to suspend to a low-power state, thereby extending the battery life and allowing for longer data communications.

power sourcing equipment (PSE)   A device that will supply DC voltage to network devices such as access points and VoIP phones. Can be either an endpoint or midspan device.

predictive site survey   A software-based site survey in which a floor plan or drawing of the area to be surveyed is imported into the program. The program then simulates the RF propagation from access points by using the attenuation properties of obstacles.

proprietary connector   Specific connector used by a manufacturer to limit the type of antenna that can be connected to a device. Prevents the possibility of using an antenna that will violate local RF regulations.

protocol   A set of rules that defines data communication between devices. TCP/IP is a common protocol set used in computer networking.

protocol analyzer   An application that allows a network engineer to view all wireless frames traversing across the air in the hearing range of the analyzing device.

push-button security   In wireless networking, a one-step process allowing users to configure wireless security by pushing a button on all devices in the network. The button may be in either hardware or software.

R

received signal strength
The minimum amount of signal a receiver must be able to receive in order to determine the data that was sent from the transmitter.

receiver   In wireless networking, a device that collects propagated RF energy from the air an antenna. It demodulates, and recovers any data included in the signal.

redundancy   Allows for fault-tolerant deployments and uninterrupted access in the event of access point or wireless LAN controller/switch failure.

reflection   Occurs when an RF signal bounces off a smooth, non-absorptive surface such as a table top and results in the original signal changing direction.

refraction   Occurs when an RF signal passes between mediums of different densities. The signal may change speed and also bend.

Remote Authentication Dial In User Service (RADIUS)   A centralized server used in computer networking providing authentication services, authorization, and accounting for devices that connect and use computer network resources. May also be known as an authentication, authorization, and accounting (AAA) server.

removable antenna   Antenna that can be disconnected from wireless LAN devices and replaced with a model with different gain either higher or lower.

RF coverage   The area in which radio frequency can be sent and received from devices providing two-way communication.

RF jamming   Disruption of communication between devices via RF interference. Jamming can be either intentional or unintentional. Used by intruders to perform denial-of-service (DoS) and hijacking attacks on wireless networks.

RF line of sight   Unobstructed radio communications between a radio transmitter and receiver.

RF spectrum analysis   A type of analysis that allows a site surveyor to view areas of RF coverage as well as interference sources using various tools currently available.

roaming   The process by which a wireless LAN device moves between basic service sets, reassociating to a new access point based on various criteria and maintaining connectivity to the network.

role-based access control (RBAC)   A security solution that relies on restricting access to only authorized users. It was designed to ease the task of security administration on large networks.

root access point mode   The default mode of most access points, allows wireless LAN users to connect to a wireless network and use network resources.

S

scattering   Occurs when an RF signal strikes an uneven surface. Wavefronts of the signal will reflect off the uneven surface in several directions.

sector antenna   Semidirectional antenna that can be configured in a group to provide omnidirectional coverage. Useful in communities, campuses, or for wireless Internet service providers.

Secure Digital Input/Output (SDIO)   Designed as a flash memory storage device with storage capacities from 8 MB to 4 GB. Now allows for connection of other devices such as cameras, global positioning system (GPS) units, FM radios, TV tuners, Ethernet networks, and Wi-Fi networks.

semidirectional antenna   Antenna used to focus the isotropic energy into a specific radiation pattern. Available in various types including patch/panel, sector, and Yagi.

serial communication   Sending computer data one bit at a time. External devices connect to a serial port.

Service Set Identifier (SSID)   The name of a wireless network to identify a basic service set and used for segmentation. It can be broadcast in beacon frames as part of the passive scanning process to allow wireless devices to locate and join the network.

shared key   An authentication method defined by the IEEE 802.11 standard, used in legacy devices. Requires the use of Wired Equivalent Privacy (WEP) for authentication and data encryption. This authentication method is flawed because it has several vulnerabilities.

signal loss   A decrease in signal strength caused by attenuation, diffusion, or interference.

signal-to-noise ratio (SNR)   The RF noise value in dBm minus the received signal strength in dBm. The minimum recommended value for wireless networking is 20dB or higher.

single channel architecture   A wireless network design in which all access points operate on the same channel and are managed by a centralized controller to avoid interference.

single input/single output (SISO)   The most basic wireless antenna technology used in a wireless LAN system. One antenna is used at the transmitter to transmit data and one antenna is used at the receiver to receive the data.

site survey   In wireless networking, a process that determines areas of RF coverage and interference as well as placement of infrastructure devices such as access points and bridges.

spatial multiplexing (SM)   Uses several antennas to transmit different pieces of the same transmission simultaneously to greatly increase throughput.

spectrum analyzer   A device used to "see" radio frequency. In wireless networking, a spectrum analyzer can be PC card–based, designed specifically for WLAN use, or a separate instrumentation device—a calibrated device that has the capability to view an entire radio spectrum.

spread spectrum   A signal spread over a frequency range, which results in a wider bandwidth.

spreading code   In wireless networking, provides redundancy of the digital data as it traverses through the air by combining a set code with the digital data prior to the transmission.

stacking   A single channel architecture management technique in which each floor or area of a building is assigned a channel to use. Spanning and blanketing are other terms used to identify managed areas based on channels.

SSID hiding   Disabling the broadcast of the Service Set Identifier in wireless LAN beacon frames. A weak and compromised method used by some as a form of wireless security.

subcarrier   A separate signal carried on a main radio frequency transmission.

T

Temporal Key Integrity Protocol (TKIP)   A firmware upgrade designed to enhance security issues with Wired Equivalent Privacy. An enhancement to WEP.

throughput   The actual rate at which information is transferred, taking into consideration factors such as overhead, interference, and contention between devices.

translational bridge   A device used to connect two or more dissimilar types of LANs together, such as wireless (802.11) and Ethernet (802.3).

transmitter   Prepares information to be sent across the air in the form of radio frequency.

U

Universal Serial Bus (USB)   USB uses a standard connector that replaces 9-pin serial, 25-pin parallel, and various other connector types. Allows for data and power with one cable.

USB 2.0   Incorporates several changes to USB, including connector types. Data rates allow for a maximum speed of 480 Mbps.

V

virtual local area networks (VLANs)   A logical separation of ports to define broadcast domains in a Layer 2 network, independent of their physical location.

Virtual Private Network (VPN)   Technology that allows for private communications over a public network infrastructure such as the Internet. A VPN creates a secure tunnel for the user and the connected endpoint.

visual line of sight   The ability of the transmitter and receiver to see each other.

voltage standing wave ratio (VSWR)   Disruption common in a wireless LAN system, caused by a mismatch in the impedance.

W

Wi-Fi Alliance   Organization formed to promote IEEE standards for wireless LAN technology and manufacturer interoperability testing.

Wi-Fi interference   Interference caused by other IEEE 802.11 wireless networks operating in the 2.4 GHz ISM or 5 GHz UNII bands.

Wi-Fi Multimedia (WMM)   A Wi-Fi Alliance certification designed as a proactive certification for the 802.11e QoS amendment to the 802.11 standard.

Wi-Fi Multimedia Power Save (WMM-PS)   A Wi-Fi Alliance certification designed for mobile devices and specific applications that require advanced power-save mechanisms for extended battery life.

Wi-Fi Protected Access (WPA)   A Wi-Fi Alliance certification designed as an interim solution until an amendment to the 802.11 standard (802.11i) addressing security improvements was released.

Wi-Fi Protected Access 2 (WPA 2.0)   A post–IEEE 802.11i amendment Wi-Fi Alliance certification addressing advanced security options for IEEE wireless LANs.

Wi-Fi Protected Setup (WPS)   A Wi-Fi Alliance certification allowing SOHO users a simple way to provide the best security possible for their deployments without the need for extensive technical knowledge of wireless networking.

wind loading   The effect of the force of wind on an antenna or other structure. In the case of an antenna, wind blowing at high speeds causes the antenna to move. Antennas designed for use in outdoor installations usually have a wind loading specification.

Wired Equivalent Privacy (WEP)   An optional authentication and/or encryption mechanism defined in the IEEE 802.11 standard designed to prevent casual eavesdropping. A weak and compromised legacy form of wireless security.

wireless bridge   Used to connect two or more local area networks together using radio frequency. Can be configured in either point-to-point or point-to-multipoint configurations.

wireless controller/switch   A device used in wireless LAN technology allowing centralized administration and control of lightweight or thin access points, including radio management, security, VLANs, and redundancy.

wireless distribution system (WDS)   A system that connects basic service sets together, making an extended service set using RF instead of cabling such as Ethernet.

wireless hotspot   A location that offers 802.11 wireless connectivity for devices (computers, PDAs, phones, etc.) to connect to and access the Internet.

wireless intrusion prevention system (WIPS)   A software and/or hardware solution designed to monitor wireless networking RF signals using sensors or access points and record events to a centralized database. It has the capability to react and prevent intrusion.

wireless LAN router   Usually consists of an Internet port, small Ethernet switch, and wireless access point. Allows SOHO and residential users to connect devices to the network and access the Internet. Also known as wireless broadband router or wireless residential gateway.

wireless mesh networking   A self-forming, self-healing, intelligent network used to route data frames between access points or "nodes" with one or more of the access points connected to a network infrastructure.

wireless repeaters   Used to extend a radio frequency cell allowing users exceeding the connection distance of an access point to still be able to connect to a wireless LAN by repeating the signal to an access point.

wireless VPN router   Usually consists of a LAN port, Internet port, and wireless port. Allows wireless LAN devices to securely connect to an access point by utilizing Layer 3 security solutions.

wireless workgroup bridge   A wireless client device that allows several Ethernet devices on an Ethernet segment to associate and connect to a wireless infrastructure through an access point. Also known as a wireless client bridge.

Wireless Zero Configuration (WZC) utility   Wireless LAN adapter client utility built into the Microsoft Windows XP and Vista operating systems, and running as a service.

wiring closet   A central and secured location where cabling is terminated and connects to infrastructure devices such as Layer 2 switches and Layer 3 routers.

Y

Yagi antenna   A semidirectional antenna typically used outdoors for short-range bridging or indoors for long hallways and corridors to provide RF coverage to a specific area.

Index

Note to the reader: Throughout this index **boldfaced** page numbers indicate primary discussions of a topic. *Italicized* page numbers indicate illustrations.

Numbers

3s and 10s Rule, 120
10BASE-T, 48
64QAM (quadrature amplitude modulation), 384
100BASE-T (Fast Ethernet), 48
802.3 Ethernet networks, CSMA/CD for access, 133
802.1X/EAP, 18, **353–354**
802.11-2007 standard (IEEE), 11, 143
    adjacent channel, 298
    on co-channel interference, 113
802.11 standard (IEEE), 10, **11–12**. *See also* IEEE (Institute of Electrical and Electronics Engineers)
802.11b devices, on 802.11g network, 15
802.11b/g Mixed mode for access point, 237
802.11b Only mode for access point, 237
802.11g Only mode for access point, 237
802.15 wireless personal area networks (WPANs), 138
1000BASE-T (Gigabit Ethernet), 48
8480-WD 802.11a/b/g, Proxim client utility for, *85*

A

AAA (authentication, authorization and accounting) server, 355
absorption, 117, *117*
AC power. *See* electrical power
access methods. *See also* spread spectrum technology
    exam essentials, 151
    review questions, 153–158
access points, **29–47**, *30*
    adding to eliminate obstacles, 409
    and antenna selection, 325
    association of survey device to, 305
    autonomous, **31–34**
    capacity of, **108–109**
    connection to distribution system, *225, 225*
    direct and distributed connectivity, 46
    distance to
        and signal strength, 393
        and throughput, **395**
    enterprise, **34–37**, *35*
    exam essentials, 52
    floor plan marked with, 300, *300*
    installation limitations, 327
    lightweight, 38, *38*, **44**
    listening for probe request frames, 218
    load balancing, **406**, *407*
    location
        and connectivity, 269
        in LANPlanner floor plan, 310
    maximum data rate, 228
    mesh, **38–39**, *39*
    for MIMO, 146
    modes for, 237
    number of users connected to, 105
    output power, and throughput, *395*
    overloading, 108
    placing in LANPlanner floor plan, *310*
    review questions, 54–59
    in site survey toolkit, 306
    testing placement, **301–302**
    upgrades, 403
    wireless bridges, **42**
    wireless controllers/switches, **43–47**
    wireless repeaters, **42–43**, *43*
    wireless routers, 40, **40–41**
Activation Code Not Found dialog box (LANPlanner), *310*, 310
active gain, **165**
active mode (AM), **234**
active scanning, **218–219**, *219*
active site survey, **305**, *305*
ad hoc networks, detecting, 211
Adapter Properties dialog box, *401*
adaptive frequency hopping (AFH), 114
    Bluetooth and, 149
adjacent channel, 298
adjacent channel interference, **112–113**, 148, 294, 298
    and wireless network planning, 149
Advanced Encryption Standard (AES), 358, 359
aesthetics, and antenna selection, 324, *325*
AFH (adaptive frequency hopping), 114
    Bluetooth and, 149

AID (association ID), 235
AirMagnet
    Spectrum Analyzer, *288*, 288, 294–298, *296*
        active site survey, *305*
        Devices tab, 297
        installation dialog box, *295*, 295–296
        passive site survey, *304*
        potential interference sources, *406*
        Spectrum tab, 297
    Survey/Planner, 312
    WiFi Analyzer, 313
Aironet Site Survey utility (Cisco), 299
Airtight Networks, 312
American Airlines Center, case study, 261–262
amplifier, 165
    for change in power, 119
amplitude, **100**, *100*, 163
antennas
    basics, **160–167**
        beamwidth, **161–162**, *162*
        polarization, 166
        RF lobes, **161**, *161*
    for building-to-building connectivity, 8
    diversity, 189
    for enterprise access points, 36
    exam essentials, 196–197
    gain, **163–165**
        active, **165**
        passive, **164–165**, *165*
    imaginary, perfect, 120
    impact on coverage area, 107
    installation, **187–189**
        limitations, 327
        placement, 187
        safety, **191**
    minimizing multipath effects using diversity, **188–189**, *189*
    mounting, **191–194**
        ceiling mount, **193**, *193*
        post/mast mount, *192*, **192–193**
        wall mount, **194**
    omnidirectional, **167–168**, *169*
        azimuth and elevation chart, *171*
        specifications, **168–170**
    removable, 32
    review questions, 198–203

semidirectional, **170**, *171*, *172–180*
  appropriate use, 173–174
  highly directional antenna, *181*, **181–183**
  highly directional antenna elevation and azimuth chart, *183*
  highly directional antenna specification, **182–183**
  patch/panel, *172*, **172**
  patch/panel elevation and azimuth charts, *175*
  sector antenna, *176*, **176–178**
  sector antenna elevation and azimuth charts, *178*
  sector antenna specifications, **176–178**
  specifications, **174–175**
  Yagi antenna, **178–181**, *179*
  Yagi antenna elevation and azimuth charts, *180*
  Yagi antenna outdoor installation, 181
  Yagi antenna specifications, **179–180**
in site survey toolkit, 307
upgrades, 404
use consideration in site survey, **271–273**, **323–325**
  selection, **324–325**
  testing multiple types, **323–324**
APIPA (Automatic Private IP Addressing), 389
applications. *See* software
Ariba, case study, 253–254
Aruba 2400 Mobility Controller, with Power over Ethernet endpoint capability, *51*
Aruba Dual-radio 802.11a/n, with antennas, *38*
Aruba Networks, case study, 253–254, 261–262
association, **223–224**
association ID (AID), 235
authentication, **219–222**, 341, **346–347**
  and association, *223*
  open system authentication, *220*, **220–221**
  shared key authentication, **221–222**, *222*
  for Wi-Fi Protected Setup certification, 19
authentication, authorization and accounting (AAA) server, 355
authentication frame, 222
authentication server, in 802.1X, 353
authenticator, 353

automatic power save delivery (APSD), **236**
Automatic Private IP Addressing (APIPA), 389
automobile, security for, 340
autonomous access points, 29, **31–34**
azimuth chart, 162–163, *163*
  for grid antenna, *183*
  for omnidirectional antenna, 170, *171*
  for patch antenna, *175*
  for sector antenna, *178*
  for Yagi antenna, 180

B

backward compatibility, of 802.11g, 13
bandwidth, shared, 107
barcode scanners, power save (ps) mode in, 236
Barker code, 140
basic service area (BSA), 212
basic service set (BSS), *212*, **212–213**
  and ESS, 214
Basic Service Set Identifier (BSSID), 215
battery life, extended, 19
battery pack, in site survey toolkit, 307
beacon frame, 217–218, 343
beamwidth, **161–162**, *162*
  of omnidirectional antenna, 167
  of Parabolic dish antennas, 181
Berkeley Varitronic Systems Swarm, 312
blank SSID, 219
blocked Fresnel zone, demonstrating, 111
blueprints
  for manual site survey, **300**
  for site surveys, 263, **266**
Bluetooth, 114, 148–149, 294
  FHSS for, 138
bottlenecks, 407
bridge mode
  enterprise access point configured as, 37
  SOHO access point configuration for, 33
bridges
  notebook computer as, 211
  translational, 225
  workgroup, **81–83**
    installation, **83**
    typical application, *82*
broadband wireless router, 40
broadcast probe request frame, 218

broadcast SSID, 219
Broadcom 802.11g wireless network adapter
  driver advanced settings page, *210*
  driver settings for, *235*
Broadcom wireless network, device driver information for, *399*
Broadcom wireless utility, for signal, noise, and data rate, *321*
BSA (basic service area), 212
BSSID (Basic Service Set Identifier), 215
building-to-building connectivity, wireless LANS for, **8–9**
Building Wizard Setup dialog box (LANPlanner), 310
BV Systems Yellowjacket, 313

C

C-Link access point, with PIN-based security, *349*
cable modem, 40
  DHCP address for, 388, *389*
cables, **184–186**, *185*
  cost of, 185
  impedance, **186**
  length, **184**
  RF connectors, **186**, *187*
  cameras, FHSS for, 138
Canada, local RF regulation, 101
cancellation effect, 100
capacity, 105
  of wireless access point, **108–109**
captive portal, 5, 45
Carrier Sense Multiple Access/ Collision Avoidance (CSMA/ CA), 132
  collision avoidance with, **134**
Carrier Sense Multiple Access/ Collision Detection (CSMA/ CD), 132
  conversation as form of, 134
  network traffic collision detection with, *133*, **133**
CCA (clear channel assessment), 408
CCMP (Cipher-block chaining meshage authentication code Protocol), 348, **359**, *359*
ceiling mount, *193*, **193**
ceiling mount antenna, *325*
cell, 33, 105
Cellynne Corporation/STEFCO Industries, case study, 256–257
centralized administration, wireless LAN controller/switch with, 44
CEPT (European Conference of Postal and Telecommunications Administrations), 11

certifications, interoperability, and 802.11 standard (IEEE), **16–19**
challenge text, in shared key authentication, 222
Chanalyzer spectrum analysis software
  demonstration, 290–293
  Sample Recordings section, *291*, 291–292
  setup wizard, 290, *290*
channel plan, 109, 148
channels
  co-channel and adjacent channel interference, 112–113
  for DSSS, 140
  DSSS and HR/DSSS, **141–143**
  multiple input/multiple output (MIMO), **147**
  orthogonal frequency division multiplexing (OFDM), *144*, 144–145
  reuse and co-location, **109–110**, *110*
China, local RF regulation, 101
Cipher-block chaining meshage authentication code Protocol (CCMP), 348, *359*, **359**
Cisco Systems
  Aironet Site Survey utility, *299*
  case study, 258
  Cisco 1200 access point security settings, *342*
  Cisco 1200 WEP key settings, *347*
  Spectrum Expert, 288
CITEL (Region A, North and South America, Inter-American Telecommunication Commission), 9
classroom deployments. *See also* educational institutions
  wireless LANS for, **6**
clear channel assessment (CCA), 408
Clear to Send (CTS) to Self option, for control frame in Mixed mode, 237
CLI (command-line interface) configuration, for enterprise access points, 37
client bridge, 81. *See also* workgroup bridges
client devices, 62
  CompactFlash (CF) devices, *73*, 73–74
  connectivity requirements, **270–271**
  drivers, 83–84
  exam essentials, 87
  ExpressCard, *68*, **68–69**, *69*
  Mini-PCI, 79, **79–81**
  no connectivity for, 386–387, *387*
  PCMCIA (Personal Computer Memory Card International Association), **62–67**, *63*

Peripheral Component Interconnect (PCI), **75–78**
  installation, 77–78
review questions, 89–94
Secure Digital (SD), 74, **74–75**
  in site survey toolkit, 307
Universal Serial Bus (USB 1.0) standard, **69–72**
  installation of devices, 71–72
upgrades, 404
client expectations for wireless LAN, 250–251
client utility software, **84–86**
  manufacturer-specific, 85
  third-party, 86
  upgrades, 402
closed network, 208, 343
co-channel interference, 112–113, 148, 294, 298
  and wireless network planning, 149
co-location, **109–110**, *110*
  of HR/DSS and ERP-OFDM systems, 147–148
coaxial bulk cable, *185*
collision avoidance
  with CSMA/CA, **134**
  with DCF, **135**
collision detection, 133
collisions, 408
Colubris wireless VPN router, *41*
command-line interface (CLI) configuration, for enterprise access points, 37
command prompt, opening, 230
communications, maintaining clear, **194–195**
CommView for WiFi (TamoSoft), 313, 314–317
CompactFlash (CF) devices, *73*, 73–74
complementary code keying (CCK), 140
configuration software, 84
Connect dialog box, 366, *366*
connections. *See also* wireless network connections
connectivity issues
  intermittent connectivity, 390–393
  no connectivity, **384–390**
    on client side, 386–387, *387*
    from IP address problems, 388–390
    from security settings, 390
  received signal strength, 391, *392*
    testing, 392–393
    weak or no signal, 393
  throughput, 394–397
    solutions to low, 396–397, *397*

connector
  for flat patch antenna, 175
  proprietary connectors, 186
  for sector antenna, 177
  for Yagi antenna, 180
contention, 133
continuous aware mode (CAM), **234**
control frames, 216
Control Panel (Windows XP), for VPN connection setup, 364
conversation, as form of CSMA/CD, 134
cordless telephones, 138
  sample spectrum analysis recording, 292–293, *293*
coverage, 105–107, *106*
  and antenna selection, 325
  requirements, **319**
  site survey information on, 263
curvature of earth, effect of, 187

D

D-Link access point, passphrase settings, *351*
D-Link Wireless N USB 2.0 adapter, installation, 71–72
data bus, PCI connection to, 76
data frames, 216–217
Data Link layer (OSI), 28
data rates, **226–227**
  vs. throughput, 228, 394
data transmission, reserving time using DCF, *135*, **135**
dB (decibel), 119
dBd (decibel dipole), 121
  vs. dBi (decibel isotropic), 121
dBi (decibel isotropic), 120
  vs. dBd (decibel dipole), 121
dBm (decibel relative to milliwatt), **119**
DCF (distributed coordination function), reserving time for data transmission, 135, *135*
dead spots, 288
deauthorization, **224–225**
Dell, and ExpressCard standard, 68
demodulation, 384
denial-of-service (DoS) attack, 225
Destination Location dialog box (CommView for WiFi), 315
detecting threats, with WIPS, 367
device drivers
  for client devices, **83–84**
  downloading, 399–400
  for PCMCIA cards, 64
  restarting Windows after installing, 317
  upgrades, **398–401**
    manual process for, 400–401

Device Manager (Windows), *84*, *400*
DHCP (Dynamic Host
    Configuration Protocol), 388,
    389
  SOHO access point as server, 33
dictionary attack, 362
diffraction, *116*, 116
diffusion, 117
digital camera, in site survey
    toolkit, 307
digital subscriber line (DSL), 40
  DHCP address for modem,
    388, *389*
direct-sequence spread spectrum
    (DSSS), **140**, *141*
  channels, **141–143**
  and data rates, 227
  Wi-Fi interference from, 294
disabling SSID broadcast, 343, *344*
disassociation, **224–225**
distance to access point, and signal
    strength, 393
distortion, from interference, 112
distributed coordination function
    (DCF), reserving time for data
    transmission, **135**, *135*
distribution system (DS), 30, 212,
    225, **225–226**
DLink DWL-2100AP SOHO access
    point, *32*
documentation
  of existing network
    characteristics, **318**
  site survey report, **328**
  for site surveys, 263, 307
    of existing network
      characteristics, **267–268**
    signal strength, 301
    site-specific, **266–267**
DoS (denial-of-service) attack, 225
downloading device drivers,
    399–400
Driver Installation Guide dialog
    box, 316, *316*
drivers. *See* device drivers
DRS (dynamic rate switching),
    231, *232*
DS. *See* distribution system (DS)
DSL (digital subscriber line), 40
  DHCP address for modem,
    388, *389*
DSSS. *See* direct-sequence spread
    spectrum (DSSS)
Dual CTS mode, for access
    points, 238
Dynamic Host Configuration
    Protocol (DHCP) server,
    388, *389*
  SOHO access point as, 33
dynamic rate selection, 231
dynamic rate switching (DRS),
    231, *232*

E

EAP (Extensible Authentication
    Protocol), 18, 353
earth curvature, effect of, 187
eavesdropping, LAN vulnerability
    to, 346
educational institutions
  antenna use consideration, 273
  gathering site survey
    requirements, **260–261**
  wireless LANS for, **6**
Ekahau Site Survey, 312
electrical power
  measuring, **118–119**
  requirements, **268–269**
  specifications, 267
elevation chart, 162–163, *163*
  for grid antenna, *183*
  for omnidirectional antenna,
    170, *171*
  for patch antenna, *175*
  for sector antenna, *178*
  for Yagi antenna, 180
encapsulation methods, for VPN,
    361, 362
encryption, **346–347**, **356–360**
  CCMP (Cipher-block chaining
    meshage authentication code
    Protocol), 348, *359*, **359**
  risk of intruder capture, 221
  TKIP (Temporal Key Integrity
    Protocol), 348, **357–358**
  with VPN, 361
  Wired Equivalent Privacy (WEP),
    342, **356–357**
endpoint devices, **51**
  for VPN, 364
enterprise access points, **34–37**, *35*
enterprise deployments, wireless
    LANS for, **4–5**
enterprise-grade client utilities, 85
enterprise mode, for wireless LAN
    security, 17, 18
environment
  and antenna selection, 324
  and azimuth and elevation
    chart, 163
  and RF range, **114–117**
ERP (extended rate physical)
    protection mechanism,
    236–237
escort, for site surveys, 265
ESSID (Extended Service Set
    Identifier), 215
Ethernet
  installation limitations, 328
  maximum distance for UTP
    cable, *50*
  standard pin assignment, *48*

ETSI (European
    Telecommunications Standards
    Institute), **11**
Europe, local RF regulation, 101
European Conference of Postal
    and Telecommunications
    Administrations (CEPT), 11
European Telecommunications
    Standards Institute (ETSI), **11**
"Exam Terms" document, 298
existing networks, wireless LANS
    for extending, 5
ExpressCard, *68*, **68–69**, *69*
  installation and configuration of
    cards, 69
extended rate physical (ERP)
    protection mechanism,
    236–237
Extended Rate Physical
    Orthogonal Frequency
    Division Multiplexing
    (ERP-OFDM), 143
  co-location, 147–148
  and data rates, 227
extended service set (ESS), *214*, **214**
Extended Service Set Identifier
    (ESSID), 215
Extensible Authentication Protocol
    (EAP), 18, **353**
extension cords, in site survey
    toolkit, 307
external adapters, 62

F

fast BSS transition, 234
Fast Ethernet (100BASE-T), 48
Federal Communications
    Commission (FCC), **10**
FHSS (frequency-hopping spread
    spectrum), 12, 114,
    138–139, *139*
  802.11 summary, 14
  for Bluetooth, 114
  and data rates, 227
  upgrade path for devices, 139
  Wi-Fi interference from, 294
firewall, 46
firmware update, 402–403, *403*
  for IEEE standards compliance, 32
  warning, 403
  on wireless LAN hardware, 359
flame rating
  of flat patch antenna, 175
  of omnidirectional antenna, 170
floor plans
  computer file for, 308
  for manual site survey, **300**
  with signal readings, *302*
  for site surveys, 263, **266**
Fluke Networks AnalyzeAir, 288

Fluke Networks InterpretAir, 312
forensics, WIPS data retention
    for, 368
four-way handshake, 222, 342
frames
    for association, 224
    null function, 216, 234
    for reassociation, 233
free space path loss (FSPL), 117
frequency, 99, **99–100**
frequency-hopping spread spectrum
    (FHSS), 12, **138–139**, *139*
    802.11 summary, 14
    for Bluetooth, 114
    and data rates, 227
    upgrade path for devices, 139
    Wi-Fi interference from, 294
frequency ranges
    for flat patch antenna, 174
    for omnidirectional antenna, 169
    for parabolic dish antenna, 182
    for sector antenna, 177
    for Yagi antenna, 179
Fresnel zone, *111*, 111–112,
    194–195, *195*
FSPL (free space path loss), 117
FTP file transfer, throughput
    differences, *396*
full duplex devices, 30
furnishings
    impact on range, 107
    site survey information on,
        266–267

G

gain in power, 100
    of antenna, 121
        flat patch, 174
        omnidirectional, 169
        parabolic dish, 182
        sector, 177
        Yagi, 179
    impact on coverage area, 107
Gigabit Ethernet (1000BASE-T), 48
Gilroy, California, 259
global problems, identifying in
    troubleshooting process, 383
government/military
    antenna use consideration, 272
    gathering site survey requirements,
        259–260
Gramm-Leach-Bliley Financial
    Services Modernization Act, 370
Greenfield mode, for access
    points, 238
grounding rods, **191**

H

half-duplex devices, 30, *31*
    effects on wireless throughput,
        135–136, *136*
handheld scanners, FHSS for, 139
hardware, device drivers for. *See*
    device drivers
Hardware Update Wizard dialog box,
    401, 401
HCF (hybrid coordination function),
    16
Health Insurance Portability and
    Accountability Act (HIPAA), 7,
    368, **370**
healthcare/medical
    antenna use consideration, 272
    furnishings information in site
        survey, 267
    gathering site survey requirements,
        257–258
    wireless LANS for, 7
    height of antenna, 195
Helium Networks Wireless
    Recon, 312
Hennepin County Medical Center,
    case study, 258
Hertz, Heinrich Rudolf, 172
Hewlett-Packard
    and ExpressCard standard, 68
    and USB, 70
hidden node, **408–411**
    based on technology, **411**, *411*
    distance as cause, **409–410**, *410*
    obstacles as cause, **408–409**, *409*
    software solution to, **411**
high frequency alternating current
    (AC) signals, 96
high rate DSSS (HR/DSSS), 12, **140**
    channels, **141–143**
    co-location, **147–148**
    and data rates, 227
high throughput (HT) protection
    mechanism, **237–238**
highly directional antennas, *181*,
    181–183
    elevation and azimuth chart, *183*
    placement, 188
    specification, **182–183**
HIPAA (Health Insurance Portability
    and Accountability Act), 7,
    368, **370**
home broadband routers, 40, *40*. *See
    also* SOHO (small office/home
    office)
horizontal beamwidth
    of flat patch antenna, 174
    of omnidirectional antenna, 169
    of Parabolic dish antennas, 182
    of sector antenna, 177

hospitality industry, gathering site
    survey requirements, **261–262**
hot-plug technology, 68
hotspots. *See* public wireless hotspots
HR/DSSS. *See* high rate DSSS (HR/
    DSSS)
HT (high throughput) 20 MHz
    protection mode, for access
    points, 238
HT (high throughput) Mixed mode,
    for access points, 238
HT (high throughput) Non-member
    protection mode, for access
    points, 238
HT-OFDM, Wi-Fi interference
    from, 294
HTTP (Hypertext Transfer
    Protocol), for SOHO access point
    configuration, 33–34
HTTPS (Hypertext Transfer Protocol
    Secure Sockets Layer), 33–34
human body, absorption of RF
    signals, 117
hybrid coordination function
    (HCF), 16

I

IEEE (Institute of Electrical and
    Electronics Engineers), **11–16**
    802.1X, *352*, **352–353**
    802.3-2005 Clause 33, 47
    802.3 standard
        802.3af, 47
        802.3at, 49
        CSMA/CD for, 132
        maximum distance for UTP
            cable, 50
    802.11-2007 standard, 11, 143
        adjacent channel, 298
        on co-channel interference, 113
    802.11 standard, 10, **11–12**
        802.11a, **12–13**
        802.11b, 12
        802.11e, 16
        802.11e on Quality of Service,
            236
        802.11f (Inter-Access Point
            Protocol), 232
        802.11g, **13–14**
        802.11i, 16, 17, 348
        802.11n, **14–15**, 237–238
        802.11n Draft 2.0 certified
            devices, 146
        802.11r, 234
        802.11s, 38
        access point response to null or
            blank SSID, 219
        channels available, 103

enterprise access points
support for, 35
on frequency bands, 102
interoperability certifications
related to, **16–19**
legacy security solutions,
265–266
maximizing throughput, 15
Mini-PCI adapter, 79
security, **341–342**
SOHO access point support
of, 32
summary, 14
unlicensed frequency ranges
for, 100
802.15 standard, and
interference, 114
impedance
cables and, **186**
of flat patch antenna, 174
of omnidirectional antenna, 169
of Parabolic dish antennas, 182
of sector antenna, 177
of Yagi antenna, 179
independent basic service set
(IBSS), *207*, **207–212**, *209*
advantages and disadvantages, **211**
radio frequency (RF) channel, **210**
security, **210**
service set identifier (SSID), **208**
terms, **210–211**
industrial networks. *See also*
manufacturing
wireless LANS for, **7–8**
industry definitions, vs.
standards, 298
Industry Standard Architecture
(ISA) bus, 76
infrared (IR) interference, 114
infrastructure devices for
wireless LAN
access points, **29–47**, *30*
autonomous, **31–34**
enterprise, **34–37**, *35*
exam essentials, 52
lightweight, **38**, *38*
mesh, **38–39**, *39*
review questions, 54–59
wireless bridges, *42*, **42**
wireless controllers/switches,
43–47
wireless repeaters, **42–43**, *43*
wireless routers, **40**, **40–41**
capacity and utilization analysis,
407–408
connectivity requirements,
320–321
power requirements, **320–321**
selection and placement, 320
optimizing, 405
upgrades, **403–404**
wired devices, 269

infrastructure mode, 207
for wireless device, 29
initialization vector (IV), 357
insertion loss, 186
InSSIDer, 166–167, 312
for identifying wireless
networks, *319*
received signal strength display,
392, *393*
installation
AirMagnet Spectrum Analyzer,
295, **295–296**
antennas, **187–189**
placement, 187
safety, **191**
CompactFlash card, 74
ExpressCard, 69
Mini-PCI, **80–81**
PCMCIA cards, **64–67**
exercise, 65–67
with wizard, *64*, *65*
USB devices, **71–72**
Institute of Electrical Electronics
Engineers. *See* IEEE (Institute
of Electrical and Electronics
Engineers)
integrated adapters, driver upgrade
for, 400
Intel
3945 IEEE 802.11a/b/g Mini-
PCIe adapter, *80*
and ExpressCard standard, 68
and USB, 70
intelligent AP, 30
Inter-Access Point Protocol, 232
interference
in hospitals, 7
in manufacturing
environments, 254
from overlapping channels,
109, *110*
and RF range, **112–114**
site survey information on, 264
sources, *289*, **289–293**
identifying, locating and
removing, 405
sunlight, 114
Wi-Fi, 294
intermittent connectivity, **390–393**
internal adapters, 62
International Telecommunication
Union-Radiocommunication
Sector (ITU-R), 9
region map, *9*
regions, geographic locations and
website URLs, 10
Internet Protocol Security
(IPSec), 363
interoperability certifications, and
802.11 standard (IEEE), **16–19**
interviewing managers and users,
for site surveys, **262–265**

intrusion prevention system (IPS), 46
tools, 225
wireless, 338, **367–368**
IP address
APIPA for, 389
no connectivity from problems
with, **388–390**
IP frame, 362
ipconfig command, *230*, 230
for MAC address display, *344*
iperf.exe program, 230
IPS. *See* intrusion prevention
system (IPS)
IPSec (Internet Protocol
Security), 363
IPX/SPX, 388
ISA (Industry Standard
Architecture) bus, 76
ISM (Industrial, Scientific, and
Medical) bands, 102
2.4 — 2.5 GHz, 12
2.4 GHz, 13
channels, 103
graph, *142*
for MIMO networks, 147
non-overlapping channels,
109, 113, *114*, *143*
overlapping channels, *113*
potential interference, 112
802.11 summary, 14
isotropic, 120
isotropic energy, 164
isotropic radiator, 120, 164
ISP (Internet service provider),
wireless, 7
Israel, local RF regulation, 101
ITU-R (International
Telecommunication Union-
Radiocommunication Sector), 9
region map, *9*
regions, geographic locations and
website URLs, 10

J

jamming, 265
Japan, local RF regulation, 101

L

L-com
2.3 GHz to 6 GHz 3 dBi omni
ceiling antenna, *193*
AL6 series 0-6 GHz coaxial
lightning and surge
protector, *190*
ceiling mount antenna, *325*
L2TP (Layer 2 Tunneling
Protocol), 363
lambda (λ), 98

LANs (local area networks). *See also* wireless LANs
  connecting wired, 42
laptop computer. *See* notebook computer
last-mile data delivery, wireless LANS for, 7
latency, 19
law enforcement networks, wireless LANS for, 7–8
Layer 2
  connectivity, 47
  security solutions, 360
Layer 3 connectivity, 47
legacy security solutions, 265–266, 343
legislative compliance requirements, and site survey, 265
lightning
  combatting effects on wireless connections, 190–191
  protection
    of sector antenna, 177
    of Yagi antenna, 179
lightning arrestors, 190, *190*
lightweight access points, 29, 38, *38*, 44
"Limited or no connectivity" meshage, 390, *391*
line of sight
  RF, **194**
  and RF range, **111**
  visual, **194**
Linksys
  access point, graphic user interface for configuring SSID, *213*
  Dual-Band Wireless-N USB client utility, *85*
  Wireless-G Notebook Adapter Setup Wizard, *65*
    profile screen, *67*
    summary screen, *67*
    Wireless Mode connection screen, *66*
  WRT54G MAC filter setup, *345*
  WRT54G wireless residential gateway/router, with push-button security, *349*
liquids, absorption of RF signals, 256
load balancing, **406**, *407*
  and number of associated users, 395
loss in power, 100

M

MAC (Media Access Control)
  address, 28
  and BSSID, 215
MAC filtering, 220
management frames, 216, 217

managers, interviewing for site surveys, **262–265**
manual site survey. *See* site surveys, manual
manufacturing
  antenna use consideration, 271
  client utility software, 85
  furnishings information in site survey, 267
  gathering site survey requirements, **254–256**
  wireless LANs for industry, 7–8
MC connectors, 186
MCA (multiple channel architecture), 325, 326, **326**
MCX connectors, 186
measurement units for radio frequency, **118–121**
  absolute measurements of power, **118–119**
  decibel relative to milliwatt (dBm), **119**
measuring tape, in site survey toolkit, 307
Media Access Control (MAC) address, 28, **344–345**, *345*
Meru MC5000 Large Scale Enterprise wireless LAN controller, 47
mesh access layer, networks with, surveying, 318
mesh access points, 29, 38–39, *39*
MetaGeek, Wi-Spy DBx spectrum analyzer, *287*, 288
mice, FHSS for, 138
Microsoft. *See also* Windows operating systems
  and ExpressCard standard, 68
  and USB, 70
  Windows built-in VPN client utility, 363, **364–366**
Microsoft Point-to-Point Encryption Protocol (MPPE), 362
Microsoft Wireless Zero Configuration (WZC) client utility, 386, 387
  data rate display, *227*
  passphrase set error, 390, *391*
  received signal strength display, *393*, *394*
  SSID in, 208, *209*
  upgrading, 402
Microsoft Wireless Zero Configuration (WZC) utility, 86, *86*
microwave oven, interference, *289*
midspan device, 49, **50–51**
milliwatt (mW), 118–119
Mini-PCI, 79, **79–81**
  installation, **80–81**
Mini-PCI Express, **79–81**
  installation, **80–81**

mitigation of threats, with WIPS, 367
mixed mode for access point, 237
MMCX connectors, 186
mobile devices, interference from, 289
mobile office, wireless LANS for, **5–6**
modem, for remote user connection, 354
modulation, 384
monitoring with WIPS, 367
Motorola
  AirDefense, 288
  AirDefense Mobile, 313
  AP7131 IEEE 802.11n access point, 35
  case study, 260–261
  CB3000 client bridge, *83*
  LA-5137 IEEE 802.11a/b/g CompactFlash card, *73*
  LANPlanner, *308*, 309–311, 312
  PSE single-port injector, *50*
  SiteScanner, 312
  WS2000 wireless LAN switch
    802.1X/EAP configuration, *354*
    disabling SSID broadcast, *344*
    firmware update screen, *403*
mounting
  antennas, **191–194**
    ceiling mount, **193**, *193*
    post/mast mount, *192*, **192–193**
    wall mount, **194**
  hardware in site survey toolkit, 307
  temporary
    for access points, 301, *302*
    for antenna, *323*
MPPE (Microsoft Point-to-Point Encryption Protocol), 362
MS-CHAP version 2, 362
multipath effects, **408**
  minimizing using antenna diversity, **188–189**, *189*
multiple access shared medium (MA), 134
multiple channel architecture (MCA), 325, **326**, *326*
multiple input/multiple output (MIMO), **146–147**, *147*
  channels, 147
multiport injectors, 51
municipal networks, wireless LANS for, 7–8

N

name, for wireless network, 208
narrowband communication, 136
National Telecommunications and Information Administration, 102
Near Field Communication (NFC) tokens, 19, 350
NEC, and USB, 70

NetBEUI, 388
Netgear
  WN311T IEEE 802.11g wireless
    PCI adapter, 76
  WN511T Wireless PCMCIA
    adapter, 63
  WNDR3300 RangeMax Dual
    Band Wireless-N router, 40
NetScout Sniffer, 313
NetStumbler, 312
  received signal strength display,
    392, 393
  to view wireless networks, 301
network access methods, 132–137
Network Instruments
  Observer, 313
Network layer (OSI), 28
network name (SSID), for wireless
  USB adapter, 72
networks
  documenting characteristics of
    existing, 318
  with mesh access layer,
    surveying, 318
New Connection Wizard dialog
  box, 364–365, 365, 366
NFC (Near Field Communication)
  tokens, 19, 350
"No Wi-Fi" policy, of government
  or military agencies, 259
noise, 322
non-overlapping channel,
  adjacent, 298
non-Wi-Fi interference, 289
notebook computer
  IBSS configuration as security
    threat, 211
  in site survey toolkit, 307
  USB 2.0 port on, 70
notification of threats, with
  WIPS, 367
null authentication, 341
null function frame, 216, 234
null SSID, 219
nulling signals, 100

O

Observer (Network
  Instruments), 313
obstacles, and range, 107
OFDM (orthogonal frequency
  division multiplexing), 12,
  143–145
  802.11 summary, 14
  channels, 144, 144–145
  and data rates, 227
  Wi-Fi interference from, 294
office/enterprise
  antenna use consideration, 271

furnishings information in site
  survey, 267
gathering site survey
  requirements, 253–254
omnidirectional antennas, 8,
  167–168, 169
  azimuth and elevation chart, 171
  placement, 188
  radiation pattern of, 168
  small office using, 253
  specifications, 168–170
OmniPeek (WildPackets), 313, 314
open networks, 208
open system authentication, 220,
  220–221, 341, 346
Open Systems Interconnection
  (OSI) model
  basics, 28–29, 29
  Layer 3
    connectivity, 388
    VPN security solution, 361
  Physical layer, 385, 385
  and TCP/IP, 388
operation modes, 206–215
  basic service set (BSS), 212,
    212–213
  for enterprise access points,
    36–37
  extended service set (ESS),
    214, 214
  independent basic service set
    (IBSS), 207, 207–212, 209
    advantages and
      disadvantages, 211
    radio frequency (RF)
      channel, 210
    security, 210
    service set identifier (SSID),
      208
    terms, 210–211
  infrastructure mode, 207
optimizing wireless networks,
  404–411
  client load balancing, 406, 407
  exam essentials, 413
  hidden node, 408–411
  infrastructure capacity and
    utilization analysis, 407–408
  infrastructure hardware selection
    and placement, 405
  interference, identifying, locating
    and removing sources, 405
  multipath effects, 408
  review questions, 414–420
orthogonal frequency division
  multiplexing (OFDM), 12,
  143–145
  802.11 summary, 14
  channels, 144, 144–145
  and data rates, 227
  Wi-Fi interference from, 294

OSI model. See Open Systems
  Interconnection (OSI) model
outdoor site survey, 195
overlapping channel, adjacent, 298
overlapping interference, 113

P

packet analyzer capture
  of association request and
    association response, 224
  of beacon frames, 218
  of disassociation and
    deauthentication frames, 224
  of four-way shared key
    authentication, 223
  of open system authentication, 221
  of probe request and probe
    response frames, 219
  of reassociation process, 233
packet analyzer, to determine
  SSID, 343
parabolic dish antennas, 181,
  181–183
  shipping, 183
parallel communication, 69
passive gain, 164–165, 165
passive scanning, 217, 217–218
passive site survey, 304, 304
passphrase, 18, 350–351, 351
password, for authentication, 341
patch/panel antennas, 172, 172
  elevation and azimuth charts, 175
  specifications, 174–175
Payment Card Industry (PCI)
  compliance, 346, 368, 369–370
PBC. See push-button
  configuration (PBC)
PC card, 63
  spectrum analysis, 294–298,
    405, 406
PCF (Point Coordination Function)
  mode, 16
PCI (Payment Card Industry)
  compliance, 346, 368, 369–370
PCI (Peripheral Component
  Interconnect), 75–78
  installation, 77–78
PCI-SIG (Peripheral Component
  Interconnect-Special Interest
  Group), 76
PCI slot, 78, 78
PCMCIA (Personal Computer
  Memory Card International
  Association), 62–67, 63
  card features, 63–64
  installation and configuration of
    cards, 64–67
    exercise, 65–67
    with wizard, 64, 65

PCO mode, for access points, 238
PD (powered device), **49–50**
performance
  baseline, 407
  and capacity, 109
  expectations, and site survey
    scope, 252
  overloaded access point and, 108
  power save mode impact, 235
Peripheral Component Interconnect
  (PCI), **75–78**
  installation, **77–78**
personal area networks (WPANs)
  coexistence with WLAN, **148–149**
  interference, 114
  wireless
    coexistence with WLAN,
      148–149
    interference, 114
Personal Computer Memory Card
  International Association
  (PCMCIA). *See* PCMCIA
  (Personal Computer Memory
  Card International Association)
personal identification number
  (PIN), 348
personal information, security for, 369
personal mode, for wireless LAN
  security, 17, 18
phase, 100, *101*
Physical layer (OSI), 28, *385*, 385
physical location size, and site survey
  scope, 251
pigtail cable, 184, *185*
PIN-based configuration, for WPS
  certification, 19
PIN-based security, **348**, *349*
ping command, 230
pins, standard assignment in
  Ethernet, *48*
placement of access points, testing,
  301–302
Plug and Play (PnP), 77
PoE Plus, 49
Point Coordination Function (PCF)
  mode, 16
point-to-multipoint link, 9, *9*
point-to-point link, 8, *8*
Point-to-Point Tunneling Protocol
  (PPTP), **362**
polarization of antenna, **166**
  example/experiment, 166–167
  for flat patch antenna, 175
  horizontal or vertical, *166*
  impact on coverage area, 107
  in manual site survey, 324
  for omnidirectional antenna, 170
  for Parabolic dish antenna, 182
  for sector antenna, 177
  for Yagi antenna, 180

portable devices. *See also* notebook
    computer
  interference from, 289
post/mast mount, *192*, **192–193**
power measurements. *See also*
    electrical power
  absolute measurements of,
    118–119, 120
  relative measurements of, **119–121**
Power over Ethernet (PoE), 45, **47–51**,
    269, 321
  Aruba 2400 Mobility Controller
    with, *51*
  benefits, 50
  endpoint devices, 51
  installation limitations, 328
  multispan devices, 50–51
  power sourcing equipment (PSE), 49
  powered device (PD), **49–50**
  site survey information on, 264
power-save mechanism, 19
power save modes, **234–236**
  in barcode scanners, 236
power sourcing equipment (PSE), **49**
powered device (PD), **49–50**
PPTP (Point-to-Point Tunneling
  Protocol), **362**
predictive site surveys, **307–312**, *308*
  demonstration, 309–311
privacy, 341
private information, security for, 369
probe request, 218
probe response frame, 218
  wireless device sending to access
    point, *219*
profile, for connection/session
    parameters, 84
propagation, and range, **107**
proprietary connectors
  for antennas, 168
  for cables, 186
protection mechanisms, **236–238**
protocol, 388
protocol analysis, **312–317**
  choices for, 313
  demonstration, 314–317
  goals of, 313
Proxim
  AP4000 access point, security
    configuration screen, *358*
  client utility for 8480-WD
    802.11a/b/g, *85*
PSE (power sourcing equipment), **49**
Psiber RF3D WiFiPlanner, 312
public access, site survey
  determination of need for, 263
Public Company Accounting Reform
  and Investor Protection Act of
  2002, 370
public infrastructure, 362
public wireless hotspots

antenna use consideration, 273
gathering site survey requirements,
  261–262
and VPN technology, *364*
wireless LANS for, **5–6**, *6*
push-button configuration (PBC),
  348–350, *349*
for WPS certification, 19

Q

QoS null frame, 216
Quality of Service amendment, to
  802.11 standard, 236
quality of service (QoS), 16, 19, 46
  site survey information on, 264

R

radiation pattern, of omnidirectional
  antenna, *168*
radio frequency, maximum distance
  for signal, 99
radio frequency (RF)
  amplification, and gain, 163
  basics, **96–104**
    amplitude, 100, *100*
    channels, *103*, **103–104**
    frequency, 99, **99–100**
    phase, 100, *101*
    range, **104**
    wavelength, **98–99**, *99*
  coverage, **270**
    cell size and, 105, *106*
    number of users connected,
      106–107
    obstacles, propagation and
      range, **107**
    wireless hardware and output
      power, 107
  exam essentials, 122
  extending cell, 42–43, *43*
  math calculation, 120
  measurement units, **118–121**
  range and speed, **110–117**
    environment and, **114–117**
    interference, **112–114**
    line of sight, **111**
  regulatory domain governing
    bodies, **9–11**
  review questions, 124–129
  uses, 97
  for wireless LANs, **101–102**
radio frequency (RF) channel, for
  IBSS, **210**
radio frequency spectrum
  management, 46
radio hardware, *62*

RADIUS (Remote Authentication
Dial-In User Service), 36,
354–355, *355*, *356*
in wireless LAN controllers/
switches, 45
range, for wireless LANs, **104**,
110–117
RBAC (role-based access
control), **360**
RC4 stream cipher, for WEP, 357
reassociation, frames for, 233
received signal strength, **321–322**,
391, *392*
testing, **392–393**
weak or no signal, 393
received signal strength indicator
(RSSI) value, 322, 391
receiver, *98*, 98
and troubleshooting, **384**, *385*
unobstructed view between
transmitter and, 111
redundancy, 46
reflected signals, MIMO process
for, 146
reflection, 115, *115*, 188
refraction, 115, *116*
Region A, North and South
America, Inter-American
Telecommunication
Commission (CITEL), 9
regulatory domain governing
bodies, on radio frequency,
9–11
relative measurements of power,
119–121
Remote Authentication Dial-In
User Service (RADIUS), 36,
354–355, *355*, *356*
in wireless LAN controllers/
switches, 45
removable antenna, for SOHO
access points, 33
repeater
enterprise access point
configured as, 37
SOHO access point as, 33
repeaters, **42–43**, *43*
wireless, **42–43**, *43*
reports, from WIPS, 368
Request to Send/Clear to Send
(RTS/CTS) process, 411
for control frame in Mixed
mode, 237
residential gateways, wireless, 40
retail/point of sale (POS)
antenna use consideration, 272
furnishings information in site
survey, 267
gathering site survey
requirements, **257**
RF. *See* radio frequency (RF)

RF connectors, **186**, *187*
RF jamming, 265
RF line of sight, 111, **194**
RF lobes, *161*, **161**
RF spectrum analysis, 270. *See
also* spectrum analysis
RJ11 connector, on Mini-PCI
card, 79
RJ45 connector, on Mini-PCI
card, 79
roaming, **232–234**, *233*
between access points, 214
improving with wireless LAN
controllers/switches, 45
site survey information on, 264
Robust Secure Network
Association (RSNA), 348
robust security network (RSN), 220
role-based access control
(RBAC), **360**
root access point mode, for
enterprise access points, **36–37**
routers, wireless, **40**, **40–41**
RP-MMCX connectors, 186
RSNA (Robust Secure Network
Association), 348
"rubber duck antenna", 168, *169*
physical specifications, *171*

S

safety, for antenna installation, **191**
San Marino Unified School
District, case study, 260–261
SanDisk, 73
SDIO Wi-Fi card, *74*
Sarbanes-Oxley Act of 2002, 370
SCA (single channel architecture),
325, **326–327**, *327*
scanning
active, **218–219**, *219*
passive, *217*, **217–218**
scattering, *117*, 117
SDIO (Secure Digital Input
Output), 74
installation, 75
sector antennas, *176*, **176–178**
elevation and azimuth
charts, *178*
specifications, **176–178**
Secure Digital Input Output
(SDIO), 74
installation, **75**
Secure Digital (SD), *74*, **74–75**
security. *See also* wireless security
for enterprise access points, 36
for IBSS, **210**
IBSS limitations, 211
site survey information on,
265–266
for SOHO access points, 33

security issues
for 802.11 standards, 17
no connectivity from, **390**
for wireless hotspots, 5
security profiles, 45
Select Program Manager Group
dialog box (CommView for
WiFi), 315
semidirectional antennas, **170**, *171*,
172–180
appropriate use, 173–174
highly directional antennas, *181*,
181–183
elevation and azimuth
chart, *183*
specification, **182–183**
patch/panel, *172*, **172**
elevation and azimuth
charts, *175*
placement, 188
sector antennas, *176*, **176–178**
elevation and azimuth
charts, *178*
specifications, **176–178**
specifications, **174–175**
Yagi antennas, **178–181**, *179*
elevation and azimuth
charts, *180*
outdoor installation, 181
specifications, **179–180**
serial communication, 69
service set identifier (SSID), 215, **343**
disabling SSID broadcast, 343, *344*
hiding, 208
for IBSS, **208**
troubleshooting connection and,
386–387
for wireless USB adapter, 72
shared key authentication,
221–222, *222*, *342*, 346
shared medium, 107, 109
signal, maximum distance, 99
signal strength
cables and, 184
documenting in site survey, 301
received signal strength,
321–322, 391, *392*
testing, **392–393**
weak or no signal, 393
signal-to-noise ratio, 322, 393
documenting in site survey, 301
sine wave, *96*, 97
Singapore, local RF regulation, 101
single channel architecture (SCA),
325, **326–327**, *327*
single input/single output (SISO),
147
MIMO compared to, 146
single port injectors, 51

site survey tools, in wireless LAN
  controllers/switches, 45–46
site surveys, 149. *See also* spectrum
  analysis
  active, 305, *305*
  antennas, use consideration,
    271–273, 323–325
  basics, **250–252**
  channel architectures, 325–327
  client connectivity requirements,
    270–271
  exam essentials, 275, 329–330
  factors impacting scope, 251–252
  gathering business requirements,
    252–262
    educational institutions,
      260–261
    general office/enterprise, *253*,
      253–254
    government/military, 259–260
    healthcare/medical, 257–258
    manufacturing, 254–256
    public wireless hotspots,
      261–262
    questions to be asked, 252
    retail/point of sale (POS), 257
    warehousing, 256–257
  infrastructure connectivity and
    power requirements, 268–269,
    320–321
  infrastructure hardware selection
    and placement, 320
  interviewing managers and users,
    262–265
  manual, 299–307
    advantages and disadvantages,
      299, 303
    floor plan with signal readings,
      302
    identifying existing wireless
      networks, 300–301
    obtaining floor plan or
      blueprint, 300
    software-assisted, 303–305
    testing access point placement,
      301–302
    toolkit for, 306–307
  outdoor, 195
  passive, *304*, 304
  physical and data security
    requirements, 265–266
  physical process, 285–286
  predictive, 307–312, *308*
    demonstration, 309–311
  received signal strength, 321–322
  report, 328
  review questions, 276–281,
    331–336
  RF coverage and capacity
    requirements, 270
  site-specific documentation,
    266–267

electrical specifications, 267
of existing network
  characteristics, **267–268**
software choices, 312
typical steps, 273
small office/home office (SOHO). *See*
  SOHO (small office/home office)
Sniffer (NetScout), 313
software
  and access point capacity, 109
  for hidden node solution, **411**
  impact on performance, 107
  for manual site survey, 303–305
  site survey information on, 264
  upgrades, **398–403**
    device drivers, **398–401**
SOHO (small office/home office)
  access points, 31–34, *32*
  client utilities, 85
  wireless LANS for, *4*, **4**
spatial multiplexing (SM), 144
spectrum analysis, 149, 286–298, *287*
  demonstration, 290–293
  interference, 289, 289–293
  as ongoing process, 288
  with WIPS, 367
spectrum analyzer, 286, *287*
  for identifying interference
    sources, 405
  for site surveys, 306
  for testing received signal
    strength, 392
speed. *See also* data rates
  of connection between sites, 269
  of RF signal, **110–117**
spoofing MAC address, 345
spread spectrum technology, 132,
  136, *136*, **138–145**
  data rates based on, 227
  direct-sequence spread spectrum
    (DSSS), 140, *141*
    channels, **141–143**
  frequency-hopping spread spectrum
    (FHSS), 12, **138–139**, *139*
    802.11 summary, 14
    for Bluetooth, 114
    upgrade path for devices, 139
    Wi-Fi interference from, 294
  high rate DSSS (HR/DSSS), 12, **140**
    channels, **141–143**
    co-location, 147–148
  multiple input/multiple output
    (MIMO), 146–147, *147*
    channels, 147
  orthogonal frequency division
    multiplexing (OFDM), 12,
    143–145
    802.11 summary, 14
    channels, *144*, 144–145
    Wi-Fi interference from, *294*
spreading code, for DSSS, 140
SSID. *See* service set identifier (SSID)

SSID hiding, **343**
stacking, 326
standards, vs. industry definitions, 298
Start Installation dialog box
  (CommView for WiFi), 315
stations (STA), access points as, 30
subcarrier, 144
sunlight interference, 114
supplicant, 84, 353

T

Taiwan, local RF regulation, 101
TamoSoft CommView for WiFi, 313,
  314–317
TCP/IP, 388
television, frequency ranges, 103
Temporal Key Integrity Protocol
  (TKIP), 348, **357–358**
temporary mounting
  for access points, 301, *302*
  for antenna, *323*
testing
  access point placement, 301–302
  received signal strength, 392–393
Thin AP, 30
third-party client utilities, 86
Thomassen Compression Systems
  (TCS), case study, 255–256
throughput, **228–231**, **394–397**
  and capacity, 109
  contention of Ethernet segment
    and, 133
  distorted signal and, 112
  half-duplex and, 30
  half duplex effects on wireless,
    135–136, *136*
  maximizing in 802.11g network, 15
  measuring for wireless network,
    229–231
  with MIMO, 146
  reduction by wireless repeaters, 43
  reflection impact on, 115
  solutions to low, **396–397**, *397*
TKIP (Temporal Key Integrity
  Protocol), 348, **357–358**
translational bridge, 225
transmit output power, adjusting in
  SOHO access point, 33
transmitter, 98, *98*
  and troubleshooting, **384**, *385*
  unobstructed view between receiver
    and, 111
transportation networks, wireless
  LANS for, 7–8
Trapeze Networks, case study,
  255–256
troubleshooting wireless networks
  basics, *382*
  exam essentials, 413

identifying problems, 382–404,
  383. See also connectivity
  issues
    receiver, **384**, *385*
    transmitter, **384**, *385*
    wired infrastructure
      problems, 383
review questions, 414–420
tunneling, with VPN, 361
two-way handshake, 341
Type I PCMCIA card, 63
Type II PCMCIA card, 63
Type III PCMCIA card, 63

U

UNII (Unlicensed National
  Information Infrastructure)
  bands, 102
  5 GHz, 12
    channel spacing, 144–145
    for MIMO networks, 147
  802.11 summary, 14
  channels, 104
United States
  Federal Communications
    Commission (FCC), **10**
  local RF regulation, 101
  unlicensed frequency bands, **102**
Universal Serial Bus (USB 1.0)
  standard, **69–72**
  installation of devices, **71–72**
unlicensed radio spectrum, 10
unshielded twisted pair (UTP)
  cable, maximum distance, 50,
  328
USB 1.0 (Universal Serial Bus)
  standard, **69–72**
USB devices, flash drive to store
  and transfer credentials, 350
USB Implementers Forum
  (USB-IF), 70
user-based security, **351–355**
username, for authentication, 341
users
  interviewing for site surveys,
    262–265
    expectations of network
      use, 263
  number of users
    connected to access point,
      105, **106–107**
    and site survey scope,
      251–252
    and throughput, **395**
UTP (unshielded twisted pair)
  cable, maximum distance for,
  50, 328

V

vertical beamwidth
  of flat patch antenna, 174
  of Parabolic dish antennas, 182
  of sector antenna, 177
VHF (very high frequency)
  band, 103
video over wireless LAN, site
  survey information on, 264
virtual LAN (VLAN), **44**, 357
virtual private networks (VPN), 6,
  360–366
  components, 363–364
  L2TP (Layer 2 Tunneling
    Protocol), 363
  PPTP (Point-to-Point Tunneling
    Protocol), 362
  setup, **364–366**
  Windows built-in client utility,
    364–366
  wireless LAN devices as
    client, 364
VisiWave - AZO Technologies, 312
visual line of sight, 111, **194**
Voice over IP (VoIP), support for, 234
voltage, for PoE, 49
voltage standing wave ratio
  (VSWR). *See* VSWR (voltage
  standing wave ratio)
VPN. *See* virtual private networks
  (VPN)
VSWR (voltage standing wave
  ratio)
  cables and, **186**
  of flat patch antenna, 174
  of omnidirectional antenna, 169
  of Parabolic dish antennas, 182
  of sector antenna, 177
  of Yagi antenna, 179

W

wall mount, **194**
walls, impact on range, 107
warehousing
  antenna use consideration,
    272, *272*
  furnishings information in site
    survey, 267
  gathering site survey
    requirements, **256–257**
watt, 118
wavelength, **98–99**, *99*
  and range, 104
WDS (wireless distribution
  system), 226, *226*
weather conditions, effects on
  wireless connection, **190–191**
web browser

for enterprise access point
  configuration, 37
for SOHO access point
  configuration, 33–34, *34*
WECA (Wireless Ethernet
  Compatibility Alliance), 17
WEP (Wired Equivalent Privacy),
  342, **346–347**, **356–357**
WEP cloaking, 368–369
Wi-Fi Alliance, **17**, 350
Wi-Fi certification
  for enterprise grade access
    points, 35–36
  for SOHO access points, 32
Wi-Fi certified logo, 17
Wi-Fi interference, **294**
Wi-Fi Internet access, 5
Wi-Fi Multimedia Power Save
  (WMM-PS) certification, **19**
Wi-Fi Multimedia (WMM)
  certification, **18–19**
Wi-Fi Protected Access 2.0
  (WPA 2.0), 18
Wi-Fi Protected Access (WPA)
  certification, **17**
  TKIP and, 358
Wi-Fi Protected Setup (WPS)
  certification, **19**, 348, 350
Wi-Spy DBx spectrum analyzer,
  287, *288*, 290, 293
WiFi Analyzer (AirMagnet), 313
wildcard SSID, 343
WildPackets OmniPeek, 313, *314*
wind
  combatting effects on wireless
    connections, **190–191**
  survival
    of flat patch antenna, 175
    of Parabolic dish
      antennas, 182
    of sector antenna, 177
    of Yagi antenna, 180
Windows operating systems
  built-in VPN client utility, 363,
    364–366
  client utility in, 86
  restarting after installing device
    drivers, 317
Windows XP, Device Manager, *84*
WIPS (wireless intrusion
  prevention systems), 338,
  367–368
Wired Equivalent Privacy (WEP),
  342, **346–347**, **356–357**
  open system authentication with,
    221
wired infrastructure,
  troubleshooting wireless
  networks and, 383
wireless bridges, **42**, *42*
wireless client bridge, 82

wireless controllers/switches, 43–47
wireless distribution system (WDS),
    226, *226*
Wireless Ethernet Compatibility
    Alliance (WECA), 17
wireless hotspots. *See* public wireless
    hotspots
wireless intrusion prevention systems
    (WIPS), 338, 367–368
wireless LANs
  advanced security for, 16
  basics
    exam essentials, 21
    review questions, 22–26
  common applications, 3–9
    building-to-building
        connectivity, 8–9
    educational institutions, 6
    enterprise deployments, 4–5
    extending existing networks, 5
    healthcare, 7
    industrial, municipal,
        law enforcement and
        transportation networks,
        7–8
    last-mile data delivery, 7
    mobile office and public
        wireless hotspots, 5–6
    small office/home office
        (SOHO), *4*, 4
  CSMA/CA as access method, 132
  early security mechanisms, 342–345
  exam essentials, 241
  identifying existing, 300–301
  intended use, and site survey
      scope, 251
  maintenance, software upgrades,
      398–403
  optimizing. *See* optimizing wireless
      networks
  radio frequency (RF) for, 101–102
  review questions, 243–248
  roaming, 232–234, *233*
wireless network adapter. *See also*
    client devices
  Broadcom 802.11g, driver advanced
      settings page, *210*
  device drivers for, 398–399
  icon for disabled, *386*

internal or external, 62
Meru MC5000 Large Scale
    Enterprise, *47*
wireless network connections,
    216–225. *See also* connectivity
    issues
  active scanning, 218–219, *219*
  association, 223–224
  authentication, 219–222
    open system authentication,
        220, 220–221
    shared key authentication,
        221–222, *222*
  deauthorization and disassociation,
      224–225
  frame types, 216–217
  infrastructure connectivity and
      power requirements, 268–269
  passive scanning, *217*, 217–218
wireless residential gateways, 40
wireless routers, *40*, 40–41
wireless security, 338
  authentication and encryption,
      346–347
  basics, 339
  early mechanisms, 342–345
    Media Access Control (MAC)
        address, 344–345
    service set identifier (SSID),
        343. *See also* service set
        identifier (SSID)
  encryption, 356–360
    CCMP (Cipher-block chaining
        meshage authentication
        code Protocol), 359, *359*
    TKIP (Temporal Key Integrity
        Protocol), 357–358
    Wired Equivalent Privacy
        (WEP), 356–357
  exam essentials, 372
  IEEE 802.11 standards, 341–342
  passphrase-based, 350–351, *351*
  PIN-based, 348, *349*
  RADIUS (Remote Authentication
      Dial-In User Service), 354–355,
      355, *356*
  regulatory compliance, 369–370
  review questions, 374–380
  role-based access control
      (RBAC), 360

SOHO and enterprise solutions, 348
threats and intrusion, 339–340, *340*
user-based, 351–355
wireless intrusion prevention
    systems (WIPS), 367–368
wireless workgroup bridge (WWB), 82
Wireless Zero Configuration (WZC)
    utility. *See* Microsoft Wireless
    Zero Configuration (WZC) client
    utility
wiring closets, 268
WMM-PS (Wi-Fi Multimedia Power
    Save) certification, **19**
WMM (Wi-Fi Multimedia)
    certification, 18–19
work-at-home professionals, 4
workgroup bridges, 81–83
  installation, 83
  typical application, *82*
WPA 2.0 (Wi-Fi Protected Access
    2.0), **18**
WPA (Wi-Fi Protected Access)
    certification, **17**
WPS. *See* Wi-Fi Protected Setup
    (WPS) certification
WZC (Wireless Zero Configuration)
    utility. *See* Microsoft Wireless
    Zero Configuration (WZC) client
    utility

X

Xirrus, case study, 256–257

Y

Yagi antennas, **178–181**, *179*, 325
  elevation and azimuth charts, *180*
  outdoor installation, 181
  specifications, **179–180**

Z

Zigbee networks, 148–149, 294

Wiley Publishing, Inc. End-User License Agreement

READ THIS. You should carefully read these terms and conditions before opening the software packet(s) included with this book "Book". This is a license agreement "Agreement" between you and Wiley Publishing, Inc. "WPI". By opening the accompanying software packet(s), you acknowledge that you have read and accept the following terms and conditions. If you do not agree and do not want to be bound by such terms and conditions, promptly return the Book and the unopened software packet(s) to the place you obtained them for a full refund.

1. **License Grant.** WPI grants to you (either an individual or entity) a nonexclusive license to use one copy of the enclosed software program(s) (collectively, the "Software," solely for your own personal or business purposes on a single computer (whether a standard computer or a workstation component of a multi-user network). The Software is in use on a computer when it is loaded into temporary memory (RAM) or installed into permanent memory (hard disk, CD-ROM, or other storage device). WPI reserves all rights not expressly granted herein.

2. **Ownership.** WPI is the owner of all right, title, and interest, including copyright, in and to the compilation of the Software recorded on the physical packet included with this Book "Software Media". Copyright to the individual programs recorded on the Software Media is owned by the author or other authorized copyright owner of each program. Ownership of the Software and all proprietary rights relating thereto remain with WPI and its licensers.

3. **Restrictions On Use and Transfer.**

(a) You may only (i) make one copy of the Software for backup or archival purposes, or (ii) transfer the Software to a single hard disk, provided that you keep the original for backup or archival purposes. You may not (i) rent or lease the Software, (ii) copy or reproduce the Software through a LAN or other network system or through any computer subscriber system or bulletin-board system, or (iii) modify, adapt, or create derivative works based on the Software.

(b) You may not reverse engineer, decompile, or disassemble the Software. You may transfer the Software and user documentation on a permanent basis, provided that the transferee agrees to accept the terms and conditions of this Agreement and you retain no copies. If the Software is an update or has been updated, any transfer must include the most recent update and all prior versions.

4. **Restrictions on Use of Individual Programs.** You must follow the individual requirements and restrictions detailed for each individual program in the About the CD-ROM appendix of this Book or on the Software Media. These limitations are also contained in the individual license agreements recorded on the Software Media. These limitations may include a requirement that after using the program for a specified period of time, the user must pay a registration fee or discontinue use. By opening the Software packet(s), you will be agreeing to abide by the licenses and restrictions for these individual programs that are detailed in the About the CD-ROM appendix and/or on the Software Media. None of the material on this Software Media or listed in this Book may ever be redistributed, in original or modified form, for commercial purposes.

5. **Limited Warranty.**

(a) WPI warrants that the Software and Software Media are free from defects in materials and workmanship under normal use for a period of sixty (60) days from the date of purchase of this Book. If WPI receives notification within the warranty period of defects in materials or workmanship, WPI will replace the defective Software Media.

(b) WPI AND THE AUTHOR(S) OF THE BOOK DISCLAIM ALL OTHER WARRANTIES, EXPRESS OR IMPLIED, INCLUDING WITHOUT LIMITATION IMPLIED WARRANTIES OF MERCHANTABILITY AND FITNESS FOR A PARTICULAR PURPOSE, WITH RESPECT TO THE SOFTWARE, THE PROGRAMS, THE SOURCE CODE CONTAINED THEREIN, AND/OR THE TECHNIQUES DESCRIBED IN THIS BOOK. WPI DOES NOT WARRANT THAT THE FUNCTIONS CONTAINED IN THE SOFTWARE WILL MEET YOUR REQUIREMENTS OR THAT THE OPERATION OF THE SOFTWARE WILL BE ERROR FREE.

(c) This limited warranty gives you specific legal rights, and you may have other rights that vary from jurisdiction to jurisdiction.

6. **Remedies.**

(a) WPI's entire liability and your exclusive remedy for defects in materials and workmanship shall be limited to replacement of the Software Media, which may be returned to WPI with a copy of your receipt at the following address: Software Media Fulfillment Department, Attn.: *CWTS: Certified Wireless Technology Specialist Official Study Guide*, Wiley Publishing, Inc., 10475 Crosspoint Blvd., Indianapolis, IN 46256, or call 1-800-762-2974. Please allow four to six weeks for delivery. This Limited Warranty is void if failure of the Software Media has resulted from accident, abuse, or misapplication. Any replacement Software Media will be warranted for the remainder of the original warranty period or thirty (30) days, whichever is longer.

(b) In no event shall WPI or the author be liable for any damages whatsoever (including without limitation damages for loss of business profits, business interruption, loss of business information, or any other pecuniary loss) arising from the use of or inability to use the Book or the Software, even if WPI has been advised of the possibility of such damages.

(c) Because some jurisdictions do not allow the exclusion or limitation of liability for consequential or incidental damages, the above limitation or exclusion may not apply to you.

7. **U.S. Government Restricted Rights.** Use, duplication, or disclosure of the Software for or on behalf of the United States of America, its agencies and/or instrumentalities "U.S. Government" is subject to restrictions as stated in paragraph (c)(1)(ii) of the Rights in Technical Data and Computer Software clause of DFARS 252.227-7013, or subparagraphs (c) (1) and (2) of the Commercial Computer Software—Restricted Rights clause at FAR 52.227-19, and in similar clauses in the NASA FAR supplement, as applicable.

8. **General.** This Agreement constitutes the entire understanding of the parties and revokes and supersedes all prior agreements, oral or written, between them and may not be modified or amended except in a writing signed by both parties hereto that specifically refers to this Agreement. This Agreement shall take precedence over any other documents that may be in conflict herewith. If any one or more provisions contained in this Agreement are held by any court or tribunal to be invalid, illegal, or otherwise unenforceable, each and every other provision shall remain in full force and effect.